THE FATE OF THE NATION-STATE

The Fate of the Nation-state

Edited by
MICHEL SEYMOUR

McGill-Queen's University Press
Montreal & Kingston · London · Ithaca

© McGill-Queen's University Press 2004
ISBN 0-7735-2685-4 (cloth)
ISBN 0-7735-2686-2 (paper)

Legal deposit second quarter 2004
Bibliothèque nationale du Québec

Printed in Canada on acid-free paper.

This book has been published with the help of a grant from the Canada Research Chair in Ethics and Political Philosophy at the Université de Montréal.

McGill-Queen's University Press acknowledges the support of the Canada Council for the Arts for its publishing program. It also acknowledges the financial support of the Government of Canada through the Book Publishing Industry Development Program (BPIDP) for its publishing activities.

National Library of Canada Cataloguing in Publication

The fate of the nation-state / Michel Seymour, editor.

Includes bibliographical references and index.
ISBN 0-7735-2685-4 (bnd)
ISBN 0-7735-2686-2 (pbk)

1. National state.   I. Seymour, Michel, 1954–

JC311.F38 2004   320.1   C2003-905703-8

This book was typeset by Dynagram Inc. in 10.5/13 Sabon.

Contents

Acknowledgements

This collection of essays is taken in part from papers given at the conference "Nation-states, Multinational States and Supranational Organizations" held in Montreal in October 2000 during the Jacques-Cartier Meetings. The Jacques-Cartier Centre has been organizing scientific meetings for researchers from France, Quebec, and other parts of the world since 1987. I am grateful for their support in the organization of the conference. I wish to express my gratitude to the Quebec government and to the University of Montreal, also major sponsors of the event.

As well, I am grateful to those who supported publication of this book. I would like to thank the Social Sciences and Humanities Research Council of Canada (SSHRC) for research grants that allowed me to work on this volume. I am indebted to my colleague Daniel Weinstock, professor in the Department of Philosophy at the University of Montreal and holder of the Canada Chair on Ethics and Political Philosophy, for sponsoring this publication. I also wish to thank those who have assisted me in the production of the work at McGill-Queen's, in particular Aurèle Parisien and Joan McGilvray for their friendliness and professional expertise. Linda Cardella-Cournoyer prepared the index with great care and attention. I also wish to thank the anonymous reviewers for their useful comments on an earlier draft of the book.

Finally, thanks to Blackwell Publishing for permission to reproduce Margaret Canovan's essay "Sleeping Dogs, Prowling Cats, and Soaring

Doves: Three Paradoxes of Nationhood." The work first appeared in *Political Studies* 49, no. 2 (June 2001). Kai Nielsen's "Are Nation-States Obsolete? The Challenge of Globalization," originally chapter 10 of his *Globalization and Justice* (Amherst, NY: Humanity Books, 2003), is reproduced by permission of Prometheus Books.

THE FATE OF THE NATION-STATE

MICHEL SEYMOUR

Introduction:
Theories and Practices

What is the most appropriate political institutional model for the next millennium? Should we look primarily to the nation-state, to the multinational state, or to supranational institutional structures that leave no real sovereignty to the component states? Has the nation-state become obsolete? Are multination states viable? Can we really create powerful supranational institutions?

There are frequent claims made nowadays about the end of the nation-state, but establishing successful multinational states has proven to be highly problematic. Indeed, there are at least two types of nation-states: "ethnic" nation-states, founded through the process known as "nation-state building" (for example, Germany), and "civic" nation-states, founded through "state-nation building" (for example, France). It would appear that certain homogeneous types of nation-states are outmoded, but others deserve to be maintained, especially those that are able to recognize their own polyethnic and pluricultural character. Whatever the specifics of each case, the redefinition of the nation-state raises complex problems because of the difficulties inherent in trying to encompass the fluidity of identities with regard to such characteristics as gender, class, and ethnicity. In addition, one cannot avoid the sometimes-antagonistic dynamics associated with national, feminist, and anti-racist movements.

Along with different ways of conceptualizing the nation-state, there are also different ways of conceptualizing the multinational state. There are de facto multinational states (such as Canada, a territorial federation based on the equality of provinces) and de jure multinational states, whose multinational character shapes their constitution and institutions (such as Belgium, a bi-multinational federation).

For some commentators, the people of the multinational state must have a common culture if it is to be viable. They thus conceived it as an inclusive cultural nation composed of several specific cultural nations. A model is here perhaps the United Kingdom. The idea is that its viability depends on a thick multinational identity. For others, the multinational state requires only a thin identity. The only common identity within this state may be the civic identity associated with it. Hence its viability requires only a constitutional patriotism, such as the one promoted by philosopher Jürgen Habermas.

There are, however, other ways to conceptualize the multinational state. One could simultaneously foster a common civic identity through the state and implement a politics of recognition towards the nations composing it. The idea is to avoid imposing a single language, a single culture, and a single history on the whole population and to avoid recourse to a thin, purely formal, civic identity, which would in the long run threaten the stability of the state. The solution is to adopt a politics of recognition as a substitute for the absence of a strong, durable, common cultural affiliation. Such recognition would induce a strong sentiment of loyalty to the encompassing state, and a relation of trust would soon follow. A final possible option involves taking a pragmatic and pluralist position. Just as there are different ways of defining the nation, and thus different populations articulating different self-representations with a different national consciousness on different territories, there are also different acceptable models of political organization. We could argue that there are several institutional political models: different acceptable forms of both nation-states and multinational states.

Beyond the nation-states and multinational states, we must also examine supranational organizations and reflect on their viability. Is there such a thing as "postnational identity," and is it a substitute or just an addition to the more usual national ties? Are supranational organizations constraining the power and influence of nation-states to an unacceptable degree? These questions surface frequently with regard to the United Nations but also, and especially, with the World Trade Organization, the World Bank, the International Monetary Fund, and, more generally, the entire range of phenomena now associated with economic globalization. These new realities are the context within which we should re-examine the traditional conflict between the nation-state and supranational organizations.

Supranational organizations may take the form of confederations of nation-states, in which the component states remain sovereign. A hybrid model involves both federative and confederative links, as is now the case in the European Union. Some observers imagine a "federation of nation-states" for the future of Europe. Europe could become a federation as a way to circumvent the insuperable obstacles facing an enlarged grouping composed of twenty-five states each with a veto. But it would still be a federation of nation-states because of the absence of a federal state.

ABOUT PART I: THEORETICAL FOUNDATIONS: NATIONAL, MULTINATIONAL, SUPRANATIONAL

These are some of the questions that are raised in this collection of essays. It is divided into two parts: one dealing with theoretical foundations and one with case studies. The nine essays in the first part could themselves be divided into two groups. Authors in the first group (Margaret Canovan, Liah Greenfeld, Daniel Weinstock, Jocelyne Couture, and Ross Poole) consider the viability of the nation-state and focus on nations and nationalism, while those in the second (Michel Seymour, David Ingram, Kai Nielsen, and Avishai Margalit) deal mostly with the viability of multinational states or supranational organizations and thus with political recognition, minority rights, and defence of the nation in a global economy.

Nations and Nationalism

Margaret Canovan's paper examines three connected paradoxes facing political theorists who try to come to terms with nationhood and nationalism. The paradoxes suggest that the topic of nations and nationalism is particularly difficult. First, during the twentieth century most Western political theorists ignored or dismissed nationhood and nationalism. But in constructing their theories, they relied tacitly on nations to provide solutions to questions that they did not explicitly address. Second, after the fall of communism woke the slumbering beasts of nationalism, many political theorists responded by working out theoretical defences of national self-determination. But, paradoxically, these theorists lay claim to universal authority, thereby actually licensing high-minded imperialism instead of the self-rule they set out to defend. Third, these self-contradictions may seem to lend support to a cosmopolitan rejection of nationhood and nationalism. But international institutions are offshoots of nation-states rather than alternatives to them. Canovan concludes that political theorists would do well, when formulating their theories, to pay more sustained attention to these crucial features of political life.

According to Liah Greenfeld, the fate of the nation-state is tied intimately to that of modernity, by which she means the specific character of social, political, and economic reality present in many societies of the past two centuries and in perhaps the majority of societies today. Modernity is modelled or constructed on the basis of national consciousness and in this sense is created by nationalism. When this form of consciousness disappears, the corresponding form of social (as well as political and economic) reality will disappear with it, to give way to a new one – of a kind that we cannot as yet imagine – modelled on a different image of reality. So nationalism is constitutive of modernity. This is the reason why, according to Greenfeld, the nation-state model was never questioned from a liberal standpoint. This view is, of course, compatible with many different ways of defining a people. It is compatible, for instance, with an understanding of the "people" as constituted by the whole population of Europe or even by the whole population of the globe. Nevertheless, the modern state has always been, according to Greenfeld, a nation-state.

Daniel Weinstock distinguishes four "ideal-types" of nation-building. He discusses some of the difficulties facing three of these types. They are all "top–down," in the sense that loyalty is imposed from above. He then suggests that a fourth model, which he terms "organic nation-building," offers a fruitful strategy for the "construction" of political communities in the future. It is a bottom–up kind of endeavour in which loyalty emerges from below. Weinstock argues against the claim that the state can reliably produce the right kind of commonality by engaging in top–down nation-building. He also sees it as problematic to suggest that the viability of institutions and the stability of society are goals of sufficient moral importance that states should be allowed to act not on the basis of what people want but on the basis of what they ought to want. He also wishes to counter the claim that the viability of the institutions of liberal democracy and the stability of its societies require that citizens view themselves as united by a shared identity. He doubts that citizens require shared identity or values in order to abstain from acting in ways harmful to the political order. So, according to Weinstock, the post-national political institutions of tomorrow will have to find ways to generate loyalties, sentiments of common purpose, and habits of co-operation among peoples who had previously thought of themselves as politically separate.

One of the challenges facing contemporary theoreticians of nationalism is to show that it could have beneficial consequences within the framework of those emerging phenomena to which we refer generically as globalization. With this desideratum in mind, Jocelyne Couture compares and evaluates, from a moral and political point of view, the arguments in favour of nationalism put forward from within communitarian, liberal, and cosmopolitan theories. She argues that these conceptions of nationalism cannot provide an adequate foundation for political organization, be it on a local or on a supranational scale. Apart from their insensitivity to the particular problems raised by the present world context, the leading contemporary conceptions of the nation manifest, in her view, a defective conception of the most general requirements of democracy. She then articulates a conception of nationalism based on solidarity, and she shows how it, while retaining certain characteristic features of the other theories, yet requires both the existence and the maintenance of both nation-states and democratic supranational institutions. The conception of the nation that should be promoted, in view of the current state of the world, is that of a nation that is at once cultural, sociological, and political. A solidaristic version of nationalism is not a barrier to globalization, but it is a condition for a globalization that is more humane and more respectful of societies; and it promises greater solidarity among peoples.

Ross Poole argues that culture is and ought to be an integral part of politics. This has important implications for people's way of thinking about multinational states and similarly significant consequences for people's way of dealing with Aboriginal peoples. His argument runs as follows. National identity has been the crucial condition of legitimacy for the modern state. The reason is that the nation has provided the form in which republican ideals of citizenship have found expression in the modern world. It thus appears that viable multinational states will have to be "multinational nation-states." Poole then argues that not all nation-state building involves assimilation of national minorities. He cites Britain as an example of a nation-state that was able to recognize to a certain extent its component national minorities. Fostering a unique common culture at the level of the encompassing state is compatible with the recognition of minority nations. The case of Aboriginal populations is another case in point. Full sovereignty is certainly not in the cards for Aboriginal peoples. But at the same time, these peoples want more than simply protection of their language and their culture. They have territorial and self-government claims. But the encompassing states that would grant them such an autonomy could very well be nation-states. So it appears problematic to argue that the social bonds that tie component nations together have to be very thin. After all, there are clear cases where this does not appear to be so.

A Larger Stage

In the second group of theoretical essays, Michel Seymour, David Ingram, Kai Nielsen, and Avishai Margalit examine alternatives to the traditional nation-state model, whether these are multinational states or supranational organizations that would limit the sovereignty of actual nation-states.

Michel Seymour investigates the conditions that would ensure the viability of multinational states. He argues that doing that should require politics of recognition towards the component nations belonging to those states. Such political recognition should lead to the entrenchment of the collective rights of nations (or peoples) in the constitution of the encompassing state. Seymour begins by trying to explain why liberal philosophers have been inclined to argue against politics of recognition. He argues that there existed historically a very close relationship between liberalism and the traditional nation-state model and that this historical connection was such that ethical individualism mistakenly came to be perceived as constitutive of liberalism. The problem is that ethical individualism enters into tension, if not into contradiction, with politics of recognition. Seymour then critically examines the view that ethical individualism can frame a liberal theory of collective rights. He criticizes Will Kymlicka's attempt to reconcile the two views. He explains defects of Kymlicka's theory of group-differentiated rights in terms of his favourable inclination towards individualism. Seymour concludes by describing an alternative theory of collective rights based on political liberalism.

David Ingram argues that talk of international justice is worthless unless it is wedded to realistic conceptions of mutually advantageous cooperation. Hence the question: can we envisage a system of international justice that is as realistic as it is utopian? Two of the world's leading political philosophers, Jürgen Habermas and John Rawls, think that we can. Ingram examines their reasons for thinking so. He shows that the disagreement between Rawls and Habermas on human rights reveals fundamental tensions in thinking about what justice demands. Their disagreement highlights their differing assessments of the cultural viability of nations and groups as unified, self-determining centres of collective agency. Rawls is right to hold that within the law of peoples nations, no less than individuals, can be holders of rights. Habermas may well be right in insisting on a strong connection between liberal democracy and respect for human rights. In conclusion, Ingram argues that neither philosopher presents an adequate account of the equal priority of economic, social, and cultural rights. Some economic rights are basic, and realizing them will require more radical changes in global governance structures than either thinker countenances. Some cultural rights are basic, too. This means – contrary to Habermas's cosmopolitan liberalism and Rawls's political liberalism – that the rights of groups, no less than the rights of individuals, will sometimes have to be politically recognized within liberal democracy.

Kai Nielsen observes that, paradoxically, during a period when there is a resurgence of nationalism and, with the politics of recognition, the importance to human beings of a sense of national identity is becoming more evident, the relentless forces of globalization and the new economic order seem at least to be undermining the ability of states to order their own affairs. Is the idea of national sovereignty slowly becoming folkloric? Nielsen states in the most forceful way possible the strongest arguments for obsolescence, and then he critically assesses their soundness. He distinguishes between weak and strong globalization. The weak variant appears to be compatible with the existence of nation-states and multinational states, while the strong version is neoliberal. Nielsen believes that neoliberal globalization poses a grave threat to democracy and to reasonable autonomy for nation-states or for multinational states. His defence of those "traditional" models does not, however, conflict with a cosmopolitan social-liberal nationalism. But he concludes that we should not dismiss the claim about the obsolescence of socially oriented nation-states as just a potful of neoliberal ideology. Globalization is becoming strong enough to require serious consideration of whether nation-states can, given capitalist globalization, have sufficient control over their affairs to provide the conditions of life in a social order that is self-determining.

Avishai Margalit critically analyses cosmopolitan ideals in the context of the urgent need for civilized and non-humiliating international institutions. To be able to do this, we have to think in terms of global decency. Cosmopolitan ideals appear to Margalit to be unrealistic, if understood as implying the existence of a world-state. Making the establishment of a decent society depend on the prior creation of a world-state is not a way of stopping institutional humiliation. The more urgent and realistic question rather involves the possibility and justification for international intervention to stop cruelty to and humiliation of persons and national minorities. The presumption is in favour of direct international intervention where cruelty is taking place. When peoples are apparently being humiliated, international intervention is to be decided on a case-by-case examination.

ABOUT PART II: CASE STUDIES: MULTINATIONAL SOCIETIES AND NATION-STATES

Multinational Societies

In the second part of the book, I have gathered case studies, which examine problems within particular societies. This part contains three groups of essay – on multinational societies and on the viability and on the fate of nation-states. In the first group (Mathew Evangelista, John McGarry, David McCrone, Montserrat Guibernau, Radha Kumar, and Michael Murphy), most authors investigate multinational societies and consider how these could be preserved. They seek to examine the internal self-determination of peoples.

Evangelista discusses the impact of the first war in Chechnya, reviews Russian President Boris Yeltsin's policies, and then considers the reforms of his successor Vladimir Putin. According to him, Putin's system of regional super-regions puts individual rights and regional autonomy at risk without providing compensating improvements in overall quality of life. Evangelista argues that Putin's attempt to recentralize Russia and do away with Yeltsin's legacy of "asymmetric federalism" could prove counterproductive. Putin should recognize that ruling the world's largest country from a single capital city is unrealistic. Some form of genuine federalism, perhaps still a negotiated, asymmetrical federalism, is Russia's best hope. The reason is that the Russian Federation is far more complicated than the Soviet Union and that its disintegration would be far messier. Evangelista concludes that Russians could end up with the worst of both worlds – an authoritarian regime yet no order and peace.

John McGarry notes that it is common for observers to see Northern Ireland as a site of rival sectarian or ethnic ideologies. It appears an ideal place therefore for the promotion of an inclusive, civic form of nationalism. But McGarry argues that the conflict there has been, in an important way, the result of a struggle between two rival civic projects – one Irish, the other British – rather than between rival, exclusionary projects. He claims that the accommodation of difference, paradoxically, is the only realistic way to construct any overarching identity in the longer term. He acknowledges that the Good Friday Agreement is fragile but argues that Northern Ireland is more stable now than it has been in thirty years. He also claims that binational compromise is a better guarantee of stability than integration into either a united Ireland or the United Kingdom.

David McCrone argues that Scotland has developed an advanced form of nationalism despite the lack of strong differences with England on language, religion, or other cultural means. The key to the Scottish question lies less in its internalist conflicts and tensions and much more in its politico-constitutional relations with the British state. Historically, the unwillingness or inability of the United Kingdom to modernize its political institutions left civil society "to its own devices," which engendered favourable conditions for a non-problematic cohabitation of the Scottish people within Britain. But by the second half of the 20th century, the contradictions inherent in the Union became more salient. The rise of nationalism in Scotland can thus be explained only in terms of geopolitics.

Montserrat Guibernau explores the political scenario set up by Spain's 1978 constitution, which recognized the existence of "nationalities and regions" and divided the country into seventeen autonomous communities. She analyses the image of Catalonia contained in the Statute of Autonomy of 1979. She also offers an account of the nationalist discourses put forward by the four major Catalan parties, emphasizing how their content differs with their political ideologies. Finally, she evaluates twenty years of Catalan political autonomy and examines the new initiatives and demands emerging from Catalan society. In conclusion, she notes that traditionally only a small minority in Catalonia has supported secession but that at present this minority is growing. The secessionist discourse of the Esquerra Republicana de Catalunya (ERC) may attract some new supporters, which could consolidate the party as Catalonia's third political force and place it in a key position, particularly if neither the Convergència i Unió (CiU) nor the Catalan Socialists achieved a majority in the Catalan election of 2003.

Radha Kumar examines partition as it occurred in five different regions: Palestine, Cyprus, India, Bosnia, and Ireland. She contrasts secessions and dissolutions of federations with partition. When an already existing unit leaves a state, that is secession. When new borders have to be carved out of existing units, it is partition. She reviews the best- and worst-case options before de jure or de facto partitions took place and she examines the best- and worst-case options after partition. She also discusses key issues of post-conflict stabilization in partition-related conflicts. She then draws five lessons from the history of partition. First, partitions do not work as a solution to ethnic conflict. Second, because partition restructures the sources of conflict, the separation of warring parties gained by partition is only temporary. Third, historical examples of alternative solutions based on a combination of human rights and devolution can be useful. Fourth, post-conflict reconstruction will be slow unless local communities are involved. Fifth, evolution with devolution has enormous potential.

Michael Murphy argues that indigenous peoples around the world are increasingly adopting the language of nationalism to describe their claims to self-determination. While this nationalist discourse has attracted attention from theorists of multicultural or multinational diversity, relatively few works focus intensively on indigenous nationalism, and fewer yet investigate the relationship between the democratic dimensions of indigenous nationalism and the distinctive challenges associated with its implementation in concrete cases and contexts. This essay attempts to fill some of these gaps. First, it develops a theoretical explanation of indigenous nationalism in terms of three interrelated dimensions of democratic self-determination: external democracy, internal democracy, and shared-ruled democracy. Second, it responds to some common criticisms of indigenous nationalism by making a clearer distinction between its normative and its empirical–institutional dimensions. Third, it explores the implications of this normative framework in concrete political terms by examining what kinds of indigenous communities will exercise the right to self-determination and what sorts of institutional possibilities are possible and/or already exist in practice. The discussion draws on examples from Australia, Canada, and New Zealand.

Nation-states: Viability and Fate

In the second group of case studies, the first three authors investigate problems related to the viability of particular nation-states; the others deal with the fate of nation-states. The first three papers (Thomas W. Pogge, Henry Milner, and Rajeev Bhargava) examine the United States, Finland, and India, respectively where the nation-state contains populations that can be described as extensions of neighbouring national majorities or as "contiguous diasporas" (Kumar's own phrase).

Thomas Pogge inquires which accommodations ought to be offered, and which refused, to native speakers of Spanish within the United States, and he investigates the moral grounds for those accommodations. Should the state protect a minority's culture by offering its children public education only in the minority language? This suggestion clashes with the best interests of children and also with liberal rights of their parents. Liberals cannot permit the interest of minority children to be sacrificed, and the preferences of their parents to be overruled, in order to help other members of this minority preserve their culture. In designing educational institutions, the interests of children must be paramount. Where the most important linguistic competence for children is fluency in English, schools should aim for such fluency first and foremost. Most minority children in the United States are served best by instruction in English. This leads to a principle not of English only, but of English first. While most minority children should be brought to full mastery of English, there is every reason to enable and encourage them to develop full mastery of their native language as well.

Henry Milner explores the various dimensions of the relationship between the Finnish majority and the Swedish minority in Finland, from constitutional rights and prerogatives to informal underlying mechanism. Among the former is the special position of the Swedish-speaking island of Åland; the latter include the role and composition of the Swedish People's Party. While no country can serve as a "model" for other countries, given the uniqueness of different experiences, Milner finds useful lessons from this country. Although the overall Finnish approach is inapplicable to Quebec – at least to a Quebec with the powers only of a Canadian province – Finland offers one major, directly applicable lesson. Anglophone Quebec needs the equivalent of the Swedish Peoples' Party, which, combined with proportional representation, would guarantee it fair political representation. Anglophones could then, over time, reject the uncompromising approach of the Equality Party and Alliance Quebec and, learning from Finland, develop leaders and policies that could contribute to creative compromises that reflected the needs and interests of both minority and majority.

Rajeev Bhargava discusses identity-dependent majority and minority issues for Muslim minorities within India. A "majority–minority syndrome" sets in when either the minority or the majority is unable to exercise power and blames the other for this disadvantage. Most of the time, of course, it is the minority that is suffering such an injustice. A majority–minority framework is one in which groups have distinct identities and are recognized as such. Bhargava believes that the syndrome may be removed by a framework that is not part of the problem but rather part of the solution. A majority–minority framework involves constitutionally protected minority rights. It may not be sufficient, but it is necessary for alleviating the source of the syndrome. In India, the issue of minority rights is tied intimately to the maintenance of Muslim personal laws. Bhargava rejects both the radical individualists who wish to abandon the framework and the conservative communitarians who seek to preserve it. He accepts personal laws in principle, but he favours a reformist position that imposes important modifications to those personal laws that violate basic human rights, and he also subscribes to an indirect form of paternalist reformism whereby the state provides conditions that facilitate reform within the community.

The next three essays (Rogers Brubaker, Ben Anderson, and Kenneth McRoberts) together provide some insights concerning the fate of nation-states.

Rogers Brubaker seeks to specify key persisting differences in the way questions of ethnicity, migration, and statehood are posed in western and eastern Europe. As far as ethnicity is concerned, western Europe endorses an immigrant-ethnicity model, in which ethnic groups arise through migration and do not make collective claims to indigeneity. Eastern Europe endorses a territorial-nationality model, in which ethnic groups are indigenous. The political claims that can be made in the name of ethnicity differ sharply in the two cases. The immigrant-ethnicity model evokes politics of anti-discrimination, civic inclusion, and "soft multiculturalism," while territorial nationality involves claims to public recognition, to resources for cultural activities, and sometimes to special immunities and exemptions. The problematics of migration in western Europe has focused on immigration, especially from outside the region, while in eastern Europe questions of migration have initially involved emigration. In conclusion, Brubaker argues that if western Europe is entering a post-national age, the political context for much of eastern Europe might more aptly be described as post-multinational. While in western Europe, the trend is towards the unbundling and re-distribution of previously concentrated powers, state-building is still very much on the agenda in eastern Europe.

Benedict Anderson argues that Indonesia is still a "real country" and that there is no good alternative to the resuscitation of its traditional nationalism. He divides his essay into three parts. He first discusses the reasons for the present deep crisis. He then explains why he thinks certain multi-ethnic nation-states, such as Indonesia, are worth recuperating and strengthening, in view of the alternatives. One key condition is that no component ethnic group should command an electoral majority or control the state apparatus. A second is that Indonesia has an accepted national language and an accepted national history that is not founded on the "legacy" of any one ethnic or religious group. He finally considers the difficulties facing national renovation at the present time, especially given the immense political, economic, cultural, and moral damage inflicted on the country for more than three decades by the Suharto regime, with almost-universal (till the last moment) international support, and he examines the various prescriptions for "cure" currently on the table – particularly "regional autonomy," and deeper deregulation of the state. His conclusion is a defence of the nineteenth-century national idea for the coming decades.

Ken McRoberts notices that nation-states are nowadays losing some of their prerogatives, but he wonders about the nations within these nation-states. In other words, what about the many "minority nations" or "nations without states" that have persisted despite the best efforts of the nation-states to absorb them? He also observes that the context of integration is fundamentally different in Europe and in North America. Europe has a collective identity, but there are no supranational North American institutions to support and foster a continental identity there. Precisely for that reason, there is a strong identification with regions and nations within the states of North America. For instance, a growing number of Quebec residents identify with Quebec more than with Canada. Forty-nine per cent of Quebecers say that they are Quebecers first. Only half of them are "proud to be Canadians." So the *state* component of the nation-state couplet may be in decline. But we should not exaggerate the decline, even for smaller nation-states, for the *nation* is not necessarily in decline. On the contrary, it seems to be faring quite well.

ABOUT THE CONCLUSION

In a concluding chapter, I draw some lessons from the twenty-one essays in this book. It seems to me that three lessons clearly emerge. First,
the nation-state can no longer count as the only model of political organization. In addition to the nation-state, we must find ways to consolidate multinational states and supranational organizations. Second, we
may also conclude that the alternatives to the traditional nation-state
model will not be viable unless the encompassing states are able to conduct themselves properly vis-à-vis their component minority nations.
Multinational (nation-)states cannot be sustainable unless they afford
political recognition to the component nations. Third, if truly liberal
and democratic minority nations are unable to gain political recognition within the multinational state, they will be morally justified in
seeking such political recognition by achieving full sovereignty or by
performing collective civil disobedience. Just as one should not adopt
the nation-state as the unique model of political organization, one
should admit that there are circumstances in which the multinational
state may no longer be viable and when the creation of a new nation-
state is morally justified.

PART ONE
Theoretical Foundations: National, Multinational, Supranational

MARGARET CANOVAN

Sleeping Dogs, Prowling Cats, and Soaring Doves: Three Paradoxes of Nationhood

Is there something particularly intractable about nationalism?[1] Many of the most long-running political conflicts are national ones, while even in the peaceful realms of political theory it seems to be hard to think about nationhood and nationalism without becoming entangled in paradox. This paper is concerned with three different paradoxes in the political theory of nationalism. For ease of reference I label them the paradoxes of the sleeping dog, the prowling cat, and the soaring dove.

The first paradox refers to the long-standing contradiction whereby political philosophers tacitly assumed the presence of nations to underpin theories that were unsympathetic or hostile to national loyalties. The recent revival of nationalist politics has brought this slumbering paradox out into the open, prompting some theorists to try to resolve it in one of two ways, either by recognizing the importance of nations and seeking to give them theoretical expression or else by denying their continuing relevance and seeking explicitly post-national solutions. My argument is that both of these opposed strategies lead their adherents into further paradoxes. Although the essay is predominantly critical, it concludes that political theorists may be able to learn important lessons from these frustrating encounters with nationhood.

THE PARADOX OF THE SLEEPING DOG

In the familiar Sherlock Holmes story, "the curious incident of the dog in the night-time" was that no incident occurred: the dog did not bark when it might have been expected to. Within mainstream Western political theory in the second half of the twentieth century, the nation was the dog that did not bark, slumbering unnoticed all the time. Not that nationalism had ever received as much attention from theorists as its practical impact might seem to warrant, as Isaiah Berlin pointed out (Berlin, 1981). But for many decades after 1945, revulsion against Nazism added disapprobation to indifference, sweeping such matters out of sight and out of mind. If mainstream political theorists considered the topic at all, they discussed it only to dismiss it as unworthy of notice (for example, Graham, 1986, 121–40; Goodin and Pettit, 1993, 3).

The paradox is that those same theorists were taking nations for granted all the time. While ignoring or dismissing nationhood, they were relying on tacit assumptions about the ubiquity of nations to make their theories work. Ernest Renan's observation on the contribution that *forgetting* can make to national unity has been much quoted during the recent revival of interest in nationalism, often to counter insistence on keeping alive the memory of ancient wrongs (Renan, 1939, 190). But amnesia is associated even more intimately with nationhood, which seems to be most influential when it has sunk so far below the threshold of social consciousness as to be almost part of the air that we breathe. Acute commentators have recently drawn attention to some of the ways in which these hidden assumptions of nationhood structure the very world that we perceive. In the words of Rogers Brubaker, we live in "a world in which nationhood is pervasively institutionalised in the practice of states and the workings of the state system. It is a world in which nation is widely, if unevenly, available and resonant as a category of social vision and division." (Brubaker, 1996, 21; cf. Billig, 1995; Calhoun, 1997).

Despite their formally universalist habits of discourse, political philosophers have shared this unconscious tendency to take nations and national boundaries for granted, with the result that crucial questions have remained unasked. Theorists of democracy have rarely worried about the boundaries of the "people" who were to generate representatives to act for them and accept majority decisions as binding, because they unconsciously took a nation with limits and unifying bonds as the norm (Canovan, 1996, 16–26). Contested national allegiances could be invoked to explain failed or problematic democracies, as in Northern Ireland, but the contribution that shared nationhood elsewhere might be making to the legitimacy of democratic representation tended not to come up for discussion.

Similarly eloquent silences can in retrospect be detected within the debates on social justice that occupied so much of the attention of political philosophers during this period. Theorists of justice rarely stopped to ask why sharing of resources should happen within *this* particular group of people, taking for granted the existence not only of a state but (more crucially) of a political community owning collective resources and sharing communal solidarity. Although the explicit purpose of John Rawls's "Original Position" and "Veil of Ignorance" was to enable him to arrive at principles of justice undistorted by "the accidents of nature and social circumstance" (such as birth into a privileged caste or race), Rawls took for granted that these principles applied only inside "a self-contained national community" recruited primarily by birth – an assumption shared unreflectively by almost all of those who debated the theory over twenty years (Rawls, 1972, 102, 357; Tamir, 1993, 117–21).[2] Rawls's subsequent elaboration of a "law of peoples" has only made this incongruous assumption more conspicuous (Rawls, 1999).

Even consciously anti-communitarian theorists helped themselves to similar assumptions by taking for granted the existence of polities of a particular and unusual kind: areas of pacified political space, enjoying sufficient generalized trust to make possible the rule of equal law inside their borders. The more cosmopolitan liberals, fixing their eyes on the broad horizon of humanity, also assumed that these cohesive polities would be so good at mobilizing popular support that they would be able to project power outside their borders in defence of human rights (Canovan, 1998). In retrospect, political theorists' failure to ask questions about the sources of *power* is particularly striking. As they explored questions of freedom, justice, and rights, almost all contemporary political philosophers have taken for granted that a modern polity can be expected to wield a great deal of power with very little use of force. They assume that states will have enough power within their own boundaries not only to maintain order, collect taxes, and provide an adequate infrastructure, but also to enforce equal laws, allocate benefits and burdens justly, and protect the rights of citizens, including members of minorities. Externally, the expectation is that the state will be able not only to defend its borders but to support liberal causes across the world. The uses that ought to be made of these internal and external powers are much debated among political theorists, but concerning the power itself – its sources, its conditions, and its limits – there is a strange silence within the literature: a reserve of consensual collective power is just there on tap, to be used as required.

Like the boundaries of their "peoples," the power of some modern liberal-democratic polities may seem part of the order of nature. But looked at in historical or comparative perspective, that view seems oddly parochial. By historical standards, these states represent astonishing concentrations of collective power, wielding a degree of control over their territory and receiving a level of co-operation from their citizens that earlier despots would have envied. Even more remarkably, these states use relatively little raw coercion: far more of their power is a matter of mobilizing consensus and directing compliance. To say this is not of course to discount the many forms of structural coercion and manipulation present in such societies (Giddens, 1985, 181–92). But what is at issue here is not so much power *over* individuals as power *to do* things by mobilizing collective action.[3] It is easy to suppose that the crucial factor is simply "modernity" itself, with all its technological implications for surveillance and indoctrination. But contemporary comparisons across the world do not bear out this idea. A number of modern states that make use of these technological devices are indeed powerful, though at the cost of exercising a great deal of coercion. A larger number are actually very weak *despite* their extensive investment in coercion – too weak to make their own laws and policies effective across their territories or to mobilize their populations and resources.[4] Their experience casts into relief the blithe assumption, made by political theorists of all persuasions, that consensual political power is easy to come by. In effect, theorists have taken for granted the power generated by communal solidarity: by the sense that "we" are a people in possession of a polity (Canovan, 1996, 68–74; 1998, 237–53).[5]

There is of course scope for argument about whether or not that communal solidarity needs to be *national*. Some observers would maintain that modern Western states have to a greater or lesser extent ceased to need such support and become self-sustaining, because they are good enough at providing the rule of law and other services to earn the respect of an increasingly cosmopolitan population of temporary residents (Parekh, 1995, 139–40). Others would follow Habermas in arguing that, despite the key role played by nationhood in the past, a polity can now be peaceful, cohesive, and powerful on the basis of "constitutional patriotism" alone (Habermas, 1990, 491–500; cf. Canovan, 2000, 413–32). Until recently, however, political theorists did not argue about this at all, simply taking for granted the presence of nations at the same time as ignoring or disparaging them. In retrospect, some might be tempted to feel that this situation was not entirely without advantages and that wise political theorists could perhaps have contrived to be more aware of the sleeping dogs while taking care to let them lie. But that option is no longer available: for the past decade the dogs have been awake and barking, roused by events outside the control of academics.

In present circumstances it is much harder simply to ignore the nations that have led a shadowy existence in the basements of political theory. Two alternative ways out of the paradox are therefore being explored. One substantial group of theorists has in the past decade sought to domesticate the prowling beasts of nationalism by providing a theoretical framework within which to judge their activities. Other political thinkers have adopted the opposite strategy, arguing that whatever the past significance of nation-states and nationalism, they are increasingly irrelevant in an age of globalization and must in any case give way to overriding cosmopolitan commitments. Unfortunately both strategies give rise to further paradoxes, in each case to do with the relation between theory and practice. I devote more space here to the first strategy, which is at the centre of current debates. I call it the paradox of the prowling cat, for reasons that become apparent below.

THE PARADOX OF THE PROWLING CAT

Following the transformation of the political agenda by the collapse of Soviet-bloc Communism, the 1990s saw an explosion of interest in the political theory of nationalism and also some rapid and revealing changes in attitudes to the topic.[6] When the sleeping dogs of nationalism first woke up at the beginning of the decade, quite a few political theorists were inclined to make pets of them, and several worked out theoretical defences of nationalism and national self-determination. While each of these defences has distinctive features, common themes are easy to find, for almost all are extensions of liberalism.

One version of nationalism turned out to follow quite readily from the familiar liberal principle of respect for individual autonomy. All that was needed was for liberal thinkers to take on board part of the communitarian critique to which they had been subjected, reinterpreting autonomy to take account of an individual's identity as a member of a particular community and bearer of a particular culture. Once they conceded that individuals commonly identify themselves as members of what Avishai Margalit and Joseph Raz call an "encompassing group" – typically, a nation – then respect for individual autonomy could be translated into rights to respect for one's distinctive culture, to self-realization as a member of the group, and to some political form of collective self-determination (Margalit and Raz, 1990; see also MacCormick, 1991; Tamir, 1993; Miller, 1995). Some theorists were cautious about the political implications of this position, but others were prepared to offer generalized defences of variants of the traditional model of the self-governing nation-state.

During a brief "springtime of the nations" in the early 1990s the tone of this new theoretical nationalism was confident and optimistic. Recent writing tends to be more guarded and hesitant (see, for example, the chapters by Moore, Miller, Nielsen, and Philpott in Moore, 1998) for reasons that are not hard to fathom. By the end of the decade events in Bosnia, Kosovo, and elsewhere had made clear that, alongside the domesticated nationalism that liberal theorists wanted to support, much more savage versions were also making use of the discourse of self-determination, and doing so in situations where mixed populations and rival claims to territory allowed vindication of such claims only through civil war and "ethnic cleansing."

We cannot hold philosophical defenders of national self-determination responsible for these horrors; even if ethnic warlords had taken the trouble to consult academic articles, they would have found that all the liberal nationalist theorists had taken great care to buttress their theories with qualifications designed to rule out any of the nasty things being done by Balkan nationalists.[7] In doing so, however, the theorists became entangled in paradoxes, undermining their own theories in the effort to guard against evil effects. Oddly enough, their dilemmas arose out of a set of highly respectable commitments. As we saw above, the new nationalist concern for self-determination is an offshoot of the liberal commitment to individual autonomy. It follows that nationalist claims must be universal – all nations have equal rights – and also that all such rights must be limited by respect for the fundamental rights of individuals and minorities. The ideal is one in which every individual enjoys self-realization and self-determination within his or her community, in harmony with other individuals enjoying the same rights within their own communities. The new theorists wanted to engage with practical politics and to influence events (for example, Miller, 1995, 2–4; Margalit and Raz, 1990, 440); they were also sensitive to the claims of different cultural traditions with clashing principles and aware that modern political territories tend to be culturally mixed. Paradoxically, it was their attempts to work out the implications of these appealing commitments that got them into trouble.

Perverse Incentives

Part of the problem is that new nationalist theories inadvertently contain perverse incentives to nationalists to do the exact opposite of what the theorist intends to authorize. It may be as well if such theorists do not gain much practical political influence, for theoretical qualifications intended specifically to avert communal violence and the wholesale redrawing of political borders would (if applied) have the effect of making these things more likely.[8]

Take a typical example of a careful theoretical proviso that could backfire in this way. In his discussion of the desirability of national self-government, David Miller rules out any licence for nationalists to secede at will from the state in which they find themselves, stipulating that such an extreme measure can be considered only "where an established state houses two or more groups with distinct and irreconcilable national identities" (Miller, 1995, 113). Nothing could seem more reasonable. But consider the incentives this proviso would create if it were translated into practice. Suppose that you are an enthusiastic and unscrupulous nationalist belonging to an amorphous minority with some degree of territorial concentration, some discontents, but considerable ties to other groups. What practical political message does this principle send to you? Surely that if you want to claim a right to secession with philosophical blessing, the way to do it is to heighten the sense of difference between your own identity and that of the majority to the point of making them "irreconcilable." As Ronald Beiner warns, "nationalist political actors can be expected to make a somewhat cynical and opportunistic use of whatever legitimising slogans are placed at their disposal" (Beiner, 1998, 161; cf. Miller, 1998, 64).

This is not merely a hypothetical possibility. We have seen in many recent cases how easily militant minorities can widen the gulf between relatively harmonious groups by provoking fear and retaliation, setting off a dynamic escalation that forces a reluctant population to choose one side (Ignatieff, 1994, supplies many examples). Furthermore, situations of this kind offer scope for irredentist agitation by neighbouring states with claims on the territory concerned (Brubaker, 1996). In other words, a principle that appears to be a reasonable way of solving a few intractable disputes could itself help to generate such problems. An even stronger incentive to nationalist militancy surfaces in the course of a defence of self-determination by Avner De-Shalit, who suggests that the best argument for the formation of new nation-states is the existence of ethnic "enmity" (De-Shalit, 1996, 914). This is precisely what much nationalist terrorism is intended to produce.

Several new nationalist theorists set up a further hurdle that nationalist movements must jump on the way to secession, stipulating that the territory in question must not contain intermingled populations that would give rise to new national minorities (Miller, 1995, 113; Moore, 1997, 910–12). Again, this looks to be an admirable principle. But what message would it send to the militants of the dominant group if they were to read it? Evidently that their most promising tactic is to induce other groups to leave: they are given an incentive to engage in "ethnic cleansing" of their territory, not necessarily by using methods as brutally effective as those employed in the former Yugoslavia, but simply by making the territory uncomfortable for the minority in the myriad ways available to an ingenious nationalist. Proposals for settling claims to secession by referendum (as proposed, for example, by Margaret Moore) provide a particularly strong practical incentive to nationalists to flood the territory with as many of their co-nationals as they can manage to recruit, while pushing out people who may vote the wrong way (Moore, 1997, 910; see also Margalit and Raz, 1990, 458). The referenda that attended the fragmentation of Yugoslavia have been described as "the battle cries of highly mobilised and desperate populations" (Brady and Kaplan, 1994, 206).

None of this is what new nationalist theorists intend as they struggle to come to terms with the practical implications of nationalism.[9] But the more ingeniously and reasonably the theorists try to cater to practical difficulties, the more they seem to undermine their own objectives. Furthermore, the paradoxes go deeper than this problem of perverse incentives. By defending national self-determination with elaborate qualifications, theorists often find themselves taking up positions that appear to license high-minded imperialism rather than self-rule.

A Mandate for NATO?

Recall that new nationalist theorists set out from concern with the politics of recognition, no doubt agreeing with Liah Greenfeld that the popular appeal of nationalism lies in its evocation of collective dignity (Greenfeld, 1992, 487): *we* will no longer be dictated to by *them*, nor defer (in the words of Isaiah Berlin) to "tutelage, however benevolent, on the part of ultimately patronising superiors from a foreign land or alien class or milieu" (quoted in Beiner, 1998, 159). Now imagine that

you are a member of a national minority with a prickly sense of national pride, and listen to some of the language in which the problems
of national self-determination have been discussed by those whose
avowed aim is to *support* it.

In their influential article on self-determination, Avishai Margalit and
Joseph Raz consider whether "encompassing groups" such as nations can
"be entrusted" with the exercise of that right. In their view such a right
would ideally be exercised only on the authorization of an impartial international court. In the absence of any such body, they argue, the right
must indeed be "entrusted" to the national group in question, but "international bodies" must also be "entrusted" with the task of seeing that it
is exercised subject to conditions. One condition is "its being exercised
for the right reasons"; another, the prospect that the establishment of the
new national state "will do good rather than add to the ills of this world"
(Margalit and Raz, 1990, 455–9. Cf. Miller, 1995, 112–13, 81; 1998, 64,
71, 75.). Use of the passive "be entrusted" leaves open the question of
who is doing the "entrusting." Other theorists are more candid. The dis-
concerting combination of a defence of self-determination with an assumption that "we" should keep control over the way it is exercised is
more explicit in Daniel Philpott's first article (1995) on the subject. According to him, "we must demand that any regime, whatever its circumstances and beliefs, seeks to protect 'basic human rights.'" No group is to
be granted self-determination without a favourable assessment of "the
group's likely potential for justice",[10] and we must be circumspect about
allowing the expression of non-liberal cultures (372, 382). Philpott crys-
tallizes the dilemma when he asks, "Which provisions for protecting culture *might we allow a self-determining group* to implement?" (374,
emphasis added).

It is a curious spectacle: a group of theorists who profess themselves
to be defenders of national self-determination, but who must seem to
nationalists to be saying, "*We* are in charge of humanity. We will *consider* authorizing you to run your own affairs, provided we are convinced that you will do it in our way, not in yours." These discussions
of what "we" will or will not allow are oddly insensitive to the way
such things must sound to a real-life nationalist.

It may be objected that the appearance of high-handedness is simply
an effect of discussing the topic in the context of an abstract, universalist discourse. Debating in general terms what actions are justified and
what "we" as political philosophers can approve is one thing; calling
for the exercise of power to stop what we disapprove of is quite

another. But the theorists concerned do appear to be (at least partly) motivated by the belief that their debates have practical implications for the policies that should be adopted by the powerful Western states in which most of them live.[11] If this is so, and if all those anxious qualifications hedging the principle of self-determination are to have any effect, then (despite the new theorists' sympathy for self-determination) commitments to more active Western intervention around the world do seem to be lurking in the small print of the very principles that are supposed to favour national autonomy.

As we saw above, those principles authorize self-government only in certain cases, definitely not in those where national groups are deeply intermingled. In such cases, we are often told, the groups involved will have to settle for power-sharing arrangements (for example, Miller, 1995, 81, 118). Discussing circumstances in which an alternative to national self-determination is required, Margaret Moore argues that her principles would have prescribed for Bosnia a confederal solution that would have recognized the equal rights of all the national groups (Moore, 1997, 912; 1998, 153). The questions begged by such arguments are whether fall-back arrangements of this kind will actually be feasible and what kind of heavy-handed intervention may be required to make them so. How might such solutions be found or made to stick? New nationalist theory itself gives this question extra urgency. By stressing the importance of shared nationality in establishing political trust, it casts doubt on the viability of power-sharing where there is no overarching nationhood to foster that trust (Miller, 1995, 91–3; Moore, 1997, 904–5). To be consistent, its authors should therefore be more prepared than liberal universalists to acknowledge the almost-insuperable difficulties of power-sharing in circumstances where some of the intermingled groups are seeking full self-determination or secession to join a neighbouring state. Putting consociational arrangements in place and preventing them from breaking down thereafter may well be possible only where they are imposed from outside (like the shaky compromise, achieved under NATO auspices, that ended the Bosnian war). It follows that one practical implication of new nationalist theory would be the establishment of many more such protectorates. But to be authorizing tutelage of mixed populations while simultaneously praising the blessings of self-determination is a confusing and politically unstable position, which seems designed almost to inflame nationalist passions among those subject to the mandate.

To sum up this section, the fundamental paradox of new nationalist theory is that the case made for self-determination cannot have the practical relevance that its authors would like it to have without authorizing paternalistic rule by the self-appointed defenders of universal liberal principles and, in effect, by those who actually have the military power to take on this role. It is a paradox reminiscent of Aesop's fable about the mice and the cat.

The Mice called a general council, and after the doors were locked, entered into a free consultation about ways and means how to render themselves more secure from the danger of the Cat. Many schemes were proposed, and much debate took place upon the matter. At last, a young Mouse, in a fine florid speech, broached an expedient, which he contended was the only one to put them entirely out of the power of the enemy, and this was, that the Cat should wear a bell about her neck, which, upon the least motion, would give the alarm, and be a signal for them to retire into their holes. This speech was received with great applause, and it was even proposed by some, that the Mouse who had made it should have the thanks of the assembly. Upon which, an old Mouse, who had sat silent hitherto, gravely observed, that the contrivance was admirable, and the author of it, without doubt, very ingenious; but he thought it would not be so proper to vote him thanks, till he should further inform them how the bell was to be fastened about the Cat's neck, and who would undertake the task. (Bewick, 1975, 193–4)

The paradox is, in short, that when liberal nationalists encourage the prowling cats of nationalism to roam, they first endanger the liberal rights that they want to defend and end by reintroducing heavy-handed tutelage. Attempting to escape from the paradox of the sleeping dog by vindicating national loyalties seems only to lead them into another impasse. As I suggested above, however, this is not the only escape route that political theorists have been exploring. The difficulties in which liberal nationalists find themselves entangled may appear to vindicate those who have chosen instead to develop cosmopolitan commitments, arguing that theory and practice must transcend nation-states altogether by building and justifying ever stronger and more effective international institutions. But cosmopolitans should not be complacent, for their chosen route leads them into yet another paradox, which I call the paradox of the soaring dove. This I explore briefly below.

THE PARADOX OF THE SOARING DOVE

One of the most striking political developments of recent decades, as cosmopolitan liberals often point out, is the enormous increase in international political action of one sort or another (Feld, Jordan, and Hurwitz, 1994). Myriad international organizations, agencies, and regimes have been established by agreements between states, making inroads on state sovereignty and acknowledging global interdependence and mutual interests in matters ranging from free trade to global warming, from avoiding nuclear war to protecting endangered species. Even more encouraging for cosmopolitans (such as Pogge, 1994; Nussbaum, 1996; Linklater, 1998) are the burgeoning growth alongside official inter-state bodies of the non-governmental organizations (NGOs) that make up "international civil society" and the upsurge of humanitarian solidarity that they and their supporters represent. The doves of universalist humanitarianism seem to be taking flight, uncertainly as yet, perhaps, but with increasing confidence and in ever-greater numbers.

No one can know what the outcome of these developments will be by the time another fifty years has passed or whether anything like the "humane" or "cosmopolitan" governance projected in some quarters will come into being (Falk, 1995; Held, 1995; see also McGrew, 1997). But the final paradox to which I want to draw attention is that most of these soaring doves are actually homing pigeons, in the sense that the international institutions are offshoots of nation-states rather than alternatives to them. International organizations and regimes rely heavily on the strong nation-states that were instrumental in setting them up; apparently footloose NGOs have their safe home bases in the liberal nation-states from which they draw most of their resources; support for universalist causes has long been a matter of national pride in a clutch of liberal nations from Sweden to the United States. Criticizing over-hasty talk about globalization and the end of the nation-state, Paul Hirst and Grahame Thompson point out that international law itself is impossible without a nucleus of states where the rule of law is already firmly established, which are usually nation-states (Hirst and Thompson, 1996, 190–4). Furthermore, the reach and influence of international organizations and regimes across the globe are uneven, as they cluster around the liberal nation-states that gave them birth.

This is not to deny the significance of these developments. There are signs that some of these international space-stations launched from national bases really are becoming more self-sustaining. International conventions on human rights may be the creations of Western states, but they have by now become sufficiently institutionalized, have built up sufficient establishments and practices, and have become so entrenched in the political discourse of those states that they can often limit the powers and affect the policies of their originators. Admittedly, this often means that the *least* oppressive states are most pilloried, whereas bloody tyrannies take no notice. But the association of human rights conventions with states that are politically and economically strong does also give them some leverage against certain states with illiberal political cultures, in so far as these states want to join Western clubs. Post-communist states eager to rejoin "Europe" have been particularly susceptible to this kind of pressure. Certain nation-states and national citizens are building new international institutions and giving rise to an international civil society that *may* eventually transcend their origins. In the meantime, however, these emergent phenomena are deeply dependent on the national polities that harbour them.

The paradox of the soaring dove may (perhaps) be a temporary predicament, but while it lasts it generates painful tensions, especially over human rights. There is no uniform global legal order from which human beings in general or nations in general can claim uniform rights. Thomas Pogge observes optimistically that "the existing global institutional framework" is not God-given, but "imposed by human beings who are collectively quite capable of changing it" (Pogge, 1994, 93). Of course *if* all human beings could be induced to act collectively, they could indeed generate the power to realize this dream. But although "humanity" (that grandest but flimsiest of contemporary imagined communities) may be able to muster enough power to fuel Greenpeace and Amnesty International, it is not nearly potent enough to bestow individual or group rights on myriad victims in China, Indonesia, much of Africa, Iraq, Colombia, and the rest of the non-liberal world. Agents ranging from small-scale NGOs to governments representing powerful nation-states are establishing *patches* of international legal order, building outwards from their national bases by means of agreements that bridge a few of the abysses of lawlessness in which so many human beings are swallowed up and bestowing on some favoured members of the human race the rights that bare humanity cannot itself convey (Arendt, 1967, 290–302; Rosas, 1995). But from a philosophical point of view the implications of political contingency are hard to accept. Rights claimed on universal grounds as the rights of all humanity belong in practice only to those fortunate enough to be citizens of liberal nation-states or to enjoy the fitful patronage of organizations based in those states. Minor infringements of the "human rights" of the fortunate are pursued with the full rigour of the law, while appalling atrocities against those outside its reach go unpunished.

One of many disquieting aspects of the paradox is that the very nation-states that most successfully defend individual rights for their own nationals, and that establish and support institutions for the protection of universal human rights, are themselves persistently and unavoidably guilty of inhumane treatment of the desperate would-be immigrants against whom they try to defend their borders. This is a problem with no obvious solution. It might even be argued that one source of the humanitarian energy that flows from Western countries into the Third World is the sheer moral strain engendered by living in one of these privileged national havens, in which "our people" enjoy rights, while looking out at a world in which more people do not. Be that as it may, the paradoxical fact is that although in some future state of the world the doves of universalist humanitarianism may roost in some kind of non-national space-station powered by its own sources of solidarity, for the moment they take flight from the bounded and exclusive havens provided by nation-states.

CONCLUSION

The paradoxes that we have been examining suggest that the topic of nations and nationalism is particularly difficult. It may be tempting to suggest that political theorists have gone astray because this is a peculiarly murky and tangled region of human affairs, a swampy jungle of irrational myths and atavistic emotions that clear thinkers enter at their peril. But our paradoxes in fact offer something rather more chastening: many political theorists have found themselves in difficulties because they failed to pay attention to some of the central phenomena of politics, which cannot really be said to be cloaked in myth and mystery. These are *power, agency,* and *contingency.* The paradox of the "sleeping dog" arises from inattention to the phenomena of collective political power; that of the "prowling cat," from insensitivity to the perspective of political agents; and that of the "soaring dove," from neglect of the contingency and patchiness of political endeavours and achievements. If the topic of nations and nationalism proves particularly intractable, the reason may be that it touches on areas in which these themes are peculiarly salient. The analysis offered here suggests that political theorists would be well advised, when formulating their theories, to pay more sustained attention to these crucial features of political life.

NOTES

1 A version of this paper appeared in *Political Studies* (2001) 49, 203–15. I
   have benefited from responses to earlier versions presented at seminars in
   London, Birmingham, and Montreal, and especially from comments by
   James Canovan, April Carter, John Horton, and the anonymous reviewers
   for *Political Studies*.
2 Some of Rawls's cosmopolitan critics did notice and dispute this tacit limitation (for example, Pogge, 1989). But evading the paradox of the sleeping
   dog only entangled them in the paradox of the soaring dove: see below
   (cf. Canovan, 1998).
3 Theorists of power regularly acknowledge a difference between power *to do*
   things and power *over* someone, but most of them are interested primarily
   in the latter (for example, Connolly, 1983, 87–8; Giddens, 1985, 7–17;
   Wrong, 1995, xiii). Those theorists who do explore the horizontal dimension of power tend to pay only marginal attention to the contribution made
   to this by national solidarity (for example, Arendt, 1967, 166; 1970, 41–9;
   Parsons, 1967, 297–354; Wrong, 1995, 138–49).
4 On the complex reasons for the weakness of most Third World states, see
   Migdal, 1988. Migdal rarely mentions national identity (even when discussing the unusual strength of the Israeli and Japanese states), but he does observe (32) that "legitimation" is "the most potent factor accounting for the
   strength of the state." Another student of Third World politics, Christopher
   Clapham, links the fragility of such states directly with lack of "a sense of
   national self-identity" (Clapham, 1985, 43). On the significance of nationhood in an era when "the people" have become the usual basis of political
   legitimacy, see Beetham, 1991, 75, 127, 132–4.
5 The most spectacular recent demonstration of power generated from the
   ground up by solidarity aided by national consciousness was the popular
   mobilization in Poland that set off the collapse of the Soviet empire in central and eastern Europe (Garton Ash, 1991, 5, 11, 14, 29, 32; Goodwyn,
   1991, 174, 253).
6 For a sample of the literature, see Margalit and Raz, 1990; MacCormick,
   1991; Nielson, 1993; Tamir, 1993; Miller, 1995; Philpott, 1995; De-Shalit,
   1996; McKim and McMahan, 1997; Moore, 1997; and Beiner, 1999. A
   particularly useful recent collection, marked by the disillusioning experiences of former Yugoslavia in the 1990s, is Moore, 1998.
7 One of the most unrepentant, Kai Nielsen, tries to avoid entanglement in
   such difficulties by restricting the scope of his argument for national

self-determination and secession to cases within "rich liberal democracies," – a category that he further narrows by excluding Spain (because of the Basque conflict) and the United Kingdom (because of Northern Ireland) (Nielsen, 1998, 104, 113, 116).

8 For incisive criticisms of the unintended practical implications of philosophical justifications of secession, see the chapters in Moore, 1998, by Ronald Beiner, Allen Buchanan, Donald Horowitz, John McGarry, and Wayne Norman, and see also Pavkovic, 2000.

9 In a footnote to a later treatment of the issue, Margaret Moore acknowledges the perverse incentive to "ethnic cleansing" and hastens to add a disclaimer; Moore, 1998, 157, note 50.

10 Commenting on qualifications of this sort, Donald Horowitz observes: "The inability to forecast the emergence of an illiberal regime with any degree of reliability renders this qualification of the right to secession illusory" (Horowitz, in Moore, 1998, 198).

11 Recent experience may have weakened or destroyed such hopes. In a disillusioned post-Bosnian treatment of the topic, Daniel Philpott concedes the dangers of self-determination in practice and the improbability of his qualifications actually being observed, because "the world's institutions are too unripe" (Philpott, 1998, 84).

REFERENCES

Arendt, H. (1967) *The Origins of Totalitarianism.* London: George Allen and Unwin.

– (1970) *On Violence.* London: Allen Lane.

Beetham, D. (1991) *The Legitimation of Power.* London: Macmillan.

Beiner, R. (1998) "National Self-determination: Some Cautionary Remarks Concerning the Rhetoric of Rights," in Moore, 1998.

– ed. (1999) *Theorizing Nationalism.* Albany, NY: SUNY Press.

Berlin, I. (1981) "Nationalism: Past Neglect and Present Power," in H. Hardy, ed., *Against the Current.* Oxford: Oxford University Press.

Bewick, T. (1975) *The Fables of Aesop.* London: Paddington Press.

Billig, M. (1995) *Banal Nationalism.* London: Sage.

Brady, H.E., and C.S. Kaplan (1994) "Eastern Europe and the Former Soviet Union," in D. Butler and A. Ranney, eds., *Referendums around the World.* London: Macmillan.

Brubaker, R. (1996) *Nationalism Reframed: Nationhood and the National Question in the New Europe.* Cambridge: Cambridge University Press.

Calhoun, C. (1997) *Nationalism.* Buckingham: Open University Press.

Canovan, M. (1996) *Nationhood and Political Theory.* Cheltenham: Edward Elgar.

– (1998) "Crusaders, Sceptics and the Nation," *Journal of Political Ideologies,* 3, 237–53.

– (2000) "Patriotism Is Not Enough," *British Journal of Political Science,* 30, 413–32.

Clapham, C. (1985) *Third World Politics: An Introduction.* London: Croom Helm.

Connolly, W.E. (1983) *The Terms of Political Discourse.* Oxford: Martin Robertson.

De-Shalit, A. (1996) "National Self-determination: Political, Not Cultural," *Political Studies* 44, 906–20.

Falk, R. (1995) *On Humane Governance: Toward a New Global Politics.* Cambridge: Polity.

Feld, W.J., and R.S. Jordan, with L. Hurwitz (1994) *International Organizations: A Comparative Approach,* 3rd ed. Westport, Conn: Praeger.

Garton Ash, T. (1991) *The Polish Revolution: Solidarity.* London: Granta Books.

Giddens, A. (1985) *The Nation-State and Violence.* Cambridge: Polity.

Goodin, R., and P. Pettit, eds. (1993) *A Companion to Contemporary Political Philosophy.* Oxford: Blackwell.

Goodwyn, L. (1991) *Breaking the Barrier: The Rise of Solidarity in Poland.* New York: Oxford University Press.

Graham, G. (1986) *Politics in Its Place.* Oxford: Oxford University Press.

Greenfeld, L. (1992) *Nationalism – Five Roads to Modernity.* Cambridge, Mass.: Harvard University Press.

Habermas, J. (1990) "Citizenship and National Identity," Appendix II in J. Habermas, *Between Facts and Norms: Contributions to a Discourse Theory of Law and Democracy.* Cambridge, Mass.: MIT Press.

Held, D. (1995) *Democracy and the Global Order: From the Modern State to Cosmopolitan Governance.* Cambridge: Polity.

Hirst, P., and G. Thompson (1996) *Globalization in Question.* Cambridge: Polity.

Ignatieff, M. (1994) *Blood and Belonging: Journeys into the New Nationalism.* London: Vintage.

Linklater, A. (1998) *The Transformation of Political Community.* Cambridge: Polity.

MacCormick, N. (1991) "Is Nationalism Philosophically Credible?" in W. Twining, ed., *Issues in Self-Determination.* Aberdeen: Aberdeen University Press.

Margalit, A., and J. Raz, (1990) "National Self-determination," *Journal of Philosophy* 87, 439–61.

McGrew, A., ed. (1997) *The Transformation of Democracy? Globalization and Territorial Democracy.* Cambridge: Polity.

McKim, R., and J. McMahan, eds. (1997) *The Morality of Nationalism.* New York: Oxford University Press.

Migdal, J.S. (1988) *Strong Societies and Weak States: State–Society Relations and State Capabilities in the Third World.* Princeton, NJ: Princeton University Press.

Miller, D. (1995) *On Nationality.* Oxford: Oxford University Press.

– (1998) "Secession and the Principle of Nationality," in Moore, 1998.

Moore, M. (1997) "On National Self-determination," *Political Studies* 45, 900–13.

– ed. (1998) *National Self-determination and Secession.* Oxford: Oxford University Press.

Nielsen, K. (1993) "Secession: The Case of Quebec," *Journal of Applied Philosophy,* 10, 29–43.

– (1998) "Liberal Nationalism and Secession," in Moore, 1998.

Nussbaum, M.C. (1996) "Patriotism and Cosmopolitanism," in J. Cohen, ed., *For Love of Country: Debating the Limits of Patriotism.* Boston, Mass.: Beacon Press.

Parekh, B. (1995) "Politics of Nationhood," in K. von Benda-Beckmann and M. Verkuyten, eds., *Nationalism, Ethnicity and Cultural Identity in Europe.* Utrecht: European Research Centre on Migration and Ethnic Relations.

Parsons, T. (1967) "On the Concept of Political Power," in Parsons, *Sociological Theory and Modern Society.* New York: Free Press.

Pavkovic, A. (2000) "Recursive Secessions in Former Yugoslavia: Too Hard a Case for Theories of Secession?" *Political Studies* 48, 485–502.

Philpott, D. (1995) "In Defense of Self-determination," *Ethics* 105, 352–85.

– (1998) "Self-determination in Practice," in Moore, 1998.

Pogge, T. (1989) *Realizing Rawls.* Ithaca, NY: Cornell University Press.

– (1994) "Cosmopolitanism and Sovereignty," in C. Brown, ed., *Political Restructuring in Europe: Ethical Perspectives.* London: Routledge.

Rawls, J. (1972) *A Theory of Justice.* Oxford: Oxford University Press.

– (1999) *The Law of Peoples.* Cambridge, Mass.: Harvard University Press.

Renan, E. (1939) "What Is a Nation?" in A. Zimmern, ed., *Modern Political Doctrines.* London: Oxford University Press.

Rosas, A. (1995) "State Sovereignty and Human Rights: Towards a Global Constitutional Project," in D. Beetham, ed., Special Issue of *Politics and Human Rights*, *Political Studies* 43, 61–78.

Tamir, Y. (1993) *Liberal Nationalism*. Princeton, NJ: Princeton University Press.

Wrong, D. (1995) *Power: Its Forms, Bases, and Uses*. New Brunswick, NJ: Transaction Publishers.

LIAH GREENFELD

Is Modernity Possible without Nationalism?

To answer the question whether modernity is possible without nationalism, one must begin by defining "modernity." A common view equates
"modernity" with "contemporaneity," regarding as "modern" any social, political, economic, and (in the narrow sense) cultural phenomenon that exists today. This view, however, is meaningless – what was
modern yesterday is no longer so today, and what is modern today will
cease being so tomorrow – and as such does not amount to a definition.
We can discard it. A related opinion defines "modernity" in terms of
certain characteristics of the so-called world order (in effect, the world
seen from a peculiarly American perspective) after the dissolution of the
Soviet Union and the collapse of communism in central and eastern Europe – specifically, the "globalization" of the economy. This opinion is
contradicted by two of the most interesting facts related to economic
globalization itself: first, judging by every possible index, it reached its
peak around a century ago and never went beyond it; and second, its
most salient expression – the multinational corporation – is, as a rule,
quintessentially national in its policies, its goals, and the constitution of
its board of trustees and stockholders alike.[1] If globalization distinguished this recent period of less than twenty years, constituted its most
distinguishing characteristic, and justified the application to it of the label "modernity," my question would have to be whether globalization
is possible without nationalism. But, as it happens, globalization does
not distinguish it, compelling us to look for a meaningful definition of
modernity elsewhere (and allowing our analysis to escape the blinding

grip of the present and very recent past). I first define modernity, then link it to nationalism, and finally characterize nationalism itself.

ELEMENTS OF MODERNITY

When we look at the population of societies that are universally considered "modern," three features – class, state, and growth – distinguish them from societies whose non-modernity is equally unambivalent. First, they have an open system of stratification, referred to as class structure, with the individual as the bearer of status; transferable resources, such as wealth and education, as its bases; and, as a result, social mobility as a built-in characteristic – which contrasts with the rigid, family–, and non-transferable resources–based stratification of non-modern societies, in which social mobility is an abnormality. Second, the impersonal and abstract, or state, form of government, in principle only represents authority presumed to reside elsewhere – as against the personal government of non-modern societies, encapsulated in the concept of "kingship," in which authority is believed to have its source in the lineage of the ruler or the direct link between the ruler and transcendental powers. Third, their economies seek sustained growth (and, as a result, a constantly growing economy), as opposed to the subsistence-oriented economies of non-modern societies caught in the unending cycle of growth and decline.

Of course, just as it is impossible to define a human being by any of the distinctive characteristics of a fully developed adult, such as bipedalism, speech, or reason, so it is impossible to define modernity – a species of society – by such characteristics. What one must find is the organizing principle that can produce, or express itself in, class structure, the state, and the growing economy, but that may not in all cases necessarily express itself in all three of these features or in all three of them to the same extent. Finding such an organizing principle would later allow us to include in our analysis of modernity such societies that could not unambivalently be defined as modern on the basis of characteristic features, lacking some of them altogether or having them insufficiently developed, just as a newborn infant, whose humanity we consider unquestionable, could not be defined as human on the basis of distinguishing characteristics of a fully developed adult, such as bipedalism or speech. The organizing principle that expresses itself in the external distinctive characteristics of a fully developed biological organism and both justifies the inclusion in the species of infants or otherwise underdeveloped specimens and necessitates such inclusion for analytical purposes is the genotype – a genetically expressed information blueprint. In society the role of the genotype is performed by culture – a symbolic system on the basis of which members construct their reality. The specific cultural system that produces various modern phenotypes – i.e., societies endowed to a greater or lesser extent with the class structure, the state form of government, and the economy oriented to sustained growth – is nationalism.

The cultural system of nationalism – like any cultural system – is a type of imagination. Specifically, it is a secular imagination of this world as ultimately meaningful and as consisting of nations, in turn imagined as sovereign communities of fundamentally equal members. The political and social principles of this cultural system – that is, the principles organizing modern politics and society – appear in the definition of the nation: these are the principles of popular sovereignty and egalitarianism (the fact that makes every nationalism a species of democracy, although this democracy may as well be of a "popular" or "socialist" variety as a "liberal democracy"). But both these two principles and other (including economic) implications of the nationalist imagination are embedded in its essential secularism and focus on this world, which we can appreciate only when we oppose them to the fundamentally religious imaginations, in which this world of empirical reality as a rule occupies but a distant and insignificant corner of the transcendental cosmic map, whose meaningful centre lies elsewhere.

LINKING MODERNITY TO NATIONALISM

How do the external characteristics of modernity, class structure, the state form of government, and the growing economy relate to the nationalist imagination? The secular focus of nationalism immediately and dramatically increases the value and significance of each human life: one's limited time on earth is all that one has (which is a belief paradoxically shared even by modern believers), and so it becomes very important that one be fulfilled in this life, necessarily reducing tolerance of social constraints and obstacles to one's fulfilment. The secularism of modernity (of the nationalist imagination that underlies it) makes one an active maker of one's destiny; it both places the responsibility for it on one's shoulders and empowers one to change it in accordance with one's individual propensities. Social ambition – a new concept, contemporary with nationalism – becomes common and legit-imate and emerges as the modern passion.

This activism, which pushes one to experiment with one's social posi-tion and constantly improve it, is reinforced by the egalitarianism of nationalism, which makes individuals in principle interchangeable. In theory, every member of the nation can occupy any position in it: social mobility (abnormal, if not inconceivable, in the framework of other cul-tural systems) is implicit in the principle of the equality of membership in the nation. As a result, the individual becomes independent from the group into which he or she is born, and status, necessarily separated from ascriptive – group – characteristics, depends on achievement and therefore on transferable resources, such as wealth or education. The class hierarchy is not simply a ladder of success, which one is invited to climb (a metaphor impossible within the imagination of a caste society, a feudal society of orders, or any other culture implying rigid stratifica-tion), but it is a flexible, swaying ladder made of such insecure materials that it is not much of a hierarchy at all. Like any system of stratifica-tion, class structure is a process, rather than a thing, but, in distinction to other systems, it is a process so fluid that the term "structure" (also, obviously, a metaphor) in application to it obscures more than it re-veals. In comparison to estate or caste categories, such as "aristocracy" or "untouchables," which refer to specific people and families, class categories of "rich" and "poor," or of "upper," "middle," and "lower" classes, are abstract concepts referring to certain market powers, whose composition may change several times in the course of one generation and which may come every five or ten years to refer to completely dif-ferent groups.

While class structure is an expression chiefly of the egalitarian princi-ple of nationalism, the state form of government is an implication of its popular sovereignty principle. The relationship between nationalism and the state is often misunderstood. Most popular theories of national-ism, which represent the dominant structuralist–materialist paradigm in the social sciences, regard nationalism as an emanation of the so-called modern state, itself quite miraculously called into being by the systemic needs of the "modern," i.e., capitalist, economy. In fact, nationalism produces the state, not the other way around. And it produces the state whether or not it (nationalism) exists in a society that can be seen as a homogeneous nation (in itself a rarity). Even in empires, nationalism produces the state. Therefore the common talk about nation-states and the demise thereof is meaningless (these imaginary entities cannot be in any danger of extinction for the simple reason that they never existed). The state is an implication of the central political principle of nationalism as such; thus government assumes its impersonal, legal–rational form in multinational entities (such as was the Soviet Union and as is, perhaps, Canada) and even in political entities formed in the age of nationalism in societies not as yet redefined and functioning as nations (not a few African states may serve as examples of this case).

Moreover, the principle of popular sovereignty, which implies that the authority of the government emanates neither from itself nor from the transcendental sources beyond the nation, but from the nation, and which therefore compels polities defined as nations or claiming membership in the community of nations to adopt the state form of government, applies equally to polities that are representative democracies in actual fact and to modern dictatorships, which dispense with representative institutions. What allows for such differences in the institutional implementation of the same principle are differences in the definition of the nation, which I address below. The principle itself, however, materially affects the experience of politics and life generally in modern society, adding to it dignity unknown to those who, in principle, could not see themselves as represented in the power wielded over them and even, theoretically speaking, to those who had no share in it. It is this in-principle impersonal and representative character of political authority in nations that permits openly authoritarian regimes to insist on their democratic nature.[2]

Finally, the sustained orientation of economic activity to growth, which so sharply distinguishes modern economies, is a result primarily of the inherent competitiveness of nations. The dignity implied in nationalism (specifically, in the principles of popular sovereignty and equality of membership) makes people invest heavily in their national identity and therefore in the dignity, or prestige, of the nation. Since prestige is a relative value, this commitment engages the population to a race with a moving finish-line. In those nations that include the economy among the areas of international competition, there emerges an economic attitude that is peculiarly irrational (contrary to common opinion, which regards it as the epitome of economic rationality) and makes the increase of wealth an end in itself, rather than a means for the satisfaction of human needs. Indeed, economic activity in a modern society serves chiefly not human needs, but an abstraction – the nation and its desire for prestige or position vis-à-vis other nations. Thus the rate of growth (productivity, competitiveness) becomes the main preoccupation, not the satisfaction of any existing demand – except, obviously, that for collective prestige. People work and do not consume products of their labour; they no longer work to live (satisfaction of material needs recedes in importance) but rather live to work.

In distinction to the class structure of the system of stratification and the state form of government – both necessary implications of nationalism – the orientation to economic growth, while a product of nationalism, is not its necessary product. This orientation occurs only where the economy ranks among a society's areas of international competition. Not every nationalism, however, defines the economy as such an area, or has a built-in component of economic nationalism. In some nationalisms, the attitude to economic activity and to its role in upholding national dignity is inconsistent – as, for instance, in France. Others may consistently oppose linking national dignity to money-making, deny any dignity to economic activity, and altogether lack economic nationalism. Such is, emphatically, the case in Russia (Greenfeld 2001).

Nationalism as such therefore does not imply sustained economic growth, but it is always nationalism that sustains it. Globalization, which is widely believed to be a trend opposed to nationalism, is a case in point. Globalization is not a new trend: it has been quite pronounced in the last 500 years. There is no basis for claiming that it was significantly modified in the last half-century, and it would be quite unreasonable to expect it suddenly to have an effect opposite to that of the first 450 years of its recorded history. During those years globalization promoted the spread of nationalism – in the first place, because a diffusion of cultural norms (of which the spread of nationalism represents a particular case) is possible only in the conditions of considerable integration. If we assume that the essential nature of the process of globalization itself has not changed, it could not contribute now to the dismantling of the social system based on nationalism, unless a new cultural system replaced nationalism, as nationalism once replaced the principles of the "society of orders." But, so far, there is no such new cultural system.

In the meantime, much of what is regarded as economic globalization – ostensibly an "objective" secular trend, required by the state of development of world economic forces and independent of particular interests and cultural values – is in fact a function of the normal working of particular national economies, guided by their particular, often explicitly national, interests and reflecting their particular cultural traditions (i.e., nationalisms). Most of the so-called global companies are both founded and run by Americans. As a rule, their objective is to succeed, to grow, rather than to advance U.S. economic interests or to contribute to the nation's prestige. If continued success requires the internationalization of a company's management, or moving the headquarters out of the United States, its American leadership will, in all probability, go forward with such changes and do so with an easy conscience. Yet such conduct is neither an expression of the iron laws of economic rationality, nor a sign of indifference to the national interest. It reflects the specific American tradition – its peculiar business ethic, which condones and encourages competition on an individual basis and which is a product of the nature and development of American national consciousness. American business people compete in their private capacity, not as representatives of their nation. There is nothing new in this: as one could observe with Rockefeller and even Colt, Americans, however attached to their country, never regarded the sphere of their activity as forever confined to it: the moment they were capable of expanding beyond its borders, they expanded.

But the situation is different in the case of multinational corporations founded and headed by nationals of other countries. While their workforce and middle management may be "global," their character remains emphatically national, with each of the companies associated with a particular nation and their success and failure – in the eyes of the respective nationals – reflecting on the nation's standing. The merger of Daimler and Chrysler, in which the German company assumed the control of the American one, was a great event in Germany. Hen Schrempp, the German CEO-elect of DaimlerChrysler, became a national hero. Citizens in no way connected to the enterprise exulted: "Finally, Germany has a global company!" There is no doubt that the reaction would be more subdued if the very same global company – which, we were assured, would remain faithful to the "key elements" at least of German business tradition and corporate culture – were a result of Chrysler's acquisition of Daimler. But the takeover involved a great American company; Germany, as we know from history, has successfully pursued "globalization" at a closer range since before the First World War.

It is doubtful that the development of the European Monetary Union, hailed as the surest sign of the demise of the state and of nationalism, represents an exception to the above interpretation. Society being an open system, everything is possible, of course, and we must wait and see. But so far it has been a union in a very limited sense, with the euro signifying neither a waning national sentiment nor a significant diminution in the authority of the participating states. In France, in Germany (and in on-the-whole-standoffish Britain), the popular mood, if not the attitudes of politicians, has been swaying in accordance with perceived opportunities for the union's leadership – namely, the possibilities of using the European Union for the advancement of the respective national interests in power and prestige. And even weaker nations, with the leadership out of reach, have not been uniformly supportive of denationalizing initiatives of any kind – including those cases in which the latter were unambivalently suggested by growth-oriented economic rationality. In 1999, Olivetti's successful bid for control of the newly privatized Telecom Italia, beating out the better-equipped Deutsche Telekom, attracted attention. The *International Herald Tribune* reported that "Olivetti won largely because it is Italian. The government was thought to have blessed its offer, and many of the institutions that tendered their shares to Olivetti are Italian."[3]

TYPES OF NATIONALISM

Clearly, then, modernity is not possible without nationalism. If defined meaningfully, modernity – with its distinguishing social, political, and economic features – is a product of the cultural system of nationalism and owes to it its character. At the same time, like nationalism, modernity is not a uniform phenomenon. There are a variety of modern societies within the broad framework of modern society, within which exist several types of modernities. These types correspond to types of nationalism that in turn are the products of distinctive initial perceptions of the nature of the nation and of criteria of membership in it.

It is common to distinguish "civic" and "ethnic," or alternatively "political" and "cultural," types of nationalism. The category "civic" ("political") emphasizes the concept and institution of citizenship, and "ethnic" (or "cultural"), preoccupations with language, history, and folklore. The latter obsessions reflect a belief in deeper, "natural" – that is, in effect, biological – underlying forces, such as race or "blood and soil," which form the ultimate reality of nationhood and national identity. The concepts "civic" and "ethnic" are useful, but they do not capture all the significant differences (i.e., those that produce different political and social institutions and behavioural patterns) between historical nationalisms. Moreover, when taken as descriptive categories,

intended to encapsulate these nationalisms – which is the inspiration behind them – they cannot explain any of these differences and thus lack
explanatory value.

Empirically, one can identify three types of nationalism, each with
distinctive implications for the ways of thinking and behaviour within
the societies that they help define: "individualistic-civic," "collectivistic-
civic," and "collectivistic-ethnic." This typology is analytical, rather
than descriptive. At its basis lie not the differences that the three types
of nationalism generate, but the differences in the initial conceptions of
the nation, which produce them.

The Nature of the Nation

The initial conception of the nation – the new, nationalist, image of society – must include two elements: the nature of the nation as a whole,
and the nature of the humans who compose the nation. The nation as a
whole can be seen either as a composite entity, a collectivity formed by
the association of individuals, or in unitary terms, as a collective individual. The former conception results in individualistic nationalism – an
individualistic vision of the new social order; the latter, in a collectivistic
vision, or collectivistic nationalism. Both categories are markers of social consciousness and of collective, or shared, representations. To bor-
row Durkheim's phrasing, both refer to the ways in which society – the
nation – is represented to its members: i.e., as a composite or as a
unitary entity, not to the motivations of the members or to the firmness
of their commitment. Historically, individualistic nations have commanded national patriotism as intense as, and more widespread than,
that of collectivistic nations. Both rates of desertion, in times of war,
and of emigration, in times of peace, have been lower in individualistic
nations than in others.

The definition of the nation as a composite entity, as was the case with
the original nationalism in England and in the other societies that adopted
the English model, assumes the moral, political, and logical primacy of
the human individual, who is seen not simply as a physical unit of society,
but as its constitutive element, in the sense that all the qualities of the latter have their source in the nature of the former. The nation – which, in
the framework of nationalism in general, is seen as a sovereign (fully independent and self-governing) community of fundamentally equal members – in the context of this composite definition derives its freedom from
the essential liberty of the individuals who compose it; its dignity, and the

dignity of national identity, reflect the natural dignity of each human being. Such dignity and liberty (which are, of course, inherently linked) make the members of the nation equal, and this equality is realized in the social and political arrangements that set individualistic nations apart from others. The principles at the foundation of individualistic nationalisms are none other than the principles of liberal democracy, which individualistic national consciousness fosters and sustains.

The definition of the nation in unitary terms, by contrast, promotes collectivist forms of social and political organization, which are conceptualized as "communism," "socialism" of one kind or another, or "socialist" and/or "popular" democracy. Collectivistic nations share in common a predilection for authoritarian politics and, as a result, for a pronounced inequality in social life, at least in the relationship between the rulers and the ruled. This authoritarianism is a logical implication of perceiving the community as an individual in its own right – and one morally superior to human individuals – with a will, interests, and purpose of its own, which have priority over and are independent of wishes and aspirations of its human members. The will, interests, and purpose of the nation are not directly known to the members and have to be deciphered and interpreted for their benefit by a specially qualified elite. This all-important service gives new meaning to the concept of representation: the elite, in such cases, represents the nation to the people, rather than representing the people. This service also establishes those who provide it in a position of vast superiority to the rest. The equality of membership that is implied in nationalism is contradicted by this superiority and is therefore reinterpreted and limited, becoming in the political sphere a matter of make-believe.

The other implication of nationalism – popular sovereignty – is also reinterpreted, becoming the attribute of the nation as separate from the people who compose it and as such lying not in political arrangements that ensure individual liberties but in collective freedom from foreign domination. Finally, the dignity of the nation, and of national identity, becomes, within collectivistic nationalisms, not a reflection of the dignity of individuals, but is instead inherent in the nation as such and is communicated to individuals only by virtue of their membership in the nation.

The Nature of Membership

The second element of the definition of the nation – the nature of the humans who compose it – rests in the criteria of membership in the nation, or nationality. It is here that one can usefully employ the conventional distinction between civic and ethnic nationalisms. One can conceive of membership in the nation either in civic or in ethnic terms. The former equates nationality with citizenship and is an essentially political and even legal category, implying a voluntarily embraced commitment to certain rights and duties. Being, at least theoretically, a matter of choice, nationality can be acquired and lost. Although it is presumed that every person at any point in time has a nationality, and that one's choice is limited to selecting among various national identities, civic nationalism means, at least in theory, that one could be without a nationality altogether. An ethnic definition of nationality, by contrast, conceives of it as an ineluctable, biological necessity. One cannot be without a nationality as one cannot be without an essential bodily organ; one is born with a particular nationality and can never lose it; at best (or at worst) one can conceal one's national identity. In some mystical, but essentially biological, natural process, completely independent of human volition, blood transmits nationality as an inherent, genetic characteristic. Nationality, it is thought, determines one's interests and sentiment and projects itself naturally and unreflectively in attachment and commitment to the nation. Ethnic homogeneity of a population (whether linguistic, racial, or other), even when seen as a characteristic of a nation, does not necessarily result in ethnic nationalism. France, perceived as ethnically homogeneous, for instance, is a civic nation.

Two Dimensions, Three Types

The two dimensions of the definition of the nation result in the three types of nationalism mentioned above, because the composite definition of the nation as a whole, with its emphasis on the logical and moral priority of the individual, implies a civic concept of nationality. Consequently, individualistic nationalism is necessarily civic. The definition of the nation in unitary terms, however, is commensurate with both civic and ethnic criteria of membership, allowing for the existence of civic and ethnic varieties of collectivistic nationalism. The components of individualistic-civic and of collectivistic-ethnic nationalism mutually reinforce each other and bolster the liberal tendencies of the former and the authoritarian proclivities of the latter. But the combination of a collectivistic definition of the nation as a whole with civic criteria of nationality unites these contradictory propensities and creates an ambivalent and inherently problematic type. In reality, the most common type is the mixed one. But the compositions of the existing mixtures vary significantly enough to justify their classification in the above terms and render these terms analytically useful.[4]

NOTES

1 Surveying the historical data on the movement of goods, services, capital, and labour, Bill Emmott (1993) observed in the *Economist*: "trade and cross-boarder investment ... boomed in 1870–1913 ... a period ... during which the world economy approached integration at an even faster pace than has been seen in the past 40 years ... One measure, the growth of world trade, is slowing rather than accelerating." The only evidence of greater economic integration was increased movement of capital (since 1980), but even this only between developing countries, where "a number of governments allowed it to." "Proper global economic integration is a distant prospect, and even continued progress toward it cannot be taken for granted." After surveying 11,678 managers (who "were not selected at random") in 25 countries, The *Harvard Business Review* (Kanter, 1991, 151, 155) concluded that the "idea of a corporate global village where a common culture of management unifies the practice of business around the world is more dream than reality ... Look at the third of the survey respondents who say that businesses should be willing to pay a premium to support domestic suppliers, or the quarter who want business owners to care more about their country's success than their company's."

2 On nationalism as the constitutive element of modernity in general, see Greenfeld 1992. On stratification and the state, specifically, see Greenfeld 1996.

3 Miller 1998, 138; Passell, 1998; Jenkins, 1999. The official guide distributed to the citizens of France on the eve of the introduction of the euro had a chart titled "L'euro fait la force" comparing the economies of France, Japan, the United States, and the "euro zone," with the last taking first place in population and falling just slightly behind the first-place United States in size of economy (as opposed to distant France). See Ministère de l'économie des finances et de l'industrie, 1998; see also Frank, 1998; see also *Economist*, 1998; finally see also de Aenlle, 1999, 19.

4 A more extended discussion of the types of nationalism and their implications appears in Greenfeld, 1992.

REFERENCES

de Aenlle, Conrad (1999) "Second Thoughts on Telecom Italia," *International Herald Tribune*, 5–6 June.

Economist (1998) "Enter the Euro," 9 May.

Emmott, Bill (1993) "Multinationals: Back in Fashion," *Economist*, 27 March.

Frank, Robert (1998) "Europe's 'On Freud's Couch' as Countries Vie for Identity," *Wall Street Journal*, 19 Oct.

Greenfeld, Liah (1992) *Nationalism: Five Roads to Modernity*. Cambridge, Mass.: Harvard University Press.

– (1996) "Nationalism and Modernity," *Social Research* 64, 4.

– (2000) "Etymology, Definitions, Types." *Encyclopedia of Nationalism*, vol. 1, 251–65.

– (2001) *The Spirit of Capitalism: Nationalism and Economic Growth*. Cambridge, Mass.: Harvard University Press.

Jenkins, Hollman W., Jr (1999) "Daimler Chrysler: Just Another German Car Company," *Wall Street Journal*, 26 May.

Miller, Karen Lowry (1998) "A Secret Weapon for German Reform," *Business Week*, 12 Oct.

Ministère de l'économie des finances et de l'industrie (1998) "Guide pratique de l'euro," Nov.

Kanter, Rosabeth Moss (1991) "Transcending Business Boundaries: 12,000 World Managers View Change," *Harvard Business Review*, May–June.

Passell, Peter (1998) "Capitalism Victorious (Thanks, Everyone)," *New York Times*, 10 May.

Wolf, Charles, Jr (1998) "All for the Currency," *Wall Street Journal*, 1 April.

DANIEL WEINSTOCK

Four Kinds of (Post-)nation-building

In a recent article, Will Kymlicka (2001b) has defended the claim that many countries in the West have developed a viable strategy for coping with the dual demands of social cohesion and recognition of diversity. In Kymlicka's view, they have embarked on deliberate policies of nation-building, while at the same time granting minorities substantial rights that have in practice abetted rather than detracted from nation-building.

In this paper,[1] I want to suggest that Kymlicka underestimates both the practical and the ethical difficulties faced by defenders of nation-building projects.

This topic is of more than purely historical and theoretical interest, as it is possible that we are now entering a new phase in the construction of political communities. The political integration of Europe is well under way, and the prospect exists of other such continental integrations in the near future.[2] Just as modern nation-states have had to take steps to make what were initially quite disparate populations feel that they "belonged together," so too post-national political institutions will have to find ways to generate loyalties, sentiments of common purpose, and habits of co-operation among peoples who had previously thought of themselves as politically separate. So we should come up with a clear sense of the kind and extent of solidarity that is required to maintain viable liberal-democratic institutions, of the types of nation-building strategies that are likely to generate such attachments, and of the moral constraints that such strategies ought to observe.

TYPES AND ASSUMPTIONS OF NATION-BUILDING

Four Types

I want in this section to distinguish four ways in which political institutions might carry out the kind of task that I described above. As will be obvious, these are ideal-types. Real-world nation-building projects in fact incorporate more than one of these types, and sometimes they include all of them. (This is also true to some degree of the different *theories* that have attempted to account for such projects). Still, it is quite clear that these ideal-types allow us to understand the different *emphases* that have characterized different theories and historical projects.

Political institutions embarking on an enterprise of nation-building must at the outset make two very fundamental decisions about the kind of project that they want to pursue. First, they must make decisions about the *end* that they are trying to reach. I refer to what seem to me to be the basic options here as *minimalism* and *maximalism*. The minimalist believes that it is sufficient that members of a political community share a basic set of political values and/or that they act in ways that support core political institutions. In liberal democracies, the minimalist nation-builder will enact measures aimed at promoting the values of equality and tolerance and at inculcating the traits of character (civility, responsibility, and so on) that are essential motivational underpinnings for these institutions.[3] The maximalist believes that it is not enough that citizens living under common political institutions merely share the kinds of political values and attitudes that the minimalist aims to realize. He or she believes that citizens must also share "deeper" aspects of culture. Different maximalists have evaluated the "depths" of the cultural commonality required in various ways. John Stuart Mill famously insisted on pre-political sentiments of national fellow-feeling as a precondition of stable institutions of representative democracy (Mill, 1991, chap. XVI). Jean-Jacques Rousseau believed that a civic religion would be necessary in order to motivate citizens to do what their civic duties require of them (Rousseau, 1966, 170–80.) And some moderate nationalists today believe that it is essential that citizens possess a shared sense of their history or at the very least that they share a language.[4] But regardless of their differences, all maximalists share the sense that political institutions require for their viability and their stability that citizens share more than simply a set of political values and/or a set of common attitudes towards political institutions.

A second decision has to do with means rather than ends. Nation-building can be pursued directly or indirectly. That is, it can be an explicit goal of public policy, or government can pursue it indirectly, in the hope that *other* aspects of the activities of the state will give rise to the required common culture. Governments can set up agencies to promote a shared national identity (as has been done in Canada), or they can gear other dimensions of policy-making and -implementation towards nation-building.

With these distinctions in hand, I would like to propose four models of nation-building that seem to me to be prevalent both in the actual policies enacted by political institutions and in the bodies of theorizing that have emerged to account for the phenomenon of nation-building – majority nation-building (MNB), constitutional (CNB), transformative (TNB), and organic (ONB).

Majority nation-building (MNB). Proponents of MNB have historically maintained a maximalist position as defined above and have believed that the culture of the majority group should serve as the focus of cultural convergence. That is, immigrants and members of indigenous minorities should ideally conform to the culture, language, and symbols, and in some countries, to the religion, of the majority national group. I would argue that the grand phase of European nation-building in the 18th and 19th centuries was driven principally by the desire to propagate the culture of the national majority. Anglo-conformity models of integration in Canada, Australia, and New Zealand have also been variants of MNB. For reasons that will become clear, very few contemporary nationalists affirm MNB, though it still finds its way into the writings even of moderate nationalists such as David Miller.[5]

Constitutional nation-building (CNB). Defenders of CNB have taken a minimalist line on cultural convergence. They have favoured enshrining the political values of a political community in a constitutional document that ought to become the focus of nation-building initiatives, which should consist only of the inculcation of these values. Note that pursuit of CNB can take a variety of forms. The political values enshrined can be more or less demanding and extensive. The more demanding the range, the more difficult it is to distinguish this type of strategy clearly from maximalist approaches to cultural convergence. (And of course, this stance may require citizens to view their "particular" identities as irrelevant in the public sphere).

In contemporary political philosophy, Jürgen Habermas is probably the most well-known defender of a version of CNB.[6] I believe that the self-understanding (if not the reality) of many French nationalists, especially of those followers of Jean-François Chevènement, who left Lionel Jospin's socialist government over the Matignon accords concerning Corsican autonomy, is also informed by this model. In Canada, the expression "Charter patriotism" captures both the intention behind and the effect of the Constitution Act of 1982, which, it was hoped, would cement Canadian identity around a set of constitutional principles.[7]

Transformative nation-building (TNB): Like defenders of MNB, proponents of TNB maintain that the cohesion of a political community depends on its members sharing a "thick" set of cultural references. But they argue not that this culture ought to privilege the cultural symbols and practices of the majority group, but rather that it should build on aspects of the cultures of the society's cultural sub-units. Gérard Bouchard has argued that "hybridation," in which "a new culture is born of the fusion of all contributions and of all heritages, no matter how heterogeneous and contradictory," represents a strategy for "new" cultures attempting to sever links with a colonial culture (Bouchard, 2000, 375; my translation) The idea that a species of European identity might be derived from the synthesis of European cultures has been discussed by a number of authors.[8]

Note that, in principle, these different types of nation-building can be pursued either directly or indirectly. In practice, however, the compatibility between nation-building and indirect strategies decreases as the requirement of cultural convergence becomes stonger, and the focus of such convergence narrower. In other words, it is difficult to see how MNB can be pursued indirectly. If a majority group's language, religion, cultural symbols, and so on, are to become mandatory for all, then they must be taught, promulgated, and enforced. The defender of MNB throws up a hostage to fortune if he or she expects that convergence around the majority's culture will occur simply as a result of the unforced interactions of the members of different social groups. To the extent that the values defended by the proponent of CNB are more demanding and culturally specific, they too are not likely to be attained through indirect strategies. Because it tolerates a broad range of acceptable cultural dispensations, it seems more likely that TNB can be pursued indirectly. This is also the case for far less demanding versions of CNB.

The types of nation-building strategies described above share the assumption that, whether directly or indirectly, the promotion of a common culture, be it "thick" or "thin," is an appropriate goal of government action. A fourth type in essence denies this premise.

Organic nation-building (ONB). Defenders of organic nation-building agree that the institutions of a political community must be underpinned by some sense of belonging and common purpose, but they hold that a common culture of the kind required can emerge as an unintended consequences of the operation of shared political institutions. Whether they like it or not, people thrown by circumstance into long-term co-operative ventures will develop habits of collaboration, sentimental attachments, and shared ways of looking at their common practices and institutions. In other words, they develop a culture or at least enough of a culture to ensure that the institutions in question will rest on something more solid and less transient than self-interest.[9]

I have drawn these sketches with a very broad brush. But I believe that they provide us with enough to consider the relative merits of the various models, both from the point of view of political morality and from that of prudence.

Comparing the Models

If we agree that nation-building must be constrained by a broadly liberal political morality, then we must reject MNB. Liberal democracy insists that citizens must be treated with equal concern and respect, regardless of their gender and sexual orientation or of their ethnic or cultural origins. Clearly, MNB violates this constraint. Making the language, history, symbols, and/or religion of one of the groups in society dominant signals to other citizens that they are not equal and that they can become so only if they shed their own cultures to take on that of the majority.

In particular, it's hard to see how MNB can be made compatible with the kinds of minority rights that Kymlicka has argued for in his other works – rights that, on the view that he now defends, fit in well with nation-building in an overall strategy that ensures social stability as well as justice towards minority groups. Minority rights create enclaves within the broader political community in which the cultures of minorities would hold sway. Yet MNB presumes that the existence of such enclaves threatens stability and that they should be eradicated so as to give pride of place to the majority's culture. So, to the extent that, as Kymlicka and others believe, their own first principles require liberal democracies to guarantee minority rights, MNB is unacceptable.

Kymlicka's claim that nation-building is compatible with recognition of substantial minority rights depends on a lack of specificity as to the *kinds* of nation-building pursued. The point is to create a common culture throughout society. For some commentators, as we have seen, nation-building must reach deep into citizens' cultural self-understanding, whereas others believe that *political* nation-building can leave citizens' deeper conceptions of themselves undisturbed. I would claim that a state that recognizes substantial minority rights has in essence stopped practising the more demanding forms of nation-building that MNB and TNB represent. To the extent that they impose norms of political and constitutional morality on the minorities to which they grant rights of self-government, states are in effect pursuing CNB.

Four Assumptions

In what follows I relate types of nation-building to underlying assumptions that may guide the process. The argument for nation-building has four elements. The *horizontality premise*: the viability of the institutions of liberal democracy and the stability of its societies require that citizens view themselves as united by a shared identity, as bound by common values, as members of the same pre-political nation, and so on. The *sceptical assumption*: we cannot expect citizens to generate this kind of commonality spontaneously. The *statist assumption*: the state can reliably produce the right kind of commonality by nation-building. The *paternalist premise*: the viability of institutions and the stability of society are goals of sufficient moral importance that their pursuit may override the liberal-democratic presumption against paternalism, defined as action undertaken by the state on the basis not of what people want but of what they ought to want. Conclusion: If the viability of the institutions of liberal democracy is an appropriate goal, the state ought, all things being equal, to engage in nation-building.

In the next section, on Canada, I attempt to refute the statist assumption. In the final sections, I question the horizontality and the sceptical premises.

CANADA: A CASE STUDY OF INTENTIONALISM

The Canadian case provides an interesting illustration here. As we see in more detail below, the Canadian state since Pierre Elliott Trudeau has put in place substantial programs of nation-building. Official bilingualism and multiculturalism instantiate a policy of TNB. The Canadian state has attempted through these two policies to generate a self-image among Canadians of a bilingual culture peopled by individuals of diverse provenance. This self-image is incompatible with that of many Quebecers, who tend to view themselves as forming a linguistically homogeneous national group within Canada. The Canadian state grants Quebec substantial self-government rights, but it does so without recognizing the existence of a minority nation in its midst, as this would conflict with its self-understanding of Canada as constituting a single bilingual and multicultural nation. The practice of the Canadian state is an indication of the tension, verging on the contradiction, between the kind of "deep" nation-building that TNB and MNB represent and the granting of minority rights.

CNB and TNB clearly mark moral progress relative to MNB. They do not unduly privilege the culture of any one group within society, and thus they do not appear to offend against the principle that all citizens in a liberal democracy should be treated with equal concern and respect. None the less, I want to argue that they pose both pragmatic and ethical problems.

Let me begin my noting that both strategies of nation-building share what I call the intentionalist premise. That is, both assume that the creation of a common culture on the basis of an initially disparate population is a legitimate, attainable goal of public policy. I question this notion for at least two reasons.

First, the promotion of a national culture for the purposes of sustaining the public institutions of the state faces obstacles that seem to me to be endemic to the state's attempts at wading into the area of culture. Living cultures are by their natures dynamic and fluid. That is, they change and evolve, as a result both of internal challenge and contestation and of contact and interaction with other cultures. Their dynamism makes it difficult to "freeze-frame" culture and to characterize it at any one time as having a set of specific properties. Such attempts at characterization will always ignore the internal complexity and the protean nature of living cultures. Now, it is one thing for the state to intervene in a national culture – for example, by funding artists and other cultural workers on the basis of suitable qualitative criteria. There is no guarantee that the un-fettered market will allow such artists to support themselves by following their muse. A society that subjected its artists to the vagaries of the mar-ket would therefore be threatening its ability to sustain a viable, living culture over time.[10] The market's imperatives are not coextensive with those of culture (although they are not completely separate from them, either), and so the state must at least to some degree immunize its culture from the logic of the marketplace.

But if market imperatives do not line up perfectly with the conditions required for a culture to survive and thrive, neither do the state's goals and requirements. When the state takes on the role of creating culture so as to foster a common identity and thereby to shore up its institu-tions, it distorts culture in at least two ways. First, it instrumentalizes culture. Cultures are not "for" anything in particular. They respond to their own internal norms, and these norms often place cultures in a tense and oppositional relation with the powers that be. When the state attempts to promote those aspects of culture that are the most condu-cive to its own needs, it disproportionately props up a very partial di-mension of a culture.

Second, the state is in any case not very good at representing com-plex, fluid phenomena such as cultural development. As James Scott (1998) has shown in *Seeing Like a State*, the state has a tendency to en-gage in administrative "simplifications" that allow it to apprehend and to bureaucratize processes that would otherwise escape its administra-tive grid. The problem is epistemological rather than ethical. It is simply that the organization of the modern state prevents it from "seeing" complex social phenomena in their full detail and complexity. The state is geared towards the control of social processes, and so it has a natural proclivity to representing social phenomena to itself *as* controllable. But in doing so it distorts these processes, often to risible, and sometimes to tragic, effect (Scott 1998).

So the intentionalist premise with respect to the creation of national cultures ought to be resisted for at least two reasons. First, in attempting to create a common culture and/or to promote aspects of existing cultures for political purposes, it necessarily distorts cultures by instrumentalizing them. And second, the fluidity and complexity of cultures necessarily es-cape the administrative and conceptual grid of the modern state. (These problems loom larger for TNB than for CNB, which aims to transform not all aspects of culture, but merely its political dimensions).

The result of this incompatibility between the desire for state control and the nature of cultures is that nation-building carried out intentionally *but within the limits and constraints imposed by a liberal-democratic political morality* often does not work.

Canada, in my view, provides an example of the limits of the intentionalist premise. Nation-building under the Trudeau governments of the 1970s and 1980s was a combination of what I have here called TNB and CNB. It sought to create a common culture for all Canadians through the combination of official bilingualism and multiculturalism. And it attempted through the repatriation of the constitution and through its Charter of Rights to create a new juridical and political self-understanding on the part of all Canadians. The intention was to break down regionalisms, including most obviously Quebec's, by creating a shared conception of citizenship, as well as a common understanding of the main pillars of Canadian culture.

Whether Trudeau's nation-building initiatives are judged a success depends on where one places the goalpost. On the one hand, the country is peaceful, prosperous, and, for the time being, still intact. On the other hand, the exacerbation of the political rift between Quebec and the rest of Canada and the failure of bilingualism to "take" either in predominantly francophone or in predominantly anglophone regions seem to me quite serious symptoms of the failure of these policies.[11]

We can explain part of their failure by invoking the fact that they took too little account of the complex "facts on the ground" concerning language in Canada. Although Canada was in many ways bilingual prior to Trudeau's policies, the subtle interplay between patterns of distribution of language use and latent political cleavages short-circuited the rather ham-fisted conception and administration of the policy. The use of the French and English languages was not distributed evenly across the Canadian territory, and so the imposition of French in English-speaking parts of the country came to appear an external imposition on the culture rather than something that arose organically from within it. The failure of bilingualism in the rest of Canada thus ended up exacerbating latent divisions that the policy had been designed to counteract.

Thus Canada's experience over the last thirty years or so provides a textbook illustration of the obstacles that face any state wanting to create or to promote an aspect of a culture. Worse, it also reveals the kind of reaction to which states lay themselves open when they venture into nation-building. The gap between the rather static and simplistic view of culture that the state promotes and the way in which cultures are experienced in real life invites a reaction from those on whom this view of culture is imposed. It creates a new source of dissatisfaction with the state. State-driven cultural initiatives meet with resistance from those who speak on behalf of "real," local cultures. Moreover, they provide a *language* in which to couch such resistance. States that take on the task of creating a common culture do so in order to foster a shared *identity* among their citizenries. Faced with plural societies divided along ethnic, linguistic, and religious lines, they attempt policies that give citizens a way of viewing themselves that might counteract the centrifugal pressures exercised by their more "particular" identities. The backlash that failed attempts at nation-building often generate thus takes on the shape of a clash of identities. The state purports to impose an identity on its citizens. But its inability to assess the different cultural dynamics playing themselves out in different segments of society make it likely that major segments of the body politic will reject this identity. And their opposition may take on the terms of the policies and nation-building measures that are being rejected. Artificial, state-sponsored identities will be opposed in the name of "real," "authentic" identities.

I have argued elsewhere that the introduction of identity-based arguments into the deliberative arena represents a danger for deliberative democracies.[12] Arguments cast in terms of recognition and respect for the identities of citizens admit less easily of compromise and accommodation than do those articulated in terms of citizens' values, interests, and preferences. While compromise is the very life-blood of democratic politics, it is difficult to see how one can compromise on a matter of identity without thereby sacrificing one's integrity.[13] It is relatively easy to see how democratic debate might lead one, consistently with the maintenance of one's sense of self-esteem, to compromise one's interests or preferences. This is, however, more difficult when arguments invoke terms of identity, even when they actually involve only interest or preference. The rhetorical force of identity claims makes democratic politics more intractable than it need be.[14]

By engaging in nation-building with a view to fostering a common identity within a diverse society, the state thus steps into a domain with which it is epistemologically ill-equipped to deal and it introduces a currency that the inevitable opponents will happily take up. The logic set in motion by the framing of political arguments in terms of identity then risks hurting democratic deliberation, as it reduces people's willingness to compromise.

The prospects for nation-building as an intentional strategy of the state therefore look grim. If this is the case, why have states chosen to engage in it at all? And haven't there been successful cases of nation-building?

I would claim that such initiatives have been successful, at least for a time, when they could rely on illiberal means – most notably, on the suppression of local languages and cultures and on other means of forced assimilation in the educational system. These have been merely the most egregious aspects of campaigns of majority nation-building that took place throughout the 18th and 19th centuries in Europe, and in the 20th century in the nation-building phase of the post-colonial world, and that also involved the imposition of the culture, language, and religion of the majority group on members of minorities.

Now, quite clearly, if a state can employ this kind of illiberal measure, it needn't worry too much about the resulting reaction. Once a local culture has been eradicated, the state no longer need fear reactions to nation-building enterprises on its behalf. Once the evolution of political morality renders the use of such measures unacceptable, however, nation-building, for the reasons pointed out above, risks being counter-productive and damaging to democratic politics. European states that in the 20th century had to limit their use of illiberal methods in their treatment of national minorities had to confront precisely the kind of reaction to identity imposition that I have described in this paper.

REJECTING PATERNALISM

I want briefly to examine another reason for liberals to look on TNB and CNB with suspicion. They involve a form of paternalism that is very difficult to justify on liberal-democratic grounds.

The paternalist assumption as phrased trades on the very vague notions of "stability" and of "viability." I think that this vagueness reflects the state of the literature on this topic.[15] What does it mean for institutions to be viable or for a society to be sufficiently stable? How do we test the hypothesis that only a requisite amount of commonality at the level of identity or value will permit attainment of major thresholds of viability and stability.

Let me consider two ways in which these concepts have been used in arguments for maintaining high levels of citizen identification in liberal democracies. The first argument comes recently from Charles Taylor (1989). Taylor, following Tocqueville, fears that the institutions of liberal democracy will turn against the very freedoms that they are designed to protect if citizens lack enough "patriotism" to take an active interest in their operation and to rise up in protest when external or internal forces threaten them. Now there are two ways to inculcate this patriotism. First, the (true) causal processes linking rising rates of apathy and privatism with institutional erosion and decay, and institutional erosion with loss of liberty and well-being, are straightforward. To the extent that citizens are motivated to safeguard their liberty and promote their well-being, they will develop the attitudes and dispositions that Taylor wants.[16] Second, citizens can be told (false) "noble lies," national myths, in the hope that they will form the belief that some deep, quasi-mystical link binds them to their fellow-citizens and that they must act so as to uphold common institutions because they are the bulwark of their common life. That is, they must learn a story about why, despite the historical accident and happenstance that lead to the creation of most, if not all, nation-states, they *actually* belong together.

A state wishing to avoid paternalism should obviously prefer the first to the second strategy. It seeks to tell citizens the truth about the ways in which the freedoms and quality of life that they cherish depend on their disposition to act for the defence of common institutions. To the extent that it attempts to bind people together through a sense of shared identity, nation-building, be it CNB or TNB, instantiates the second type of strategy. The would-be nation-builder believes that it would be in the interest of citizens to possess dispositions that would lead them to defend their institutions in times of threat and therefore that it would also be in their interest to imbibe the kind of history that, regardless of its connection to the actual historical record, would be likely to lead to the development of such dispositions. But this is the very definition of state paternalism. To the extent that liberal democracies must eschew paternalism when its avoidance is compatible with the attainment of valuable social goals (and the existence of the republican alternative suggests that paternalism can be avoided in the quest for institutional viability), the state must for ethical reasons avoid engaging in national myth-making.[17]

The second argument has to do with the threat of secession of territorially concentrated groups within the broader society. It claims that societies with national minorities must engage in nation-building to offset the threat that these minorities might attempt to set up their own state. Now, if nation-building involves the promulgation by the state of a common identity, and if the inculcation of such an identity necessitates claims about the broader society that are answerable not before the bar of historical truth but before that of political efficacy, then nation-building involves a noxious form of paternalism. As I suggest below, nation-states often exaggerate the risk that the lack of a strong common identity poses for their unity. Secession is a costly and traumatic affair, and only national minorities that are truly oppressed are likely to choose to subject themselves to the dislocation and uncertainty that it wreaks. But, analogous to the claim that I made about the viability of institutions, a nation-state wishing to keep its constituent populations together should treat its citizens justly and point to the real advantages and virtues that maintenance of the state represents for its members. The kind of nation-building alluded to above, which attempts to forge a common identity for the state's varied population, seems to me to place a state on the horns of a dilemma. Either there are real tensions, created by injustice, that can be papered over only through the creation of a sense of common belonging; or the society is stable and just and devoid of major tensions and rifts. In the former case, nation-building is objectionable, because it attempts to purchase stability for the wrong reasons.[18] People will be inclined to remain together because they are led to believe that they belong together in some deep sense, rather than because their union instantiates real political values and norms of justice. In the latter case, it is simply superfluous.

AGAINST HORIZONTALITY

I have argued above that, while liberal-democratic political morality rules out MNB a priori, CNB and TNB are also vulnerable to objections. I have proposed that, when they cannot avail themselves of illiberal, coercive methods, they may be counterproductive, and, to the extent that they may set in motion conflicts of identity, they risk hardening democratic deliberation and making compromise more difficult. I have also suggested that they instantiate a form of state paternalism that liberal democracies ought to avoid.

If these arguments hold, is the appropriate inference that liberal democracies are helpless in the face of the centrifugal forces that may tear them apart? Must they stand idly by if ethnic, cultural, and religious conflicts rage?

I want to suggest, drawing on some of my previous work (Weinstock, 1999), that these fears trade on an assumption that can and should be questioned. The "horizontality assumption," claims that the unity, stability, and viability of modern societies depends on their citizens being bound together by shared values and/or by a shared sense of identity. Thus the viability of institutions requires the prior, "horizontal" integration of the citizens who live under them.

In my view, the hypothesis assumes that what is required to establish a viable state is that citizens have the same reasons to remain committed to their political institutions, and thereby to their fellow citizens, as they would have to set up new political institutions with people with whom they had no prior ties. And this assumption strikes me as mistaken.

It is a truism conceded even by nationalist authors that modern nation-states emerged in their present form and with their present boundaries as a result of historical accident and happenstance. Many of these states have failed miserably to ensure the well-being and security of their citizens, while some have succeeded quite admirably. Now, when a state ensures a decent standard of living for its citizens, its disruption may involve considerable costs. There are great disincentives to breaking up or disrupting a state that functions tolerably well, and this is so regardless of whether or not its citizens share a common identity or a strong set of shared values. As Wayne Norman (1995) has ably shown, many of the world's most stable states vary considerably at the level of people's values, while states with much greater uniformity at the level of values have been notoriously unstable. Shared or divergent values are weak predictors of the overall level of stability of a state.

So while individuals might want a case to be made in terms of shared values or identity in order to join in political union (resistance to greater European integration certainly at times seems to invoke the lack of any overriding European identity), I doubt that they require shared identity or values in order to abstain from harming the political order to which they find themselves belonging.

In my previous work, I have tried to cash out in terms of social trust the kind of horizontal integration that might be required. Trust, as I have defined it, requires not that citizens share an identity or a set of values, but rather that they believe that their fellow-citizens are not ill-disposed towards their realizing their particular conception of the good life. Now, the state can act in ways that promote trust – for example, by making trusting behaviour attractive or untrusting behaviour unattractive, even in the absence of a psychological attitude of trust – in the hope that the bootstrapping mechanisms to which trust might be amenable will "kick in." If what I have said about trust is correct, nation-building initiatives may very well be the *worst* way to promote social cohesion. By imposing aspects of a culture on all citizens, it risks making some groups of citizens fearful that the state to which they belong is inhospitable to their particular culture. And to the extent that members of such minority groups see the state as "belonging" to the majority, it may create distrust between groups.

CONCLUSION

I close by suggesting that we ought to be much more willing than we have been historically to affirm the radical historical contingency of the nation-states that we have inherited from such arational processes as war, migration, conquest, treaty, and dynastic marriage. Rather than attempting to impose self-conceptions on a potentially recalcitrant citizen body, we ought to accept that citizens living under common institutions may very well share nothing *but* a stake in those institutions. When these institutions function well and justly for the good of all, this may very well be enough to ensure institutional viability and social stability. Individuals working and living together under common institutions may very well end up spontaneously developing habits of co-operation, affective links, and shared ways of thinking of their common institutions. That is, they may end up engaging in organic nation-building. Such a way of engendering a sense of shared belonging would, in virtue of not having been piloted by the state, be immune from the pragmatic and ethical difficulties that we have identified in the case of state-driven initiatives. With the prospect looming of new political formations in Europe, the Americas, and elsewhere, perhaps the possibility of this bottom–up way of creating political community ought to be taken more seriously than it has been in the heyday of the nation-state.

NOTES

1 I first presented this paper in the course of a debate with Will Kymlicka at the City University of Hong Kong. I wish to thank the participants at the session for their questions and Will Kymlicka and Daniel A. Bell for many probing comments and challenges.

2 According to recent reports, a surprisingly high number of Canadians believe that Canada and the United States will eventually integrate politically.

3 The most abundantly discussed minimalist project in contemporary political philosophy is undoubtedly John Rawls, 1993. This book can be read as the confessions of an erstwhile maximalist.

4 For history, see David Miller, 1995; for the importance of language, see Will Kymlicka, 2001a, chaps. 10 and 17.

5 For an interesting account of the evolution of Australian conceptions of citizenship, see Stephen Castles, 1994.

6 The notion of "constitutional patriotism" is discussed by Habermas in a number of places, including 1998,225–6.

7 For a critique of the French republican self-understanding in the face of the debates over Corsica, see Jean-Marie Colombani, 2000.

8 Some of the proposals are discussed in Jean-Marc Ferry, 2000, chap. 1.

9 In some of his most recent writing on Europe, Jürgen Habermas has pointed to this kind of "organic" process as a plausible way in which to envisage the gradual emergence of a European political community. See Habermas, 2000, 146–7.

10 That the market does not provide a "neutral" setting for cultural production offers a clue for the defence of arts funding in the liberal state. For rival views on this issue, see Sam Black, 1992, and Ronald Dworkin, 1985.

11 The best study of the federal government's nation-building strategy is Kenneth McRoberts, 1997.

12 See Weinstock, 2001.

13 The rhetorical and conceptuel link between integrity and compromise is discussed at length in Martin Benjamin, 1990.

14 For a fascinating, yet in my view ultimately failed, attempt at showing the deep compatibility between deliberative democracy and identity politics, see Anthony Simon Laden, 2001.

15 For more on this point, see Weinstock, 1999.

16 A healthy appreciation of these links lies, according to some commentators, at the heart of the classical republican conception of civic virtue. See Quentin Skinner, 1984. See also Maurizio Viroli, 1995.

17 For a defence of the use of national myths, see David Archard, 1995.

18 For the idea of "stability for the right reasons," see John Rawls, 1999, 12–13.

REFERENCES

Archard, David (1995) "Myths, Lies and Historical Truth: A Defence of Nationalism," *Political Studies*, 43.

Benjamin, Martin (1990) *Splitting the Difference: Compromise and Integrity in Ethics and Politics*. Lawrence: University of Kansas Press.

Black, Sam (1992) "Revisionist Liberalism and the Decline of Culture," *Ethics* 102, no. 2.

Bouchard, Gérard (2000) *Genèse des nations et cultures du nouveau monde*. Montreal: Éditions Boréal.

Castles, Stephen (1994) "Democracy and Multicultural Citizenship: Australian Debates and Their Relevance for Western Europe," in Rainer Bauböck, ed., *From Aliens to Citizens: Redefining the Status of Immigrants in Europe*. Aldershot: Avebury.

Colombani, Jean-Marie (2000) *Les infortunes de la république*. Paris: Bernard Grasset.

Dworkin, Ronald (1985) "Can a Liberal State Support Art?" in *A Matter of Principle*. Oxford: Oxford University Press.

Habermas, Jürgen (1998) *The Inclusion of the Other*. Cambridge, Mass.: MIT Press.

– (2000) "L'État-nation européen sous la pression de la mondialisation," in *Après l'État-nation*. Paris: Fayard.

Ferry, Jean-Marc (2000) *La question de l'État européen*. Paris: Gallimard.

Kymlicka, Will (2001a) *Politics in the Vernacular*. Oxford: Oxford University Press.

– (2001b) "Western Political Theory and Ethnic Relations in Eastern Europe," in Will Kymlicka and Magda Opalski, eds., *Can Liberal Pluralism Be Exported? Western Political Theory and Ethnic Relations in Eastern Europe*. Oxford: Oxford University Press.

Laden, Anthony Simon (2001) *Reasonably Radical: Deliberative Liberalism and the Politics of Identity*. Ithaca, NY: Cornell University Press.

McRoberts, Kenneth (1997) *Misconceiving Canada: The Struggle for National Unity*. Oxford: Oxford University Press.

Mill, John Stuart (1991) *Considerations on Representative Government*. Amherst: Prometheus Books.

Miller, David (1995) *On Nationality*. Oxford: Oxford University Press.

Norman, Wayne (1995) "The Ideology of Shared Values: A Myopic Vision of Unity in the Multi-nation State," in Joseph Carens, ed., *Is Quebec Nationalism Just? Perspectives from Anglophone Canada*. Montreal: McGill-Queen's University Press.

Rawls, John (1993) *Political Liberalism*. New York: Columbia University Press.

– (1999) *The Law of Peoples*. New York: Columbia University Press.

Rousseau, Jean-Jacques (1966) *Du contrat social*. Paris: Garnier-Flammarion.

Scott, James C. (1998) *Seeing Like a State. How Certain Schemes to Improve the Human Condition Have Failed*. New Haven, Conn.: Yale University Press.

Skinner, Quentin (1984) "The Idea of Negative Liberty: Philosophical and Historical Perspectives." in R. Rorty, J.B. Schneewind, and Q. Skinner, eds., *Philosophy in History*. Cambridge: Cambridge University Press.

Taylor, Charles (1989) "Cross-Purposes: The Liberal–Communitarian Debate," in N. Rosenblum, ed., *Liberalism and the Moral Life*. Cambridge, Mass.: Harvard University Press.

Viroli, Maurizio (1995) *For Love of Country*. Oxford: Oxford University Press.

Weinstock, Daniel (1999) "Building Trust in Divided Societies," *Journal of Political Philosophy*, 7, no. 3.

– (2001) "Les arguments identitaires sont-ils dangereux pour la démocratie?" in J. Maclure and A. Gagnon, dirs., *Repères en mutation*. Montreal: Québec Amérique, 227–50.

JOCELYNE COUTURE

Nationalism and Global Democracy: Between the Myth of Community and the Mirage of the Global Village

For a number of years, philosophical theorizing on the subject of nationalism has focused on exploring its normative grounds. For instance, the ideal conception of civic nationalism was first developed as a response to ethnic nationalism, rightly considered to be morally unacceptable. Then, to avoid the excesses of that ideal, which was criticized for being unable to avoid the pitfalls of ethnic nationalism except at the cost of denying the moral value of cultural belonging, emerged the liberal, communitarian, and even cosmopolitan versions of nationalism, along with combinations of various components of those diverse normative conceptions.

The question of nationalism's moral legitimacy is not closed – far from it. Yet, while this issue continues to torment philosophers, political scientists, jurists, and sociologists,[1] another is becoming more pressing: the *relevance* of nationalism in the current geopolitical context. Of course, that question we cannot understand unless we already have a reasonably precise idea of what nationalism is and of the different forms in which it may manifest itself. On this point the various normative conceptions of nationalism articulated in recent years are of great assistance. Yet what good is it to establish the moral legitimacy of certain forms of nationalism if those forms are not realizable – perhaps not even desirable – in the world of today? One of the key challenges facing theoreticians of nationalism is to show that nationalism could become a reality and yet have beneficial consequences within the framework of those emerging phenomena to which we generically refer as globalization.

For the last few years, I have been suggesting (Couture 1997, 1999) that one of the characteristic features of globalization – such as we are now experiencing it, that is, as a chiefly economic phenomenon[2] – is that it profits from a weakening of democracy. It "profits" from it in the sense that it takes advantage of citizens' increasing lack of interest in democracy, which allows national leaders to consent to the demands of globalization or to orchestrate its advances, but also in the sense that globalization's progression precipitates the erosion of the social bonds that form the very basis of democracy.[3]

The relevance of nationalism in this context does not depend solely on its ability to satisfy certain general moral principles. Its relevance also relies on its capacity to play a positive role, rather than a negative one, in the evolution of democratic societies and on its capacity to develop and maintain itself within existing or foreseeable institutional structures. A nationalism that seems desirable and feasible does not have to impede all forms of globalization, but it ought to be thought of as a condition – perhaps the main condition – of a globalization that is more humane, is more respectful of societies, and makes for greater solidarity among peoples.

Before showing how a form of liberal nationalism can meet these requirements, I would like to indicate how the principal current conceptualizations of nationalism, which tend to establish its moral legitimacy remain impervious to the conditions that should make it relevant today. To that end I examine three of the principal arguments underpinning normative conceptions of nationalism: the first is based on the value of cultural belonging; the second, on the values of political liberalism, and the third, on the value of a cosmopolitanism that nationalism ought to endorse.[4]

THREE ARGUMENTS FOR NATIONALISM

The Moral Value of Cultural Belonging

According to this first argument, a culture constitutes, for those who belong to it, the "context of choice" that is indispensable to their development as moral persons – that is, as free and responsible human beings. A culture provides the realm in which people can make free, responsible choices because it exemplifies, in the form of various modes of activity or social roles, the range of options open to its members, and provides the standards by which people can judge the relative value of those options and devise life plans that to them seem worthy of being carried out. Hence, the moral value of cultural belonging does not depend on whether a culture satisfies, in its specific contents, certain distinctive criteria of morality, but rather on whether it puts in place and structures a set of parameters without which the idea of choice would be meaningless. Will Kymlicka (1989) concludes that a culturally non-homogeneous society has a moral obligation to be open and receptive towards the social manifestations of cultural diversity.

There is no need to examine how this argument could have led to a normative conception, which I call "cultural," of the nation. A nation, the locus par excellence of a culture, constitutes a context of choice for its members and thus possesses a moral status that commands the respect and consideration of other nations. The argument that confers moral accreditation on the nation so defined does not, however, support the idea that it would be possible – and a fortiori legitimate – for a nation, simply because it constitutes a cultural nation, to endow itself with the attributes that would make it a political entity in its own right. This can be seen from two components of Kymlicka's argument.

First, the value of cultural belonging depends solely on the individual benefits – defined in terms of autonomy, self-esteem, and freedom – that people obtain from it. This individualistic logic remains quite incapable of explaining how people who have enjoyed the benefits of their cultural belonging might want to perpetuate their own culture for future generations (rather than, for example, encouraging their children to assimilate into another culture whose benefits would be just as great).[5] In relying only on this logic of choice – made by individuals and for themselves – Kymlicka's argument dismisses the possibility that, within a given community, precisely because it is a community, there could emerge a collective will to preserve its own culture or to develop it in accordance with collectively accepted parameters. It is in this first sense that the argument shows itself to be impervious to the very idea of political community, that is, of a community – that wants to take charge of its own destiny. Applied without qualifications to the nation, the argument has the same implications: the moral value of national belonging cannot be, for members of the same nation, a reason to take charge of their collective destiny.

The context in which this argument was first formulated gives credit – but still no justification – to the idea that cultural communities capable of being invested with a moral value have no legitimate claims to full-fledged political status. Kymlicka advances this position to show that a liberal state not only can but should concern itself with the cultures, especially the minority ones, that exist within its territory. Naturally, the argument focuses on the duties of the state and the rights of the cultural communities but does not otherwise concern itself with identifying the duties of members to their own culture. That is precisely the rub, for, to subscribe to the argument, one must admit at the outset that the responsible political power is outside the communities: the liberal state should offer political guarantees to its cultural communities, which themselves would have no morally valid reason, under Kymlicka's argument, to give themselves the political means that they consider capable of preserving their own culture. Faced with possible state inertia, they would have the duty only to encourage their members, who are entitled to the individual benefits of cultural belonging, to assimilate to a new "context of choice".[6] The cultural nation, legitimized by this same reasoning, also lacks any political dimension, and its conditions of existence depend on an external political power. The Québécois nation, for example, should be protected by the Canadian state just like any other cultural community living in its territory, but it would not be justified in asserting itself as a political community dedicated to protecting its own culture by giving itself, relatively to the parent state, the autonomy required for that purpose .[7]

Should we, in the present world context, promote the point of view that nations are just cultural entities and not also political ones? The implications of this position would be the same whether nations constitute majorities within a state or minorities without a state of their own. In either case, it would be necessary to abandon the ideas first that nations can constitute valid sources of democratic claims and thus that they can, as such, be legitimately represented by a political power. They could certainly enjoy political representation as sources of morally valuable belongings, but since this standpoint casts all nations as perfectly interchangeable, no reasonable argument could be advanced by a political power to promote at the international level the specific interests of the particular nation or nations that it represents.

The view that nations are merely cultural entities, deserving to be neither defended nor represented at the international level, could be of great comfort to governments that, faced with the advances of economic globalization, claim to be less and less capable – or are less and less desirous – of respecting and asserting internationally the democratically expressed wills of the nations that they represent. The same is true for all states that contain minority nations whose existence they deny or to whom they refuse to grant the measure of political autonomy that befits their status as nations. Moreover, the individualist perspective that inspires the conception of a cultural, non-political nation might also please architects of an economic globalization that is insensitive both to democracy and to the bonds of solidarity on which it is based. If the value of a culture rests only on the individual advantages that people derive from it, and not on its providing members with the basis of social bound and human solidarities, then a merely cultural nation is nothing more than the sum of its individuals. In the world today, this conception of the nation can only bolster the anti-democratic effects of capitalist globalization.

The Values of Political Liberalism

A second argument aims at establishing the moral relevance of nations by appealing to the moral value of a liberal-style constitution. The moral value of such a constitution finds expression in the ideals that it explicitly sets forth, such as tolerance, democratic equality, freedoms, and fundamental rights, and in the capacities that those ideals presuppose and maintain in citizens, such as autonomy, mutual respect, and a sense of political justice. By analogy with the first argument, this perspective presents belonging to a political community governed by a liberal constitution as a good for its individual members.

A nation that can be morally justified with such an argument is therefore a liberal nation, founded on citizens' allegiance to a liberal constitution and centred on realization of the ideals that it sets forth and the capacities that it presupposes. This conception of the nation, unlike the purely cultural version discussed above, promotes the practice of civic virtues; it can account for citizens' interest in advancing and perpetuating their political "culture" in their own society, since belonging to that specific culture is for them a good. Yet liberal nationalism so understood must avoid relying on cultural elements such as language, ways of life, religious beliefs, concepts of good, aesthetic values, or worldviews – in short, on all those elements that characterize the cultural nation and make it a "context of choice."

The argument for such an exclusion is simple. Its author, John Rawls, explains that in contemporary societies marked by pluralistic conceptions of good, the only commonly shared values are political ones, which are therefore the only ones on which one can rely to build societal cohesion (Rawls 1993, 173–211). Rawls does not deny that various elements of a culture, in the broad sense of the term, can constitute a good for individuals, but the realization of this type of good must remain an individual matter, and a liberal society, beyond the tolerance that it must show in this regard, has no obligation towards particular conceptions of good. According to Rawls, the only common culture shared by all members of a society is political in nature. Liberal nationalism, so understood, is heir to that exclusion: the only values that it can advance are political, and the only nations that it can attempt to promote are political ones, united by their sole allegiance to the principles of liberalism.[8]

It is therefore on such allegiance, and only on such allegiance, that one can rely to maintain the vitality of the liberal nation and, in particular, to encourage democratic participation in it. Yet, and still according to Rawls's rationale, allegiance to the liberal principles would be secured and reinforced when citizens enjoy the fruits of their political investment – that is, when they have a society that is more just, more egalitarian, and more respectful of rights. The question that arises – and crucially so in the world of today – is what can still guarantee allegiance to a liberal nation, taken in that sense, when so-called liberal states are now incapable of or unconcerned about providing the benefits that citizens have every right to expect from a liberal constitution? In such circumstances there is no reason for citizens, ideology aside, to be loyal to a liberal constitution. Allegiance to liberal values means merely an allegiance to ideas,[9] incapable by itself of inducing the sustained practice of democracy that the existence of an authentic liberal nation requires.

Rooted Cosmopolitanism

The third argument used to justify nationalism – and the last one that I examine here – is based on the value of national belonging as a necessary condition of its self-overcoming. This reasoning has a cosmopolitan premise – that recognizing the equal value of persons, regardless of "nationality, ethnicity, religion [or] class," implies, first, an "allegiance ... to the world-wide community of human beings" and, second, the obligation to "do [something] with and for the rest of the world" (Nussbaum, 1996, 4–13). The argument's other premise is that if one wants to do something with and for the rest of the world, one must first acquire the experience of what it is to be in the world, which each person acquires only within a particular community, in a given place, and at a given time.

These two premises form the basis of what has been called rooted cosmopolitanism.[10] Based on them, the argument for nationalism asserts, under the second premise, the moral value of national belonging and, under the first premise, its instrumental role in the formation of cosmopolitan solidarities. In the perspective set by rooted cosmopolitism, a nationalism that can satisfy these two conditions is open, tolerant, concerned about the fate of members of other nations, and respectful of their national culture.

Among the expected benefits of this normative conception of the nation and nationalism, proponents of rooted cosmopolitanism often give a prominent place to its democratic potential. According to them, the duty that falls to the "citizens of the world" – to help improve the lot of peoples, whoever and wherever they are – implies democratic participation that extends beyond political life and transcends the borders drawn by the traditional institutions of democracy. Thus, as cosmopolitan commitment finds its basis in solidarities first experienced within a nation, it would see democratic participation at the global scale as parasitic on the democratic awareness acquired within a nation.

But the idea of global democracy as an extension of local democracy receives no support from the institutional models of cosmopolitan democracy proposed to this day.[11] These models in effect stress democratic participation within international or supranational institutions or in the framework of associations emerging from the global civil society, but they also would limit the role of traditional – national – democratic institutions. Moreover, their proponents explicitly count the weakening of the usual democratic forums as essential for the emergence and the sustaining of a truly cosmopolitan type of democracy. Freed from the yoke of traditional nation-states, from their control over the organization of political life, and from their constraints on the exercise of democracy, the citizens of the world would revive the profound and stimulating meaning of democratic commitment and would find in it the impetus for sustained and vigorous practice of democracy.

It is, I think, to institutional cosmopolitanism's credit that it points out the role that states have played, and are still playing, in inhibiting the advent of global democracy. It is also to its credit, in the context of economic globalization, that it emphasizes that the solution to the problems associated with democracy can no longer be strictly local. It has nothing to propose, however, as loci for global democracy except supranational and international institutions and voluntary associations of global civil society – in effect, world governance "without government" and a world democratic base deprived of genuine democratic institutions. Even its most carefully articulated models hinge the "duties" of the citizens of the world ultimately on their individual initiatives and on their capacity to form associations.

The proponents of institutional cosmopolitanism thus stress the discrepancy that exists between democracy as it should, in their view, be practised world-wide and democracy as it takes place within societies. As for explaining the emergence of a global democracy, rooted cosmopolitanism, like the normative conception of the open nation based on it, is heir to a problematic point of view. Rooted cosmopolitanism rightly stresses the role that nations can play as the founding locus of a global democracy – that is, as the place where democracy must first be realized, with the aid of the solidarity that unites the citizens of a nation – before it develops into solidarity among peoples. But if, as the proponents claim, global democracy conflicts – in its principles, in its practice, in the conditions under which it is practised and even in the attitudes on which it is based – with democracy within national institutions, then it requires the citizens of the world to transcend and abandon any conception of democracy that they may have formed within these institutions. This position renders open nationalism a conflicting option: the "citizen of the world" is not the one who, having realized, from his or her own experience, the significance of national belonging for democratic involvement makes a commitment to respect other's people sense of belonging and have it respected. Rather, the citizen of the world is the one who has rejected the very idea of national belonging and the conception of the bases of democracy that it presupposes.

This criticism does not suggest that it is impossible to reconcile rooted cosmopolitanism and a form of institutional cosmopolitanism within a conception more sensitive to the links between global democracy and democracy within national institutions. My position here is rather that a cosmopolitan perspective can account for these links and for the link between nation and democracy, provided that it breaks firmly with the conception of global democracy currently endorsed by the proponents of institutional cosmopolitanism. By minimizing the role that nations can play in the advent of a global democracy, cosmopolitanism deprives itself of its own most immediate and most vigorous base. The democratic practice of citizens of the world, cut off from their democratic investment in their society, risks going for naught, leaving of the plan originally set out by institutional cosmopolitanism nothing but an authoritarian world governance – that is, more or less the same thing that globalization of the economy has brought us to date. Yet if this normative conception of democracy were to be realized in the manner expected by its authors, nations themselves would be reduced to insignificance as loci of democratic investment.

LIBERAL NATIONALISM:
FINDING AN APPROPRIATE FORM

Nations and Democracy

None of these three normative conceptions of the nation leads to the conclusion that nations could contribute to making the world in which we live more democratic. Their central – and common – shortcoming in this respect is that they fail to account for the possibility that a nation that is otherwise considered morally legitimate would satisfy the conditions that could make it a full-fledged political entity. This is true of the cultural nation, dependent on a political will that is outside it; of the liberal nation, whose stability is impaired by the circumstances of today; and of the cosmopolitan-inspired nation, whose institutions should play only a secondary role in the political life of the citizens.

This shortcoming clearly shows that these conceptualizations are insensitive to the existence of primarily economic – and certainly undemocratic – authority structures and to the concomitant erosion of the political sphere as a locus of democratic action. The conclusion to which they should lead is that the nation, since it is not a full-fledged political entity, has no role to play in the evolution of democracy. Nations and nationalisms, legitimate as they may be from the moral standpoint, would be simply devoid of relevance today. Yet such a conclusion is not normatively neutral. The view that nations are not political entities or the inability to define the conditions today under which they might become political entities could have undesirable consequences. One of them would be to minimize the importance of national demands in what remains of the democratic forum and thus to help legitimize the anti-democratic effects of economic globalization. In particular, trivializing national demands would endorse the process of economic globalization, in which national cultures become diluted or intermixed or even vanish for the benefit of a dominant "culture." If one believes at all that cultural belonging has a moral value, denying the political status of nations appears to be, at the very least, paradoxical.

Apart from their insensitivity to particular current problems, and beyond their predictable consequences, the leading conceptions of the nation fail to comprehend the most general requirements of democracy. A democratic political organization presupposes at least the existence of democratic institutions – that is, of loci for democratic interventions and decision-making. When one denies the political nature of nations, one denies them the relevance to equip themselves with such institutions. The cultural and the cosmopolitan conceptions of the nation, for example, both presuppose that the loci of democratic action and decision-making do not belong specifically to the nation, that they are situated elsewhere. Both are content with the facts that such loci exist and that they are open to all, including individuals who profess allegiance to their own nation. Hence both measure democracy against the yardstick of the possibility for citizens to express their wills and, let us assume, the possibility of their being heard in the democratic forum.[12]

However, the problem raised by democracy, especially in so-called democratic societies, has nothing to do with possibilities; rather, it relates to the fact that what is possible is not actualized. The loci of democratic action may well exist, but, deserted by the citizens and diverted from their purposes, they no longer fulfil the role that led to their creation. If the mere existence of democratic loci in no way demonstrates the vitality of a democracy, neither is it a sufficient condition of that vitality. This observation brings us to an aspect of democracy that the cultural and cosmopolitan conceptions seem to ignore: democracy presupposes not only the right of citizens to express themselves and be heard but also their duty to support the democratic institutions, to promote them as a means to reach understandings, and to practise vigilance so that the institutions are not used for partisan ends. The liberal conception takes this second aspect into account when it asserts that the citizens who love liberal values and the benefits that they receive from a society that conforms to those values must ensure the vitality of democratic institutions. Yet, as we saw above, the liberal conception assumes a motivational basis that is not strong enough to guarantee citizens participation, especially in the current situation. Love for liberal values is a powerful force, but, confronted with repeated denials of freedom, justice, and equality, it no longer arouses in citizens a sense of duty towards their democratic institutions.

It therefore seems that democracy needs to take root in a more vital and concrete way in the lives and concerns of citizens, so that they may believe that its institutions will enable them to reach decisions about themselves and about subjects that matter to them. The cultural and cosmopolitan conceptions of the nation take for granted that democratic loci that are "open to all" can obtain the support that they need. Yet what democratic advantages lie in promoting democratic loci whose existence, without popular support, can entertain only the illusion of democracy? These formal conceptions of democracy, and the idealistic conception that underlies liberal nationalism, necessitate creation of a more realistic vision of democracy, of its bases, and of the circumstances that make its actualization possible.

The circumstances cannot be entirely determined within the framework of a theory of democracy; they depend largely on an empirical analysis of the historical and sociological context. But if, as I believe, the bases of democracy lie in the will of citizens to realize their own aspirations and plans, then it should be recognized that the members of a nation, who share a historical awareness, certain common values, a common culture and language, and certain common plans, can, when they have democratic institutions and thus form a viable political entity, help revitalize democracy.

Towards the Cultural, Sociological, and Political Nation

The conception of the nation that I believe should be promoted, in view of the current state of the world, is at once cultural, sociological, and political. It is cultural, first because people usually attach particular importance to the ways of life that are current in their society, a fortiori if that society is their community of origin,[13] and are generally concerned with the evolution of those ways of life. Second, culture, in view of its crucial role in asserting national identity, is the central pillar of citizens' involvement in their society. Third, the common cultural references that characterize a nation constitute a universe of shared meanings within which citizens have a better chance of understanding and getting along with one another. Thus the first reason for promoting a cultural conception of the nation relates to the moral value of cultural belonging for autonomous, responsible people; the second and third derive from the role of shared cultural belonging as the creator of democratic commitment.

The nation is also a sociological reality,[14] which does not presuppose that the common culture is the native culture of all its members. The history of most contemporary nations shows that, at each stage in their evolution, they became the home societies of groups and individuals of diverse origins who, though eager to integrate into their new society, did not want to renounce their own values and culture. From a normative standpoint, positing the sociological nature of nations implies that they have three obligations – first, to be open to those who wish to join them and who are prepared to abide by the society's fundamental laws; second, to facilitate actively their inclusion in the national culture and their participation in every level of the social structure; and, third, to promote and maintain, in the society as a whole, interactions based on tolerance and equity.

Cultural nations constitute a richer human environment than the so-called liberal nations. That is why cultural nations, when they espouse liberal values and become sociological entities in the normative sense of the word, are genuine home societies, not only respectful of the diversity of their members but also capable of providing them with an environment in which they can become full-fledged social actors. When the nation is sociological, as well as cultural, it nurtures new solidarities based on the search for, definition of, and sharing of a new collective space. Combined with the solidarities that bind individuals on the basis of their native culture, they make the cultural and sociological society the hotbed par excellence of democratic participation.

Finally, the cultural and sociological nation must also be political, for three reasons – first, it is within the framework of its particular institutions that citizens' sense of democracy can be turned into concrete action; second, the use of such institutions and the benefits that they produce for life in society help to strengthen the bonds of solidarity between citizens and consequently to deepen their commitment to democracy; and, third, such institutions allow nations to participate with other nations in the decisions that concern them.

This characterization of the nation readily subscribes to the moral values that severally underlie the cultural, liberal, and cosmopolitan conceptions of the nation. Yet by subscribing to those values simultaneously, it gains a moral credibility that none of those conceptions possesses separately. By putting the value of cultural belonging into the context of a sociological reality, it avoids the pitfalls of marginalizing minorities, and it asserts more consistently than the liberal nations the equality of all citizens as social actors. For the same reason, such a nation presupposes social relationships based on "the will to cooperate with all those with whom we are compelled to live", – a vision that, for Kant, lay at the heart of the cosmopolitan spirit.[15] Moreover, by putting the value of cultural belonging into a political context, this characterization embraces a principle of equal respect for the peoples of the world and of their right to self-determination, which does not follow directly from either the cosmopolitan ideal or the ideal of the so-called cultural nation. Finally, this characterization of the nation, coupling liberal values with the more communitarian-style values that underlie its cultural and sociological components, adds a further dimension to the cosmopolitan ideal by justifying the moral obligation for each nation actively to promote democratic equality and tolerance in the world's other nations and in their relations with one another. The nation thus characterized is not elitist or exclusivist or assimilationist or expansionist, as a nation that is only cultural and political might be. It is not self-centred and limited by a strict policy of non-interference, as the liberal nation might be. And it enriches rather than restricts the cosmopolitan ideals.

Nations thus characterized also have a relevance, in the present geopolitical context, that none of the three conceptions discussed above has. That relevance comes from the role that they can play in revitalizing democracy both locally and globally. At the local level, nations that are at once cultural, sociological, and political possess the optimum conditions for sustained democratic participation. Their cultural component guarantees the existence of a shared space of meanings that arouses citizens' interest in their own society and nurtures their expectations of reaching agreements democratically, and within which certain collective plans can take shape. Their sociological component is based on and reinforces the sense of the social co-operation, reciprocity, and mutual respect that are central to the idea of citizenship and that, because they confirm the equality of citizens, form one of the essential motivational bases of their democratic participation. Finally, the political component of nations provides citizens with a set of institutions that facilitate democratic exchange and deliberation, making possible the effective implementation of agreements that they have reached with one another and guaranteeing them adequate representation in decisions that also involve nations other than their own. These ideas, while expressing democracy in concrete terms, would consolidate citizens' sense of democracy and encourage their involvement in its processes.

At the world level, cultural, sociological, and political nations take their place as the prime loci of genuine democratic practice, as entities with the will to achieve self-determination, and as valid sources of demands. The effective existence of such nations would help cut off the leading source of anti-democratic interference afflicting the world these days – the globalization of the capitalist economy. A nation that is at the height of its powers and driven by the democratic will of its members does not have to yield to economic imperatives that jeopardize its culture, its institutions, the welfare of its citizens, and their sense of social co-operation. These are the interests that its representatives must defend and, supported or impelled by democratic will, will defend.

It would be utopian to think that a nation in the sense intended here could succeed alone in curbing the anti-democratic interference of capitalist globalization. But cultural, sociological, and political nations have common interests and political means that enable them to put up concerted resistance. They also have the political means to supervise jointly the establishment and operation of international or supranational bodies to orchestrate democratic control of the decisions that concern them. Furthermore, they have the means to require that that control also be applied to peoples whom circumstances have prevented from reaching the democratic ideal. It is, in any case, in the interest of the nations in the sense that I intend to ensure that undemocratic governments stop encouraging the free riders of capitalist globalization. But it is also in their interest to create a global democratic base that is sufficiently robust to advance the interests of all peoples without exception. Thus consideration of social utility converge with the cosmopolitan requirements that, for the sake of consistency, peoples who care about their own lot must apply to all other peoples.

In the world of today, the citizen of a cultural, sociological, and political nation will soon also be forced to become a citizen of the world. From the standpoint of this conception of the nation, however, the transition will be that much smoother if he or she knows from experience the value of his or her own national belonging, based on openness to others, co-operation within a cultural, sociological, and political space, and sustained practice of democracy.[16]

Transition Issues

Philosophers often leave it up to others to explore how to make the transition from the current state of the world to the state that they believe we should aim for. Be it wisdom or modesty, this attitude does not excuse them from attempting to show that the current state of the world makes such a transition at least plausible. So how does my conception of the nation measure up in that respect?

This conception of the nation borrows from the model, familiar but suspect in many respects, of the nation-state.[17] The familiarity of the model indicates that it is realizable at least partly within institutions that already exist or, if they do not, whose scope, methods of operation, and goals are well understood.

However, the model of the nation-state is being undermined by two related difficulties. One is the disjunction, in two separate bodies, of the political and of what should form its democratic basis. In economic globalization, citizens are neither present nor represented in the decision-making forums where their individual and collective interests are at stake. Yet they are also kept out of other decision-making forums on the pretext that the decisions being made there either do not concern them or exceed their competence. Such is the case for issues relating to, for example, the global environment, the health of populations, the rearmament of world powers, famine in Africa and India, respect for human rights, and international justice. Characteristically, the heads of government making such decisions have neither the pretension nor the desire to represent the views of their citizens on all those issues. When citizens want to express their opinions on those subjects, they have to do so in non-governmental organizations, whose democratic status is, at the very least, fragile[18] and which, in any case, have no decision-making powers.

The second difficulty has to do with citizens' perception of their own national belonging. It is hardly surprising that citizens of nation-states no longer have a very clear sense of what brings them together in their institutions or of the role that they can play there. Nor is it surprising that stateless nations are losing their confidence in the democratic potential of institutions that seem promising in theory but prove ineffective in practice.

I attempted above to show that the solution to the first problem – that of disjunction – depends largely on solving the second problem – that is, on finding a coherent national awareness. That awareness should encompass the various aspects of the condition of contemporary citizens: the sense of belonging to a historical culture, the sharing – by chance or otherwise – of certain ways of life, the resulting forms of solidarity, and an undying shared belief in the value of democracy. I have argued that it is national awareness thus defined that most effectively nurtures citizens' will to reappropriate their democratic institutions and, if necessary, to create them.

Is it utopian to think that such a national awareness could emerge today? It seems to me that it is already forming, though still too timidly and patchily, in a number of European and North and South American nation-states. We take note of that emergence when governments are reminded that the interests of citizens come before those of multinationals and where concern is expressed about the consequences of decisions that supposedly have to do only with the regulation of relations between states. Nor does it seem utopian to me to think that citizens who no longer have any idea what unites them within their own institutions will soon discover, spurred on by their governments' off-hand attitude towards them, the value of revitalizing those institutions and of facilitating their emergence within nations that still lack them.

On this last point, it may seem as if the model of the nation-state presents insurmountable difficulties. The state system, as actualized since its creation, completely dominates relations between peoples and subsumes those relations under a generalized principle of non-interference. The democratization of non-democratic states would therefore be a goal outside the scope of political action of citizens not belonging to these states and would require that the states themselves, on their own initiative, renounce the principle of non-interference. The problem would obviously not be solved by the mere fact that democratic states alone, under pressure from their citizens, expressed willingness to conclude such an agreement. Yet this problem does not seem to me to be very different in form from the problems raised by global environment, international justice, or world hunger. If democratic states do not have the power to force undemocratic states to halt unacceptable practices – whether in the environment, distribution of wealth, or democracy – in their own territory, they do have the power to demand the establishment of international agencies to eradicate such practices. The citizens of democratic states have the power to require from their states a commitment to promote and maintain such agencies, and they have the duty to see to it that those agencies operate effectively. It seems to me that again here we can take a few lessons from cosmopolitan wisdom, which urges us to create many loci of democratic participation, both between states, where citizens can develop and maintain bonds of solidarity with other nations of the world, and above states, where institutions are accountable to the court of nations for their representatives' actions.

Before actually starting down such paths, however, citizens need to become fully aware of the power that they represent as members of a nation and not just as individual electors, of the resources that a nation has at its disposal to carry out its plans, and of the solidarities on which it can rely to ensure its existence as a nation. That is how national awareness, in the sense in which I understand it, can effectively serve global democracy.

NOTES

1 For a sample of the various ways in which this question has been formulated, see Couture, Nielsen, and Seymour, 1996.

2 When I say that globalization is an economic phenomenon, I am not assuming that its effects are exclusively, or even mostly, economic.

3 One example is the way in which the collective imagination has made a clean break with the idea of social responsibility – the central idea of the welfare state – after states, taking on the role of the IMF's messengers, began sacrificing social programs in order to repay the national debt and implement other types of so-called economic cleansing.

4 The space allowed here does not permit a full discussion of these arguments and their impications for a conception of nations. Detailed discussions, however, appear in Couture, 1997; 1999; and in Couture, Nielsen, and Seymour, 1996, 579–661.

5 A frequent criticism of Kymlicka (which he himself notes) is that, as mere "contexts of choice," all cultures would be interchangeable, which would make a state policy of assimilation, rather than a policy based on respect for particular cultures, morally acceptable (Kymlicka, 1989, 173ff). My point is different: even from the standpoint of the individuals concerned (the members of the cultural communities), assimilation would be, under Kymlicka's argument, a morally acceptable choice. In a communitarian-style response to the first criticism, and to oppose any assimilationist policy, Kymlicka argued that culture is valuable as a context of choice to the extent that it is people's *home* (or native) culture (Kymlicka, 1989, 175). First, this response is at odds with the theses concerning autonomy of the person and effective freedom of choice that are at the heart of the original argument. Second, it does not resolve the issue that I have raised here, which concerns a decision that affects future generations, and it can be expressed just as easily in terms of home culture.

6 Kymlicka later adopted this perspective to characterize the state's role vis-à-vis cultural communities. In a subsequent book, he proposes to interpret the demands of cultural communities as demands for inclusion in the majority culture (Kymlicka, 1995, chap. 9).

7 Unlike the demands for inclusion in the majority culture, those regarding full governmental autonomy cannot be justified, according to Kymlicka. Granting these demands, he argues, would jeopardize social unity. But since denying them would have the same effect, Kymlicka admits that, in certain circumstances, they must, for pragmatic reasons, be acceded to; see Kymlicka, 1995, 192. Elsewhere (Kymlicka, 1999, 138) he raises the following

questions: "Why isn't freedom of speech and association sufficient to allow people to express their cultural identity? Why is the state needed for people to share a language, memorize their past, cherish their heroes, living a fulfilling national life?" He answers: "If a national group has full language rights and control over immigration, education, and resource development policy, then its long term viability is secured. If [national minorities] lack these rights and powers ... and do not wish to assimilate, they must struggle either through secession of regional autonomy ... whose result is longstanding national divisions, sometimes flaring into violence" (140). Yet "[i]t is unclear why liberals should see the political expression of national identity as a virtue to be promoted" (139). So, although Kymlicka's position seems to many with liberal commitments to be very sympathetic to and with that to make sense of liberal nationalism, these quotations show that he is not endorsing in any way the idea that a nation that forms a minority within a liberal state can become a sovereign political entity.

8 A nation conceived in such a way would be close in scope and attributes to what Kymlicka characterizes as a liberal society. According to both Kymlicka and Rawls, the state of a liberal society should not seek to give a particular culture public expression. The state, says Kymlicka, "must be seen as equally belonging to all people who are governed by it, regardless of their nationality" (1999, 139). Kymlicka departs from Rawls, as we saw above, in that he asserts the moral duty, for a liberal society, to grant cultural minorities (including national minorities) special rights and powers that would, in Rawls's terms, help realize their particular conceptions of the good.

9 One might argue that, under Rawls's argument of overlapping consensus, allegiance to the *doctrine* of political liberalism should guarantee the stability of liberal society. But before concluding that that is Rawls's position, one must consider that, under that argument, consensus is created within a well-ordered society, whose members already enjoy all the benefits of a constitution consistent with political liberalism. From this perspective, allegiance to liberal *ideas* is the confirmation, not the condition, of sustained liberal practice. See Rawls, 1993, 133–72.

10 For a description and defence of this position, see Cohen, 1994, and Nielsen, 1999.

11 Not all theoreticians of cosmopolitanism give equal value to questions relatived to democracy. Some advocate cosmopolitanism as a moral doctrine or as a general attitude in matters of justice, without stressing its possible implications for democracy or, if they do so, without articulating an institutional model likely to actualize its ideals as much as its democratic potential. What I call here "the cosmopolitan conception of democracy" refers to such

an institutional model – the one proposed by Held, 1995 – and whose general outline is still inspiring theoreticians of cosmopolitan democracy.

12 This assumption may seem too generous towards these conceptions of the democratic forum. Indeed, it rules out the quite real possibility that, in such a context, entire groups of citizens may be permanently marginalized in their specific demands by a majority that has different demands. This suggests that the members of those marginalized groups may not feel any sense of duty to the democratic institutions. While I do not wish to deny the strength of that argument, mine is different. Rather than focusing on the possibility of citizens' expressing demands (or their being heard), I wish to emphasize the nature of the agreements that may be reached in the democratic forum. For the purposes of this argument, it is simpler to assume initially that citizens "are heard"; if that assumption is unrealistic – and I think that it is – then we should conclude that the two arguments converge on the same conclusion and strengthen one another.

13 That importance can be reflected in attachment to those ways of life or in the assertion of a particular identity or even of loyalty to those who participate in them. Hence it may vary in intensity from one person to another and does not prevent a citizen from recognizing the importance of other ways of life or from deciding to adopt ways of life that prevail in another culture. Moreover, the particular importance one attaches to those ways of life does not imply that one approves of them; certain ways of life may arouse feelings of indignation or shame that would not arise if these ways of acting were not those of one's fellow citizens.

14 The concept of the sociological nation was put forward by Michel Seymour, 1999, but my characterization of it differs appreciably from his.

15 Kant expounds on this idea primarily in "On the Common Saying: This may be true in theory but it does not apply in practice" (in Reiss, 1991, 89–92), in "Perpetual Peace: A Philosophical Sketch" (104–8), and in "Idea for a Universal History with a Cosmopolitan Purpose" (44–8).

16 An anonymous referee asked: "Is there evidence that the countries that are doing a better job of coping with globalization are ones with a high level of national awareness?" My attempt to answer that empirical question is twofold. First, the question presupposes that some countries cope better – that is, I take it, that their economy, working conditions, social welfare policies, domestic cultural policies, democratic institutions, and levels of employment and wealth are not as badly affected by capitalist globalization as are those of other countries. That would be hard to deny. Some countries have more resilient institutions and policies than others – for example, Sweden than Indonesia, Taiwan than South Korea.

Now the question is how, if at all, is that related to the degree of national awareness in these countries? My answer here is that the resilience of institutions and policies in a given country depends on many factors, such as wealth, level of education, resources, and environmental conditions. But the resilience of its institutions and policies also depends substantially on citizens' support. Many kinds of solidarities would be at work here, springing from worker's unions, business lobbies, cultural associations, community action groups, environmental associations, and so on. One does not have to deny that these associations and groups often concern themselves with international issues in order to admit, first, that they are likely to stem from a basic solidarity within a nation and, second, that a high degree of national awareness in a country will tend to fuel all kinds of solidarities that render institutions and local policies more resilient.

My point, however, is not that national awareness in a country helps *that* country to cope better with globalization – which would amount to dismissing the other factors that I mentioned above and, moreover, to saying that a global problem could receive a local solution. My point is rather that national awareness will generate solidarities that would tend to cross the borders of a country and then aid world-wide resistance to capitalist globalization. This is the cosmopolitan side – and an important one – of the nationalism that I defend.

This is not a full empirical answer to this empirical question, but it seems at least a plausible one, supported by examples such as the debates initiated in France, over the so-called cultural exception; in Canada, over the wood industry; in Ecuador, over coffee plantations; and in Argentina, over dollarization. It would be hard not to recognize that these debates originated in national forums, with peoples aware not only of their common interests but also of their common belonging and of the value of their solidaristic action. That they then extended across national borders and that some of them at least are slowing or even stopping the advances of multinationals support the normative claim that I am making here.

17 Contrary to what some believe, this model also encompasses multinational states or federations of nation-states.

18 The central problem with the democratic status of such associations is, for all practical purposes, the same as the problem with pressure groups in constitutional democracies, except that, in the latter case, their actions are in principle limited by public reason, while in the former, they are not.

REFERENCES

Cohen, Mitchell (1994) "Rooted Cosmopolitanism," in Michel Walzer, ed., *Toward a Global Civil Society*. Providence, RI: Bergham Books, 223–33.

Couture, Jocelyne (1997) "An Ethical Response to Globalization: Justice or Solidarity?" in J. Drydyk and P. Pentz, eds., *Global Justice, Global Democracy*. Winnipeg: Society for Socialist Studies/Fendwood Publishing, 123–39.

– (1999) "Facing Globalization: Cosmopolitan Democracy and Liberal Nationalism," *Monist* 82, no. 3, 491–515.

Couture, Jocelyne, Kai Nielsen, and Michel Seymour, eds. (1996) *Rethinking Nationalism*. Calgary: University of Calgary Press.

Held, David (1995) *Democracy and the Global Order; From the Modern State to Cosmopolitan Governance*. Cambridge: Polity Press, 1995.

Kymlicka, Will (1989) *Liberalism Community, and Culture*. Oxford: Clarendon Press.

– (1995) *Multicultural Citizenship*. Oxford: Clarendon Press.

– (1999) "Misunderstanding Nationalism," in Ronald Beiner, ed., *Theorizing Nationalism*. New York: State University of New York Press, 131–40.

Nielsen, Kai (1999) "Cosmopolitan Nationalism," *Monist* 82, no. 1, 446–90.

Nussbaum, Martha (1996) "Patriotism and Cosmopolitanism," in Joshua Cohen, ed., *For Love of Country*. Boston: Beacon Press.

Rawls, John (1993) *Political Liberalism*. New York: Columbia University Press.

Reiss, Hans, ed. (1991) *Kant: Political Writings*. Cambridge: Cambridge University Press.

Seymour, Michel (1999) "Plaidoyer pour la nation sociopolitique," in Michel Seymour, ed., *Nationalité, citoyenneté et solidarité*. Montreal: Liber.

ROSS POOLE

The Nation-state and Aboriginal Self-determination

This paper has three sections. In the first, I state and defend the thesis – which I take to be the major theoretical insight of nationalism – that in the modern world culture is and ought to be an integral part of politics. This thesis is embodied in the concept of the nation-state. In the second, I discuss some of the implications of the nationalist thesis, particularly with respect to "multi-nation states." In the third, I make some suggestions as to how to meet the claims of indigenous peoples within the nation-state.

CULTURE AND POLITICS

There are sociological arguments that attempt to show why the modern world has been uniquely hospitable to nationalism (see Gellner, 1983; Anderson, 1991; and Poole, 1999, chap. 1). The argument I sketch here occupies a different terrain: that of normative political philosophy. Its aim is to show that there are good reasons why the modern state *ought* to be a nation-state.

If a liberal is someone who is concerned to protect the rights of the person and a republican is someone who emphasizes the responsibilities of the citizen, then there are good reasons for liberals to become republicans. The argument here is familiar (see Skinner, 1984; 1991; Taylor, 1989; Macedo, 1990; Galston, 1991; and Pettit, 1997). The rights celebrated by liberals presuppose certain social and political conditions. There must be an appropriate framework of law and law enforcement through which laws are defined and protected, disputes adjudicated, and so on. There must also be some form of constitutional democracy in place. A legal framework of right will decay unless there are political institutions and procedures through which citizens can criticize and change the laws and their administration. However, the mere existence of these institutions is not on its own sufficient to sustain the regime of rights. They must also receive confirmation in the behaviour and attitudes of those subject to them. There are two major conditions here. The first involves some measure of *activity*. Those subject to the institutions – or at least enough of them, enough of the time – must make use of the opportunities that they provide to participate in public affairs and to criticize or support political, legal, and administrative decisions; they must take the time to understand and participate in political debates, and so on. Second, they must have some measure of *commitment* to the results of political processes. They must accept the legitimacy of the state and the authority of its representatives. In other words, liberal persons – or enough of them – must take on the responsibilities of citizenship: they must be both active and committed members of the body politic.

The need for some measure of activity on the part of citizens has been increasingly recognized by liberal philosophers and is an aspect of the voluminous literature on civil society. The requirement of commitment has not received so much attention. But it is crucial. Activity on the part of those who do not accept the legitimacy of the system would undermine it, not sustain it. Unless there is a widely shared commitment to the system, a passive citizenship is the only way in which it can survive. But then the system will erode from within. Although the most striking illustrations of this malaise are societies constructed on the Soviet model, it is also a problem for liberal-democratic societies, which face special difficulties in achieving political commitment. This is partly because citizens are inclined to devote their main energies to private life and thus to view the demands of public life as alien intrusions (Walzer, 1989). But it is also because democracy relies on a certain schizophrenia in public life itself. On the one hand, it expects citizens to be committed to their own views; good democrats will work to mobilize support for their views, provide reasons why others should support them, and so on. But it also asks that they respect the results of the democratic process, even when this goes against them. If this is not quite a paradox (as argued by Wollheim, 1962), it is a tension that is both constitutive of the practice of democracy and a potential threat to it.

Just what level of activity and commitment is required of citizens depends very much on one's expectation of the state. Neoliberals, for example, envisage a diminished role for the state. This conception necessitates a minimum of activity and commitment; the citizen is (more or less) the taxpayer, whose major responsibility is to rein in the wasteful expenditure of the state. Social-democratic policies, in contrast, require a much stronger practice of citizenship. Government strategies need to be criticized and informed, and citizens must accept a higher degree of state expenditure and interference. So finding the resources to sustain a practice of citizenship poses a greater problem for social democrats than for neoliberals. Neoliberals may welcome a decline in the citizenship activities encouraged by social democrats as a sign of healthy individualism. However, the decline cannot go too far: even the most austere neoliberal state needs some support in the attitudes and activities of those subject to it.

If there is good reason for liberal theory to move in the direction of republicanism, what reason is there for the liberal individual to become an active and committed citizen? Here the argument is not so straightforward. The activity and commitment of citizens cannot be matters of enforceable duty. While some citizen responsibilities can be compelled (for example, jury service, paying taxes, voting in some countries), not all can be (for example, one can hardly be forced to participate in political debates). And even those that can be enforced need to be carried out conscientiously, and this lies outside the provenance of the law. So not all the responsibilities of citizenship can be made compulsory. But neither can they be left to the unformed choice of the individual. This may have been possible in the classical city-state imagined by many republicans, where citizenship was an elite way of life and its responsibilities went along with a number of privileges. Given the smallness of these communities, there was also a close connection between the acts of the individual and the overall social good, while failure to perform was likely to result in stigma or worse. In these circumstances, there may have been sufficient motivation for most citizens to carry out their responsibilities of their own free will. In the modern world, however, citizenship is universal; politics is not a way of life (except for professional politicians). Citizenship is marginal to the main business of life, and freedom points towards private life, not public duty (Constant, 1988; Walzer, 1989). Given that the responsibilities of citizenship will usually involve some sacrifice of one's other interests and concerns, there is little reason to suppose that many people will choose them.

Citizenship responsibilities fall in the area between the legally enforce-able and the freely chosen. A healthy liberal polity requires a widespread propensity to perform these responsibilities, so that citizens – enough of them, enough of the time – carry them out. Citizens must have the appro-priate *virtues*. The Aristotelian background of the term *virtue* reminds us that these propensities must be connected, systematically though defeasi-bly, with some notion of the good life, both for the citizen and for the pol-ity to which he or she belongs. For Aristotle, the practice of the virtues is both constitutive of and conducive to the well-being of the individual and of the state (although he recognized that things could go badly wrong). If modern citizens are to practise the virtues necessary to sustain political life, these must be related not merely to a distant public benefit but to in-dividual well-being. The individual must get something out of acting as a citizen. Unless they are associated with certain rewards, the virtues will not be carried out and the liberal-democratic state will decay. But how can these rewards be provided in the modern world?

One part of the answer lies in the role of culture and identity. It is through culture – language, stories about land and history, art forms, modes of dress and communication, common rituals, customs, and so on – that individuals form a sense of themselves as belonging to a *na-tion*, and it is this identity that provides the link between the individual and the state (see Miller, 1995; Tamir, 1995; Canovan, 1996; Poole, 1999). The formation of a national identity not only contributes to the fellow feeling and trust that are necessary between citizens; but it also – and perhaps more fundamentally – allows the individual to iden-tify with a larger and more satisfying narrative than that provided by his or her private affairs. It provides a sense of oneself as belonging to a historical community, such that one's own well-being is bound up with that of the community. It offers a glimpse – indeed, an experience – of the powers and triumphs, glories and tragedies, that are part of the nation's histories and achievements. It even allows, for a moment, the transcendence of one's finitude (cf. Anderson, 1991). It is because one's national identity provides for pleasures, for meanings, and for a sense of fulfilment lacking in other avenues of life that it directs the will of the individual towards the responsibilities of citizenship.

It is a necessary condition of the operations of the modern state that it bring to bear sufficient cultural resources to ensure the commitment and sustain the activity of its citizens.[1] Although nationalisms have of-ten enough been anti-liberal and anti-democratic, the nationalist insight applies especially strongly to liberal democracies. These require a more complex form of commitment than do authoritarian governments. Nor can they rely on overt coercion to the same extent. Although a range of other factors have played a part, national identity has been the crucial condition for the legitimacy of the modern state. It is through the nation that the state has gathered together cultural resources to attract the commitment of its citizens. So far, neither history nor theory has presented a workable alternative. If liberals ought to become republicans, both ought to become nationalists. The modern state – especially the liberal and democratic state – is and ought to be the nation-state.

IMPLICATIONS OF NATIONALISM

Historically, there have been two routes towards the nation-state. The first, approximating roughly to the history of England (later Britain) in the sixteenth, seventeenth and eighteenth centuries, and to France and the United States somewhat later (see Colley, 1992; Greenfeld, 1992), involves a state establishing the political environment within which national cultures develop. In the nineteenth century, "nation-building" became an explicit project of the state. The second route – "national self-determination" – involves the formation of national communities with political aspirations that challenge the existing order.[2] Both processes are still going on. Both may reasonably appeal to the nationalist thesis for support. But what happens when the two movements clash – that is, when the nation-building of an existing state conflicts with the political aspirations of a national minority? Which should prevail?

Will Kymlicka and Christine Straehle (1999, 76) describe the situation: "If it is indeed desirable for states to be nation-states, then this seems to leave two unattractive options in countries where there are two or more national groups: either (a) split up multination states so as to enable all national groups to form their own nation-state; or (b) enable the largest or most powerful national group within each multination state to use state-nationalism to destroy all competing national identities." As Kymlicka and Straehle depict the alternatives, they certainly seem unattractive. If every national minority were to achieve statehood, there would be an unwieldy number of states. Worse, the process would create national minorities within the proliferating states, and the problems that they were intended to resolve would recur within the new state. But a policy of forcing national minorities to assimilate with the majority nation would be unjust and, as recent history indicates, unlikely to succeed.

Kymlicka and Straehle's (1999, 78) solution is as follows: "We need to think of a world, not of nation-states, but of multi-nation states. If liberal nationalism is to be a viable and defensible approach in today's world, we need to renounce the traditional aim of liberal nationalism – namely, the aspiration to common nationhood within each state – and instead think of states as federations of self-governing peoples, in which boundaries have been drawn and powers distributed as to allow all national groups to exercise some degree of self-government."

However, this is not so much a solution as a restatement of the problem. The nationalist insight that a state must deploy the cultural resources necessary to secure the active support of its citizens applies to any form of the state – including the multinational. A multi-nation state, especially one that is attempting to deal justly with the demands of national minorities within the minorities, not to speak of other cultural claimants, will have to be an interventionist one. If it is to be democratic, there will need to be a public sphere for debate of matters of common concern, and this will limit the number of publicly recognized languages. Like any other states, it will make demands on its citizens, and it will need to mobilize or create the cultural resources to ensure than they respond to these demands. If there are to be viable multi-nation-states they will have to be multi-nation nation-states.

This possibility suggests that we should look more closely at the "nation-building" alternative that Kymlicka and Straehle reject.[3] Fortunately, this option is not as unattractive as they suggest. For them, nation-building means that "the largest or most powerful national group within each multination state … [will] use state-nationalism to destroy all competing national identities." But this formulation is far too simple. Consider, for example, the ways in which a British national identity was formed out of a dominant English identity and ancillary Scottish and Welsh identities, with the three components each containing considerable internal complexity (see Hobsbawm and Ranger, 1983; Colley, 1992), and the way in which the Soviet Union provided limited but significant recognition of the various national minorities that it inherited from its predecessor (Brubaker 1996). While there is a lot to object to in the ways in which national difference was recognized in these cases, state-nationalisms do not always "destroy" minority nationalisms. While most have aimed at their subordination (Switzerland is a notable exception), relatively few have aimed at, let alone achieved, their complete destruction. If we are to explore the possibility of nation-states that do – both politically and culturally – recognize and even enable difference, we must carefully examine the actual history of multinational nations. We should not simply rule the possibility out of court.

It may be that underlying Kymlicka and Straehle's position is the temptation to conceive cultures – especially national cultures – as much more unitary and homogeneous than they are. However, as cultural theorists have long recognized (for example, Geertz, 1973; Said, 1994), cultures are relational, internally differentiated, and conflictual.[4] Elsewhere, when he discusses the problem of social unity in a multinational federation, Kymlicka (1998, chap. 13) adopts a more nuanced position. He cites with approval Jeremy Webber's (1994) valuable argument that national identity is an ongoing debate that contests and modifies, among other things, the terms of membership. To be British, French, or Canadian is to be part of a continuing debate about what it means to be British, French, or Canadian, and this involves discussion of the terms in which Caribbeans, Africans, and Québécois, for example, might be counted as full members of the nation. A national identity is an ongoing dialogue through which difference is accommodated – or not. Of course, dialogue may turn into conflict, and accommodation into assimilation or repudiation. But we should not build this worst-case scenario into the definition of national culture. Nor should we assume that the outcome of this debate will be one homogeneous identity. On the contrary: most national cultures provide for different ways in which one can find one's identity in that culture, and there is no reason to suppose that they might not contain national differences. Indeed, the British and Swiss examples show that they can.

Because he operates with too unified a conception of national culture, Kymlicka assumes that the bonds of social unity in a multi-nation state must always be weaker and more conditional than those that are possible in a single nation-state. But there is no necessity here. Multinational Britain (though not the United Kingdom!) and Switzerland have been able to construct strong national identities; so too has the United States, despite the enormous diversity – including national diversity – that it contains. To understand the strength of these bonds, and also their occasional vulnerability, we must recognize the ways in which cultures are formed through their engagement with each other. For over two centuries, for example, the Scottish and Welsh national identities were formed in a complex relationship with English identities, as different ways in which one might be British. Sometimes the interrelationship may be or become a source of antagonism – as, for example, that between anglophone and francophone Canadians. In these cases, the differences may be so great that a weak sense of overriding national identity is the best for which one can hope, at least for the time being. But this is not an inevitable feature of multinational nations.

Of course, if multinational nations are to be viable and legitimate, they must meet certain conditions. Their political institutions must provide for the political claims of the minority, and these will usually include some measure of self-government. Historical claims must be arbitrated in ways that are acceptable to members of both the minority and the majority groups. The national culture must provide an appropriate place for the component cultures, not merely express the identity of the dominant group. Given the conflictual situations in which many multinational nation-states come into existence, it will be enormously difficult to achieve these goals. But it would be a political mistake of the first order to rule out the possibility of strong forms of commitment. To understand how this might be possible, theorists must explore the patterns of flexibility and accommodation that have existed within multinational nations. If there are to be viable multi-nation states – multinational nation-states – it is not merely of theoretical, but of crucial political, importance to reject the assumption that national cultures are discrete, self-contained, and unified.

ABORIGINAL CLAIMS

Responding to the claims of minority groups within the nation takes on an especially stark and intransigent form in the case of aboriginal people. In this section, I describe some of the resources available within the nation-state to do justice to this issue.

Fundamental to the self-conception of indigenous peoples of Canada, the United States, Australia, and other "post-colonial" states is the belief that they were the original inhabitants of the land and were dispossessed by European settlement. For them, justice requires return of or compensation for what they have lost. But how to conceptualize that loss? One view is that the loss was of something analogous to property: the indigenous people were once the owners of their land, and it was taken from them. This is clearly part of the story. But another – complementary – way to envisage the loss is as that of something analogous to sovereignty. What aboriginal people lost was not merely an economic or even a cultural resource: it was the right of self-determination. This does not mean that they had the right to lead their lives in ways completely unaffected by the enormous changes that were taking place in the rest of the world. Nor does it mean even that they had a right to sole occupancy of all the vast lands that they had occupied prior to European encroachment. No political rights can be so sweeping and absolute. What self-determination does mean is that indigenous people should have been allowed to work out for themselves how they were to respond to the changes taking place in the rest of the world. It was inevitable that these changes were going to impinge on indigenous people. Their relative isolation could not continue. However, they should have been provided with the opportunity to make and remake their lives in the larger world within which they were henceforth going to live. The basic claim of indigenous people is that the right of self-determination, so brutally overridden in past centuries, should be restored and respected now.

But what form might self-determination take? In the modern world, political power has always had a territorial basis (a "ground," in a literal sense), so it is natural to suppose that indigenous self-determination will mean the return of large areas of land to traditional owners and the provision of strong forms of territorial autonomy (Kymlicka, 1996, chap. 2; Reynolds, 1996). The centrality of land in almost all indigenous religion and culture reinforces this project. There have been notable achievements along these lines (Nunavut is a recent and striking example), and there is reason to hope for more. But self-governing indigenous regions cannot be the whole story. Most traditional land cannot be returned to descendants of the original owners without enormous disruption and injustice to the current occupants. Many indigenous people now live largely non-traditional lives distant from their place of origin.[5] It cannot be a condition of their rights that they maintain a traditional and non-urban way of life. Even if self-determination is a right of *all* indigenous people, territorial self-government cannot be the only form that it takes.

There is a further problem with this solution, though largely one of emphasis. Territorial autonomy promises a discrete space – in a literal sense – in which indigenous cultures and ways of life can be recuperated. But geographical separation may obscure the extent to which the relation to non-indigenous people remains one of dependence (indeed interdependence, as I suggest below). Indigenous territories will be reliant on federal and state or provincial authorities for economic support, medical aid, educational resources, and other kinds of assistance. This dependence is not merely material; it is also cultural. For better or worse, the fate of aboriginal cultures is now inextricably tied up with that of the pervasive national cultures within which they are now thoroughly embedded. The form and content of the self-determination sought by indigenous people are inevitably shaped by the experience of colonization.

In Australia, for example, prior to British settlement there were perhaps two hundred and fifty distinct language groups and six hundred dialects (Bourke, 1994). The European invaders defined these many peoples as one (and gave them the initially pejorative title of "Aborigines"). Yet these indigenous peoples have made themselves one in their ongoing struggle for self-determination.[6] The common language in which indigenous groups organize their struggle for self-determination is that which they have acquired from the dominant colonial culture. The astonishing achievements of Aboriginal artists in recent years involve the transformation of traditional forms, making use of new materials, techniques, and themes. These developments are sources of regret only if one's model of self-determination is the recovery or reinvention of a past way of life. But this is not an appropriate model. Self-determination is a process of self-transformation: of finding the forms in which one can make one's destiny within a context shaped by events that one cannot control. The context of indigenous struggles is the post-colonial nation-state. Self-determination requires interaction and absorption, as well as recovery and repudiation.

The dependence of indigenous people on the post-colonial state is obvious. But the dependence is of a special kind. What indigenous people demand is not charity, but justice. They ask for no more than is their due. Indeed, since their power in conventional terms is very limited, their major political resource is the justice of their claims. But this resource is considerable. Almost all the citizens of post-colonial countries[7] are uncomfortably aware of the immense injustice that lies at the core of their nation's history. This awareness is a deeply troubling one. Recognition of the genocidal nature of the founding moment places any sense of national legitimacy in doubt. The task of doing justice to indigenous claims is also that of recovering a sense of national identity – of what it is to be Australian, Canadian, or whatever – in the light of the shameful nature of one's national inheritance. Of course, repression and denial are possible responses – and have been the dominant response in the past. But these have their costs. To reject the claims of justice means that one can no longer take pride in one's national identity and in the history and sense of place associated with it. It contributes to a diminished public discourse in which self-interest and power displace considerations of justice and responsibility. To reject the national project of justice is to deny the larger meanings, purposes, and fulfilments provided by a shared identity.

The relationship between indigenous and non-indigenous citizens of the post-colonial state is one of interdependence or – perhaps better – symbiosis. The groups share a history and a land; but it is precisely the history and the land that divide them. Separation is not possible, and denial and repudiation are possible only at massive social and moral cost. Both parties have an enormous stake in finding a just solution. Paradoxically, it is the division and the need to overcome it that unite them. In general terms, the solution is obvious. Ultimately, indigenous and non-indigenous people must find a way of sharing the land, of constructing a history that they can both recognize as theirs, and thus of finding their identity in the same nation. It hardly needs saying that this is an enormously difficult undertaking. Post-colonial nations must come to terms with their past and make the injustice of the past part of their present understanding. The national identity must provide a place for indigenous people that recognizes their historical priority. The history of the nation must include the time before European encroachment and recognize the heroism and tenacity with which that invasion was resisted. The rituals and symbols of public life must embody representations of indigenous history. There is of course the considerable risk that indigenous cultural forms will be diminished by alien forms of representation. Nevertheless, the risk must be taken if indigenous citizens are to have a place in the public culture of the nation.

Changes in public culture are a necessary part of the project of justice to indigenous people. But they cannot be the whole of it. Political and legal forms must be constructed that facilitate indigenous self-determination. Land rights will be part of the inventory. They will provide space within which many indigenous people will live their lives, and they will be of crucial symbolic value to all indigenous people. But they are not sufficient. To place too much weight on them draws attention away from the most important avenues of political and theoretical development. The residual sovereignty of the indigenous people must be worked out through the formation of independent political institutions, which represent all indigenous people and have authority over certain aspects of their lives. There must be some recognition of indigenous laws ands customs, as well as tribunals to deal with conflicts between indigenous and non-indigenous traditions. Many of the problems here are practical ones. But underlying them is the difficulty of conceptualizing a form of political power that is not grounded on discrete territories. This raises quite fundamental questions in political and legal philosophy, and, despite parallels with the pre-modern world (especially the overlapping jurisdictions of the medieval period) and with certain features of globalization, most of the work remains to be done.[8]

Justice to indigenous people is a project, not a program. It makes demands on non-indigenous people: to come to terms with the past; to acquire some understanding of indigenous cultures and ways of life; to provide the legal, political, social, and cultural space for indigenous people to reproduce their culture; and to transfer the massive resources necessary to make aboriginal self-determination possible. It makes much greater demands on indigenous people: they have the task of remaking their cultures and lives in the new environment that has been imposed on them; they must recognize that some form of justice is possible, if their lives are not to be irredeemably structured by the difficulties, injustices, and tragedies of the past. Perhaps equally demanding, the two groups must come to terms with each other and work towards a resolution that each has reason to accept. If recognition of the historical injustices suffered by indigenous people places post-colonial national identities in question, arriving at a new understanding of that history and dealing with those injustices are tantamount to rebuilding those identities.

One of the many difficulties in that area is that the activity and commitment that will be required demand a strong sense of national identity, when the very problem that needs to be addressed is one that erodes the legitimacy of that identity. This difficulty would amount to an impossibility if, as Kymlicka suggests, the commitments associated with multi-nation states must always be weak and contingent. But we are dealing with necessity here, albeit of a historical kind. There is no way in which the indigenous and non-indigenous members of post-colonial societies can separate: divorce is not an option. The resolution, if there can be one, must involve reciprocal awareness of the need to live together – to share the same land and history and to construct an understanding of that land and history that does justice to the presence of each. This challenge is inescapable.

NOTES

1 This claim is not intended to hold for every form of power. Economic power, for example, whether exercised by an individual, by a corporate

body, or by the impersonal forces of the market, does not need the commitment and support of those subject to it. All it requires is that they have wants and needs that can be serviced or exploited. Nor do military rulers or invading armies need much to support their power: force and the fear that it inspires are sufficient, at least for a while.

2 This distinction is often blurred. The various nation-states that emerged out of the breakup of the Soviet Union were formed largely within the institutional spaces created by Soviet policies; see Brubaker, 1996, especially chapter 2. The Scotland that may yet assume independence was culturally if not politically an artifact of British rule; see Hobsbawm and Ranger, 1983. The distinction is often used to draw a line between good, "civic" (or "territorial") nations and bad, "ethnic" nations. This is not my intention. For criticisms of that distinction, see Kymlicka, 1995; Yack, 1996; Nielsen, 1996–97; and Poole, 1999, 41–3.

3 In some circumstances secession will be appropriate. However, as Kymlicka and Straehle point out, we must always ask how the resulting nation-state would treat its minorities. Secession does not avoid but rather requires a solution to the problems of the "nation-building" alternative. The other problem noted by Kymlicka and Straehle – that secession would generate an impractically large number of mini-states – is overstated. As Gellner (1983, 43–4) noted, what is remarkable about the number of potential nations is how few have made the claim to statehood. One criterion of the strength of a culture is its political will. We do not need to wait on a principle to tell us which cultures deserve independence and which do not. The first and most important question is: which ones *want* it? Given the costs and inconveniences of secession, not to speak of residual loyalty to the larger state, it does not seem inevitable that secession will generate an impractical deluge of new mini-states.

4 Tully, 1995, and Brubaker, 1996, are interesting examples of theorists who are fully aware of the internal complexity of cultures; Tully (9–12) gives an exemplary account of the way in which cultures are differentiated, conflictual, and constituted in relation to other cultures. However, they do not extend this insight to national cultures, where they assume that uniformity is the norm.

5 In Australia, for example, some 75 percent of indigenous people live in cities and towns; there is no reason to suppose that the numbers in other countries would be much different.

6 There are two major indigenous groups in Australia – the Aborigines and the ethnically distinct Torres Strait Islanders. They have different political agendas and also have internal differences.

7 The United States is probably an exception. There, the experience of slavery and racism directed against African Americans tends to occlude the equal moral catastrophe of the expropriation and subsequent treatment of native Americans.

8 The "bicultural" policy followed in New Zealand is a promising development; see Poole, 2000, for some discussion – though not nearly enough – and references.

REFERENCES

Anderson, Benedict (1991) *Imagined Communities: Reflections on the Origins and Spread of Nationalism*, 2nd ed. London: Verso.

Beiner, Ronald, ed. (1999) *Theorizing Nationalism*. Albany: State University of New York Press.

Bourke, Eleanor (1994) "Australia's First People: Identity and Population," in Colin Bourke et al. eds., *Aboriginal Australia*. St Lucia: University of Queensland Press, 38–55.

Brubaker, Rogers (1996) *Nationalism Reframed: Nationhood and the National Question in the New Europe*. Cambridge: Cambridge University Press.

Canovan, Margaret (1996) *Nationhood and Political Theory*. Cheltenham: Edward Elgar.

Colley, Linda (1992) *Britons: Forging the Nation 1707–1837*. New Haven, Conn.: Yale University Press.

Constant, Benjamin (1988) "The Liberty of the Ancients Compared with the Moderns," in Biancamaria Fontana, ed., *Political Writings*. Cambridge: Cambridge University Press.

Galston, William (1991) *Liberal Purposes: Goods, Virtues, and Duties in the Liberal State*. Cambridge: Cambridge University Press.

Geertz, Clifford (1973) *The Interpretation of Cultures*. New York: Basic Books.

Gellner, Ernest (1983) *Nations and Nationalism*. Oxford: Basil Blackwell.

Greenfeld, Liah (1992) *Nationalism: Five Roads to Modernity*. Cambridge, Mass.: Harvard University Press.

Hobsbawm, Eric, and Terrence Ranger, eds. (1983) *The Invention of Tradition*. Cambridge: Cambridge University Press.

Kymlicka, Will (1995) "Misunderstanding Nationalism," *Dissent* (winter), 130–7; reprinted in Beiner, 1999, 131–40.

– (1996) *Multicultural Citizenship: A Liberal Theory of Minority Rights*. Oxford: Clarendon Press.

– (1998) *Finding Our Way: Rethinking Ethnocultural Relations in Canada.* Toronto: Oxford University Press.

Kymlicka, Will, and Christine Straehle (1999) "Cosmopolitanism, Nation-States, and Minority Nationalism: A Critical Review of Recent Literature," *European Journal of Philosophy* 7, no. 1, 65–88.

Macedo, Stephen (1990) *Liberal Virtues: Citizenship, Virtue and Community in Liberal Constitutionalism.* Oxford: Oxford University Press.

Miller, David (1995) *On Nationality.* Oxford: Clarendon Press.

Nielsen, Kai (1996–97) "Cultural Nationalism, Neither Ethnic nor Civic," *Philosophical Forum* 28. nos. 1–2, 42–52; reprinted in Beiner, 1999, 119–30.

Pettit, Philip (1997) *Republicanism: A Theory of Freedom and Government.* Oxford: Oxford University Press.

Poole, Ross (1999) *Nation and Identity.* London: Routledge.

– (2000) "Justice or Appropriation? Indigenous Claims and Liberal Theory," *Radical Philosophy* (May/June), 5–17.

Reynolds, Henry (1996) *Aboriginal Sovereignty: Reflections on Race, State and Nation.* St Leonards, NSW: Allen & Unwin.

Said, Edward (1994) *Culture and Imperialism.* New York: Vintage Books.

Skinner, Quentin (1984) "The Idea of Negative Liberty: Philosophical and Historical Perspectives," in Richard Rorty et al., eds., *Philosophy in History.* Cambridge: Cambridge University Press, 193–221.

– (1991) "The Paradoxes of Political Liberty," in David Miller, ed., *Liberty.* Oxford: Oxford University Press, 183–205.

Tamir, Yael (1995) *Liberal Nationalism,* 2nd ed. Princeton, NJ: Princeton University Press.

Taylor, Charles (1989) "Cross-Purposes: The Liberal–Communitarian Debate," in Nancy L. Rosenblum, ed., *Liberalism and the Moral Life.* Cambridge, Mass.: Harvard University Press, 159–82.

Tully, James (1995) *Strange Multiplicity: Constitutionalism in an Age of Diversity.* Cambridge: Cambridge University Press.

Walzer, Michael (1989) "Citizenship," in Terence Ball et al., eds., *Political Innovation and Conceptual Change.* Cambridge: Cambridge University Press.

Webber, Jeremy (1994) *Reimagining Canada: Language, Culture, Community and the Canadian Constitution.* Montreal: McGill–Queen's University Press.

Wollheim, Richard (1962) "A Paradox in the Theory of Democracy," in Peter Laslett and W.G. Runciman, eds., *Philosophy, Politics and Society (Second Series).* Oxford: Basil Blackwell.

Yack, Bernard (1996) "The Myth of the Civic Nation," *Critical Review.* 10, no. 2 (spring), 193–211; reprinted in Beiner, 1999, 103–18.

MICHEL SEYMOUR

Collective Rights in Multi-nation States: From Ethical Individualism to the Law of Peoples

In this paper, I wish to discuss foundational issues concerning collective rights in the context of multi-nation states. I assume throughout that the viability of multi-nation states requires implementation of politics of recognition for component nations. I also take for granted the idea that politics of recognition should include the entrenchment of the collective rights of nations (or peoples) in the constitution of the encompassing state. I also assume that the appropriate foundation must be sought within the liberal tradition. My main purpose is to ask whether ethical individualism provides the appropriate framework for a liberal theory of collective rights.

I look first at liberalism and its integred relationship with the nation-state and then at its basis in ethical individualism. Many philosophers – perhaps most notably Will Kymlicka – believe that ethical individualism is compatible with politics of recognition. I describe Kymlicka's theory of group-differentiated rights and then explain its defects in terms of his favourable inclination towards individualism. I finally outline an alternative liberal theory of collective rights that could serve as a foundation for an effective law of peoples.

LIBERALISM, THE NATION-STATE, AND ETHICAL INDIVIDUALISM

Liberalism and the Nation-State

I said above that politics of recognition have to be implemented in order to ensure the stability of multi-nation states. One cannot expect a nation to accept the devolution of its sovereignty to an encompassing state and at the same time agree that it will not have any recognition at all as a nation within that state. In my view, those who defend multination states and argue against politics of recognition defend a position that leads to political instability. I do not, however, provide in this paper an argument for this point. My main concern is not with stability but with justice. Thus I take it for granted that nations (or peoples) seek some kind of political recognition and that, if they cannot obtain it from the encompassing state, they will seek it from the international community by becoming a sovereign state. So I assume that the viability of multi-nation states is intimately related to the successful application of politics of recognition.

In this section, I try to explain why liberal philosophers have been inclined to argue both for the integration of some nations into multination states and against politics of recognition. There existed a very close relationship between liberalism and the traditional nation-state model, which supposes the state to be composed of an ethnically or culturally homogeneous society. This relationship has until recently escaped most liberal philosophers, for reasons that I outline briefly. We can then explain the philosophical conservatism of many liberal philosophers vis-à-vis politics of recognition. I show that if one sees the homogeneous nation-state as the only acceptable form of political organization, one is then extremely reluctant to recognize the collective rights of groups. The reason is that the traditional nation-state has led to acceptance of ethical individualism as an apparent constitutive doctrine of liberalism. And it is ethical individualism that most philosophers invoke in their arguments against the admission of collective rights. Finally, I claim that ethical individualism still influences those who discuss political recognition, even when they look for alternative models such as the multi-nation state. Let us examine these issues more closely.

Given the increasing importance of multi-nation states in the context of global exchanges occurring within the Western world and some parts of Asia, liberal philosophers should have been inclined to adopt politics of recognition towards nations, yet many among them are still hesitant. Why are they so uneasy about recognizing collective rights of peoples? The explanation that I favour runs as follows. If one is a liberal, one must argue for the fundamental character of individual rights and liberties. These principles cannot be overruled by any other principles and must therefore have an absolute priority over the particular interests of groups. And as long as we are considering society through the lens of an ethnically or culturally homogeneous nation-state, no other principles can compete with them. Within homogeneous nation-states, the only groups are particular interest groups defending their own views about the good life. These interests must be resisted for the sake of preserving liberal neutrality and the primacy of justice over particular conceptions of the good.

In multinational societies, however, the society as a whole consists not only of individual citizens and particular interest groups, but also of different nations. However, liberal philosophers have been influenced by a deep connection between liberalism and the nation-state and have thus failed to appreciate the demands made by particular sub-groups. So they tend, even within multi-nation states, to conflate nations with particular interest groups. My conclusion is that liberal philosophers are still very much under the influence of the traditional nation-state model, and this is why they are so reluctant to accept collective rights.

But has there been a historical connection between liberalism and the traditional nation-state model? Why should that be so? Is it not paradoxical to suggest a profound link between liberalism and nationalism? There appears, as Will Kymlicka argues (2001b), to be a "paradox of liberal nationalism," for liberal ideals are universal in character, while nationalism seems to go hand in hand with a certain form of particularism. And some people will then want to argue on that basis that liberalism must transcend all forms of particularism. But we should perhaps not draw these conclusions too hastily. Nation-states are not bound to remain particularistic, parochial, and atavistic, and we do not need to invoke a post-national identity or hail the virtues of constitutional patriotism to overcome such narrow inclinations. Nation-states may welcome universal principles. Moreover, they may even be good illustrations of what Kymlicka calls "societal cultures" – societies with a common language, a common history, and a common set of institutions (2001a, 25; and see 1995, 76–9). Within these institutions, societal cultures provide a wide range of options, described by Kymlicka as a "context of choice" (see 1989, 13–17, 47–8, 50–1; 1995, 82–4). Thus only a societal culture, with its common language, history, and context of choice, can realize those universal liberal principles. This context of choice – and hence liberalism – would not exist without a particular societal culture.

Historically, societal cultures have tended to take the form of nation-states. So nation-states might have been initially the sole providers of the liberty to choose from a rich variety of moral, cultural, and political goods. Consequently, the nation-state has been a condition of possibility for the exercise of individual freedoms and liberties. And so, far from constraining liberties and individual choices, nation-states, understood as involving complete societal cultures, appeared to provide a necessary condition for the existence of individual choices and liberties. The presence of a societal culture is not a sufficient condition for the presence of a wide context of choice, for there can be non-liberal societal cultures, but it is certainly a necessary condition.

Of course societal cultures are in some mild sense "particularistic." A common public language (compatible with the existence of minority languages), a common public history (interpreted and criticized in different ways), and a common set of institutions (with a specific context of choice) are contingent and historical features of a society. But these must not be confused with other particularistic features such as traditions, customs, habits, moral ends, and conceptions about the common good and about the good life. The former features relate to what Kymlicka calls a "structure of culture," and the latter, to the "character of culture" (see 1989, 79–81, 165–7, 169–71; 1995, 77). Nation-states may in a sense coherently be "particularistic" and "liberal" when they are seen as having a particular structure of culture, but they cease to be liberal as soon as they become intimately associated with a unique character of culture. Liberalism is, by definition, compatible only with societies that allow for an irreducible plurality of cultural characters.

The importance of whole societal cultures is precisely what a liberal philosopher trained in the tradition of the nation-state model may have failed to see. The framework of the nation-state has always been taken for granted, and for that reason the motivation for protecting whole societal cultures was not always explicit (Canovan, 1996). Many liberal philosophers were thus never able to explain why, historically, the nation-state was considered as the only good form of political organization. But now that we question this traditional model, some commentators are eager to engage in such a critical assessment without reflecting on the importance of whole societal cultures, which were after all implicitly recognized when nation-states were accepted without criticism. Liberal philosophers do not always pay enough attention to the writings of classic liberal thinkers such as Mill, Green, Hobhouse, and Dewey (Kymlicka, 1989, 207), and so they do not develop arguments to illustrate the virtues of societal cultures. At the same time, the nation-state model still very much influences their attitude towards subgroups. They adopt the attitude of those philosophers who always looked at the world from within the nation-state and thus interpret the demands of whole societal cultures as similar to those of particular interest groups.

Some liberals also defended their own state without even raising any questions concerning the nation-state model. But now that the state faces demands from minority nations, they have begun to argue in favour of multi-nation states and have used these arguments as an alibi against the demands from minority nations in Canada, Spain, and the United Kingdom. It is the increasing demands of recognition formulated by minority nations that explain their newly discovered interest in the multi-nation state. But their inability to think about these demands outside the framework of the nation-state leads them to confuse these demands with those of particular interest groups. So their somewhat confused defence of the multi-nation state replicates the one that they used to take for granted concerning the traditional nation-state. For practical purposes, they still support the status quo, but the labels have changed: instead of promoting the nation-state, they hail the virtues of the same political order, but now describe it as a "multi-nation state."

As we saw above, the source of the problem is that liberal philosophers still take for granted many aspects of the traditional nation-state model. They do not explicitly reflect on the importance of societal cultures, and so they do not accept any form of political recognition for particular sub-groups in a multi-nation state, even if these happen to be whole societal cultures, and they react against the demands of those groups in a conservative way in order to maintain the integrity of the encompassing state. Therefore, even if they pay lip service to multi-nation states, their policies echo those that were made from the perspective of the traditional nation-state.

Liberalism and Ethical Individualism

I have tried to explain liberal philosophers' reluctance to recognize collective rights for groups belonging to societal cultures. They failed to remove themselves intellectually from the traditional nation-state model, which cast groups as merely particular interests. Their mistaken assimilation of societal cultures with pressure groups is the source of this neglect. Within the confines of a homogeneous nation-state, the only possible group interests are those of particular interest groups, and they cannot conceivably be those of full societal cultures.[1] But the more the connection between liberalism and the nation-state is made explicit, the more liberal philosophers claim that liberalism need not logically entail the nation-state model. Unfortunately, since they are still in the thrall of this model, they usually reject any kind of political recognition for groups.

However, most liberal philosophers now accept a historical connection between liberalism and nationalism, and some agree even that it is at least partly responsible for the failure to accommodate the demands of minorities. But very few are also willing to question ethical individualism – that is, a comprehensive doctrine according to which personal identity is prior to moral identity, individuals are the ultimate sources of moral worth, and autonomy is the most basic liberal value. Most liberals are still committed to ethical individualism, and they do not realize that this doctrine is a side effect of the historical connection between liberalism and nationalism. They do not see that it is precisely because of the continuous influence of the nation-state model that the individual is seen as the basic unit of the liberal state. Within homogeneous nation-states there are no sub-groups forming whole societal cultures: there are just individuals and associations of individuals. So within the nation state model, groups do not appear to be autonomous sources of valid moral claims, for the only groups that make claims are particular interests groups. Since these groups are associations of individuals, the validity of their claims depends on the validity of the claims made by the individuals that compose them. It is also because of the nation-state model that individual rights appear to be the only rights enjoying an absolute priority. If liberals endorse the primacy of justice over conceptions of the good, they have to assert the absolute priority of individual rights over the collective rights of particular interest groups.

If we take the nation-state for granted, and accept the crucial role of societal cultures without making it explicit, we are able to show that individuals are the ultimate source of moral worth and individual autonomy is the most important value. We can do so only because we are assuming the nation-state model. The nation is not, within such a model, seeking recognition, for it has been given full political expression. It enjoys full sovereignty, and so political recognition is not a relevant issue. It is thus this model that enables one to derive the doctrine of ethical individualism from very general liberal principles. This doctrine may then appear constitutive of liberalism.

But if we can separate liberalism from the traditional nation-state model, we should also disconnect it from ethical individualism. The nation-state is a particular historical model of political organization that is not logically constitutive of liberalism – or of ethical individualism. It is at best only a historical product of liberalism. If we explicitly acknowledged the crucial role of societal cultures, instead of simply assuming it, then we could see societal cultures in the framework of a multi-nation state as autonomous sources of moral worth and their autonomy as valuable as the autonomy of individuals. So there would no longer be any reason to hold that individuals have an absolute priority over societal cultures.

Unfortunately, most contemporary philosophers treat ethical individualism as constitutive of liberalism. They fail to see that the doctrine is the natural expression of liberalism only within the traditional nation-state. So adopting politics of recognition will require abandoning ethical individualism. And it might be argued that this move is compatible with liberalism as long as one does not subscribe to the opposite doctrine of "ethical collectivism" – that is, the view that the rights of societal cultures must override those of individuals. We must seek instead an ethical pluralism that can accommodate both individuals and societal cultures. If the rights and liberties of individuals remain fundamental, then there is perhaps nothing wrong in asserting that the rights of peoples must also be treated as fundamental.

Of course, this argument presupposes that ethical individualism is incompatible with a genuine political recognition of peoples. And as we all know, Will Kymlicka believes that this is not true. Kymlicka wants to show that it is possible to defend simultaneously ethical individualism and the political recognition of peoples (1989, 177–8). So let us now turn to this particular point of view.

KYMLICKA'S THEORY
OF GROUP-DIFFERENTIATED RIGHTS

Kymlicka argues that liberal philosophers have ignored the problems raised by the protection of minority cultures, and he claims that they have done so because those philosophers belong to nation-states. Their own particular political experiences have influenced their judgment on these issues. Kymlicka seems to confirm my own diagnosis (Kymlicka, 1995, 50–7 and 93). He sees the nation-state as an external influence that affects the judgment of liberal theorists, and this also explains why that model grounds their theoretical work. Kymlicka not only alludes to sociopolitical circumstances that explain their lack of theoretical concern for minorities, he also thinks that it explains the prevalence of that model within their theories. So Kymlicka acknowledges somewhat the historical connection between that model and liberalism. But he also thinks that ethical individualism remains a fundamental doctrine and that it has nothing to do with the historical influence of the model. He believes that ethical individualism does not explain the reluctance of liberal philosophers about politics of recognition. This is why he invokes historical circumstances, such as the failure of minority treaties, the demands of Afro-Americans for racial desegregation, and the ethnic revival in the United States, as the main explanations.[2]

Kymlicka wants to blame something other than ethical individualism, because he endorses the doctrine. He believes that ethical individualism is not responsible for the negative attitude, since he sees adoption of a regime of collective rights as compatible with it. He also makes it abundantly clear that he remains an individualist. He maintains that individuals are the ultimate source of legitimate claims and the ultimate unit of moral worth. He presents a version of liberalism explicitly understood as a comprehensive doctrine based on individual autonomy. He is thus committed to ethical individualism.[3]

I now want to show that Kymlicka's philosophical position influences his account of collective rights and causes important difficulties in his theory. I show also that his individualistic account does not do full justice to the political recognition of peoples.

Let us look at his account more closely. First, Kymlicka discards "collective rights" in favour of "group-differentiated rights." This might seem only a terminological matter, but it conceals deeper issues. For instance, he restricts the application of such rights to minorities, and he does not allow it to describe the rights of majorities or whole communities. This is surprising, since, by definition, collective rights involve collectivities such as whole nations, not just what Kymlicka calls "national minorities." After all, shouldn't national majorities as well as national minorities have collective rights within a society? In Belgium, for instance, should the Walloons have collective rights, but not the Flemish? Some nations are majorities, and this is not a reason to deny them collective rights.

Furthermore, Kymlicka articulates two sorts of "collective" rights – internal restrictions on the individual liberties of citizens and external protections for minorities in their relationship to majority cultures – and he accepts only the latter as legitimate (1995, 35–44; 2001a, 22). This normative distinction assumes that it is impossible to independently justify restrictions on individual rights made for the sake of fostering a common civic identity. Not only does he wish to treat individual rights as fundamental, he also apparently sees them as not available for any restriction whatsoever, not even cultural restrictions that stem from the structure of the culture (1995, 36, 202 footnote 1).

Kymlicka is also forced to deny that collective rights must be individuated partly by reference to the subject of the right (1995, 46). For him, the ultimate subject of those rights may in many cases be the individual. Of course, most collective rights are not about the primacy of the collectivity over individuals (47), but he also wants them compatible with the primacy of the individual. Instead of defending equally respect for the group and respect for the individual, he argues that "both sides of the dilemma concern respect for the individual" (150). He therefore seems to individuate collective rights with reference only to their objects – i.e., institutional or participatory goods – not to their subject. Collective rights, according to him, concern institutional goods that are claimed by individuals.

Finally, since collective rights are ultimately rights that individuals can claim, the justification for their inclusion in a constitution must rest on the value that individuals ascribe to their own culture. Kymlicka must therefore postulate a rational preference of the individual for his or her own culture, and he must suppose that individuals treat their cultural allegiances as primary goods (1989, 166). So he endorses major claims in moral psychology (1995, chap. 8, especially 158–63).

A Critical Assessment of Kymlicka's Theory

One may wonder whether Kymlicka's notion of group-differentiated rights has anything to do with what is usually meant by "collective rights." He sees group-differentiated rights as meant for individuals, enjoyed by individuals, and claimed by individuals. One cannot impose any cultural restrictions whatsoever on individuals, for they are the true, ultimate subject of valid moral claims concerning group-differentiated rights, according to Kymlicka. In short, this approach appears to provide justification not for collective rights but for special kinds of individual rights – those that concern institutional goods. So it is perhaps for that reason that Kymlicka uses a new label to describe the relevant sort of right.

Quite apart from this general line of criticism, we must look very closely at the different theses involved in the argument. Unfortunately, most of them are false. First, it is simply not true, as Kymlicka some-times writes, that liberals must somehow commit themselves to ethical individualism. There are liberal philosophers – most notably, John Rawls, 1993b, and Joseph Raz, 1986 – who have developed liberal theories that avoid commitment to ethical individualism. As Kymlicka himself now seems prepared to agree, liberal philosophers can coher-ently reject that particular doctrine.

Let us, however, consider more urgent difficulties. The distinction be-tween external protections and internal restrictions cannot stand. A re-gime of collective rights for a minority nation within the state cannot avoid imposing some (reasonable) restrictions on the rights of individu-als within the nation. External protections inevitably lead to internal re-strictions, and so the distinction between these two sorts of collective rights becomes problematic. For example, language laws in Quebec in-volve simultaneously external protections and internal restrictions.[4] They can be justified as means of protecting French Quebecers from the majority of anglophones living in North America, but they force immi-grants to send their children to French schools, they impose a certain predominance of French on commercial signs, and they insist on French as the language used at work. Of course, Kymlicka accepts Quebec's language laws and rightly sees them as legitimate, but he tries to ac-count for them only in terms of external protections, and this does not seem to be possible.

Kymlicka is well aware of this difficulty and tries to solve it. His ar-gument appears to be that internal restrictions cannot autonomously be justified and are acceptable only if they are instrumental for external protection. So group-differentiated rights whose main justification in-vokes external protections are acceptable; those justified solely on the basis of being internal restrictions are not. Kymlicka is willing to accept internal restrictions, but only in so far as they serve to protect the mi-nority from the majority. But this tack fails to capture an essential di-mension of collective rights. Whether they are majorities or minorities and whether they require external protections or not, peoples have the right to impose reasonable restrictions such as the promotion and pro-tection of a common public language (compatible with the protection and promotion of minority languages), a common public culture (com-patible with the promotion and protection of minority cultures), and a common public history (compatible with the promotion and protection of the historical minorities). These policies amount to the fostering of a common civic identity.

Kymlicka should know that the fragmentation of the nation may come not only from outside but also from inside forces and that social cohesion requires at least a minimal common civic identity. But he prefers to describe policies purporting to secure social cohesion as instances of "nationalism" and not as policies that promote and protect the collective rights of peoples. For him, they appear to be merely nation-building policies, and collective rights are meant to preserve minorities from nation-building policies (Kymlicka, 2001a). Of course, I agree that minorities are very often subjected to the tyranny of the majority and to nation-building policies, and I also agree that a system of collective rights can serve to counterbalance these external forces. But only Kymlicka's obsession with ethical individualism can explain why he feels compelled to avoid the terminology of collective rights for national majorities or whole peoples.

Most citizens in liberal societies agree to live with restrictions on their individual liberties such as those that are involved in a common civic identity. They agree to use a common public language and a common public structure of culture, and they relate to the same common public history. They do not see these policies as unacceptable restrictions on their individual liberties, for they are reasonable requirements for the exercise of a full citizenship. Moreover, suggesting that the society as a whole has the right to impose such restrictions on the liberties of its citizens must not be interpreted as a case where collective rights override individual rights. It is more like striking an appropriate balance between the fundamental interests of individuals and those of whole communities. Societal cultures cannot survive without a minimal common civic identity. This imposes reasonable restrictions on the liberties of individuals, just as fundamental liberties of individuals impose reasonable limitations on the collective rights of peoples. And it will not do not to reply that imposing a common civic identity can be interpreted as merely instrumental for individual liberties, for there are independent justifications for the protection of whole societal cultures that have nothing to do with individual values.[5]

Of course, Kymlicka agrees completely with most of this. He is perfectly aware that external protection always comes with internal restrictions and that there are good arguments for reasonable restrictions on individual liberties such as those to which I have been alluding. So why does he refuse to describe those internal restrictions as an acceptable form of collective rights? The only answer that I can come up with is his endorsement of ethical individualism.

Kymlicka uses some rhetorical arguments in his campaign against internal restrictions. In order to oppose these sorts of collective rights more convincingly, he characterizes them as involving the imposition of traditions, ways of life, and illiberal customs. He gives a communitarian twist to the idea of an internal restriction in order to make it clearly unacceptable (1995, 37–44; 2001, 22). He suggests that internal restrictions impose limitations on "the right of individuals within the group to revise their conception of the good" (1995, 161). But what about "imposing" a common public language, public history, and public culture? Most citizens accept such internal restrictions within each societal culture. Do these internal restrictions impose particular views about the good life? Must they be rejected even if they are appropriately constrained by a charter of individual rights and by policies that seek to protect the collective rights of minority cultures within such a society?

Moreover, the notion of an unrestricted fundamental individual right is a pure abstraction that never exists in practice. Freedom of speech is constrained by laws against hate literature; freedom of association, by anti-gang laws; the right to physical integrity, by the right to self-defence; the right of the public to be informed, by the right to privacy; and even the right to life, by laws on abortion and euthanasia and perhaps eventually on assisted suicide. So similarly, we can acknowledge the need to constrain the rights of citizens by "imposing" a common public structure of culture, as long as it is compatible with the preservation of minority cultures within the nation. In other words, by allowing for collective rights that would impose reasonable restrictions on individual rights, we are doing nothing more than applying some additional reasonable restrictions on individual liberties.

Most societal cultures impose a common public language, public history, and public culture, and it is not necessary to abandon those policies in order to go beyond the traditional nation-state model, for a multi-nation state must also allow each societal culture to foster its own civic identity. Allowing component nations to do so is precisely what can ensure the viability of the multi-nation state itself. It may not be possible to impose a single lingua franca, a single common culture, and a single common history when the state is multinational, and so citizens must rely only on a very "thin" common civic identity. How then could such a state survive? Adopting politics of recognition towards the component nations may allow them to impose reasonable restrictions, such as those that result from fostering a common civic identity. Kymlicka sees the importance of societal cultures and sees that they must have self-determination, but he denies that reasonable internal restrictions of minority societal cultures can be justified in their own right. They are apparently acceptable for him only if they are instrumental for their external protection, and he does not seem to consider the promotion and protection of a societal culture for a majority or for a whole people as promotion and protection of their collective rights.

Some want to assess internal restrictions imposed by a societal culture on its members as depending on whether it is the rights of other individuals or the collective rights of an encompassing group that create them. The former can be tolerated, because they increase individual liberties for everyone; the latter do not meet this requirement. But this answer won't do as an argument against collective rights if the problem is that they impose restrictions on liberties. It displaces the problem, since the issue was initially whether individual rights and liberties may reasonably be restricted or not. The argument was supposed to be against there being restrictions on individual liberties. But it now appears that individual liberties cannot, according to the individualist, be restricted by collective rights, and this amounts to expressing qualms about collective rights as such, not about there being restrictions on individual liberties. One cannot have it both ways. If the argument concerns restrictions on individual liberties, we can reply that systems of individual liberties themselves always constrain individual liberties. But if the argument concerns the source of the restriction, then the problem is about collective rights as such, not about their imposing restrictions. Of course, the ultimate argument is that the particular restrictions imposed on individual liberties by a system of collective rights are precisely the restrictions that one finds unacceptable. But I have suggested above that we must distinguish between the restrictions that stem from the requirement of a common language, structure of culture, and history and those that flow from imposing a particular character of culture. And I have argued that the former are acceptable in principle, as well as accepted in practice in most, if not all, societies.

Even if Kymlicka makes the distinction between the character and the structure of culture, he tends to conflate the two notions when he determines whether or not some internal restrictions are intrinsically acceptable. He surprisingly chooses to interpret internal restrictions as the imposition of cultural characters and not as the imposition of a particular structure of culture. I have claimed that this stance does not do justice to a reasonable regime of collective rights aiming to implement a common civic identity. In other places, Kymlicka simply describes the imposition of common languages, cultures, and histories as instances of "nationalism," but he offers no reasons for distinguishing between nationalism and the defence of the collective rights of a people. If we accept this equation, we have to accept the reasonable character of some internal restrictions whether or not they are also instrumental for external protection. But if we do so, then collective rights seem to compete with individual rights and no particular hierarchy holds between these two sorts of rights. This logic, in turn, casts some doubt on the possibility of defending collective rights with individualistic arguments.

By ruling out reasonable internal restrictions, Kymlicka gives a truncated picture of collective rights. He fails to show that individual rights must in no way be culturally restricted at all.[6] He accepts nation-building policies as long as they are appropriately constrained by individual liberties and by group-differentiated rights for minorities. But he fails to notice that nation-building policies provide the best instance of the exercise of collective rights, for they seek to secure the self-determination of the people as a whole. Since Kymlicka does not argue against such policies, but rather seeks to constrain them, he should not have rejected collective rights that impose internal restrictions on individual liberties. So why does he think otherwise? It is because he theoretically wants to restrict the use of group-differentiated rights to minorities. This is more than just a terminological fiat, for it fails to do justice to a very important class of collective rights, and it provides a distorted picture of the issue in order to force collective rights into an individualistic, Procustean bed.

Another difficulty is this. If we try to individuate collective rights by reference to the object of the right and not also partly by reference to its subject, we cannot explain the difference between the cultural demands made by individual immigrants and those made by the members of welcoming national communities, for both could in principle have equal legitimate moral claims to cultural protection. How can we decide who must be integrated into whose community if, in either case, individuals claim protection for their own societal culture? We are naturally inclined to resolve this contentious issue by saying that immigrants have an obligation to integrate within the welcoming community, since it has the collective right to survive and flourish, and it could not do this if immigrants failed to integrate. At least this is true of immigrant societies such as Canada and the United States. We are naturally inclined to believe that integration policies are reasonable internal restrictions on the individual liberties of immigrants. But as we saw above, this option is not available to Kymlicka, and not only because he does not allow for internal restrictions. The subject of the right is irrelevant, according to him. He must try to justify the integration of immigrants without having recourse to the welcoming community, as a genuine bearer of rights, for he wants to say that the subject of group-differentiated rights need not be collective entities. But how then can he explain the intuition that the immigrant clearly has an obligation to integrate?

Kymlicka tries to avoid the issue by proposing that an immigrant is someone who has renounced his or her linguistic and cultural affiliations.[7] Being an immigrant in effect amounts to a renouncement of one's rights. Of course, most immigrants are willing to integrate. Most of them learn the language of their welcoming community and are willing to be part of its culture, but, in countries of immigration such as Australia, Canada, and the United States, a growing number of immigrants are able to live in local immigrant communities, where they can keep their own language, culture, and history. So it is wrong to suggest that they have renounced their own language and their attachment to their own culture or history. Most immigrants do not realize the great pains that are associated with adopting a new country and a new language, a new culture, and a new history. So it cannot be claimed that they have renounced their allegiance to their own national identity. Even if they are willing to integrate, they are not willing to assimilate.

So Kymlicka's hypothesis is empirically false. He is wrong to interpret the willingness of immigrants to integrate as a proof that they have decided to abandon their language, culture, and history. And he is wrong to interpret this criticism as suggesting that immigrants are unwilling to integrate. Everyone agrees that most immigrants are willing to integrate. The question is whether they also wish to abandon their own language, culture, and history. I believe that they don't. And so I believe that members of an immigrant community and members of the welcoming community both want to keep their own language, culture, and history. And if we consider only individuals and their moral claims, we are unable to distinguish between the two sorts of claims and thus unable to derive an obligation to integrate on the part of immigrants. Once again, ethical individualism proves to be a rather shaky foundation for a theory of collective rights, for we are unable to justify on this basis an obligation to integrate on the part of immigrants without introducing additional, false, empirical hypotheses.

We ask immigrants to integrate (but not necessarily assimilate) into their welcoming community. But why can we do so? Why can't they refuse such integration? Couldn't it be the other way around? The members of the welcoming community should perhaps be the ones who have to integrate in the immigrant communities. Why not? The answer is obviously related to the collective rights of the welcoming societal culture. But since Kymlicka sees the individual as the ultimate bearer of the collective right, and since he is unwilling to accept internal restrictions, he must somehow try to explain why the individual right of someone belonging to a welcoming community should supersede the individual right of the immigrant to cultural protection. And here, I am afraid, no answer is forthcoming. Since he is unable to distinguish between the claims of welcomers and the claims of immigrants, Kymlicka cannot explain why we intuitively tend to think that immigrants must integrate.[8] This is why he postulates an ad hoc and convenient empirical hypothesis to the effect that immigrants by definition are people who have renounced their own linguistic and cultural affiliations. But this ad hoc stipulation is false and conceals a genuine defect of the theory.

Let us consider one last difficulty. Kymlicka wants to derive the justification for a regime of group-differentiated rights by relying solely on individualistic grounds. But he cannot just invoke the importance of societal cultures for individuals in general by saying that they provide the necessary condition for the implementation of a system of liberties. Such an argument would indeed be ultimately founded on individual values, but it is clearly insufficient: it cannot serve as a basis for the protection of each particular societal culture. It is compatible with the existence of just one large societal culture embracing all the citizens of the world. If we argue simply that societal cultures are valuable in general for the individual, we cannot rule out the possibility of having only one societal culture for everyone. The problem is that we seek to justify the protection of each particular societal culture. True, we could translate initially a normative argument to the effect that societal cultures are important in general into institutional measures that could ensure the protection of each one of them. But we could not rule out as morally problematic the assimilation of these cultures into a single assimilating society. The social fact of assimilation and even assimilation policies could be pursued in perfect accordance with the principle.

So we need to add an additional principle. Could it be simply that individuals want their own culture to be protected? This, I am afraid, will not do either, at least in those societies in which individuals have many different allegiances. In societies where individuals have multiple identities, they may want to preserve many different allegiances and not just

their own societal culture. If the groups that can be promoted and protected are all of those groups that citizens want to preserve, then we are
not in a position to identify societal cultures as the main groups that are
entitled to a regime of collective rights. The problem is that we seek to
justify rights only for societal cultures and not for all the groups. Since
rational preferences concerning group allegiances vary from one citizen
to another and vary through time for a single individual, we cannot
simply rely on the willingness of individuals to preserve all their particular group allegiances in order to justify a regime of collective rights
for societal cultures. Kymlicka thinks that among all groups, only the
members of societal cultures can legitimately claim group-differentiated
rights. So there must be an additional premise in the argument that enables him to filter out all those groups that cannot legitimately claim
cultural protection. The appropriate missing premise is that individuals
rationally prefer a regime that can guarantee protection for their own
national affiliations – that is, for their own societal culture. In other
words, the moral psychology of individuals confirms the role of societal
cultures as a primary social good for individuals. If we are to provide an
individualistic justification for the protection only for societal cultures,
then Kymlicka must claim that their cultural affiliations occupy the first
position in the minds of everyone (1989, 166).

Unfortunately, Allen Buchanan and many others have argued convincingly that individuals do not always see their own societal culture as a
primary good (Buchanan, 1996). So it is wrong to suggest that people
agree on the primacy of their own affiliation to their societal culture. Rational preferences may vary from person to person, and from time to time
for a single individual. Some people even give a very low priority to their
own societal affiliation. So we cannot justify a regime of collective rights
for societal cultures by considerations pertaining to the existence of a
rational preference in the moral psychology of citizens. Even worse, if
we were trying to impose a single ranking of allegiances on that basis, we
would be violating the principle of equal respect for individuals. We
would be imposing a particular hierarchy of group affiliations that would
conflict with the particular hierarchies of many individuals.

Buchanan's argument presupposes that Kymlicka is right in seeking
an individualistic justification for collective rights, which he finds in the
rational preferences of individuals. And he agrees with Kymlicka that
individuals do give the highest priority to their different "cultural" affiliations (Buchanan, 1994). But he disagrees with Kymlicka concerning
the privilege afforded to societal cultures, for there are many other

cultural groups (religious, ideological, and so on) that can also claim cultural protection. He believes that there are no individualistic justifications for the privilege afforded to nations, or to societal cultures, among all cultural groups. Thomas Pogge makes a similar argument based on the principle of equal respect (Pogge 1997).

This line of argument can also be pursued even further, and it can be shown to have many other damaging effects for collective rights. If Buchanan and Pogge are right, the only way to harmonize a theory of collective rights with the rational preferences of individuals would be to allow for the recognition of many different cultural, linguistic, religious, ethnic, and ideological groups in the public realm. There are thus many equally good candidates for a regime of collective rights. But now the problem is this. If the justification has to be founded on the rational preferences of individuals, we inevitably face a proliferation of groups competing with each other for recognition. It will then be very tempting to conclude that this leads to a *reductio ad absurdum* of most theories of collective rights (Weinstock, 1999).

So we have every reason to believe that Kymlicka's individualistic justification for collective rights fails. He is unable to account for a large class of collective rights – namely, those that involve reasonable internal restrictions – and for the collective rights of national majorities or whole peoples. He is unable to justify theoretically the obligation of immigrants to integrate and unable to provide an individualistic justification for the privilege afforded to societal cultures. The conclusion is that one may have to choose between ethical individualism and politics of recognition. This in a way is not a very happy outcome, for we have all the reason to believe that most liberals will choose the former, but it is not a reason for failing to have the courage to defend the latter. Liberal philosophers must have the courage to abandon ethical individualism and to embrace politics of recognition for peoples. Kymlicka is right to claim that, among all the groups, societal cultures are special. But he is wrong in trying to derive this claim from ethical individualism.

AN ALTERNATIVE LIBERAL THEORY OF COLLECTIVE RIGHTS

Let me outline the kinds of arguments that one could make for collective rights for peoples. As we have seen above, there are reasons to believe that Will Kymlicka has failed to show that ethical individualism could provide a secure foundation for politics of recognition. The problem is perhaps that Kymlicka wants to deploy arguments for liberalism that engage us into a comprehensive doctrine. He gives the impression that we do not have choice in this regard, and he seldom acknowledges alternative approaches. In my opinion, the appropriate liberal framework is Rawls's political liberalism (Rawls, 1993b). This is an approach that avoids any commitment to ethical individualism. It can also account for the equal importance of individuals and peoples, and it assumes that peoples and individuals are autonomous sources of moral worth. It has led Rawls to accept a second original position involving peoples; see Rawls, 1993a; 1999.

There are defects in Rawls's version of the law of peoples, identified by many commentators.[9] Rawls fails to provide a true liberal law of peoples, he tolerates non-liberal regimes, and he defends a "realistic" conception of international relations dominated by sovereign states. Although I cannot go into details here, I believe that a version of political liberalism is possible that avoids these unwanted consequences (Seymour, 2004). I want, however, to say this. Political liberalism allows us to acknowledge the public or institutional identity of persons and peoples and to treat persons and peoples as having a genuine moral character. Principles of justice must therefore apply equally to persons and to peoples. *Pace* Rawls, all these principles should apply both in the international arena and on the domestic scene. This entails that the two principles of justice must be applied at the international level and that the principles contained in the law of peoples must have application at the local level. There is no reason why the principles on which we agree at the international level should not be those that apply at the local level, and no reason why the principles on which we agree at the local level should not be those that apply at the international level. There are many differences between this account and Rawls's, but the major difference concerns the fact that the two dimensions of justice, international and domestic, contain a single set of principles. Political liberalism can thus be accepted as a truly universal doctrine. The law of peoples that I wish to defend is one that incorporates the two fundamental principles on which a consensus had been achieved at the domestic level. Under such a version, tolerance remains crucial, but it applies only to the different conceptions of persons and of peoples. This tolerance is what justifies the introduction of political conceptions of the person and of peoples. But it does not yield tolerance towards non-liberal regimes. It seeks to achieve a more appropriate balance between the interests of individuals, peoples, and sovereign states.

Rawls did not analyse the possible application of the law of peoples within multi-nation states. His eight principles hold for peoples with their own states, not for stateless peoples. But Rawls sees his law as only a first approximation. It is a simplified version, to be complemented by rules for creating federations of peoples and for self-determination and secession. So it is not a final, definitive account. Just as, in the domestic case, Rawls chose to consider only a closed society forming a nation-state, with no immigration and no contact with other peoples, and one that people enter by birth and leave by death, he also works within idealized assumptions at the level of international relations, for he now assumes that all peoples have their own states. This is an extreme simplification, and Rawls knows it. Rawls believes that the law of peoples has an application within the confines of actual multi-nation states. Any suggestion to the contrary would amount to ignoring the fact that Rawls meant to provide only an extremely simplified model.

But how can we justify a regime of collective rights for peoples if we cannot account for their importance in terms of the value that individuals attach to them? What is the additional, missing premise that we must add to the claims that societal cultures are crucial for individual liberties and that individuals want their societal culture to be protected? As we have seen above, these two claims do not by themselves justify politics of recognition for peoples. The first cannot justify protections for each societal culture, and the second does not identify peoples as the main bearers of collective rights.

So what can we add to those two initial claims? First, the value of societal cultures is implicitly accepted by those who wish to defend the equal respect that we owe to the different charts of allegiances in the minds of each citizen. Without a societal culture, there would not be many groups for us to plead allegiance to. It would not even be possible to create one's own chart of allegiances, for that too is a function of the existence of a liberal societal culture. One can also perhaps explain the importance of societal culture partly by noting its presence in everyone's charts. Even if it does not always occupy first place and is not for everyone a primary social good, it is the only allegiance that appears in every charts. Some philosophers will not mention their allegiance to their philosophical association, or workers, theirs to a trade union, but everyone belonging to a given societal culture will mention it somewhere in their own chart. Paradoxically, this is possible because we allow for multiple identities. Usually, it is thought that multiple identities may put one's national identity in jeopardy, for it now appears only one among many other allegiances. But the truth is quite the opposite. If we have only one affiliation to choose, we may want to exclude our national affiliation. But if the choice is open, chances are that we will mention our affiliation to a societal culture sooner or later. Most, if not all, other affiliations appear only in some charts and not in others. Many Christians will not mention that affiliation at all. The reason is that even if we can imagine ourselves without being affiliated to any association, we cannot easily imagine ourselves removed from societal cultures in general. Many Canadians do not see themselves as part of the Canadian societal culture – for instance, aboriginal peoples and Quebecers – but that is so because they have their own societal culture, which, they believe, Canadians do not sufficiently recognize. No one will reasonably be inclined to plead allegiance to his or her wider society if this society does not recognize his or her own local societal culture. Of course, one can have identities vis-à-vis several societal cultures, but some people will reasonably be reluctant to plead allegiance to the wider society if it does not recognize their own local societal culture.

The above remarks concerning the importance of societal cultures are interesting and important and must be accepted if there is to be a certain amount of respect towards each citizen, but they do not yet provide the justification that we seek. At best, they serve to pave the way for a solution that would not violate the principle of equal respect. If we endorse the sociological thesis that societal cultures are in general a necessary condition for individual liberties, this commits us only to protecting at least one societal culture. We can of course also acknowledge the importance of societal cultures by noting their presence in the charts of everyone. But then again, these rational preferences are compatible with the adoption of a single big societal culture for everyone. So what is the missing premise? The answer is that peoples, and societal cultures in general, help ensure cultural diversity. We wish to remain neutral on whether cultural diversity is intrinsically valuable or merely instrumental for the survival of the human species. But if cultural diversity is thus indispensable in this sense, then we should protect and promote each particular societal culture. Some will want to assert the intrinsic value of cultural diversity (Parekh, 2000). Others will claim that cultural diversity is instrumental for individualistic reasons or that it is instrumental for the survival of the human species. We wish to remain neutral on the normative grounds for endorsing the value of cultural diversity.

In *Multicultural Citizenship*, Kymlicka does consider justifying collective rights by relying on cultural diversity, but he discards the idea

(1995, 121–3). However, his negative reaction begs the question, for his arguments against it presuppose the truth of ethical individualism. He proposes that cultural diversity can be accepted as a value only if it benefits the individual. In this formulation, cultural diversity could hardly justify collective rights, for the demonstration must show that politics of recognition enhance the benefits of cultural diversity for the individuals belonging to the majority and to the minority. If the members of a majority culture accept a regime of collective rights for a minority group, the individual belonging to this group will not integrate in the majority culture, and so the members of the majority will not benefit from the culture of the minority. Simultaneously, since the members of the minority will be less inclined to integrate into the majority, they will not benefit from the culture of the majority. So it seems that such a regime reduces the benefits of cultural diversity for the individual instead of enhancing them. For that reason, Kymlicka believes that the value of cultural diversity is of no help as a justification for collective protection. But this is because he understands its benefits only in individualistic terms.

We could say instead that the beneficiary of cultural diversity must be humanity as a whole and not necessarily the individual. We could then argue that societal cultures have an autonomous moral worth, when compared with that of individuals, whether it derives its value from its intrinsic worth or from its instrumental role in preserving the survival of the human species. So Kymlicka misunderstands the import of the argument from cultural diversity. It must, according to him, benefit the individuals belonging either to the majority or to the minority cultures. This bias distorts his appreciation of the value of cultural diversity.

CONCLUSION

Given the importance of societal cultures for individual freedoms and liberties, Kymlicka has forcefully and, in my view, rightly argued that liberal philosophers must leave some room for the recognition of the collective rights of those groups that can be described as societal cultures. But he was misled to believe that the only way to harmonize liberalism and collective rights was by trying to show that they are compatible with ethical individualism. Liberalism is no more logically linked to ethical individualism than it is to the traditional nation-state model. If we are to understand liberalism apart from that model, we can and must do so apart from ethical individualism.

There are different ways of trying to accommodate collective rights within liberal theory. Kymlicka's brand of liberalism is one attempt to do so. As we have seen above his comprehensive version presupposes substantial individualistic claims in moral psychology (see Kymlicka, 2001a, 23, footnote 14). He subscribes to the idea that individuals are the ultimate sources of valid moral claims (1989, 140). He also treats individual autonomy as the only fundamental liberal value (1995, chap. 8). And he makes the dubious claim that individuals see their own cultural belonging as a primary good. This approach leads him to reject autonomously accepted collective rights, for they must derive from individual rights and are valid only as external protections, not as internal restrictions. Individual liberties and freedoms cannot, according to him, reasonably be internally constrained by group rights. Finally, these need not be understood by reference to the subject of the right, since the bearers can be individuals. Unfortunately, numerous arguments have shown that the individualistic derivation of collective rights fails because ethical individualism cannot do justice to a genuine recognition of collective rights.

Because of the importance of whole societal cultures, it appears that the state in a multi-nation society must protect not only individual citizens but also societal cultures. It must safeguard not only individual rights and liberties but also and equally the collective rights of societal cultures. The appropriate justification is one that invokes the value of cultural diversity and that acknowledges the instrumental role played by peoples in securing cultural diversity.

NOTES

1 The connection between nation-state building and the rejection of collective rights for minority groups is strikingly illustrated by the recent judgment of the Constitutional Council in France. It justifies its refusal to recognize the existence of a Corsican people or to ratify the European convention on minority languages by arguing that recognition of collective rights for minority groups would threaten the existence of a single French people.

2 See, for instance, Kymlicka, 1995, 57–69.

3 Kymlicka rejects "abstract individualism," understood as an atomistic view that supposes the absence of ties that bind the individual to his or her community (1995, 127–8), but he endorses ethical individualism, which sees individuals as the "ultimate units of moral worth." See also Kymlicka, 1989, 140.

4 For a similar argument, see Brighouse, 1996, 401. I agree with Brighouse on this point, even if he is wrong to use this argument against politics of recognition and against nationalism in general. On those crucial political issues of nationalism and politics of recognition, I side with Kymlicka and against Brighouse.

5 As we see below, societal cultures must be protected and promoted for the sake of cultural diversity. Here, I am not claiming that cultural diversity has an intrinsic value. It may have only an instrumental value for the survival of the human species.

6 For a discussion, see Kymlicka, 1995, 152; see also 42–4. The overall idea is that collective rights, to be acceptable, must first and foremost be external protections.

7 Kymlicka writes: "After all, most immigrants (as distinct from refugees) choose to leave their own culture. They have uprooted themselves ... In deciding to uproot themselves, immigrants voluntarily relinquish some of the rights that go along with their original national membership" (1995, 95–6).

8 There are places where Kymlicka writes that the bearer of the right must be the group (1995, 45), but these rights seem to be instrumental for the protection of more fundamental individual rights.

9 See, for instance, Beitz, 2000; Buchanan, 2000; Kuper, 2000.

REFERENCES

Beitz, Charles (2000) "Rawls's Law of Peoples," *Ethics* 110, 669–96.

Brighouse, Harry (1996) "Against Nationalism," in J. Couture, K. Nielsen, and M. Seymour, eds. *Rethinking Nationalism, Canadian Journal of Philosophy*, Supplementary Volume, 365–405.

Buchanan, Allen (1994), "Liberalism and Group Rights," in J. Coleman, eds., *In Harm's Way: Essays in Honour of Joel Feinberg*. Cambridge: Cambridge University Press, 1–15.

– (1996) "What's So Special about Nations?" in J. Couture, K. Nielsen, and M. Seymour, eds., *Rethinking Nationalism Canadian Journal of Philosophy*. Supplementary Volume.

– (2000) "Rawls's Law of Peoples: Rules for a Vanished Westphalian World," *Ethics* 110, 697–721.

Canovan, Margaret (1996) *Nationhood and Political Theory*. Cheltenham: Edward Elgar.

Kuper, Andrew (2000) "Rawlsian Global Justice: Beyond the Law of Peoples to a Cosmopolitan Law of Persons," *Political Theory* 28, no. 5, 640–74.

Kymlicka, Will (1989) *Liberalism, Community and Culture*. Oxford: Clarendon Press.

– (1995) *Multicultural Citizenship*. Oxford: Clarendon Press.

– (2001a) "The New Debate over Minority Rights," in Kymlicka, *Politics in the Vernacular*. Oxford: Oxford University Press.

– (2001b) "The Paradox of Liberal Nationalism," in Kymlicka, *Politics in the Vernacular*. Oxford: Oxford University Press, 254–64; originally published in *Literary Review of Canada* 4, no. 10 (1995), 13–15.

Parekh, Bhikhu (2000) *Rethinking Multiculturalism: Cultural Diversity and Political Theory*. London: Macmillan.

Pogge, Thomas (1994), "An Egalitarian Law of Peoples," *Philosophy and Public Affairs* 23, no. 3, 195–224.

– (1997) "Group Rights and Ethnicity," in Will Kymlicka and Shapiro, eds., *Ethnicity and Group Rights*. New York: New York University Press.

– (2001) "Rawls on International Justice," *Philosophical Quarterly* 51, 203 and 246–53.

Rawls, John (1993a) "The Law of Peoples," in Stephen Shute and Susan Hurley, eds., *On Human Rights. The Oxford Amnesty Lectures 1993*. New York, Basic Books, 41–82.

– (1993b) *Political Liberalism*. New York: Columbia University Press.

– (1999) *The Law of Peoples*. Cambridge, Mass.: Harvard University Press.

Raz, Joseph (1986) *The Morality of Freedom*. Oxford: Oxford University Press.

Seymour, Michel (2004) "Rethinking Political Recognition," in Alain-G. Gagnon, Montserrat Guibernau, and François Rocher, eds., *Conditions of Diversity in Multinational Democracies*. Montreal: IRPP, 59–84.

Weinstock, Daniel (1999) "Le problème de la boîte de Pandore," in Michel Seymour, ed., *Nationalité, citoyenneté et solidarité*. Montreal: Liber, 17–40.

DAVID INGRAM

The Complementarity of Rights: Rawls and Habermas on International Justice for Individuals and Groups

Political scientists continually remind us that we live in a world in which respect for human rights necessarily takes a back seat to the exigencies of realpolitik. Political philosophers, however, urge us to consider the morally unconscionable costs of conducting international relations in this mode. According to them, if the lessons of the Cold War have taught us anything, it is that foreign policies geared towards advancing narrow conceptions of national interest are self-defeating. No strategic equilibrium or power-based modus vivendi can be stable for long. Worse, such a system of international peace allows considerations of national security to countermand human rights and duties to assist the destitute.

Moral outrage directed against such evil seems futile, however, unless informed by realistic conceptions of international justice. Responding to this challenge, Jürgen Habermas and John Rawls have each developed conceptions that are as realistic as they are utopian. Departing from Kant's famous treatise, *Perpetual Peace* (1795), they agree, first, that national sovereignty must be limited by respect for universal human rights rather than simply being replaced by a global state and, second, that differing peoples must be allowed to interpret these rights in accordance with their own particular political traditions, at least within limits. At the same time, they disagree about the precise nature of these limits, with Habermas affirming and Rawls denying their essential liberal-democratic content. This disagreement in turn helps determine what they regard as the minimally acceptable level of economic inequality between nations.

In this paper I first outline the differences between Rawls and Habermas and then show how they crucially neglect economic and cultural rights. I next look at the rights of minorities and immigrants and then consider what I see as the complementarity of civil and political rights with cultural, economic, and social rights.

RAWLS VERSUS HABERMAS

In his essay *The Law of Peoples*, Rawls (1999) proposes to base international respect for human rights, just principles of war, and principles of economic assistance vis-à-vis burdened nations on a conception of mutual respect between decent "peoples," or nations. Accepting the idea that nations, unlike states, are self-limiting moral agents, he sees no reason why they should not be fully respected so long as they in turn respect basic human rights,[1] refrain from expansionist policies, and institutionalize a conception of justice based on reciprocal duties and the rule of law. Significantly, Rawls holds that even illiberal, undemocratic nations that do not allow equal civil and political freedom and whose legal institutions embody a conception of justice that privileges one particular comprehensive conception of the common good over others (what he calls a "common good conception of justice "as distinct from a liberal, or "political conception of justice") can be minimally decent (1999, 64–5). Consonant with this view, he maintains that human rights can be assigned to persons as members of subgroups, which can be accorded unequal freedoms as required by the common good (66). In his opinion, legitimacy – if not full justice – is maintained to the degree that minority groups are tolerated, dissenting groups are adequately responded to, and each group is fairly represented in a consultation hierarchy (69).[2] Seen from the vantage point of economic justice, a minimally just Rawlsian world would also tolerate decent societies that do not possess the material support for state-funded services and socioeconomic equality normally thought to be essential to maintaining a healthy democracy. Hence, it would tolerate significantly large differences in economic well-being among decent and liberal democratic regimes.

Habermas, in *The Inclusion of the Other* (1998a) and *The Postnational Constellation* (1998b), presents a different case for human rights. Like Rawls, he recognizes that rights are empty apart from being interpreted by particular communities in accordance with their unique constitutional traditions. Unlike Rawls, however, he views nations as inappropriate agents of such traditions. In his opinion, nations – or nationalities – typically designate artificially constructed loci of identification whose moral agency is questionable. Conceding the positive role played by nationalism in struggles for liberation and democracy, he notes that nationality today has all too often justified illiberal forms of nationalism and stands discredited by the multicultural migrations set in motion by globalization. Concomitant with this understanding of nationality as ideology, Habermas believes that "popular sovereignty and [individual] human rights go hand in hand" (1996, 127). According to this view, rights devolve principally on individuals rather than on groups because individuals alone generate legitimate moral and legal norms in the course of deliberating together as free and equal participants in democratic dialogue. Because Habermas believes that individual rights flourish only within liberal democracies, which in his view require relatively high levels of government welfare and socioeconomic equality, he insists that a just world composed entirely of liberal democracies would (and should) tolerate much less inequality between nations than one not so composed.

The disagreement between Rawls and Habermas undoubtedly reflects differences in their respective understandings of reasonable agreement on universal principles of justice. Rawls assumes that reasonable people living in illiberal, non-democratic societies will disagree about the superiority of liberal-democratic conceptions of equality and freedom relative to other schemes of justice, just as reasonable people living in liberal-democratic societies will disagree about the superiority of this or that conception of equality and freedom. Therefore it would be unreasonable and intolerant of liberal-democratic societies to press these other societies into adopting a liberal-democratic interpretation of rights as a prerequisite for mutual co-operation. In any case, the mere fact that these other societies do not extend equal political rights to all their members is no argument against respecting them as equals, since illiberal, hierarchical organizations, such as churches and universities, are often treated as equals by more liberal, egalitarian groups (Rawls, 1999, 69). Despite disagreeing on liberal-democratic ideals, decent peoples, Rawls believes, will agree on "thinner" principles of justice possessing weaker prescriptive content, albeit for very different and possibly incommensurable reasons. The incommensurability of these culture-bound reasons implies that any serious attempt to persuade others into accepting a liberal-democratic interpretation of these principles will very probably seem to them futile, if not utterly disrespectful.[3]

Habermas, in contrast, denies that cultural differences reflect a "reasonable pluralism" of belief unless they are the product of an open and unlimited dialogue. The liberal and egalitarian presuppositions underlying such dialogue distinguish rational suasion from prejudicial discourse and manipulative rhetoric. Fully trustworthy agreements, in which both parties have good reasons to respect one another, must be based on shared reasons. The mere fact that I observe that other persons agree to the same principle that I endorse – and for reasons that I can, if at all, barely fathom – would not entitle me to infer that their reasons were moral reasons, let alone fully reasonable (i.e., justifiable) ones (Habermas, 1998a, 62, 90). But unless I can be sure that the reasons why you (a citizen of, for example, an illiberal Islamic theocracy) and I (a citizen of a liberal democracy) agree are both morally justifiable – and thus equally reliable and stable – for roughly the same reasons, I have no grounds for trusting you. For all I know, your faith in rights could be trumped by fundamentalist ardour; for all you know, my secular support of the same could be trumped by economic greed. Therefore, instead of tolerating trenchant and unsolvable cultural disagreement in this area – and instead of simply accepting some general but largely meaningless platitudes about human rights – we should rather insist on a fully inclusive and open dialogue aimed at creating a fully determinate and prescriptive understanding of rights. Ultimately, the reasons underlying our shared understanding of rights must themselves hark back to the liberal and egalitarian assumptions of rational dialogue. Therefore a global consensus on thicker liberal-democratic ideals can be expected to emerge as international relations become settled in rational dialogue.

ENGAGING ECONOMIC AND CULTURAL RIGHTS

I have argued elsewhere (Ingram, 2003) that Habermas's understanding of the desirable kind of rational agreement is preferable in the long run if only because it provides a global democratic procedure to discuss human rights fully, to modify them progressively in a liberal-democratic direction, and to give them the kind of concrete, prescriptive meaning associated with legally enforceable rights. By contrast, Rawls's method of agreement leaves us with abstract categories of rights whose generality renders them virtually unenforceable. Habermas's theory thus presents a method of agreement that offers both the universalizability and the prescriptive determinacy required for enforceable human rights. However, in this paper I argue that neither thinker provides a satisfactory account of two other requirements: completeness and priority. This failure is reflected in their downplaying of economic and cultural rights.

A complete theory of rights includes all the categories of rights that are necessary for the full exercise of any right. I propose that Habermas's theory is more complete than Rawls's, in so far as it insists on complementarity between property, security, and civil rights, on one side, and democratic rights, on the other. Like Rawls, Habermas denies that human rights can be directly derived from a priori morality (natural law), since they are "structured" as enforceable statutes under the auspices of the United Nations (Habermas, 1998a, 190–2). However, unlike Rawls, he argues that rights refer beyond the contingent moral reasons given in support of them by the signatories to the United Nations' (UN's) Universal Declaration of Human Rights to include the necessary and universal presuppositions of speech that condition rational moral agency (191). In speaking to one another, persons are obligated to recognize one another as free and equal. Because equality and autonomy are deeply embedded in our (communicative) nature, laws sanctioning rights cannot be bestowed on citizens paternalistically without violating their own humanity as self-legislating bearers of rights (261). Hence, liberal democracy is not simply one possible form that a legitimate regime can take: it is the only one – and the only one, too, for any transnational federation that seeks to protect the fragile social democracies of member nation states against the destructive impact of economic globalization (80–4, 120–6).

Unlike political rights, human rights possess intrinsic moral worth, applying to everyone regardless of their political status (Habermas, 1998a, 259–60). Yet their actualization as fully legitimate and enforceable depends on the institutionalization of political rights. But how do human and political rights relate to economic, cultural, and social rights?

Sometimes Habermas agrees with Rawls in holding that these latter rights guarantee positive access to goods and capacities that realize the fair value of "political civil" and "classical human" rights. According to Habermas, the negative freedom to "pursue one's private conception of the good" without interference is meaningless apart from the positive freedom to be protected and supported in this endeavour by the state (1996, 41–2). In institutionalizing negative rights, the state is conceptually committed to a host of other rights, including rights to membership in equal standing and rights to due process. These basic categories of right – to "the greatest possible measure of equal liberties that are mutually compatible," to equal membership (including freedom to emigrate and immigrate), and to free access to impartial courts – constitute an abstract legal code that must be interpreted by citizens exercising their political rights. Habermas concludes that citizens must have "equal opportunities to utilize" the four "absolutely justified categories" of rights – to personal liberty, citizenship, due process, and political participation. These equal opportunities imply "basic rights to the provision of living conditions that are social, technologically, and ecologically safeguarded."

Like Rawls, Habermas insists that this fifth category of social rights "can be justified only in relative terms" with respect to the four "absolutely justifiable" categories of civil and political rights. Contrary to both Rawls and Habermas, I argue that at least some economic, cultural, and social rights – far from merely guaranteeing auxiliary goods and capacities instrumental for realizing the fair value of human, civil, and political rights – are identical to them. Thus the right to self-preservation (the right to life) is a classical human right that is intimately connected to a right to economic subsistence, if not (as John Locke thought) to a right to acquire and exchange private property. And, as I argue below, some social and cultural rights are explicitly "civil and political" in nature, just as some civil and political rights are inherently social and cultural, enabling not only individuals but also groups to preserve their society and culture.

Following Henry Shue (1996), I would argue that any society that grants individuals rights of one kind or another – and there are virtually none that don't – are theoretically committed to granting them more basic rights to subsistence, security, freedom, democratic participation, and – missing from Shue's account – culture (Ingram, 2000a, 249). Rights are enforceable demands placed on others, and they cannot be made good without decent subsistence, security, freedom, and political power.

The U.S. State Department's continual refusal to endorse the UN's International Covenant on Economic, Social, and Cultural Rights of 1966 parallels the theoretical obtuseness of both Rawls (despite his belated recognition of subsistence rights) and Habermas (despite his belated recognition of social and cultural rights). The State Department urged that the UN Declaration of Human Rights be split into two independently ratifiable treaties: the International Covenant on Civil and Political Rights and the International Covenant on Economic, Social, and Cultural Rights. While supporting the former, the State Department has refused to endorse the latter on the grounds that these rights are less binding. Clearly, even if we accept the view, espoused by Habermas

(1998b, 181), that liberal-democratic rights are intrinsic to a universal process of modernization[4] and that cultural and social rights cannot have priority over civil and political rights, since the former only serve to guarantee (in Rawls's words) the "fair value" of civil and political rights, it doesn't follow that political and civil rights have priority over cultural and social rights. The mere facts that we can agree on civil and political rights with greater facility and that negative rights to non-interference are often easier to discern and enforce are not reasons to privilege them over economic, social, and cultural rights.

In any case, the UN's division of civil and political rights on one hand and economic, social, and cultural rights on the other hand is arbitrary and incoherent. Some rights, like the right to join labour unions, straddle the distinction, while most rights that fall under one covenant are ineffectual apart from being conjoined with rights falling under the other. Even as a marker of priorities, the distinction fails to take into account that within each division there are rights that are more basic (meriting greater protection) than others. Thus the economic right to acquire land and productive capacity for profit is less basic than the economic right to bare subsistence, just as the political right to contribute money to political campaigns and parties is less basic than the right to vote. By not taking into account the priority of subsistence over market freedom, the State Department has imposed its own hyper-libertarian, hyper-individualist interpretation of basic rights in a manner that subverts – rather than promotes – the aims of liberal democracy.

Another unfortunate consequence of the way in which Rawls and Habermas draw the distinction between basic and non-basic rights is that it excludes cultural rights from the class of basic rights, thereby also neglecting the place of group rights. Although they recognize the validity of group rights in their own fashion, they cannot explain how such rights are necessary features of liberal-democratic societies. This oversight stems from the individualism implicit in discourse theory and political liberalism (as applied to individual persons or individual nations). Rawls, for instance, understands the importance of group representation in illiberal, hierarchical societies (such as his idealized Islamic theocracy, Kazanistan), but he does not grasp its role in liberal democracy, which he continues to interpret primarily in terms of aggregating individual preferences. He thus sees group representation as subordinate to the integrity of individuals – be they persons or nations. Habermas likewise views democratic political life as centred on individual contributions to discussion. Indeed, neither political liberalism nor discourse theory satisfactorily accounts for group identity, and so neither establishes a satisfactory basis for group rights. But lacking a sound basis for group rights, neither can present a fully satisfactory theory of individual rights. This becomes evident when we turn to what Rawls and Habermas say about sub-nationalities and immigrants.

RIGHTS OF MINORITIES AND IMMIGRANTS

As we saw above, Rawls presumes incommensurability between what he regards as essentially self-contained political cultures. Traces of the kind of racially inspired cultural determinism that fuelled the nationalism that swept Europe during the nineteenth and twentieth centuries surprisingly resurface in Rawls's appeal to nations rather than to individuals or to states as the pre-eminent moral agents (individuals) underwriting international rights. To be sure, his appeal rests partly on other grounds – namely, his view that the law of peoples is arrived at through first working out the principles of justice for domestic societies. In regarding a domestic liberal society from the standpoint of the original position, we make the simplifying assumption that it is closed. We regard it as "self-contained and as having no relations with other societies," in such a way that it "reproduces itself and its institutions and culture over generations" (Rawls, 1993, 12, 18) and that its members "enter only by birth and exit only by death" (26).

Rawls, of course, is aware that, despite his abstraction of a closed society bound together by a self-perpetuating national political culture, "historical conquests and immigration have caused the intermingling of groups with different cultures and historical memories" within the same territory. Yet he continues to hold this assumption as if it were descriptive of historical reality, even to the extent of endorsing John Stuart Mill's deterministic definition of national identity as "common sympathies" rooted in "race and descent" (Rawls, 1993, 23).

Habermas finds such essentialist notions of national identity highly suspect. As he points out, national identities are ideological fictions (Habermas, 1998b, 37) that, having once helped pave the way for democratic political integration at a local level, now threaten to obstruct it at the international level (1998a, 112–15). Hence they must be radically transformed and subordinated to less all-encompassing, cosmopolitan-friendly cultural identities that are maintained and generated more or less reflectively and voluntarily. Moreover, as Iris Young (2000) and others have pointed out, the very identification of peoples with closed territorial groups needs to be rethought, especially for cases of overlapping peoples, as in Northern Ireland and Israel/Palestine. Partitioning is not always the best solution in these cases, since the contending parties essentially share the economies and spaces being contested. A better solution would combine cosmopolitan forms of governance (sometimes involving third parties) with more local forms. The larger lesson to be drawn here, as in the case of economic assistance, is that local forms of participatory and/or advisory government at metropolitan and regional levels must be strengthened in tandem with more global, cosmopolitan forms.

Despite his salubrious critique of cultural essentialism, Habermas goes overboard in criticizing cultural nationalism. For instance, in contrast to Rawls, he insists that states must be absolutely neutral with respect to religion in order to guarantee full religious toleration (Habermas, 1998b, 187). By equating legitimacy with a rational constitutional consensus on rights, which by definition are impartial and neutral with respect to competing cultures and their respective conceptions of the good, Habermas demands that citizens "uncouple" their national cultural identities from the universal political culture that they all share as rational individuals (227). Whether democratic (procedural) impartiality requires such a strong conception of neutrality is certainly doubtful, and for two reasons. First, no institutional specification of justice can be culturally neutral. Habermas himself notes that political cultures invariably gravitate around a national culture, and this applies to liberal multicultural democracies no less than to illiberal hierarchies. Second, to the extent that he appreciates this fact, he is forced to concede that national political cultures are the essential medium in which largely abstract constitutional principles are interpreted.

This fact alone does not vitiate constitutional impartiality. Nor does the fact that different sub-nationalities within the same national political culture interpret the constitution somewhat differently (Seymour, 1999). The concern here is that too much sub-national (or ethnic) diversity in the interpretation of a constitution will simply multiply the number of effective constitutions, thereby resulting in a sort of lawless anarchy. Habermas clearly thinks that nationalism is divisive in this bad sense. But he thinks that cultural pluralism is good. So the question arises, can he clearly distinguish between divisive and closed national identities, on one hand, and unifying and open cultural identities, on the other? I doubt it. The distinction stems from Habermas's assumption that identities that are "merely cultural" rather than quasi-racial can be sustained in their integrity through rational scrutiny in a way that national identities that are ostensibly quasi-racial cannot (Pensky, 2000). Yet even he admits that opening up cultural "lifeworlds" to global communication threatens them with pathological disintegration (Habermas, 1998b, 127). As he points out in his comments on Quebec's cultural laws, cultural instability is the price that liberal societies pay for allowing immigration.

There the distinction between cultural and national groups totally collapses. Québécois nationalism is not racial but cultural. The education law requiring immigrants to send their children to French-speaking schools was intended to include them in Quebec's public life; and the language laws that applied to work spaces and signs eliminated discriminatory preferences in favour of English rather than limiting fundamental freedoms. More important, the laws had a thoroughly rational basis: the protection of a common language essential to political life. In discussing these laws, Habermas argued that legal efforts to preserve a culture inevitably run up against the freedom of expression so necessary for identity formation in liberal societies (Habermas, 1998a, 222). He could have concluded just as easily that without such laws the very medium of free expression itself would have been imperilled. Again, his optimistic belief that multicultural immigration poses no danger to the preservation of liberal democracy accords with the view that unregulated multicultural communication always revitalizes otherwise-ossified cultures. But, given what Habermas knows about the disintegrative effects of global mass culture and "postmodern neoliberalism" on smaller national-linguistic cultures (Habermas, 1998b, 115, 124), this view seems naïve.

Habermas's defence of individuals' rights of access to their own particular cultures did not lead him to endorse group rights, which he found "unnecessary" and "normatively questionable." However, he later changed his mind, including "group-specific rights" – along with a "federalist delegation of powers, a functionally specified transfer or decentralization of state competencies, above all guarantees of cultural autonomy ..., compensatory policies, and other arrangements for effectively protecting minorities" (Habermas, 1998a, 145–6) – among the "difference sensitive" strategies for protecting cultural minorities. Unfortunately, he never tells us how we move from a theory of individual rights to a theory of group rights.

One way to do it is to show that cultural rights are among the list of basic, mutually complementary rights. Cultural rights may take the general form of a right to education, which is essential to exercising and politically defending one's other rights. However, they can also take a particular form. Because culture is passed down principally in the form of a particular heritage, the right to culture is more than the right to education (culture in general); it is the right to access to the culture of one's people(s). So political rights entail rights to political representation as members of cultural groups (broadly construed).

Cultural and political rights are among the rights mentioned in articles 21, 22, and 27 of the Universal Declaration of Human Rights that apply to groups as well as to individuals.[5] Others include the rights to nationality (Article 15), to trade-union membership (Article 23), to free association (Article 20), and to religion (Article 18). More relevant to our purposes, Article 29.1 notes that the exercise of rights is linked to duties "to the community in which alone the free and full development of [one's] personality is possible." Now, within liberal democracy the tension between "duties to the community," which are often specified as group rights, and individual rights is almost invariably resolved in favour of the latter. Since individuality is regarded as an irrepressible part of common humanity, the rights of individuals are esteemed above the rights of groups. For Habermas, one of the trademarks of any legal right (as distinct from a purely moral right) is that it is merely permissive, imposing no corresponding duty on those who have them other than the duty to allow their free exercise. Having individual rights doesn't depend, therefore, on fulfilling any broader duties to the community. However, "liberals" as divergent as Will Kymlicka and Charles Taylor have persuasively argued that one's cultural- and ethnic-group affiliations are also an irrepressible part of one's individuality. In the words of Kymlicka, cultural membership "affects our very sense of identity and capacity" in so far as it is "the context within which we choose our ends, and come to see their value, and this is a precondition of self-respect, of the sense that one's ends are worth pursuing" (Kymlicka, 1991).

Because cultural identity is experienced as group identity, the cultural right that people have as individuals will typically be asserted in the form of a group right whenever one of the cultural groups to which they belong is singled out for discrimination. For instance, the appropriate remedy for dealing with anti-Semitic violence – which is directed against Jews not as individuals but as members of a group – is a group right, as exemplified by the New York legislature's establishment of a separate school district for the Kiryas Joel Hasidim community (Ingram, 2000a, 1–27). The same thinking applies to Quebec's language laws. One's freedom to participate as an equal in Quebec's democracy may very well require that one share a common language with others; and since this language is threatened by the incursion of a more dominant (English) language – and for some French speakers, the incursion of English in the workplace functions to discriminate against them – laws that "impose" French in private and public spaces also protect individuals in the free exercise of their civil and political rights. Again, as John Stuart Mill argued in *Representative Government*, any democracy that underrepresents political groups (such as African Americans) also oppresses the individuals within those groups. So, despite Habermas, group rights *are* sometimes necessary for protecting individual rights.

Habermas and Rawls (Rawls, 1999, 72) view political rights within liberal democracies as applying equally (and in a purely formal way) to individuals, not to groups. Rawls is correct that protecting women's individual civil and political rights – not to mention their basic subsistence and security rights – will often require guaranteeing them representation as women, and in ways that seem to violate the formal demand for equal participation and representation, as interpreted by a principle of majority rule suitably qualified by constitutionally entrenched civil rights. But he sees this special group right as applying to women mainly in illiberal, undemocratic societies, where they lack equal political rights (1999, 75, 110). On the contrary, the need to secure proportional group representation for women applies equally to liberal-democratic societies, possibly requiring them to post a certain percentage of women candidates for contested offices (as in France) or reserving a certain percentage of seats for them. It might even require the use of supermajoritarian procedures, such as office rotation and veto privileges, that aim to compensate women and oppressed minorities for their political disadvantage (Ingram, 2000a, 199).

But what about the potential domination of groups over their own dissident minorities? The groups to which they belong may view dissident minorities as external threats to the self-determination of the groups' majority membership. Very often this conflict seems like a tug of war between the individual rights of dissidents and the group rights of the majority. Within an illiberal, undemocratic society it very often is – tragically so. But within liberal democracy – and within an ideally open global community – dissident individuals should have the right to exit and form new groups if they cannot negotiate a reasonable compromise with the majority. The right to exit does not resolve all conflicts between individual and group – a reality powerfully brought home to us by the example of women inhabiting patriarchal religious communities who must confront the hard choice of leaving their families and spiritual support groups or suffering sexist discrimination (Ingram, 2000a, 115). But the right to exit does allow for a freedom of association that can promise empowerment as well as emancipation.

Immigrants and refugees who take advantage of this right are the classical addressees of human rights, since they are often denied the rights of citizenship. One might be tempted to justify strong immigration rights by applying the Rawlsian device of an original position to cosmopolitan individuals on the grounds that citizenship and place of residence are as morally arbitrary as other undeserved features affecting their fortunes. Ignorant of their citizenship or residence, cosmopolitan individuals placed in an original position would relate to one another as fully free and equal and so would incline towards a liberal-democratic interpretation of basic rights. They would also probably opt for principles of justice allowing for relatively unrestricted freedom of movement across borders, since that would maximize the overall well-being of the most oppressed and most numerous among them. Assuming that Rawls is right that equal and free persons placed in a domestic (liberal-democratic) original position would reject utilitarian principles in favour of strongly egalitarian ones such as his difference principle – which allows economic inequalities only to the extent that they benefit the worst-off – then it is not unreasonable to suppose that free and equal persons placed in an international original position would choose the same way, thereby necessitating massive transfers of wealth from rich individuals to poor individuals (Rawls, 1999, 119–20).

Things look very different if the contractors are imagined to be peoples rather than cosmopolitan citizens. Self-interested peoples, Rawls insists, have good moral reasons to protect themselves, their culture, and the territory that they inhabit by instituting restrictive immigration policies – at least so long as they coexist in a world of security risks, epidemics, multicultural conflicts, and economic scarcities. These views of immigration and economic redistribution are ones that Rawls draws – somewhat surprisingly – from one of his staunchest critics, Michael Walzer. As an opponent of cosmopolitan liberalism, Walzer holds that protection of a people's property, no less than of its political culture, is sufficient to limit immigration. Although Rawls is probably right to argue that the political and economic causes that drive immigration would be greatly mitigated under his proposed law of peoples, he gives no reason why the survival needs of desperate individuals should not outweigh the culturally perfectionist expectations of affluent peoples anxious to maintain a costly political culture and way of life. Like Walzer, he thinks that a global state without borders would be a cosmopolitan dystopia of deracinated men and women, and he adds that under its regime, global capitalism would have free rein to overwhelm local communities (Rawls, 1999, 39). But elsewhere he seems more sanguine about the benefits of free trade; and although he is hardly oblivious to the harsh inequalities generated by global capitalism, he fails to note that the political evils contributing to bad resource management, overpopulation, lack of investment, and other factors driving immigration are partly if not mainly attributable to a global system that has disproportionately benefited affluent, border-conscious countries.

Habermas, with his cosmopolitan liberal approach to international relations and more sophisticated understanding of global interdependence and political diversity, identifies at least as strongly with the rights of individuals (such as desperate immigrants and stateless refugees) as with the rights of nations. His endorsement of a relatively open immigration policy of the sort recommended by Joseph Carens (1987), coupled with a more egalitarian plan of global economic redistribution, flows from his recognition that the First World has benefited disproportionately from "the history of colonization and the uprooting of regional cultures by the incursion of capitalist modernization" (Habermas, 1998a, 230–1). It also follows from his discourse theory, which de-essentializes national identities and places a high premium on democracy. Treating immigrants as equals in this context means, among other things, allowing them to assimilate to a constitutional political culture without having to "give up the cultural form of life of their origins," even if their doing so "changes the character of the community" (229–30). Such a view needs to be qualified. As in the case of Quebec, changes in the linguistic fabric of the community cannot be allowed to extend so far that they undermine the integrity of the political culture.

COMPLEMENTARY RIGHTS

Our discussion of the group rights of immigrants again recalls the complex complementarity of political, cultural, and economic rights. Economic rights, too, are basic. Yet neither Rawls nor Habermas provides fully adequate accounts of them; both seem to presume the legitimacy of capitalist markets. Rawls urges decent peoples to assist burdened nations to the extent needed for relations of peaceable mutual co-operation. But, he adds, many decent nations could reasonably refuse to give up wealth and resources simply for the sake of equalizing the lives of cosmopolitan individuals. Hence he opposes global distributive principles of the sort that have been advanced by Charles Beitz and Thomas Pogge (Rawls, 1999, 116–20).[6]

Rawls does so because, as we have seen above, he does not think that all decent peoples can agree on such principles. But, as Beitz notes (2000, 681), such deference to factual disagreements is not as such morally compelling. No more compelling is Rawls's view that moral psychology dictates limited expectations regarding the capacity of persons to think of themselves from a cosmopolitan view. The idea that we must protect the economic sovereignty of peoples respecting individuals' economic rights simply because individuals identify themselves first and foremost as fellow members of a territorially bounded scheme of mutual co-operation and responsibility confuses (in the words of Beitz) "questions about justification and those about institutional design" (683). Even if territorial states happen to be the most efficient mechanism for managing resources for mutual benefit and so provide an exemplary basis for determining our primary obligations as citizens, this fact alone says nothing about our psychological capacity to identify with, and care for, strangers as human beings. If persons in large multicultural states can identify with one another for this reason, surely they can identify with outsiders for the same reason (indeed, we may depend on, and have more in common with, people who live outside our nation than on and with people who live within it). In any case, Rawls is wrong to adopt the communitarian maxim that moral psychology – or feelings of solidarity with fellow members (whoever they might be) – ought to determine the extent of our moral duties; for allowing this is tantamount to caving in to ethnocentric prejudice.

Rawls's privileging of peoples over individuals as the principal subjects of international law also undermines his defence of a principle of assistance to burdened societies. Rawls insists that this principle be understood not as a requirement of international distributive justice to be implemented continuously, but merely as a duty to raise all societies to a minimum level of political culture and economic sustainability commensurate with requirements of minimal decency. As such, the duty has a definite "cut-off point." Here again, Rawls offers scant justification for the duty, other than the possible global security risks that unstable societies pose to the rest of the world. Although he remarks that liberal-democratic societies will be morally required to relieve absolute poverty so that people can live decent lives, to mitigate the stigma of inferiority that comes with differences in wealth, and to secure fair conditions for democratic politics, he notes that these reasons do not apply directly to the international arena, except in so far as any well-ordered, decent people will have met the basic needs of all citizens so that they, as equal and autonomous members of the "Society of Well-ordered Peoples," can decide for themselves "the significance and importance of the wealth of [their] own society" (1999, 114–15). So, unlike in the individual-centred theory of justice that he developed with respect to liberal democracy, Rawls here makes no mention of the unfairness of allowing arbitrary circumstances, such as one's being born in a poor, resource-starved country, to diminish one's *equal* chances for a free and fulfilling life.

Rawls's resistance to a global theory of distributive justice is also revealing, in that it reflects his questionable views about the capacity of states to be economically independent and autonomous in their distribution of resources. Rawls asserts that "there is no society anywhere in the world – except in marginal cases – with resources so scarce that it could not, were it reasonably and rationally organized and governed, become well-ordered" (1999, 108). Leaving aside the questionableness of this assertion, Rawls makes no reference to causes other than lack of resources that contribute to the impoverishment of nations, except perhaps unfair trade agreements (69). This is surprising, given his understanding of how capitalist economies in liberal democracies generate inequalities whose effects on the life chances of disadvantaged persons are both arbitrary and unjust and therefore require correction through redistributive means. Thus, to take the example of trade, there is now a voluminous literature on how inequalities in capital and other resources enable developed countries to implement free trade agreements that condemn underdeveloped countries to perpetual neocolonial dependence; weakened health, education, and welfare services; ecological devastation; political corruption; class warfare; resource depletion; and (for most inhabitants) poverty. In sum, the national resource sufficiency and international fair trade that Rawls maintains are necessary for bringing about a global Society of Well-ordered Peoples are undermined by a capitalist global structure.

Rawls gives additional reasons why a principle of global distributive justice is unfeasible – none of them convincing. He argues, for instance, that it would be unjust to demand that well-ordered nations that have managed their economies responsibly – through hard work, population control, and savings – transfer some of their wealth to poorer, well-ordered nations that have not been as industrious or thrifty. As Beitz notes, the appeal of this argument tacitly depends "on an analogy with individual morality, where we typically believe that society has no obligation to hold people harmless from the adverse consequences of their own informed, uncoerced choices" (2000, 691). The full force of this argument becomes apparent once we realize that individuals inhabiting most underdeveloped nations had much less choice in determining their economic fates than people living in developed ones. For example, many heavily indebted poor countries (HIPCs) in Africa, Asia, and Central America accrued their debt and, along with it, a corresponding poor credit rating that discouraged outside investment during the Cold War, when the U.S. government and its allies persuaded their leaders (some of them military dictators) to take out loans intended for defence and commercial infrastructure. The average citizen in these countries had little say in these decisions and received few, if any, benefits from the loans (many of the loans were pilfered by corrupt officials or invested in bad projects, often with the knowing acquiescence of U.S. officials). Not only was the choice to accept these loans constrained (if not coerced) by the U.S. government – thereby making Americans co-responsible for the loans – but the deregulation of currencies and the decline in the value of the U.S. dollar (and dollar-pegged exports, such as oil) resulted in inflationary interest rates that increased the debt burden of client states to the oppressive levels of today. Only a blanket forgiveness of that burden – not the structural readjustment policies dictated by the International Monetary Fund and World Bank as conditions for receiving further multilateral loans – will save these nations from total ruin.

Perhaps it is unfair to saddle Rawls's theory of economic assistance with the burden of having to deal with "marginal" cases such as these; perhaps his strictures about fair trade might reach all the way down to regulating, in some form, the background structures and institutions constraining trade. Granting that, it is presuming a lot to suppose that representatives of peoples in the global original position of choice seeking to advance the corporate interests of their respective peoples would settle for a weak principle of charity (the duty to assist burdened peoples) instead of a more egalitarian principle of distributive justice. Would not knowledge of the short-term (and very possibly long-term) detrimental effects of a global market system on the most vulnerable nations lead them to view continuous economic redistribution as a matter of right, necessary for guaranteeing the equality and autonomy of all trading partners? As Thomas Pogge (1999) argues, even more egalitarian principles of distributive justice, such as like the difference principle that Rawls invokes for liberal-democratic societies, would be preferred if the representatives in the global original position represented individual heads of households instead of peoples.

It would be wrong to think that Rawls's anti-egalitarian views on global economic justice simply follow from his privileging "special responsibilities to the members of our own families, communities, and societies" over "general responsibilities" to needy others and humanity at large (Scheffler, 1999). An emphasis on general responsibilities – as the neoliberal defence of free markets shows – can be no less anti-egalitarian than an emphasis on special responsibilities can be egalitarian – as the protectionist defence of local economies likewise shows. Rawls's appeal to the rights of peoples imposes limits on any global egalitarian redistribution but is not hostile to egalitarian outcomes achieved through protectionist means. However, it is a very large question whether nation-states can protect their domestic economies without banding together in larger, supranational organizations that are democratically empowered to regulate market inequalities and externalities. Here again, economic self-determination at the level of the group (or community) rather than of the nation might be the most efficacious way to protect economic rights. Regional and metropolitan self-determination, however, needs to be coupled with inter-regional and, ultimately, supranational regulatory bodies in order to rein in multinational corporations and ensure equitable development.

In the current era of globalization, liberal democracies across the board are under increasing pressure from financial institutions – and, yes, from global economic entities such as the European Union – to embrace structural adjustment policies that exact a heavy toll on social services and other security nets essential to egalitarian democracy. As Allen Buchanan observes (2000, 701), Rawls's protectionist understanding seems to reflect a "vanished Westphalian world" that overestimates religious and cultural differences while underestimating global interdependence. Specifically, Rawls overestimates the extent to which states are "economically self-sufficient" and "distributionally autonomous"[7] while idealizing the degree to which they are "politically homogeneous" and lack internal politico-cultural divisions.

Habermas, by contrast, tends to view international justice as an extension of domestic justice; in his opinion, relationships of mutual

dependence and mutual effect implicate something like a "basic structure" whose injustices require rectification. This suggestion – as salu-
tary as it is – might not go far enough, however. Habermas often
comes close to associating modernization (and therewith moral and
legal enlightenment) with the development of market systems that
have a strongly capitalistic flavour. He seldom acknowledges the possibility of market-based socialism and usually couches his criticism of
globalization in terms of "taming" the capitalist economic system.[8]
Furthermore, because of his neglect of group rights, he underestimates
the possible economic benefits that might flow from a two-tiered
strategy combining local democratic oversight of regional economies
(protectionism) with supranational democratic oversight of global
economies.

CONCLUSION

In summary, neither Habermas nor Rawls presents an adequate account
of the equal priority of economic, social, and cultural rights. Some economic rights are basic, and realizing them will require more radical
changes in global governance structures than either man countenances.
Some cultural rights are basic, too. This means – contrary to Habermas's cosmopolitan liberalism and Rawls's political liberalism – that the
rights of groups no less than the rights of individuals will sometimes
have to be politically recognized within liberal democracy. Ultimately,
Habermas is right that an international democratic federation of liberal
democracies and political groups is really the only lasting basis on
which to build peace and justice. His recommendation to restructure
the UN – perhaps by abolishing the vetoes of the permanent members of
the Security Council or by adding new permanent members – is also
worthy of consideration. In addition to this reform, however, the
General Assembly should also be supplemented with a People's Assembly, composed of persons, elected directly from all over the world, who
would represent vulnerable sub-groups, including women, indigenous
people, poor people, vulnerable ethnic groups, immigrants, and refugees (Young, 2000, 273). Last but not least, can anyone seriously
imagine a world safe from terrorism without the democratization and
opening up of global banking and trading institutions, such as the International Monetary Fund, the Organization for Economic Cooperation
and Development, the World Bank, and the World Trade Organization?
And can we imagine a world safe from disease, pollution, and ecologi-

cal devastation without full multilateral co-operation on the part of the most powerful nations? Until these reforms are implemented, unconscionable suffering will continue unabated and trust among peoples will remain elusive.

NOTES

1 Among the human rights mentioned by Rawls are "the right to life (to the means of subsistence and security); to liberty (to freedom from slavery, serfdom, and forced occupation, and to a sufficient measure of liberty of conscience to ensure freedom of religion and thought); to property (personal property); and to formal equality as expressed by the rules of natural justice (that is, that similar cases be treated similarly)." Elsewhere Rawls notes that articles 3–18 of the Universal Declaration of Human Rights (1948) detail universal human rights in his sense, whereas article 1, which asserts that "all human beings are born free and equal in dignity and rights," expresses a particular liberal interpretation of human rights (Rawls, 1999, 65, 80).

2 Rawls excludes from the Society of Well-ordered Peoples (i.e., peoples that are guaranteed protection from international sanction) such unreasonable peoples as outlaw states that violate human rights and benevolent dictatorships that respect human rights but deny their citizens a meaningful role in making political decisions. Also excluded are reasonable societies burdened by unfavourable economic or cultural circumstances (4).

Rawls includes in the society decent-consultation hierarchies, in which only some persons are allowed to run for and hold office. Persons choose members of their own group (occupational, religious, and so on) to represent them in an assembly of group representatives but do not vote directly as individuals for government officers. Government leaders (some of whom might be chosen by a clerical hierarchy) consult the higher assembly, balancing fairly the interests of all groups (72).

3 Although Rawls normally talks about a plurality of "opposing" and "irreconcilable" doctrines (1993, 3), he refers occasionally to a "plurality of conflicting and incommensurable doctrines" (135). By "irreconcilable" he seems to mean "uncompromising" (138); "incommensurable," in contrast, suggests that doctrines are incapable of being translated into a common language by which they might be discussed and modified. If so, incommensurability would serve to immunize doctrines from the demands of public accountability. But it is doubtful whether such incommensurability is conceptually coherent, as Donald Davidson and Habermas contend.

4 Contrary to Habermas but in agreement with Rawls, Charles Taylor proposes the idea of "alternative modernities" to capture the different legal forms by which diverse nations will institutionalize universal "norms of action," along with industrial market economies and bureaucratic administrations. He thinks that neither these legal forms nor the specific rationales by which they are justified need refer to "subjective" or "individual" rights in the possessive liberal sense (Taylor, 1996; 1997). For a critique of Taylor's views that is sympathetic to Habermas's position, see McCarthy, 1997.

5 Following Germany's notorious appeal – in justification of its expansionist policies in the late 1930s – to bilateral and multilateral treaty provisions under the League of Nations (granting irredentist Germans living in Poland and Czechoslovakia special privileges and rights), the UN deleted all references to the rights of ethnic and national minorities in its Universal Declaration of Human Rights. Nevertheless, some of the individual rights that it mentions are rights that are typically exercised in groups (see below). Furthermore, the UN has been debating both a Declaration on the Rights of Persons Belonging to National or Ethnic, Religious and Linguistic Minorities (1993) and a draft Universal Declaration on Indigenous Rights (1988).

6 Rawls finds Charles Beitz's "resource redistribution principle" (Beitz, 1979, 137, 141) inconsequential because he thinks that a nation's political culture is more decisive in hindering its capacity to achieve economic independence than its level of resources (Rawls, 1999, 116). He rejects Beitz's "global distribution principle" (Beitz, 1979, 153–163), which applies the difference principle to peoples, because it would penalize unfairly a nation that had voluntarily controlled its population or increased its rate of savings and industrial development in comparison to another nation similarly situated that had chosen not to do so. Rawls is willing to accept Thomas Pogge's global resources tax on resource use (Pogge, 1999), but only if it specifies as its cut-off point the elevation of the world's poorest peoples to the level where their citizens' basic needs are fulfilled and they can stand on their own (119). For criticisms of Pogge's proposal, see Roger Crisp and Dale Jamieson, "Egalitarianism and a Global Resources Tax: Pogge on Rawls" (in Davion and Wolf, 2000, 90–101); and Hillel Steiner, "Just Taxation and International Redistribution" (in Shapiro and Brilmayer, 1999, 171–91).

7 For Buchanan, "states are more or less economically self-sufficient if and only if they can … provide adequately for the material needs of their population … A state is distributionally autonomous if and only if it can determine how wealth is distributed within its borders" (2000, 702).

8 For further discussion of Habermas's ambivalent attitude towards market economies, see Ingram, 2000b.

REFERENCES

Beitz, Charles (1979) *Political Theory and International Relations.* Princeton, NJ: Princeton University Press.

– (2000) "Rawls's Law of Peoples," *Ethics* 110, 669–96.

Buchanan, Allen (2000) "Rawls's Law of Peoples: Rules for a Vanished Westphalian World," *Ethics* 110, 670–721.

Carens, Joseph (1987) "Aliens and Citizens: The Case for Open Borders," *Review of Politics* 49, no. 92, 251–73.

Davion, V., and C. Wolf, eds. (2000) *The Idea of a Political Liberalism.* Lanham, Md.: Rowman and Littlefield.

Habermas, Jurgen (1996) *Between Facts and Norms: Contributions to a Discourse Theory of Law and Democracy.* Cambridge, Mass.: MIT Press.

– (1998a) *The Inclusion of the Other: Studies in Political Theory.* Cambridge, Mass.: MIT Press.

– (1998b), *Die Postnationale Konstellation. Politische Essays.* Frankfurt am Main: Suhrkamp.

Ingram, David (2000a) *Group Rights: Reconciling Equality and Difference.* Lawrence: University Press of Kansas.

– (2000b) "Individual Freedom and Social Equality: Habermas's Democratic Revolution in the Social Contractarian Justification of Law," in L. Hahn, ed., *Perspectives on Habermas.* Chicago: Open Court, 289–308.

– (2003) "Between Political Liberalism and Postnational Cosmopolitanism: Toward an Alternative Theory of Human Rights," *Political Theory,* June.

Kymlicka, Will (1991) *Liberalism, Community and Culture.* Oxford: Oxford University Press.

McCarthy, Thomas (1997) "On Reconciling Cosmopolitan Unity and Multicultural Diversity," *Public Culture* 11, no. 1.

Pensky, Max (2000) "Cosmopolitanism and the Solidarity Problem: Habermas on National and Cultural Identities," *Constellations* 7, no. 1, 64–79.

Pogge, Thomas (1989) *Realizing Rawls.* Ithaca, NY: Cornell University Press.

– (1994) "An Egalitarian Law of Peoples," *Philosophy and Public Affairs* 23, 195–224.

– (1999) "Human Flourishing and Universal Justice," *Social Philosophy* 16, no. 1.

Rawls, John (1971) *A Theory of Justice.* Rev. 1999. Cambridge, Mass.: Harvard University Press.

– (1993) *Political Liberalism.* New York: Cambridge University Press.

– (1999) *The Law of Peoples.* Cambridge, Mass.: Harvard University Press.

Scheffler, S. (1999) "The Conflict between Justice and Responsibility," in Shapiro and Brilmayer, 1999.

Seymour, Michel (1999) "On Redefining the Nation," *Monist* 82, no. 3, 427.

Shapiro, I, and L. Brilmayer, eds. (1999) *Global Justice.* NOMOS XLI. New York: New York University Press.

Shue, Henry (1996) *Basic Rights: Subsistence, Affluence, and U.S. Foreign Policy.* 2nd ed. Princeton, NJ: Princeton University Press.

Taylor, Charles (1996) "A World Consensus on Human Rights?" *Dissent*, summer, 15–21.

– (1997) "Nationalism and Modernity," in R. McKim and J. McMahon, eds., *The Morality of Nationalism.* Oxford: Oxford University Press.

Young, I.M. (2000) *Inclusion and Democracy.* Oxford: Oxford University Press.

KAI NIELSEN

Are Nation-states Obsolete?
The Challenge of Globalization

The bourgeoisie has through its exploitation of the world-market given a cosmopolitan character to production and consumption in every country. To the great chagrin of Reactionists, it has drawn from under the feet of industry the national ground on which it stood. All old-established national industries have been destroyed or are daily being destroyed. They are dislodged by new industries, whose introduction becomes a life-and-death question for all civilized nations, by industries that no longer work up indigenous raw material, but raw material drawn from the remotest zones; industries whose products are consumed, not only at home, but in every quarter of the globe. In place of the old wants, satisfied by the productions of the country, we find new wants, requiring for their satisfaction the products of distant lands and climes. In place of the old local and national seclusion and self-sufficiency, we have intercourse in every direction, universal interdependence of nations.

– *The Communist Manifesto*

If this is not a good description of globalization then what is?

– David Harvey

INTRODUCTION

Economic globalization obtains when transterritorial organizations steer and importantly control the economic structures of the world. We have, in addition to economic globalization, cultural, social, and political globalization when transterritorial organizations on a similar scale steer and importantly control these domains. We have strong globalization – some call it "hyperglobalization" – when these transterritorial organizations so tightly steer and control the economic, cultural, social, and political life of nation-states that they have no feasible way of developing and sustaining policy-options or programs that the peoples of these nation-states might desire as answering to what they regard as being in their interests where they stand in conflict with global economic imperatives conceived as neoliberal capitalism conceives of them. No nation-state, the strong globalist claim goes, can successfully set itself against these imperatives. Nation-states must rather march in lock step to the mandates of these transnational organizations over most fundamental economic, political, social, and cultural matters (Teeple, 1995). With that the autonomy of nation-states is significantly eviscerated.

We have weaker forms of globalization when there is only the extensive influence of these transterritorial organizations limiting, to one degree or another, the capacity of nation-states to determine in these crucial dimensions the direction in which they would go. We have no globalization at all when there are no transterritorial organizations exerting such influence.

There is no dichotomy here and no difference in *kind* between strong and weak globalization. But there are important differences in degree. And we can and do have different conceptualizations of globalization that take it to be a stronger or weaker process in the ways that I have specified. It is clearly the stronger conceptions of globalization that, if instantiated as actual processes in the world or, if these processes have a strong possibility of being instantiated, pose a threat to democracy and to the capacity of nations to be self-determining. But still keep in mind that we have a difference in degree here. Some weak globalizations also could be extensively undermining of the powers of nation-states.

I am concerned here with actually existing globalization and importantly with the trajectory that it may very well take in the near future. Such a globalization is a capitalist globalization and not only that but a neoliberal capitalist globalization. Absent a world-state or a reasonably strong and effective world federation, anything like a Keynesian or neo-Keynesian capitalist globalization seems at least to be impossible. Actually existing globalization or something reasonably close to it, I argue, as have many others, is a threat to democracy and a threat to any nation-state that would be more than a conduit for such a capitalism (Teeple, 1995; Scholte, 1997).

Defenders of weak globalization point out, and rightly, that we do not quite have our neoliberal Brave New World yet. Most multinationals, though transterritorial, are not genuinely transnational, for they are still based in home countries; there are regional trading blocs; most of the world's trading goes on between the rich capitalist states of the North, and much labour is not tradable or mobile. So we are not quite there yet. (For a strong globalist response, see Miyoshi, 1998, 248–50.) But neoliberalism, with its anti-statist ideology and its conception of economic rationality, is seeking to make such a strong globalization a reality, and, as I try to show, there are abundant signs of something like it coming into being. My argument is that actually existing neoliberal globalization, as it stands, and even more so as it is pregnant with becoming, poses a grave threat to democracy and to a reasonable autonomy for nation-states or for that matter for multi-nation-states.

This does not stand in conflict with the cosmopolitan social liberal nationalism that I have defended elsewhere.[1] That, as distinct from what I principally do here, was a bit of normative political theorizing. But ought implies can. Here I raise a problem about the can in effect posed by the challenge of strong globalization. Can nation-states, I ask, given the reality of the global economic order (if there is such a reality), exercise much in the way of effective self-determination?[2]

One further preliminary. I am against capitalist globalization, but not against globalization per se. Barring a nuclear war or some great economic collapse culminating in an extended world-wide depression, globalization, though perhaps tamable, is irreversible. Or at least arguably so. (For some reasons for questioning this, see Weiss, 1997, 1999a, and 1999b.) Moreover, a democratic globalization – a globalization from below rather than from above – and most particularly a thoroughly democratic socialist globalization – would – or so I would argue – be a very good thing indeed. Democracy would not be threatened by such a globalization. Moreover, democracy would not, with the advent of such a socialism, stop, as it does now, at the workplace gate. With democratic control of the workplace, socialism would extend democracy in a far deeper way than can now be achieved in even the best of the social liberal capitalist democracies. But the argument for that is for another time and place.

Here I am concerned with the at least putative challenge to nation-states posed by neoliberal capitalist globalization. We need to take a careful look at such a challenge. I do not want it to be the case, if we can avoid it, that we social liberal nationalists achieve our country only to find it so beholden to global capitalism that our nation-state is little more than a conduit for a neoliberal or some other form of capitalist global economic order.

THE STRONG GLOBALIST CHALLENGE

Strong globalists maintain that there is no rational alternative to a global capitalist order, with the lean and mean social regime that it requires. With new technologies in place, economic markets can transfer cash anywhere at the push of a button. Financial capital, that is, is incredibly mobile. This has changed things for governments and their ability to make policy and most particularly macroeconomic policy. As the *Economist* put it, "when a government makes a false move markets vote against it with ruthless speed" (May 1996, 30). What we increasingly have now, the claim for strong globalization goes, instead of political governance, democratic or undemocratic, is rule by the market with economics not politics in command, or, if not quite "rule by the market," for reasons that Paul Bairoch and Noam Chomsky have made clear, rule by the giant multinationals (Bairoch, 1993; Chomsky, 1998). With the global mobility of financial capital, and to a substantial but lesser degree industrial capital, governments have, and increasingly so, little room to manoeuvre independently of business-driven imperatives, at least where what is substantially at issue effects capital accumulation: the restless and endless search throughout the world for maximum profits. Here where the fundamental direction of the global economy, and national economies as well, is at issue, capitalists, not politicians, have the decisive say. A country, for example, with social-democratic commitments, that taxes corporations highly or by its policies pushes up labour costs, will find the multinationals and other large corporations taking their business elsewhere. Quebec, for example, which has a number of the pharmaceuticals, is forced to have legislation favourable to them, but hardly favourable to consumers, to keep the pharmaceuticals from making the short trip to Ontario or New York or perhaps the longer trip to Taiwan. This is a familiar story that, with minor variations, gets told over and over again all over the world. (*Pace* this, see Therborn, 2000.)

With the globalizing agenda of neoliberalism we have what is in effect, and perhaps in intention, an anti-statist individualistic liberalism distant from the social liberalism of John Dewey and John Rawls. As Paul Hirst and Grahame Thompson put it: "Set free from politics, the new globalized economy allows companies and markets to allocate the factors of production to greatest advantage, and without the distortions of state intervention. Free trade, transnational companies and world capital markets have liberated business from the constraints of politics, and are able to provide the world's consumers with the cheapest and most efficient products ... Business activity is primary and political power has no other task than the protection of the world free-trading system" (Hirst and Thompson, 1996, 176, characterizing, though not defending, this view).

The rich capitalist democracies (most extensively the United States) have deeply apolitical populations (Boggs, 2000). In much of what goes for public discourse politics is marginalized and trivialized. People do not think about politics, have little understanding of the political forces that affect (some would say drive) their lives, and do not care about politics. As Evans, McBride, and Shields put it, "the idea of duly elected governments empowered to manage their own affairs and control their policy agenda within their territorial boundaries – a precondition of democratic governance itself – has been eroded" (Held, 1993; Evans, McBride, and Shields, 1998, 6).

If this picture of globalization is near to being accurate, there is little future for the nation-state or the multi-nation state except as a hand-maiden to help smooth the path for possible development of global capitalism. Is this strong "globalization picture" telling it like it is? Have we with globalization an uncontrollable transnational suprana-tional force against which national governments are impotent?

The claim of strong globalists, as Thomas R. Donahue graphically puts it, is that "the world has become a huge bazaar with nations ped-dling their workforce in competition one against another offering the lowest prices for doing business" (Donahue, 1994, 47). Here we have a race to the bottom under the pressure of an emerging international cap-italist class that is able to bypass the policies, laws, and regulations of nation-states and place irresistible pressures to lower wages, labour standards, and social and environmental regulations across the globe. The claim by strong globalists is that "this new global capitalist order neutralizes the policy capacity of the nation-state which must increas-ingly dance to the tune set by competitive world market forces" (Evans, McBride, and Shields, 1998, 10).

Is this "globaloney," as David Harvey called it, or is it a *realpolitik* telling it like it is? Or is it something in between, to wit, a somewhat hy-perbolic statement of a phenomenon that is very real, and becoming more so everyday, presenting a real and present danger to the viability of a nation-state that would be more than a conduit for global capitalism? Moreover, would it not as well present a threat to the very possibility of their coming into being any form of global "cosmopolitan democracy" that would be more than a conduit for global capitalism?

What is centrally at issue between strong and weak globalization here concerns the type of international economy that exists or is inexorably coming into being. Do we have an economy that is essentially transnational, or do we have an economy that, despite high levels of international trade and investment, is still an economy that is nationally located: an economy in which "nationally located processes and economic actions still remain central"? (Hirst and Thompson, 1996, 176).

COMMON GROUND BETWEEN STRONG AND WEAK GLOBALIZATION

There is some common ground between proponents of strong and weak globalization that should first be noted. What facilitates globalization, whether strong or weak, is 1) financial deregulation following from the abandonment of the Bretton Woods Accord in 1970. With its abandonment we came to have an international economic system that is more volatile, with its accompanying decentralization and with a system that is co-ordinated through the market and not overtly politically controlled as it was in the old Bretton Woods system. 2) The reduction in costs rooted in technological change has collapsed, or at least is collapsing, prior distance and time constraints (Scheuerman, 1999a and 1999b). It is now possible to move information and commodities with a speed and cost-effectiveness that would have hardly even been thinkable a few years back. Financial transfers affecting deeply the economic situation of a whole country can be made practically instantaneously with the pressing of a button. 3) There has been an extensive change in economic organizational and production forms. There has been a geographical dispersal and fragmentation of systems of economic organization, divisions of labour, and specialization of tasks. And this not infrequently, and paradoxically, has been accompanied by increased levels of corporate concentration (Harvey 1995, 1). That these things have occurred is not in dispute, though their depth and extent are disputed.

There are a number of related facts that are also not in dispute: 1) that there has been since the 1980s a rapid growth in world trade, 2) that during the same period foreign direct investment has risen rapidly, 3) that the production of goods and services is occurring in a more international manner, and 4) that less developed nations have increased, though hardly dramatically, their presence in the world economy. Strong globalists think that these facts confirm the emergence of a radically different socioeconomic order. This is the claim that those favouring weak globalization oppose.

What is their case against strong globalization? First, look at the labour force world-wide. While there has been a significant rise in the number of workers engaged in global activity, it remains the case that in the industrialized nations approximately 70 per cent of the labour force is employed in the service sector, and most of this labour is not tradable. In the developing countries, with the pervasiveness there of low-income workers, most employment is still in subsistence farming or other forms of traditional agriculture or (in the urban centres) in informal-sector activities that are for the most part non-tradable. In these developing countries – India and China, for example – under 15 per cent of the workers are engaged in the tradable sector (ILO, World Employment, 1996/97, 5).

Second, consider direct foreign investment. It continues to grow, but it still constitutes only 5 per cent of total world investment (Moody, 1997, 7). And most OECD trade is between members of the OECD themselves rather than with the developing countries. Moreover, "foreign branches of multinational corporations account for about 15 percent of the world's industrial output, while 85 percent is produced by domestic corporations in single geographical locales" (Wood, 1997, 24).

Third, consider the mobility of capital. Financial capital is indeed, as I have noted, very mobile, but industrial capital is less so. Industrial capital is "still far more constrained in its capacity to pick up and move" (Wood, 1997, 24–5). There is going on a great migration of populations, but that notwithstanding "labor as a factor of production is largely immobile" (Evans, McBride, and Shields, 1998, 101).[3] This certainly gives us grounds for believing that it has not become genuinely transnational.

There, fourth, are also problems concerning the ability of current multinational corporations (MNCs) to transform themselves into transnational corporations (Evans, McBride, and Shields, 1998, 10). The MNCs still are home based in distinct countries, and they are integrated into and dependent upon these home-based countries. They are not free-floating transnational corporations. The "ultimate symbol of the global economy – the transnational corporation operating world-wide without any national identity – is still more image than reality: most MNCs continue to have a strong home-country attachment where the majority of assets, employees and decision-makers remain" (Betcherman, 1993, 5). Moreover, most of the MNCs are based in the United States.

Fifth, there is indeed an increase in the number and power of international governmental and non-governmental organizations – for example, the World Bank, the World Trade Organization, the International Momentary Fund. These organizations, without doubt, have become important institutions for helping to manage international economic relations (Evans, McBride, and Shields, 1998, 11). But this does not show, or even legitimately give us to understand, "that there exists a unified international capitalist class or any organization that serves as a kind of capitalist international" (McNally, 1990, 237). We need to realize, as Evans, McBride, and Shields put it, that the "movement towards greater international economic interaction was sponsored by nation-states; they created bodies such as the IMF" (1998, 11). What we need to acknowledge, they claim, is that the nation-state remains "the main conduit through which national (or indeed multinational) capital is inserted into the global market" (Wood, 1997, 28). The major economic powers (the United States, Germany, and Japan) are "particularly important policy actors in shaping the trends and conditions of international trade" (Evans, McBride, and Shields, 1998, 11).

Sixth, and last, we need to consider the actually existing major trading blocs. They show, as clearly as clear can be, that there is no one unified global capitalist system.

Rather than constituting one highly integrated global economy, current economic developments might better be described as the emergence of a tripolar world economic order. The three major economic blocs, namely the European Union (with Germany as the dominant partner), North America (centered on the United States), and the Asian Pacific Rim (focused on Japan), are not designed to operate "as autarkic economic entities, but as large liberalized trading spheres which will serve as launching pads for intensified competition in world markets. The trend towards trading blocs thus embodies elements of both internationalism and protectionism". There is a geographical reorganization of capitalism underway as embodied in these regionalized trading zones; however, this does not imply the end of the nation-state. (Evans, McBride, and Shields, 1998, 11, quoting McNally, 1997, 237; see also Thompson, 2000.)

We have nothing like a global economic union. Again – or so at least it appears – we do not have a global economic order that brushes aside the nation-state as *passé*.

A STRONG GLOBALIST RESPONSE

Is this defence of the viability of nation-states sound? Is weak globalization – or perhaps no globalization at all – the winner over strong globalization? I argue that things are not as settled as the critics of strong
globalization believe. Sometimes their criticisms rest on straw-man
arguments, as when they take strong globalists to be in effect advocating a form of economic determinism and functionalism that, in reality,
though hardly in intent, is a metaphysical account. But there is no such
a priori refutation of strong globalization. Strong globalists need not,
and should not, claim that they are either making any such strong, and
arguably incoherent, contention or presupposing it. What strong globalists are arguing is that they have identified a trend in the way contemporary economies are going and can reasonably be conjectured to
continue to go in an increasingly more intensified and consistent form.
They add, moreover, that this trend (barring some catastrophe such as a
nuclear war) appears at least to be irreversible in a similar empirical
way to that of the tractor replacing the horse in ploughing practices is
irreversible once we have the tractor and stable economic and environmental conditions. We do not have a unified global order in place yet,
the claim goes, but we are getting there.

The claim is that the economies of the world are becoming increasingly integrated and increasingly responsive on a world-wide scale to
the imperatives of neoliberal conceptions of economic rationality and
that with this it is becoming increasingly difficult for nation-states to
steer their own national economies or to develop social polices that are
out of sync with a global neoliberal economic agenda: an agenda that,
in neoliberal ideology at least, is expressive of what "economic
rationality" comes to (Chomsky, 1998).[4] Without courting economic
and with it social disaster, there is, the strong globalist claim goes, no
longer the possibility of delinking national economies and social
policies from the emerging global economy, with its strict neoliberal
economic rationale–dependent imperatives. (See, however, Therborn,
2000.) The strong globalist need not assert that the economies of the
world are yet so strongly integrated, but only that there is an observable

trend going in that direction, that that trend is growing stronger, and that it is probably as a matter of fact irreversible.

What is sensibly at issue here is not metaphysics – some nonsense about historical inevitability – but the *empirical plausibility* of such a strong globalist claim concerning the trajectory of the societies of the world (Popper, 1945; Berlin, 1954).

To claim, as strong globalists do, that the nation-state has lost much of its relevance, and predictably will lose still more with the continued development of global capitalism, is to say that central powers that states once had have been eroded. This is true particularly of welfare states and states approaching welfare states (for example, United States during the Roosevelt era). They have become, with a few honourable exceptions (for example, Sweden and Finland), or are on their way to becoming, servants of global capitalism, things that capitalist non-welfare states more patently are. In the hands of transterritorial systems of organization, nation-states have lost much of the power that the social-democratic ones once had.[5] They are no longer able to set out – or so the strong globalist claim goes – social policies that could make for the well-being of citizens of those states. And this is true in very central areas of their lives. Production to meet basic human needs is an idea that will now not even get on the political agenda. In important areas of our social lives, we have, as political actors, lost control over the direction in which our ship of state can go. What, for the most part, calls the tune, at least in ideology, in our increasingly globalized world, is the imperatives of economic rationality interpreted along neoliberal, economistic lines (Chomsky, 1998). These imperatives and democracy or any vital policy initiatives that a nation-state might venture stand in conflict (Scholte, 1997). And so far at least economistic globalized capitalism is winning out, with states being more and more transformed into facilitators for capitalism.

Evans, McBrides, and Shields resist this. They argue that "while it is true that nation-states have less control over macroeconomic policy, they retain exclusive control over their physical territory and national population – capital may be highly mobile but people and land are not" (1998, 19).

This is an unpersuasive contention. What kind of control do they have over their physical territory and their population when they cannot control health policy, taxation policy, cultural policy, investment policy, trade policy, banking policy, industrial employment policy, and the like? They can put people in jail and in some places execute them, put them in the armed forces, force them to go to school to a certain age, prohibit violence to individuals and property, require them to obey traffic regulations and the like: things that are essentially night-watchman functions, or capital-enhancement functions (for example, capitalism needs a trained, disciplined, and politically passive work-force). And although people are not as mobile as capital, particularly finance capital, still there are increasingly great movements of popula-tions in search of work and security. And if the state prohibits the out-ward flow or inward flow of people, people will still find illegal ways of doing so, and capitalism will not stand opposed (Hobsbawm, 1995).[6] This comes pretty close to being a piddling sovereignty.

There is, however, a second argument that they bring forward: " 'Though nation-states can no longer claim to have an exclusive mo-nopoly on governance, nation-states' are far from irrelevant. 'Even in a liberalized and market-dominated order, public power is crucial to pro-tect property.' Moreover, to maintain financial economic and social sta-bility, some measure of public regulation is essential. 'Stability in the international economy can only be had if states combine to regulate it and to agree on common objectives and standards of governance.' " (Evans, McBride, and Shields, 1998, 19, quoting Hirst and Thompson, 1996, 186–8).

Again, as with the first objection to the claims of strong globalists about the weakening of the nation-state, we have little more here than a state with its night-watchman and capitalist-facilitation powers: a state in the service of capitalism and severely constrained by capitalism's eco-nomic imperatives. Strong globalists argue that we no longer have states, like the old welfare states of the social democracies, functioning both to sustain capitalism and to tame it a bit in the interests of its citi-zenry.[7] Contemporary nation-states, the claim goes, have lost their abil-ity to develop policies answering to the needs and expectations of their citizens. Their sovereignty (if that is what we should call it) is not such that they can stand against the economic forces and devices of global-ized capitalism. Moreover, it is crucial to note the kind of regulation in which they engage. The state's own exercise of regulations is essentially, as F.H. Hayek insists, only to maintain a secure atmosphere for unregu-lated markets. But we have a very minimal state indeed, one whose powers have been so severely curtailed that we in fact have a very weak-ened state. It is hardly a state that can answer to the interests of it citi-zens, a few capitalists apart. There is, for example, no room for social policy – for the state to even consider something like a social wage – or for it to have objectives such as governing for the commonweal.[8] All "the commonweal" that we will get, strong globalizers have it, is what we get from a free-flowing, unregulated market economy. All the state should be concerned with, on this neoliberal conception, is the maintenance of some measure of stability and keeping out of the way of the market. Policy initiatives to secure social welfare will just muck up the market. And in doing so, neoliberals claim, harm the very people that the policies are designed to help.

It is with talk, and the transforming of that talk into reality, of states co-operating to regulate the international economy and to agree on common objectives and standards of governance that would meet the needs of their citizens, that we would get something robust enough to be called an effective nation-state. If some nation-states, working together, can pull this off, they will show some reasonable measure of self-governance. But it is just that kind of state that is anathema to neoliberalism, with its commitment to a global free-market economy constrained only by the imperatives of economic rationality (the maximizing of profit and the minimizing of losses) and by some very weakened version of the rule of law (Scheuerman, 1999a). If states can regulate the economy and come to have common objectives, the neoliberal, market-oriented global economic rules will be undermined. But it is just this neoliberal order that seems at least to be gaining global hegemony, and it cannot, to maintain that hegemony, have such policy-oriented nation-states interfering with the very rationale of a market economy (Teeple, 1995). If we watch the economic actors on the world stage in action, we will see them, again and again, undermining – or trying to undermine – such state formations in order maximally to further capital accumulation operating with unfettered markets. The innovation and freedom that such markets make possible, provide, strong globalizers claim, conditions that would make for the maximum satisfaction of human wants. The economy cannot, to run at maximum efficiency, have states interfering with consumer sovereignty. *Perhaps* this is so – although I for one do not think so – but what is relevant here is that, if this is how things go, we have a radical diminishment of the power of a state to act. And we do not have democracy. Even if (a very dubious if) neoliberalism can deliver consumer sovereignty, that does not add up to democracy.

I turn now to a third argument of Evans, McBride, and Shields: "if the central role of the state in our contemporary world is so diminished, this is not so much due to the inexorable pattern of the restructuring of the global economy on a neo-liberal model as to the political choices made by nation-states and their rulers" (1998, 14).

The active rule of the state, the argument continues, in isolating governance mechanisms and constructing a new state form congruent with a system of neoliberal global capitalism and its free-market imperatives has been masked by neoliberal anti-statist ideology. The states themselves or their leaders are overt actors who, in tune with a neoliberal economic agenda, act in accordance with what they take, or at least proclaim, to be economic rationality (Chomsky, 1998). This is particularly obvious with a global power such as the United States. Some have even gone so far as to say that globalization should be called Americanization (Berndtson, 2000; Hutton and Giddens, 2000). But this view about globalization coming to Americanization aside, a view that I think is a superficial view of the matter, consider Evans, McBride, and Shields's further important argument. "One of the most glaring contradictions associated with this transformative period is that a strong state is a prerequisite to a flexible state as a means of managing the construction of a regime more appropriate to the new conditions. To accomplish this successfully political leaders now require a strengthening of the political arm of the government if they are to cope with the demands of the transformed political systems they must govern. The state's more coercive hand must be sufficiently strengthened to enable it to effectively resist and counteract the 'democratic pressures' seeking to prevent the dismantling of the protective welfare state, in order that the neo-liberal goal of market dominance can be realized" (1998, 19, quoting Aucoin, 1995, 126). They conclude, "Freed from the 'self denying ordinance' of neo-liberal anti-statism, the nation-state could play a much stronger role, operating at a variety of levels, in controlling the impact of international markets" (1998, 19).

This conclusion might be right. Indeed I think it is. But it certainly does not follow from the fact, if it is a fact, that it was the actions of leaders of nation-states and their capitalist cohorts that brought about, in line with neoliberal imperatives, the diminishment of nation-state sovereignty, that this shows that the nation-state is sustained and remains viable, anymore than the fact that Gorbachev, a communist, brought about the demise of an oligarchic Soviet Communism shows that Soviet Communism is viable. A strong nation-state might be necessary to bring about a neoliberal minimal state with the powers of the strong nation-state passing to transnational institutions. However, only if such strong nation-states are necessary not only to bring about a neoliberal minimal state, but that we need a strong state to continue to sustain the minimalist state in that very society, do we get the contradiction of which Evans McBride, and Shields speak – namely, that we require a strong state that is not a strong state. While they give evidence that it was often state actors who brought about, in the near term at least, the neoliberal minimal state, they give no evidence at all that such a strong state – a state having more than night-watchman and capitalism-facilitating powers – is necessary, once the neoliberal state is securely in place, to sustain it and to give people who live in such a regime a sense of its viability.[9] What they claim might be so, but we have been given no reason to believe that it is. What is plausible to believe is that strong state actors are necessary to bring about such a neoliberal social order and in the short term to sustain it, but, as neoliberal ideology becomes very thoroughly socialized into people – into the citizenry generally – such a strong state may no longer be necessary. After years of the tides of neoliberal ideology running high, neoliberal minimal states arguably "will seem to just come naturally," to be thought of as the way things are and must be if we are to live at all rationally. Or perhaps even, "rationally or not," with cynicism setting in, this will pervasively be taken to be the way things are and must be. Anything else will be taken to be a spitting into the wind. There will be no need to have a state form where we have a state that is at the same time and in the same important respects both a strong state and a weak one: one that at one and the same time determines social policy and does not. But there is no need for the strong globalist to make that incoherent claim. What we might have – such a notion is not incoherent and may well be true – is the need for a strong state at time $T1$ to usher in a weak state at time $T2$.

CONCLUSION

My brief has been to argue that it is not unreasonable to believe that globalization is becoming sufficiently strong so as to require us seriously to consider whether nation-states have, or even can have, given capitalist globalization sufficient control over their affairs so as to justify our believing that they have the power to provide the conditions of life where we can flourish and live in a social order that is self-determining (Scholte, 1997). I do not now know enough – and perhaps I never shall – to be able to say what is warrantedly assertable here. Perhaps no one does? But I do say that we should not dismiss the above claim about the obsolesence of socially oriented nation-states as just a potful of neoliberal ideology or to treat it as involving an "unanswerable question," although perhaps it poses a question that needs to be focused into a more precise question to have a determinate answer.

One short coda. It should be obvious from "my logical tone of voice" (to adopt Gilbert Ryle's metaphor) that I do not much like what I have called strong globalization, to wit neoliberal capitalist globalization. I think that it would, if it obtained, be a disaster for us. The world that we live in is already a moral wilderness. And such globalization would just make the moral wilderness even denser, darker, and more encompassing. But to come to grips with that has not been my task here, but trying to keep our heads out of the sand, to point to the challenge that neoliberal capitalist globalization poses for us. We should not blinker ourselves concerning its threat or to the disasters that it would bring to us, and we should resolutely and intelligently look for strategies of resistance and overcoming: something that will enable us to create a better world than capitalism, and the distinctive globalization that is its contemporary form, yields.

NOTES

1 Kai Nielsen, 1996–9, 1998, 1998–99, 1999–2000; Kai Nielsen, with Jocelyne Couture and Michel Seymour, 1996.

2 For careful arguments that there is no such a reality, see Hirst and Thompson, 1996, and Thompson, 2000.

3 See here, 2000, 13, and Bauman, 1998, 77–127.

4 In coming to see how neoliberalism works, we must distinguish between the ideology of neoliberalism and actually existing neoliberalism. As Paul Bairoch, 1993, and Noam Chomsky, 1998, have argued, there is a gulf here between ideology and practice. The ideology is all about unregulated free markets with no state guidance, protection, or intervention allowed. The reality is the practice of strong protectionism for the powerful states, at least until they have gained secure hegemony, and "free markets" for the poor or poorer and vulnerable or more vulnerable states. British capitalism prospered and grew stronger by protection from, for example, Indian and Egyptian goods and by compelling in the eighteenth-century deindustrialization of India. The United States did much the same thing by imposing prohibitively high tariffs on British steel and British textiles. Japan did similar things. The capitalist countries that became developed countries were precisely the ones that did not follow free-market practices.

5 This neoliberal thesis is very similar to a Marxist thesis about the state. But I think that the Marxist thesis, which only partly applied in former times, perhaps now, because of the way capitalist globalization affects our lives, applies with added force. It is an irony of the twists and turns of our thought how strong globalists committed to a neoliberal agenda espouse in a bald form a vulgarization of a classical Marxist thesis.

6 That in the present situation the flow of populations is as extensive as it is claimed above or as Hobsbawm claims has been challenged empirically. It, the counter goes, is mainly well-trained professionals in demand in the various economies who have such mobility (Bauman, 1998, 77–127; Sivanandan, 2000, 13). Even if this is true, this is a temporary slowing down. Given their demographics, all the rich capitalist democracies, with their declining populations, will in a very little while need massive numbers of immigrants to keep their economies stable.

7 For a plausible empirical challenge to this, which is also a challenge to Gray's flat assertion that social democracies are not sustainable, see Therborn, 2000.

8 But for some strong arguments that things may not be that dismal for First Way social democracies (such as Finland and Sweden), as distinct from Third Way "social democracies" (such as Britain and New Zealand), see Therborn, 2000. This runs strongly against a major claim of Gray, 1999.

9 It may be, as Gray argues, that the neoliberal state will never be securely in place over any length of time (1999).

REFERENCES

Aucoin, Peter (1995) "Politicians, Public Servants and Public Management: Getting Government Right," in B. Roy Peters and Donald J. Savoie, eds., *Governance in a Changing Environment*. Montreal: McGill-Queen's University Press, 115–32.

Bairoch, Paul (1993) *Economics and World History*. Chicago: University of Chicago Press.

Barkins, Joanne (2000) "Reply to Goodhart," *Dissent* (summer), 86–8.

Bauman, Zygmant (1998) *Globalization: The Human Consequences*. New York: Columbia University Press.

Berlin, Isaiah (1954) *Historical Inevitability*. London: Oxford University Press.

Berndtson, Erkki (2000) "Globalization as Americanization," in Henri Goverde et al., eds., *Power in Contemporary Politics*. London: Sage Publications, 155–69.

Betcherman, Gordon (1993) *Labour in a More Global Economy*. Ottawa: Office of International Affairs, Human Resources and Labour Canada.

Blair, Tony, and Gerhard Schroeder (2000) "The Third Way/Die Neue Mitte," *Dissent* (spring), 51–65.

Boggs, Carl (2000) *The End of Politics*. New York: Guilford Press.

Bond, Patrick (1997) "Globalization and Social Change in South Africa," *Socialist Studies Bulletin*, no. 47, 54–75.

Bromley, Simon (1996) "Globalization?" *Radical Philosophy*, no. 80, 2–5.

Chomsky, Noam (1998) "Free Trade and Free Market: Pretense and Practice," in Frederic Jameson and Masao Miyoshi, eds., *The Cultures of Globalization*. Durham, NC: Duke University Press, 356–70.

Cohen, G.A. (1978) *Karl Marx's Theory of History: A Defense*. Oxford: Clarendon Press.

– (1988) *History, Labour, and Freedom*. Oxford: Clarendon Press.

Couture, Jocelyne (2000) "Cosmopolitan Democracy and Liberal Nationalism," in Nenad Miscevic, ed., *Nationalism and Ethnic Conflict: Philosophical Perspectives*. La Salle, Ill.: Open Court, 261–82.

Donahue, Thomas R. (1994) "International Labour Standards: The Perspective of Labour," In *International Labour Standards and Global Economic Integration: Proceedings of a Symposium*. Washington, DC: U.S. Department of Labour.

Evans, Mitchell B., Stephen McBride, and John Shields (1998) "National Governance versus Globalization: Canadian Democracy in Question," *Socialist Studies Bulletin*, no. 54, 5–26.

Foot, Philippa (1978) *Virtues and Vices*. Berkeley: University of California Press.

Frost, Rainer (1999) "Transcultural Human Rights," *Constellations* 6, 35–60.

Glyn, Andrew, and Bob Sutcliffe (1992) "Global but Leaderless? The New Capital World Order," *Socialist Register*, 134–83.

Goodhart, David (2000) "Having It All," *Dissent* (summer), 83–5.

Gray, John (1999) *False Dawn*. London: Granta Books.

Harvey, David (1995) "Globalization in Question," *Rethinking Marxism* 8, no. 4, 1–10.

Hayek, Friedrich A. (1944) *The Road to Serfdom*. London: Routledge and Kegan Paul.

Held, David (1993) "Democracy from City-States to a Cosmopolitan Order," in David Held, ed., *Prospects for Democracy: North, South, East, West*. Stanford: Stanford University Press.

Hirst, Paul, and Grahame Thompson (1996) *Globalization in Question: The International Economy and the Possibilities of Governance*. Cambridge: Polity Press.

Hobsbawm, Eric (1995) "Ethnicity Migration and the Validity of the Nation-State," in Michael Walzer, ed., *Toward a Global Civil Society*. Oxford: Berghahn Brooks, 235–40.

– (1998) "The Nation and Globalization," *Constellations* 5, no 1, 1–9.

Hutton, Will, and Anthony Giddens (2000) "Is Globalization Americanization?" *Dissent* (summer), 58–63.

Kumar, Chandra (2000) "Power, Freedom, Ideology and Explanation: A Marxian View." PhD dissertation, University of Toronto.

Kymlicka, Will (1998) *Finding Our Way: Rethinking Ethnocultural Relations in Canada*. Toronto: Oxford University Press.

Lamora, Stephen (1989) "Is There Customary International Economic Law?" *German Yearbook of International Law* 32, 10–25.

Levine, Andrew (1981) *Liberal Democracy: A Critique of Its Theory*. New York: Columbia University Press.

McNally, David (1990) *Political Economy and the Rise of Capitalism: A Reinterpretation*. Berkeley: University of California Press.

– (1997) "Beyond Nationalism, beyond Protectionism: Labour and the Canada–US Free Trade Agreement," *Capital and Class* (spring), 230–43.

– (1998) "Globalization, Trade Pacts and Working Class Resistance," *Socialist Studies Bulletin*, no. 53, 22–37.

Miyoshi, Masao (1998) "'Globalization,' Culture, and the University," in Fredric Jameson and Masao Miyoshi, eds., *The Cultures of Globalization*. Durham, NC: Duke University Press, 247–70.

Moody, Kim (1997) *Workers in a Lean World: Unions in the International Economy*. London: Verso.

Mooers, Colin (1998) "Can We Still Resist? Globalization, Citizenship Rights and Class Formation," *Socialist Studies Bulletin* no. 53, 38–53

Nielsen, Kai (1982) "Political Violence," *Indian Political Science Review* 16, 165–78.

– (1990) "State Authority and Legitimation," in Paul Harris, ed., *On Political Obligation*. London: Routledge, 218–51.

– (1992) "Global Justice, Capitalism and the Third World," in Robin Attfield and Barry Wilkens, eds., *International Justice and the Third World*. London: Routledge, 17–34.

– (1996–97) "Cultural Nationalism, Neither Ethnic Nor Civic," *Philosophical Forum* 28, nos. 1–2, 42–52.

– (1998) "Is Global Justice Impossible?" *Res Publica* 4, no. 2, 131–66.

– (1998) "Liberal Nationalism, Liberal Democracies, and Secession," *University of Toronto Law Journal* 28, 253–95.

- (1998–99) "Cosmopolitanism, Universalism and Particularlism in an Age of Nationalism and Multiculturalism," *Philosophic Exchange*, 4–39.
- (1999) "Cosmopolitan Nationalism," *Monist* 82, no. 2, 446–68.
- (1999–2000) "Nationalism, Socialism and the Case of Quebec," *Arena Journal* new series no. 14, 83–98.
- (2001) "Socialism and Egalitarian Justice." *Windsor Yearbook of Access to Justice*, forthcoming.

Nielsen, Kai, with Jocelyne Couture and Michel Seymour (1996) "Liberal Nationalism Both Cosmopolitan and Rooted," in Jocelyne Couture et al., *Rethinking Nationalism*. Calgary: University of Calgary Press, 579–663.

Popper, Karl (1945) *The Open Society and Its Enemies, Vol. II*. London: Routledge & Kegan Paul.

Putnam, Hilary (1990) *Realism with a Human Face*. Cambridge, Mass.: Harvard University Press.

Rawls, John (1999) *The Law of Peoples*. Cambridge, Mass.: Harvard University Press.

Robinson, Jan (1993) "North American Free Trade As If Democracy Mattered." Ottawa and Washington, DC: Canadian Centre for Policy Alternatives and International Labour Rights Education and Research Fund.

Roemer, John E. (1994) *A Future For Socialism*. Cambridge, Mass.: Harvard University Press.

Rorty, Richard (1998) *Against Bosses, against Oligarchies: A Conversation with Richard Rorty*. Charlottesville, Va.: Prickly Pear Pamphlets.

Scheuerman, William E. (1999a) "Corporations against the Rule of Law," *Constellations* 6, no. 1, 3–25.

- (1999b) "Globalization, Exceptional Powers and the Erosion of Liberal Democracy," *Radical Philosophy* 93, 14–23.

Scholte, Jan Aart (1997) "Global Capitalism and the State," *International Affairs* 73, 427–53.

Schweickart, David (1993) *Against Capitalism*. Cambridge: Cambridge University Press.

Sivanandan, Ambalavaner (1997) "Capitalism, Globalization, and Epochal Shifts," *Monthly Review* 8, no. 9, 19–23

- (2000) "Casualties of Globalism," *Manchester Guardian Weekly* 163, no. 8, 13.

Teeple, Gary (1995) *Globalization and the Decline of Social Reform*. Toronto: Garamond Press.

Therborn, Göran (2000) "Social Democracy in One Country?" *Dissent*, 59–65.

Thompson, Grahame (2000) "Economic Globalization?" in David Held, ed., *A Globalizing World? Culture, Economics, Politics*. London: Routledge, 85–126.

Weiss, Linda (1997) "Globalization and the Myth of the Powerless State," *New Left Review*, no. 225, 3–27.

– (1999a) "Globalization and National Governance: Antinomy or Interdependence?" *Review of International Studies* 23, no. 5, 59–88.

– (1999b) "Managed Openness beyond Neo-liberal Globalism," *New Left Review*, no. 228, 126–40.

Wood, Ellen Meiksins (1997) "A Reply to A. Sivanandan: 'Globalization' or 'Globaloney'?" *Monthly Review* 8, no. 9, 23–5.

AVISHAI MARGALIT

Global Decency

Can humanity at large constitute a decent society – that is, a society whose institutions do not humiliate people? I make a distinction between a decent and a civilized society. In a civilized society, people do not humiliate one another. In a decent society, the stress is on the behaviour of institutions rather than on personal relations. So my question about a potentially decent society is really about developing global, world-wide, non-humiliating institutions. (For an extensive discussion, see Margalit, 1996.)

In describing a decent society as non-humiliating, I use "humiliation" in a rather strong sense – in the sense not of lowering one's *social* position in one's own eyes, as well as in those of others, but of lowering one's position of being human. Treating humans as machines or as "numbers," treating them as beasts or sub-humans or permanent children, are some of the ways to injure their human dignity. Could or should humanity at large form a non-humiliating society?

An air of tautology may seem to attach to the question whether humanity should treat each of its members as a human being. How else should it treat its members? But humanity is not a society. The individuals who constitute the aggregate called humanity do not interact enough, or in sufficiently systematic ways, to turn such an aggregate into a society with state-like institutions. Our cosmos is not enough of a body-polity to constitute a cosmopolitan reality. There are of course extensive international relations and institutions, as well as expanding transnational relations and organizations, but there are no cosmopolitan relations and institutions. Thus to talk about turning humanity into a decent society is to put the cart before the horses. The right order of the question is: should we turn humanity into a society with full-fledged institutions? In short, should we strive to create a cosmopolitan reality?

One argument for doing so is that in order to make the world safe for human dignity and free from humiliation, we should constitute a political society based on the single morally relevant attribute – being human. Only humanity at large is a society that meets this moral condition. Parochially charged labels such as "tribe", "class," "sect," and "nation" usually turn classifications into conflicts, labels into moral liability. Local political labels are not neutral as to what falls under the label and what falls out of it: there is a strong tendency to turn labels into distinctions between friends and foes.

In politics, as in negative theology, participants understand the negation – who they are *not* – better than who they are. The stress on negation for the sake of self-understanding may turn the other into an enemy. And on that slippery slope the enemy may become non-human. Divisive labels produce dehumanization, usually through demonization. (Witness the recent cases of Serbia and of East Timor.) If this is true, the only safeguard against the perils of parochial political labelling – cruelty and humiliation – is to establish a society based on the single non-exclusionary label, of being a human being. The idea is not that there is safety in large numbers, but that the only label that qualifies one to belong to the human commonwealth is the very label that the decent society tries to protect – namely, being human.

On this argument there is an internal relation between the idea of the decent society as a non-humiliating society and the idea of the cosmopolitan society that comprises all human beings under the label of human beings. The appropriate version of cosmopolitanism is very strong – it comes at the expense of all political organizations based on exclusionary labels.

The appeal to humanity as a safeguard against humiliation requires hedging. An ideology that appeals to "true" humanity can exclude some real people as parasites, and thus as sub-humans. Bolshevism was such an ideology. It was universalistic and used strong exclusionary labelling in the name of true humanity, exemplified only by the working class. For humanity to be a safeguard against exclusion, it should be taken not in a normative sense, but simply as humanity as it is. Where there are Ubermenschen, there are Untermenschen too.

The argument that I present for cosmopolitanism as a foundation for attaining a society that does not humiliate, while not the same as Immanuel Kant's for cosmopolitanism as a condition for administering justice universally, is Kantian in spirit. A decent society for me is second best to a just society. And if we need cosmopolitanism for the stable, decent society, we need it so much more for the just society.

Cosmopolitanism is, I believe, a noble idea. It appeals to the best in us. But is it also a good idea? The idea of the decent society is governed by a sense of urgency and by political realism. We should not conflate urgency with significance. To have a just society is more important than to have a decent society, but less urgent. Stopping cruelty, in the sense of physical cruelty, is even more urgent than stopping humiliation. Urgency means calling for immediate attention and action. Making establishment of a decent society depend on the creation of a world-state first is not a way of responding to the urgency of stopping institutional humiliation. Even if a cosmopolitan society is a better foundation for the creation of a decent society, it is colossally unrealistic.

What is needed for the idea of the decent society is political realism, which means scrupulous attention to what is possible in a foreseeable future – given the knowledge that in the long run we shall all be dead. No matter how extensive globalism becomes, Kantian cosmopolitanism, in my judgment, is not in the cards. Urgency is not in and of itself an argument against aspiring and working towards such a society, but it is an argument for not making the decent society depend on creating a world-state as a pre-condition for a decent society. After I outline two puzzles concerning the decent society, I turn to the crucial question – intervention.

TWO PUZZLES

The idea of the decent society, especially that of the world as a decent society, is puzzling on two counts. First, what does it mean to treat the other as human? We know vaguely what it means to treat someone as a carpenter, as a churchgoer, as a citizen, and even as a mother of two children, but what does it mean to treat him or her as a human being? Treating someone as a human being is a by-product of treating him or her as a carpenter, churchgoer, and so on. Treating them also as human seems to have no independent content of its own. Second, and even more troubling, humanity consists of too many cultures that differ widely and wildly from each other for us to believe in a universal notion of what it is to be human. And adding enigma to our puzzles, how can we justify imposing any parochial notion of universal humanity on a cosmopolitan society? Isn't Kantian cosmopolitanism a mere manifestation of the moral imperialism of the Enlightenment? It is benign to be sure, but imperialism all the same.

The two puzzles are connected. It is far from clear what makes up the treatment of the other as a human being. At the minimum it means respecting others' rights, no matter who they are. This is a possible gloss on treating the other as human. My account of a decent society is a negative one. We may be unsure about what treating others as humans entails, but we know all too well what treating them as non-human – i.e., humiliating them – consists of. Even respecting the human rights of others should be construed negatively: we know what violations of human rights look like better than we know what respecting them consists of, or even than what human rights are.

So I base my account of the decent society on the idea of avoiding institutional humiliation rather than on recognizing humans as humans. Humiliation, I submit, has a wider scope than the violation of human rights. Humiliation has to do with gestures and with symbolic acts and, in general, with acts that call for cultural interpretation. But then we have to take into account that there are many cultures and that they may render humiliation very differently. Take an insulting gesture that Europeans are very familiar with: the act of holding the hand up to the nose so that the thumb touches the tip of the nose with fingers spread out, pointing forwards. This insult, the shrewd observer Desmond Morris tells us, is perhaps the best known in Europe. Europeans tend to believe that it is universal. But It is not so. In Tunisia, for example, it is unknown.

Shouldn't such a trivial example warn us against making humiliation, insult, mockery, and so on into universal notions? Not quite. Tunisians may use different gestures to insult people, as they use abusive terms that differ linguistically from ours, but this does not mean that our notion of humiliation is alien to them. While manifestations of humiliation are indigenous to a culture, the very notion of humiliation travels well and crosses cultural boundaries quite easily. So I do not take the variety of cultures as an obstacle to promoting the notion of the decent society, be it on a retail basis, in each society, or on a wholesale, global scale.

INTERVENTION

There is a question that I find morally urgent and politically germane, given an ever-expanding social and economic world, and it involves something more down to earth than the idea of cosmopolitanism. It is couched in international terms: is humiliation a solid ground for international intervention in the internal affairs of a sovereign state? By intervention I mean not exerting influence but rather violating the territorial integrity of the humiliating state.

The moral pendulum in international relations is at the moment swinging towards more intervention. Once there was a time when empires did not have to justify their expansions and interventions. Glory and self-interest were self-evident motives for such behaviour. The modern age of imperialism used the spreading of civilization as such justification, meaning the injection of "superior" culture into inferior natives, usually with the right doses of Christianity and by a "superior" – i.e., white – race. It took these palliatives to justify intervention and domination. The process whereby the "mother country" gives up its colonies and grants them the status of sovereign state – in short, decolonization – resulted partly from rising awareness that colonialism is a strong form of humiliation. The status of unassailable sovereignty was an expression of the idea that the former colonized people are responsible human beings who are entitled to run their own lives and make their own mistakes, free from the paternalism of their former masters.

Against the background of decolonization, the pendulum swung vigorously towards non-intervention in the "internal affairs" of independent states. But "internal affairs," often covered up acts of brutal cruelty and humiliation in countries freed from colonialism. Former-colonial states find themselves in a double bind: when others interfere, it invokes the evil spirit of humiliation from the past; when they do not, horrendous behaviour, including genocide, ethnic cleansing, torture, and systematic humiliation, may result.

The troubling history of colonialism created a strong presumption against intervention. A presumption – like that of innocence in criminal law – can be rebutted. And I believe that in the case of serious physical cruelty and destruction the presumption should not just be rebutted but reversed altogether and turned into a presumption for intervention, where the burden of proof is on those who oppose it. Preventing cruelty should be the top political priority. Stopping humiliation comes second.

In cases of humiliation, I maintain, unlike in cases of cruelty, where the presumption transforms itself into one in favour of intervention, there is no presumption either way. The presumption is altogether cancelled, and the issue of intervention should be dealt with on the merits of each case, on the balance of reason for or against intervention.

The urgent issue is not cosmopolitanism for the sake of decency, but interventionism.

PART TWO
Case Studies: Multinational Societies and Nation-states

MATTHEW EVANGELISTA

Will Russia Go the Way
of the Soviet Union?

The first effect of centralization ... is to make any kind of indigenous character
in the diverse regions of the country disappear ... all of the provincial and
municipal freedoms are confiscated to benefit the supreme power that is the
government.
  – Pierre-Joseph Proudhon, *La Fédération et L'Unité en Italie*, 1862[1]

The state lies, it is unable to offer any cogent policies or enforce its decisions.
But citizens still believe in the state.
  – Representative of a non-governmental organization in Pskov, 1999[2]

In August 1990 President Boris Yeltsin travelled to Kazan', capital of Tatarstan, to urge local authorities to "take as much autonomy as you can
swallow."[3] Ten years later, newly elected President Vladimir Putin visited
the same city during a festival and dunked his head into a bucket of fer-
mented mare's milk as part of a local folk ritual. But he was not swallow-
ing any of his predecessor's pro-autonomy rhetoric. Propelled into office
by popular support for revival of war against the separatist republic of
Chechnya, Putin pledged from the start to bring the rest of the regions
into line as well. Though a noticeable departure from Yeltsin's laissez-
faire approach, Putin's intention to strengthen the centre at the expense of
the regions was hardly unprecedented. His stated views were consistent
with those of most of the prime ministers who served under Yeltsin, as
well as of national political leaders across the spectrum.

Russian leaders' preoccupation with the weakness of the centre vis-à-vis the regions is part of the explanation for the outbreak of two brutal wars in Chechnya. Yeltsin evidently believed that he had gone too far in his rhetorical embrace of regional autonomy. He tried to draw the line at Chechnya. For Putin, who insisted on rebuilding a strong state, regaining Russian control over Chechnya was the sine qua non of statehood, defined in Weberian terms as the monopoly of force over a given territory.

Putin's attempt to recentralize Russia and do away with Yeltsin's legacy of "asymmetric federalism" could prove counterproductive – reintroducing authoritarian methods but without improving the quality of life, which has been a key source of legitimacy for post-Soviet governments. An alternative to Putin's approach would require the recognition that ruling the world's largest country from a single capital city is unrealistic. Some form of genuine federalism, perhaps still a negotiated, asymmetric federalism, is Russia's best hope.

The worst-case scenario for Boris Yeltsin and Vladimir Putin was a breakup of the Russian Federation along the lines of what happened to the Soviet Union. That country was also nominally a federation, consisting of 15 so-called union republics, and when it collapsed each one of them became an independent country. The Russian Federation is far more complicated, and its disintegration would be far messier.

As a federation, Russia consists of 89 "subjects," in a wide diversity of sizes and political designations. They include 49 provinces (*oblasti*), 21 ethnically defined republics, 6 territories (*kraia*), 11 ethnically defined autonomous districts (*okrugi*) and provinces located within Russian-majority *kraia* or *oblasti*, and 2 cities (Moscow and St Petersburg).[4] Some "subjects" are large enough to be independent countries. Tatarstan and Bashkortostan, for example, have populations greater than seventy member states of the United Nations, including such countries as Panama, Ireland, and New Zealand.[5]

Unlike the Soviet Union, however, where barely half the population was Russian, some 80 per cent of the Russian Federation's citizens are ethnic Russians. Perhaps another 8 or 9 per cent identify themselves culturally as Russian, with Russian as their first or only language. David Laitin captured the picture well with the Russian ditty, "*Mama tatarka, otets grek, a ia russkii chelovek*" – "My mom's a Tatar, my father's a Greek, and I'm a Russian."[6] Given the predominance of Russians and Russian speakers throughout the federation, people concerned about separatism have focused on the 21 republics, even though they constitute just

28.6 per cent of the country's territory and 15.2 per cent of its population.[7] For the pessimists, Chechnya's declaration of independence, and the war that followed, sounded the tocsin of the federation's demise.

This chapter reviews Russian approaches to federalism since the demise of the Soviet Union. The first section outlines two aspects of Boris Yeltsin's presidency: the impact of the first war in Chechnya and the impact of Yeltsin's policies. It then considers Vladimir Putin's project: regional reform, the recent decline in regions' self-confidence, and Putin's system of super-regions – headed mainly by former KGB officers, police, and military officials. These super-regions, I argue, put individual rights and regional autonomy at risk without providing compensating improvements in overall quality of life.

THE YELTSIN YEARS

The Chechen Brush-fire

Boris Yeltsin explained the 1994 invasion of Chechnya as necessary to maintain the territorial integrity of the Russian Federation and prevent further secessions. Vladmir Putin made the same case to justify renewal of the war in 1999. Yet when Russian army forces began attacking Chechnya in December 1994, they seemed more likely to precipitate the further loss of much of the Russian North Caucasus than the reintegration of Chechnya.

Opposition to Moscow's invasion was immediate and widespread throughout Russian society, but particularly along the invasion route and even within the armed forces themselves. As the Russian armoured columns advanced through Ingushetiia and Dagestan they were constantly blocked by crowds of civilians, including women and children. Snipers shot at Russian tanks and armoured personnel carriers and were in turn attacked by Russian helicopters.[8]

The widespread, sometimes violent opposition to the Russian invasion of Chechnya led many observers – politicians, military leaders, and scholars – to make dire predictions about the future integrity of the Russian Federation. Galina Starovoitova, leader of the Democratic Russia party, and a former adviser to Yeltsin on ethnic affairs, predicted that Russia's resort to force would "produce mistrust of the centre's policy and centrifugal tendencies in Tatarstan, Bashkortostan, Yakutia, Karelia," and other parts of the Russian Federation. Colonel-General Eduard Vorob'ev, a Russian army officer who resigned his command in

December 1994 rather than lead the ill-prepared invasion of Chechnya, also offered a gloomy prognosis: "Russia has lost in every respect in Chechnya: politically, militarily, morally. Russia has more than a hundred ethnic groups. Will it resolve all disputes through force?" A Russian scholar summarized a common view – that Chechen secession could set a dangerous precedent: "the 'brush-fire' of drives for independence may pick up elsewhere across Russia, leading to the eventual destruction of Russian territorial integrity."[9]

But the drive for independence did not spread, despite the damage that Russia inflicted on itself by its brutal, ultimately futile, use of military force. In the wake of nearly two years of devastating warfare and wholesale destruction of Grozny and many other Chechen villages and towns, one could understand why leaders of Russia's regions might deem the cost of Chechnya's seeming independence too high. As an official from Tatarstan told me in November 1998, the "lessons of Chechnya should be a warning to everybody" – "to radicals in Tatarstan or any other republic, to radicals in Russia, governmental or nongovernmental radicals" – that military conflict between the centre and the regions "should not be repeated in any form." He maintained that "too big a price was paid in Chechnya" on both sides.[10]

Yet, even without the negative example of Chechnya's destruction in the first war, and even through Russia reneged on its subsequent commitment to peaceful negotiation of the republic's future, the prospects for a "brush-fire" of independence movements was never great. Nevertheless, the Chechen example has proved a potent one for justifying the efforts of Boris Yeltsin, and especially of his successor, Vladimir Putin, to recentralize the Russian state and limit the rights of the regions.

Yeltsin's Legacy

In 1990 Yeltsin was president of a Russian republic still formally part of the Soviet Union. He seemed so intent on rattling his rival, Soviet President Mikhail Gorbachev, that he was willing to fan the flames of separatist sentiment in order to do so. Once he had helped destroy the Soviet Union and emerged as leader of an independent Russia, Yeltsin still faced serious political opposition – this time from the Russian parliament. In October 1993 he disbanded the parliament by military force and then sought to remove regional leaders who had supported the opposition. But overall his message to the regions, especially those that had remained loyal, only served to encourage their aspirations for further autonomy: "The regions have to deal with their own problems on their own, by, among other things, raising their own status." He acknowledged that "the government has no coherent regional policy."[11] Yeltsin's approach led to a situation of "asymmetrical federalism," with regions seeking to establish special privileges vis-à-vis the central government, particularly in tax collection and control and sale of natural resources.

Yeltsin's indulgence of the regions, especially the national republics (with the glaring exception of Chechnya), owed less to ideological conviction than to political and economic expediency. He turned a blind eye to regional leaders who engaged in fraud and other undemocratic means to maintain their power, as long as they supported his political aspirations – particularly his re-election campaign in 1996. Under Yeltsin the federal government signed "treaties" with many of Russia's 21 ethnically defined and self-styled sovereign republics to govern matters such as taxation and trade that normally would have fallen under the purview of routine domestic (federal) legislation. Moscow's concessions to rich industrial powerhouses such as Tatarstan and Bashkortostan seemed driven by weakness. Better to give them some benefits than to risk provoking further separatist tendencies. Better to allow the relatively wealthy "donor" regions to keep a substantial portion of their tax revenues than to risk receiving none to redistribute among the vast majority of poorer regions – particularly if the central government lacked the means for efficient taxation anyhow.

Political and economic incentives motivated the regional leaders as well in their contribution to the evolution of asymmetric federalism. Figures such as Tatarstan's president, Mintimer Shaimiev, used the threat of radical separatism to extract more resources from the centre and used those resources to buy off the separatist opposition. Tatarstan's ambiguous status bolstered his own position. In the wake of the financial crisis of August 1998, Tatarstan sought improved relations with the centre; its representatives in Moscow seemed committed to working with the government, for example, to reconcile major discrepancies between the constitutions of the Russian Federation and the Tatar Republic.[12] At the same time Shaimiev began to exhibit ambitions for a national political role, as a leader of the All Russia–Fatherland bloc.

Whatever conciliatory effect the crisis of August 1998 had on formerly recalcitrant regions, it was not enough to satisfy central government officials. In September, newly appointed Prime Minister Evgenii Primakov insisted that his "government must first and foremost pay special attention to preserving Russia as a single state ... We are facing a serious threat of disintegration of our country."[13] In January 1999, anticipating the language that Putin would use just months later, Primakov called for the "restoration of the vertical state power structure, where all matters would be solved jointly by the centre and local authorities" and insisted that separatist trends "must be quelled, liquidated, and uprooted."[14] Primakov did not remain in office long enough to carry out that agenda. It was left to his successor, Vladimir Putin, to relaunch a brutal war against Chechnya in August 1999 and, once elected president in March 2000, to begin an ambitious reform of centre-regional relations.

PUTIN'S PROJECT

Regional Reform

Putin enunciated several goals for regional reform: to bring regional laws into compliance with federal legislation and the Russian constitution; to provide for impeachment of regional leaders who abused their power; to redistribute tax revenues to favour poorer regions, by revoking the special tax status of many of the republics; to limit the regions' ability to conduct foreign trade independent of Moscow and to solicit foreign credits; and to reform the Federation Council, the upper chamber of the parliament, where most of the regional leaders sit, along with representatives from regional legislatures. Putin wanted especially to remove governors and republic presidents from the Federation Council, not least to remove the parliamentary immunity that protected them from the law.

The initiative that created the biggest impression was Putin's presidential decree of May 2000. It established seven federal districts among which all of the 89 "subjects" of the Russian Federation would be divided. The seven districts have designated capital cities, which serve as bases for the president's "plenipotentiary representatives" and their staffs. The new districts correspond fairly closely to the economic regions known as "associations of economic co-operation," but even more closely with the country's military districts – with only a couple of capital cities differing.

Proposals for replacing the system of ethnic–territorial divisions that characterized both the old Soviet Union and the present Russian Federation have been around for some time. Perhaps the best-known one came nearly a decade earlier from the fascist politician Vladimir Zhirinovskii, who suggested a return to the tsarist system of *gubernii*. Democratic political figures, such as the late Galina Starovoitova, were also sympathetic to proposals to reorganize Russian political divisions to de-emphasize the ethnic factor – although she had come to believe that such a reform would be impossible to implement.[15]

Zhirinovskii claimed that Putin's decree coincided exactly with what he had proposed, but in fact it differed in a key respect: the new federal districts did not replace the existing 89 subjects of the Federation, but rather imposed an additional layer of administration between them and the central government in Moscow. As the *Economist* quoted one observer from Bashkortostan, "the decree just creates one more bureaucracy with thousands more employees."[16]

Regional leaders responded to Putin's initiatives in various ways, depending apparently on the same sorts of economic and political considerations that had influenced their behaviour during the Yelstin years. Many were understandably unnerved at the prospect of losing parliamentary immunity, as anticipated in Putin's proposal for reform of the Federation Council. Concern for maintaining their own political status seemed to loom large in their calculations – as Putin evidently recognized.

The potential for conflict over the economic implications of Putin's reforms came in September 2000 when the president revealed his budget and tax proposals. Some sixteen of the poorest regions – the recipients of federal subsidies – expressed support for Putin's budget because it appeared to entail a redistribution of funds in their favour. However, leaders of economically successful regions, such as Novgorod's governor Mikhail Prusak, were incensed that the government sought to revise the provision of the Tax Code that allowed for a 50–50 split in the distribution of tax revenue. Bashkortostan's leaders were even more upset. They were obliged to void previous agreements with Moscow and, for the first time in years, to turn over tax revenues to the central government; previously they had retained those funds in lieu of various payments and subsidies from Moscow.

As opposition mounted from the wealthier "donor" regions, the national finance ministry evidently began cutting side deals, making promises – to St Petersburg and Tiumen, for example – to provide additional subsidies to make up for the decline in receipt of tax revenues. Smoothing over such potential conflicts through bilateral negotiations was a hallmark of Yeltsin's regional policy, but too many exceptions of this sort could undermine the coherence of Putin's reforms.

The End of the "Parade of Sovereignties"

In the wake of the August 1998 financial crisis, well before Putin and his reforms, fissiparous tendencies in the Russian Federation showed a marked decline. As Vladimir Shapoval, representative to Moscow of the far eastern *oblast'* of Sakhalin, told me in November of that year, "the crisis showed that not one of us, even the richest, is yet ready to survive independently in today's world." He believed that "the period of the 'parade of sovereignties' is over." The government has "a real chance to create a normal structure of a federal state, in which each unit will know the rights it has and the responsibilities it bears." Shapoval criticized "the rosy democratic slogan our President [Yeltsin] put forward: 'Take just as much sovereignty as you can swallow.' I consider that this was simply a populist slogan and it hasn't the remotest relationship to real life."[17]

Tatarstan's experience confirms Shapoval's judgment that even the richest regions suffered from the August meltdown.[18] Mikhail Stoliarov, first deputy plenipotentiary of Tatarstan to the Russian Federation, expressed similar views. As for the August crisis, "we really suffered from it, and we do suffer it from now. We are not separate; we cannot close the border and seclude ourselves from the economy of the Russian Federation." The crisis confirmed that "we are part of Russia, and we are Russian, and therefore all the problems that have been faced by the Russian Federation are also the problems of Tatarstan." Moreover, "being in the centre of the Russian Federation, we cannot separate." Stoliarov expressed confidence that Tatarstan would be able to work out its differences with Moscow, including reconciling divergent constitutions and laws.[19]

The leadership in Bashkortostan also took a fairly conciliatory line in the wake of the August crisis. It was particularly anxious to defend itself against charges that the republic had secured unwarranted privileges through its negotiated agreements with the centre, in the realm of taxes, for example. Irek Ablaev, Bashkortostan's representative to Moscow, explained that the republic's decisions to withhold certain tax payments to the centre were usually intended to offset subsidies that Moscow was no longer providing. For instance, a major industrial complex in Blagoveshchensk that produced valuable polyether compounds for construction and for the military had not received funds for modernization or even to cover basic social services for employees. Whatever funds the republic provided to make up for what Moscow failed to send would then be withheld from its tax obligation.[20] The situation with Blagoveshchensk resembles on a smaller scale what Tatarstan faces in its efforts to maintain the enormous Kamskii automobile works (KAMAZ) in Naberezhnye Chelny. Without support from the federal centre to maintain production, unemployment could threaten the livelihoods of thousands of people – about 100,000 in the case of KAMAZ, including workers and their families.[21] Dependence on the federal government in these cases tends to mute any calls for secession.

Despite their insistence on their republic's "sovereignty," Bashkortostan's officials, like those of Tatarstan, acknowledge how completely the region is integrated into the Russian system. As Ablaev pointed out, in a population of 4.1 million, nearly one million are pensioners. They spent their lives working throughout the Soviet Union and then returned home to retire. Who should pay their pensions – the republic or the centre? On these sorts of matters, Bashkortostan is happy to maintain its links with Moscow. Even in areas where the republic does enjoy advantages, as in industrial development and natural resources, its officials are willing to admit that "we perfectly well understand that these are not the achievements of our republic alone. They were created in the course of seventy years by the entire Soviet people." Ablaev drew particular attention to the scores of factories that were moved into Bashkortostan during the Second World War to escape destruction by the German armies and the vast investments in oil processing "created by the efforts of the entire Soviet Union." Ablaev was sensitive to the charge that Bakhkortostan's wealth accords it a certain privileged position in its relations with Moscow. But he also stressed the negative side of his republic's Soviet-era economic development. Industrial pollution poisons the land, water, and air. According to Ablaev, every second child is born unhealthy, the victim of an environmental disaster that the central government in Moscow ignores. "And they speak of 'privileges,'" he complained. "If we had healthy children, that would be a privilege."[22]

It is evident that there was no great rush by the regions to secede from the Russian Federation – not in the early years of the Yeltsin regime and certainly not at the dawn of the Putin era. No other region sought to emulate the Chechen example. Moreover, the overall level of integration and mutual dependence between the centre and the regions was recognized by the leadership of even the most privileged republics. They sought to use whatever leverage they had to improve their status, but they had no intention to abandon the federation.

Freedom versus Order?

Yet the jockeying for privilege among the richer regions caused considerable resentment elsewhere in the Russian Federation. Thus Putin's intention to rationalize Russia's governing institutions and to bring regional laws into compliance with the federal constitution seemed to command widespread support. His initial choices for plenipotentiary representatives caused some observers to wonder, however, whether his imposition of order comes at the expense of individual freedom and democracy. Five of the seven were former military, police, or security service officials, including KGB and Interior Ministry officers and two generals who had commanded forces in Chechnya. One of the two exceptions (the other is a former diplomat) was Sergei Kirienko, who served under Yeltsin in 1998 as acting prime minister and before that in Nizhnii Novgorod, now the centre of the new Volga federal district. But even Kirienko has former KGB officials on his staff, including most notably Major-General Marsel Gafurovich Galimardanov, who was appointed federal inspector in Tatarstan.

Many observers have speculated that the backgrounds of the people whom Putin appointed (and his own experience as an intelligence officer in the KGB), in combination with his own inclinations, make it likely that the president's regional reforms will favour imposition of order rather than the strengthening of democracy. For some of his supporters, this aspect of Putin's regional policy is the most attractive. In a radio interview Valerii Velichko, head of an association of former KGB officials, maintained that officers of the Federal Security Service are best suited for imposing top–down authority on the regions. They are the best hope for helping Putin establish an "enlightened autocracy." Such a political system would be "neither the coarse militarized communism of Pol Pot, nor the fascist or half-fascist regime of Pinochet" (although some of what transpired in the course of Putin's war in Chechnya would be familiar to the victims of those regimes).[23]

In February 2000, then Acting President Putin told Ministry of Justice officials that "the only sort of dictatorship to which we must be subject is the dictatorship of law." He complained that "the system of state authority is neglected, slack and ill-disciplined," and he stressed the need to relieve popular anxiety and insecurity. "There is only one way to achieve this – by turning Russia into a strong state."

Many commentators have given Putin's neo-tsarist/military/KGB plan for regional reform the benefit of the doubt. They hoped that it would help build a strong law-governed state to protect the freedom and economic well-being of Russia's citizens. But an "enlightened autocracy," even one that avoids the extremes of Pol Pot and Pinochet, would be another matter. Russians could end up with the worst of both worlds – an authoritarian regime that fails to bring order and peace to the fractured Russian Federation.

NOTES

1 See Proudhon, 1862, 25.
2 Representative of a non-governmental organization in Pskov, quoted in Dinello, 2001, 8.
3 Quoted in Sagitova, 2001.
4 For a good overview, see DeBardeleben, 1997, chap. 2.
5 See Treisman, 1999, 21.
6 See Laitin, 1998, 191.
7 See DeBardeleben, 1997, 38.
8 See Socor, 1994b.
9 Starovoitova quoted in Socor, 1994a; Vorob'ev, in Remnick, 1997, 283; "brush-fire" quote from Shumikhin, 1995, 29.
10 Transcript of my interview with Mikhail Stoliarov, at the office of the permanent representative of the Republic of Tatarstan in Moscow, 4 Nov. 1998.
11 Quoted in Treisman, 1999, 15.
12 Stoliarov interview.
13 Quoted in Alexseev, 1999, 2.
14 Quoted in Evangelista, 1999b.
15 Evangelista, 1999a.
16 "Russia's Regions: Beyond the Kremlin's Walls," *Economist*, 20–26 May 2000.
17 My interview with Vladimir Shapoval, 4 Nov. 1998, Moscow.
18 Khakimov, 1999.
19 Stoliarov interview.
20 Transcript with my interview with Irek Ablaev, plenipotentiary representative of Bashkortostan in Moscow, 13 Nov. 1998.
21 R.G. Akhmetov, "KAMAZ – uzel protivorechii mezhdu Moskvoi i Kazan'iu" [KAMAZ – A Knot of Contradictions between Moscow and Kazan], in Drobizheva, 1998, 95.
22 Ablaev interview.
23 Quoted in *RFE/RL Russian Federation Report* 2, no. 24, 28 June 2000.

REFERENCES

Alexseev, Mikhail A., ed. (1999) *Centre–Periphery Conflict in Post-Soviet Russia: A Federation Imperilled*. London: Macmillan.

DeBardeleben, Joan (1997) "The Development of Federalism in Russia," in Peter J. Stavrakis, Joan DeBardeleben, and Larry Black, with Jodi Koehn, eds., *Beyond the Monolith: The Emergence of Regionalism in Post-Soviet Russia*. Washington, DC: Woodrow Wilson Center Press, chap. 2.

Dinello, Natalia (2001) "What's So Great about Novgorod-the-Great? Trisectoral Cooperation and Symbolic Management," Report to the National Council for Eurasian and East European Research, Washington, DC, 3 June.

Drobizheva, L.M. (1998) *Asimmetrichnaia federatsiia: vzgliad iz tsentra, respublik i oblastei* [Asymmetrical Federation: The View from the Centre, the Republics, and the Provinces]. Moscow: Institute of Sociology of the Russian Academy of Sciences.

Evangelista, Matthew (1999a) "An Interview with Galina Starovoytova," *Post-Soviet Affairs* 15, no. 3 (July–Sept.). www.vhwinston.com/psa/abstract/af990304.html

– (1999b) "Russia's Fragile Union," *Bulletin of the Atomic Scientists* 55, no. 3 (May/June). www.bullatomsci.org/issues/1999/mj99/mj99evangelista.html

Khakimov, Rafael', ed. (1999) *Ekonomika Tatarstana posle 17 avgusta* [Tatarstan's Economy after 17 August], special issue of *Panorama-Forum* (Kazan'), no. 21.

Laitin, David D. (1998) *Identity in Formation: The Russian-Speaking Populations in the Near Abroad*. Ithaca, NY: Cornell University Press.

Proudhon, Pierre-Joseph (1862) *La fédération et l'unité en Italie* [Federation and Unity in Italy]. Paris: E. Dentu.

Remnick, David (1997) *Resurrection: The Struggle for a New Russia*. New York: Random House.

Sagitova, Lilia V. (2001) "Interesy sotsial'nykh grupp v kontekste etnokul'turnoi i etnopoliticheskoi integratsii Tatarstanskogo soobshchestva" [The Interests of Social Groups in the Context of Ethnocultural and Ethnopolitical Integration in Tatarstan Society], Institute of History, Tatarstan Academy of Sciences, Kazan', June.

Shumikhin, Andrei (1995) "The Chechen Crisis and the Future of Russia," in Roald Z. Sagdeev and Susan Eisenhower, eds., *Central Asia: Conflict, Resolution, and Change*. Chevy Chase, Md.: CPSS Press.

Socor, Vladimir (1994a) "Critical Voices," RFE/RL *Daily Report*, no. 236, 15 Dec.

– (1994b) "Resistance in Ingushetiia ... and Dagestan," RFE/RL *Daily Report*, no. 234, 13 Dec.

Treisman, Daniel S. (1999) *After the Deluge: Regional Crises and Political Consolidation in Russia*. Ann Arbor: University of Michigan Press.

JOHN McGARRY

Civic Nationalism
and the Northern Ireland Conflict

Civic nationalism is the doctrine that everyone in the state, regardless of race or ethnicity, is a member of the nation, entitled to full and equal citizenship.[1] It originated with the Jacobins during the French Revolution and has since spread throughout the world. It comes in multiculturalist and assimilationist ideal types. The former is compatible with respect for the culture of minorities and resembles the practice of "multiculturalism" in the United States, Australia, and Canada. The latter requires ethnic minorities to embrace the culture of the dominant group and is associated with the republican approach used in France. Civic nationalists believe that a state with a diverse population cannot be stable unless its people share a common civic identity. They see this commonality as underpinning the social solidarity required for welfare-state redistribution and for deliberative democracy.[2]

Civic nationalists usually attribute conflict to the existence of ethnic (or racial) nationalism, which restricts membership in the nation to members of the relevant ethnic group.[3] They see conflict in Nazi Germany, in apartheid-era South Africa, and in post-Communist central and eastern Europe as flowing from ethnocentric or racist practices by state authorities. They ascribe the relative tranquillity of Western democracies to their civic inclusiveness. Where conflict occurs in liberal democracies, as in the case of the United Kingdom (Northern Ireland), Canada (Quebec), or Spain (the Basque country), it is frequently imputed to ethnic sentiment among minorities.[4]

The civic nationalist prescription for conflict is the erosion of ethnic identities and the promotion of a common civic identity through integrationist policies. This often seems a practical proposal, as ethnic attachments are thought to be malleable.[5] The civic nationalist tool-box includes the propagation of an ideology of inclusion through catch-all political parties, trade unions, and other civic associations; the banning of discrimination; economic growth; integration in schools, workplaces, and residential neighbourhoods; training in the dominant language for immigrant minorities; and – sometimes, according to multicultural civic nationalists – cultural rights for minorities, as long as these are consistent with a common national identity. Civic nationalists usually oppose political institutions that distinguish citizens along ethnic lines for fear that these will entrench divisions and create power bases for ethno-nationalist elites.

Some civic nationalists point to the South African "miracle" as an example of the promise of their message even in unpropitious circumstances.[6] South Africa was once a society deeply divided along racial lines, embroiled in seemingly intractable conflict. Its central political institutions were divided along racial lines, among whites, Asians, and "coloureds," with blacks excluded, often in ethnic "Bantustans." As long as whites thought in racial terms, it is argued, they could not conceive of surrendering power, which would have involved handing it over to a black majority. The civic nationalist/non-racial message of Nelson Mandela and the African National Congress (ANC) lessened whites' fears about the consequences of majority rule and made possible a transition to a reasonably stable and unified state. From this perspective, the lesson of the 1990s is that divided societies have a clear and easy choice: they can choose the civic message of Mandela, which leads to ethnic and racial harmony, or the ethnic message of Slobodan Milosevic in Serbia, which produces "ethnic cleansing" and catastrophe.

It is common for observers to see Northern Ireland as similar to pre-1994 South Africa or to the pre-1960s U.S. deep south – a site of exclusionary ideologies and an obvious setting for civic prescriptions of the type outlined above. I argue, however, that Northern Ireland illustrates the flaws in civic nationalist thinking. Its conflict has been, in an important way, between two rival, inclusionary projects – one Irish, the other British – rather than between two exclusionary projects. The first section of this paper outlines those two projects; the second shows how they led to longstanding stalemate. We see in the third section that it was only when powerful actors in both communities moved away from the idea of stretching their nation over their rivals and embraced a binational compromise that a settlement became possible – the Good Friday Agreement of 1998.

NORTHERN IRELAND: A HOTBED OF INCLUSIVENESS

While journalists and others have written of (and written off) Northern Ireland as a site of ethnic (or "sectarian") hatreds, many of its politicians and intellectuals have sought to include their rivals within their nation. They have aired two distinct views – civic (Irish) and unionist.

Civic (Irish) Nationalism

The first view, the one most consistently argued throughout the period, insists on the construction of an Irish civic nation capable of transcending rival sectarian identities. This position has been put forward since the 1790s, when Wolfe Tone, following the Jacobins, called for the people of Ireland "to substitute the common name of Irishman in place of the denominations Catholic, Protestant and Dissenter."[7] It was represented by Young Ireland in the 1840s, with its support for the "multicultural" tricolour as the flag of an independent Ireland. Throughout parts of the last two centuries, it has competed with a rival Catholic and Gaelic ethnic nationalism. In its early decades, the Irish Free State gave a privileged position to the Catholic church, and its most influential politician, Eamon de Valera, who was supposedly committed to ending partition, proclaimed that Ireland was a "Catholic state." However, in recent history, a civic nationalist discourse has been hegemonic. Every nationalist party in Ireland expresses a commitment to a tolerant and pluralist united Ireland.

The traditional republican position – that associated with Sinn Fein for most of the past thirty years – is that sectarian division in Ireland is not the result of primordial hatreds or deep-rooted sentiments. Rather, it is a consequence of Britain's historic policy of "divide and rule."[8] British imperialists governed Ireland, it is claimed, by bestowing privileges on Irish Protestants. When the issue of Home Rule for Ireland arose at Westminster after 1886, Conservatives "played the Orange Card," stirring up Protestant opposition to Home Rule for reasons to do with partisan domestic politics. In the face of an Irish nationalist rebellion, the British government partitioned Ireland without the formal support of a single Irish MP, Protestant or Catholic. The result had two dimensions, although the first is discussed more frequently than the second. On the one hand, a statelet emerged in Northern Ireland, with an in-built Protestant majority. Protestants could monopolize government as long as they stressed zero–sum politics and maintained ethnic solidarity, and this is what they did. On the other hand, partition resulted in an almost homogeneously Catholic state in the south of Ireland. For most of its history, it pursued a public policy consistent with its religious make-up, elevating the position of the Catholic church and imposing Catholic morality in the regulation of sexuality and the body. Britain's partition of Ireland therefore produced two sectarian identities and made impossible the realization of Tone's civic ideal. Ireland remains partitioned in this exogenous account because Protestants continue to fear for their religious identity under Dublin rule and because of the benefits of a large British subvention.

This analysis contributed to the use by republican militants of armed struggle between 1969 and 1994. They believed that the British state, as the chief cause of sectarianism in Ireland, should be removed by force. At that point, they thought, Protestants would accept their destiny as Irish people in a united Ireland. It may appear odd to outsiders, given republican attacks on Protestants, but the official republican ideology was profoundly civic and inclusionary in character.

Some nationalist intellectuals place less stress on Britain's responsibility for sectarian division and more on endogenous factors. They also regard the militant tactics of republican paramilitaries as wrong-headed and counterproductive. Rupert Taylor, who supports a "non-sectarian democratic society … in a united 'New Ireland,'" sees social segregation, particularly in the school system, as a cause of division. He blames divisions also on sectarian politicians and on social elites who stress difference for their own self-interested purposes.[9] Instead of armed insurrection, Taylor calls for increased public spending to tackle the "material" basis of sectarian strife. He wants sectarian elites to be challenged by civil society, particularly by those organizations that "cross-cut social divisions and challenge and erode the clash of opposing ethnonationalisms." This does not seem to him a utopian task: he finds evidence already of increasing integration in housing and schools and claims that a significant number of voluntary associations are working to break down "Orange and Green stereotypes" and to promote a new inclusiveness.[10]

Irish integrationists have traditionally opposed political structures that they believe will entrench divisions in Ireland. Prior to 1998, Sinn Fein would not accept any settlement that maintained the British presence in Ireland, which it saw as incompatible with the erosion of sectarianism. It would also not support a devolved assembly and executive in Northern Ireland, even one erected on power-sharing principles, because it believed that this would be a forum for zero–sum politics. A republican campaign of violence helped to destroy the Sunningdale Agreement of 1973, which included such an assembly, as well as a power-sharing executive and a Council of Ireland. Republicans have generally been prepared to accommodate unionist culture, and of course the Protestant religion, but only within a united and sovereign Ireland. In this sense, they are civic nationalists of the multiculturalist rather than of the assimilationist variety.

Civic Unionism

The Irish civic nationalist project has come to be matched in recent years by a civic unionist project. Traditionally, unionism in Ireland has been ethnic and exclusionary. While William Pitt sought to build a civic United Kingdom by linking the Act of Union with Catholic Emancipation, he was frustrated by Anglo–Irish Protestants, Tories, and King George III.[11] Some of those who opposed Home Rule for Ireland at the end of the nineteenth century did so on civic grounds, although civic unionists were more conspicuous in Britain (and in southern Ireland) than in Ulster. For most of the period between 1921 and the 1970s, the dominant Ulster Unionist Party (UUP) made no attempt to reach out to Catholics, although smaller (small "u") unionist parties such as the Northern Ireland Labour Party did. Northern Ireland's first prime minister, Sir James Craig, professed that he was proud to have constructed a "Protestant parliament for a Protestant people,"[12] and the UUP did not appoint a Catholic cabinet minister until its regime was on the verge of collapse in 1968.

Integrationist arguments became more popular in the Unionist party after the "proroguing" of the Stormont Parliament in 1972. The UUP began to espouse the integration of Northern Ireland into the United Kingdom, particularly after Enoch Powell entered the party in 1974 and James Molyneaux became leader in 1979. In the wake of the Anglo–Irish Agreement of 1985, a number of civic unionist organizations were formed outside of conventional politics, such as the Campaign for Equal Citizenship and the Campaign for Labour Representation in Northern Ireland. These took the position that if the Union was to be sold to both Catholics and Protestants, it would have to be detached from traditional unionist political parties, which were seen as too closely associated with sectarianism.[13] In recent years, this version of civic unionism has been most closely identified with Robert McCartney, founder of the Campaign for Equal Citizenship and current leader of the United Kingdom Unionist Party (UKUP). It has also received support from Ireland's most famous intellectual, Conor Cruise O'Brien, from the Scottish journalist John Lloyd, and from a number of academics, such as Arthur Aughey, Hugh Roberts, and Patrick Roche.[14] By the later 1990s, it was *de rigeur* for politicians from all unionist parties to defend the union as something that could accommodate Catholics and even Irish nationalists.

While republicans argued that divisions in Ireland were not deeply-rooted, civic unionists made the same argument about divisions in Northern Ireland. They saw the roots of the conflict as lying in Britain's decision, first, to withdraw from the rest of Ireland in the face of an ethnically motivated Irish rebellion and, second, to establish a devolved parliament in Belfast, against the wishes of unionist leaders, rather than integrating Northern Ireland into the United Kingdom. In a position similar to their Irish counterparts, civic unionists agree that the establishment of a devolved parliament in Northern Ireland encouraged divisive sectarian politics. However, they claim that the situation was exacerbated by the Irish Republic's irredentism; by the refusal of nationalist elites to accept the state; by the British government's lack of commitment to the Union and its lack of interest in what was going on in Northern Ireland; and some blame the failure of British political parties to organize in Northern Ireland, which left the province isolated from Britain's civic political culture.[15]

Until 1998, unionist integrationists proposed a straightforward remedy for Northern Ireland: it should be politically integrated with the rest of the United Kingdom. Civic unionists asked that the government in London abandon attempts to devolve power to a regional assembly in Belfast. They pushed for legislation affecting Northern Ireland to be incorporated into British legislation or, if separate legislation was necessary, for it to be passed by normal parliamentary procedures, rather than by order in council; for its representation at Westminster to increase; and for it to be administered in the same way as regions in Britain. Some lobbied for the main British parties – Conservative and Labour – to organize in Northern Ireland. During the height of "electoral integrationism" in the late 1980s, its supporters believed that this would bring two benefits: it would help Northern Ireland to import

Britain's more rational and modern political culture, and it would allow its electorate to vote for the only two parties able to form a British government, thereby democratizing rule from London and undermining the appeal of devolution. The overall aim was to replace rival sectarian identities with a transcendent British civic identity, to make the region, as Margaret Thatcher once put it, "as British as Finchley" – her suburban London constituency.

This integrationist platform was incompatible with the demands of even moderate nationalists, which included a power-sharing regional government and institutional links with the Republic of Ireland. Such measures, unionist intellectuals claimed, would not only appease ethnic chauvinists, including IRA murderers, but would damage progressive elements in unionist politics, increase the popularity of chauvinistic Protestant politicians, and/or drive people to join the loyalist paramilitaries. They would also jeopardize the rights and liberties of Northern Ireland's citizens by facilitating their transfer from a modern and secular United Kingdom to a still relatively backward and priest-dominated united Ireland. Unionist politicians and intellectuals, including Marxists, used these "progressive" propositions to argue throughout much of the conflict against any compromise with Irish nationalists.[16]

In a view that mirrors Irish nationalist criticisms, unionists argued that Catholics and even nationalists could accept the union, given that the United Kingdom was no longer a Protestant state and that it provided a home for Scottish and Welsh nationalists. They pointed out that many Catholics already supported the Union and that more would do so but for the propaganda of nationalist elites and intimidation by republican militants. What was needed to win over more Catholics was not concessions to separatist nationalism, but for London to make clear its commitment to the Union and to military victory over the IRA, and for Dublin to abandon its irredentism.[17] Like their nationalist counterparts, unionists espoused multiculturalism: they were happy to accommodate Catholicism, the Irish culture, and even Irish nationalism, as long as this was squarely within the United Kingdom.

CIVIC PROJECTS AND POLITICAL STALEMATE

Northern Ireland indicates at least three difficulties with civic nationalism as a method of conflict resolution in nationally divided societies. First, the choice is not always the easy one depicted by many civic nationalists, between civic and ethnic nationalism. Rather, it is sometimes between two rival inclusionary projects. Such a choice presents itself not only in Northern Ireland. Quebec nationalists offer a Quebec civic nationalism as an alternative to a Canadian civic nationalism. Scottish nationalists promote their own brand of civic nationalism against the British version. In Catalonia and the Basque Country, Catalonian and Basque civic nationalist projects compete with a Spanish counterpart. It is not easy for impartial liberals to pick between these rival inclusionary projects, claims by partisans notwithstanding. In Northern Ireland, there is no clear evidence that a united Ireland would be any more or less civic than the United Kingdom. Both the Irish republic and the United Kingdom have some illiberal failings, but both are clearly liberal democracies.[18]

Second, the targets of civic nationalist appeals may interpret these as insincere, and sometimes for good reasons. Thus, as both civic Yugoslavs and ethnocentric Serbs wanted the same broad constitutional goals – a united Yugoslavia – many Croats and Bosniaks interpreted civic appeals as ethnic chauvinism in tactical guise. Similarly, in Northern Ireland, both sides regard the civic nationalism of their rivals as "politically correct" smokescreens for traditional ethnic goals, designed mainly for external consumption and not meant to be taken seriously by their ostensible targets. Unionists note that the republican plea for them to "embrace the common name of Irishman" coincided with a campaign of violence in which republicans killed and injured thousands of Protestants. They believe that what republicans, or at least the republican rank and file, are attached to is the land that unionists occupy – Ireland's fourth green field – rather than the unionist people. Nationalists note that unionists did not enunciate civic principles during the Stormont regime between 1921 and 1972, when they had the power to implement them. Civic unionism, everyone is aware, became popular only after the British government abolished Stormont and pressed unionists to accommodate nationalists. It became particularly prominent only after 1985, after a series of political and international defeats for unionists, including the Anglo–Irish Agreement, which international opinion enthusiastically endorsed.

Third, civic nationalism, even in its multicultural variant, is incompatible with the substantive institutional recognition that minority national communities want. Minority nations, whether in Quebec, Scotland, Catalonia, or the Basque Country, seek more than to be treated as equal individuals within someone else's nation-state or to receive a limited form of cultural recognition on a par with immigrant (for example,

Mexican or Buddhist) minorities. They want far-reaching institutional recognition of their national identity, with precise demands varying from place to place.[19]

Traditional British and Irish civic projects in Northern Ireland are inconsistent with the aspirations of even moderate members of the other national community. Moderate Irish nationalists reject equal citizenship within the United Kingdom. They seek, at a minimum, a consociational government in Northern Ireland, parity of esteem between nationalists and unionists, and political institutions that link Northern Ireland and the Irish republic. Until 1994, republicans demanded a united Ireland and supported the use of force to achieve it. Even the most moderate unionists reject equal citizenship in a united Ireland. They insist on the retention of British sovereignty in Northern Ireland, although they are prepared to countenance institutional links with the Irish Republic to accommodate Irish nationalists. Other unionists reject such concessions.

The evidence suggests that these aspirations, and the identities on which they are based, are deeply rooted and unlikely to dissipate in the foreseeable future. For over a century, Northern Ireland's electorate has been divided into two ethnonational blocs, with virtually all Protestants supporting unionist parties and most Catholics backing nationalist parties. There has been little or no swing voting between the two blocs. Electoral polarization has become even more pronounced during the past thirty years. While nationalist and unionist parties won an average of 82 per cent of the vote during the five elections held in Northern Ireland between 1973 and 1975, they received an average of 90.6 per cent in Northern Ireland's five elections between 1996 and 1999. Within the nationalist bloc, the republican (radical nationalist) share of the vote has been increasing. In its first five election campaigns (1982–87), Sinn Fein won an average of 37.3 per cent of the nationalist vote. In the five campaigns from 1996 to 1999, its average increased to 41.8 per cent.[20] The trend within the unionist bloc is more difficult to measure, as both major unionist parties have been equally intransigent for most of the period. There is some evidence, however, that the UUP's increased moderation in recent years has cost it electoral support to the advantage of more intransigent unionist parties.

One response to this evidence is to argue that it reflects "elite" politics and does not measure the preferences of the large number of people who are alienated from Northern Ireland's confrontational politics. However, electoral turnout is higher in Northern Ireland than in Britain. The position of political parties on constitutional issues also broadly reflects the preferences reported in survey data.[21] Nor do the constitutional goals of Northern Ireland's "civil society" – its many civic associations – appear dramatically different from those of its political parties. The most popular such organizations – the Orange Order and the Gaelic Athletic Association – are solidly unionist and nationalist, respectively. Several smaller peace and conflict-resolution organizations reach across the national divide and seek to promote a transcendent identity. However, just as many, according to the academic who has most closely studied them, are nationalist or unionist groups that want an honourable bi-national compromise.[22] Finally, civic integrationists exaggerate both the willingness of both communities to integrate socially and its political consequences. There is no clear evidence of a desire for social integration,[23] and even if there was, it would not necessarily translate into a desire for political (national) integration.[24]

While they are often depicted as solutions to Northern Ireland's conflict, it makes more sense to see its rival inclusionary projects as responsible for its political stalemate before 1998. For much of this time, republicans and unionists remained wedded to their respective versions of national integration and were not prepared to accept the other's preferences or to split the difference. Only the moderate nationalists of the Social Democratic and Labour Party (SDLP) and small parties, such as Alliance, were willing to endorse a settlement that accommodated both national communities. Agreement became possible in 1998 when leaders in the republican and unionist communities abandoned traditional positions and compromised along the lines suggested by the SDLP.

THE 1990S: FROM NATIONAL INTEGRATION TO A BI-NATIONAL COMPROMISE

Republicans' path to a settlement began with the Hume–Adams talks of 1988–94, when the SDLP leader, John Hume, sought to convince Sinn Fein's Gerry Adams that a strategy of violence was counterproductive, alienating not just unionists, but Britain and potential Irish supporters in the United States. A "learning curve," aided by the vehemence of loyalist attacks on republicans in the early 1990s, increased republicans' respect for the resilience of unionism and for its independence from metropolitan manipulation. It was also clear that the military struggle had resulted in stalemate and that it was compromising Sinn Fein's electoral strategy.

At the same time, republicans' faith in constitutional politics increased because of support from an increasingly interventionist U.S. administration. Influenced by a large Irish-American lobby and by the end of the Cold War, the U.S. government gave unprecedented attention to Northern Ireland after President Bill Clinton took office in 1993. Clinton sent a special envoy to Northern Ireland during the early stages of the peace process; put several of his senior advisers to work on the Northern Ireland peace process, including his national security adviser, Anthony Lake; visited the province three times in five years; regularly invited party leaders to Washington; persuaded former Senate majority leader George Mitchell to preside over the negotiations that led to the Good Friday Agreement; and intervened personally in the political negotiations on several occasions. American pressure for an equitable settlement helped to boost the position of the Irish government in negotiations with Britain. It also increased the confidence of republicans about the utility of talks.[25] Clinton's decision in early 1994 to issue a visa to Gerry Adams is credited with giving Adams the standing that he needed to bring hard-line republicans behind his peace strategy. Adams himself claimed that it brought forward the IRA cease-fire, which occurred in August 1994, by one year.[26]

A decision by republicans to embrace constitutional politics was also helped by demographic change. Between 1961 and 1991, the number of those who gave their religion as Catholic increased from 34.9 per cent to 38.4 per cent, while those who declared themselves Protestant declined from 63.2 per cent to 50.6 per cent. The remainder (11 per cent in 1991) gave no religion. At the same time, the nationalist share of the vote increased steadily, from an average of 31 per cent in four elections for various levels of government between 1982 and 1985 to an average of 38 per cent in the four elections (1996–97) before the agreement. Both nationalist parties grew – the SDLP, from 20 per cent to 23.7 per cent, and Sinn Fein, from 11.5 per cent to 14.2 per cent. The Unionist vote declined during the same period, from 57.5 per cent to 52 per cent, with the UUP's vote dropping from 28.5 per cent to 26.5 per cent, and the Democratic Unionist Party (DUP), from 25.2 per cent to 19.5 per cent.[27] Both the rising Catholic share of the population and a corresponding increase in Sinn Fein's vote helped to convince its leaders that they could exercise meaningful influence within Northern Ireland.[28] It also allowed them to sell compromise to their followers while claiming that a united Ireland had been postponed rather than cancelled.

The volte face by David Trimble's UUP resulted from several related factors. After a brief fling with integration in the late 1970s, the British government made it increasingly clear that this was no longer an option. After 1985, it indicated that unalloyed direct rule was not on offer either. Unionists had always considered this preferable to the risks of a settlement with nationalists. In the Anglo–Irish Agreement of 1985, however, Britain gave the Republic of Ireland a role in policy-making in Northern Ireland, while offering to reduce this in the event of an agreement on devolution between nationalists and unionists. The default to compromise shifted from direct rule from Westminster to London–Dublin co-operation in the governance of Northern Ireland, with the danger, for the unionists, that this would be consolidated in the absence of agreement between the Northern Ireland parties.

There was no immediate movement. At first, unionists thought that they could destroy the agreement by protest, but it proved impervious. They also hoped that the agreement could be resisted or turned back while the Conservatives were in power in London, particularly during the 1992–97 parliament, when the government depended on unionist support in the House of Commons. The UUP began to negotiate seriously with the SDLP and Sinn Fein only following Labour's landslide victory in 1997 and Tony Blair's signal that he was committed to achieving a settlement by May 1998.

Another factor that induced unionist flexibility was the increasing Catholic share of the population and the matching increase in support for nationalist parties, particularly Sinn Fein. This trend underlined that time was not on the side of unionist negotiators. The rising nationalist vote also undercut the integrationist argument that nationalism was superficial. It showed not only that civic unionism was falling on deaf Catholic ears, but that the continuing failure to accommodate nationalists was squeezing moderates.[29] Unionist intellectuals, including Paul Bew, a key adviser to David Trimble, switched subtly from the integrationist position that any accommodation of nationalists was a boon to Protestant sectarianism to the argument that a (minimalist) accommodation of nationalism was necessary for peace and the erosion of extremism.[30] The changing demography also undermined traditional unionist opposition to power-sharing. As advisers to the UUP pointed out in the wake of the agreement, with the nationalist share of the population continuing to increase, unionists might soon be "grateful" that they had agreed to mandatory power sharing.[31]

The case for integration with Britain also lost momentum when the Labour government decided in 1997 to devolve power to a Scottish parliament and a Welsh assembly. Integrationists had resisted devolution partly on the basis that it created a political distinction between Northern Ireland and the rest of Britain and had insisted in their rhetoric that Northern Ireland be treated the same as Scotland and Wales. Devolution to Scotland and Wales made it easier for unionist moderates to accept devolution for Northern Ireland. Moreover, as the Scottish and Welsh devolution packages were asymmetrical, reflecting the desire of Scots for more radical decentralization, a *sui generis* package suited to Northern Ireland's peculiar needs, including mandatory power-sharing and cross-border political institutions, seemed less objectionable.

Finally, UUP leader David Trimble's decision to negotiate was facilitated by the novel flexibility of republicans. It would have been impossible for Trimble to negotiate with Sinn Fein if the IRA had not declared a ceasefire in 1994, although he did not enter negotiations with Sinn Fein until three years later. The IRA's ceasefire ushered in loyalist counterparts and the participation of two refreshingly flexible loyalist parties in the political negotiations. Their presence acted as a crucial cushion for Trimble against DUP accusations that his involvement in talks jeopardized the union.

In the 1998 Agreement, both republicans and unionists stepped away from previous absolutisms. Sinn Fein dropped its insistence that a settlement must include British withdrawal and a united Ireland. The Agreement left these matters to Northern Ireland's electorate to decide, by simple majority, at an unspecified time. Sinn Fein also agreed that a referendum be put to voters in the Irish republic proposing the amendment of clauses in its constitution that expressed sovereignty over Northern Ireland. The UUP agreed that the United Kingdom must substantively accommodate the identity of Northern Ireland's nationalists and that a united Ireland could come about as soon as a majority in Northern Ireland wanted. Both sides settled on the compromise of power-sharing devolution and new political institutions linking north and south and east and west over integration into their respective nation-states. The latter element represented evolution from the fixation of both sides with the Westphalian sovereign state. While each used to claim that its nationalism was progressive and that the other's was reactionary, the Agreement acknowledged that both unionism and Irish nationalism should enjoy "parity of esteem."

This account of the background to Northern Ireland's settlement highlights the differences between it and South Africa – differences that civic nationalists overlook.[32] In South Africa, the conflict was caused by whites blocking the integration of blacks, who wanted to be included as equal citizens in a South African nation-state. In Northern Ireland, the conflict was a result of rival national communities attempting to impose their preferred form of integration on groups that did not want it. The respective settlements reflected this difference. While South Africa's accord provided for an integrated nation-state constructed on principles of equal citizenship, Northern Ireland's created institutions that sought to accommodate two distinct national communities and that spanned two states.

CONCLUSION

The case of Northern Ireland suggests a number of serious problems with what I have identified as a civic nationalist approach to conflict resolution in nationally divided societies. One is that the choice is not always the clear one depicted in many accounts – between civic and ethnic nationalism. Rather, it is often between two projects, both of which claim to be civic. It is not always straightforward for impartial liberals to choose between these rival projects, despite claims by partisans.

Another problem is that appeals in civic language often seem to the targeted minority as ethnocentrism in "politically correct" garb – an impression that is often correct. In Northern Ireland both sides make civic appeals, but the other side decodes them as merely shrewd forms of sectarianism. In Canada, also, while both Anglo-Quebecers and Quebec nationalists describe their respective nationalisms as civic, many in each camp sees the other side's nationalism as ethnically based. This helps to explain why in both places projects that are civic in their language are ethnically homogeneous in their support base

If we leave suspicions about sincerity aside, it is also clear that civic nationalism, even in its multicultural variant, is incompatible with the substantive institutional recognition that national minorities want. Such minorities seek a bi-national (or multinational) state or their own state. They do not want incorporation in someone else's nation-state.

NOTES

1 This chapter is based on a paper entitled "Northern Ireland as a Site of Conflicting Civic Nationalisms," presented at a conference on "Nation-states, Multi-national States and Supranational Organisations," Thirteenth Jacques Cartier Meetings, Montreal, 6 October 2000. My thanks to Michel Seymour for organizing the conference and for editing the collection in which this chapter appears. I would also like to thank the Social Sciences and Humanities Research Council of Canada and the Carnegie Corporation of New York for funding my research.

2 As J.S. Mill wrote, "Free institutions are next to impossible in a country made up of different nationalities. Among a people without fellow-feeling, especially if they read and speak different languages, the united public opinion, necessary to the workings of representative government cannot exist" (1993, 392). For the importance of civic nationalism to the welfare state, see Miller, 1995.

3 The distinction between civic and ethnic nationalism is made by a number of academics, including Ignatieff, 1992, and Pfaff, 1993. Others make a similar distinction using different terms. Kohn, 1994, distinguishes between "western" and "eastern" nationalism; Franck, 1997, between civic and "tribal" nationalism; Taylor, 1997, between "patriotism" and nationalism; and Fukuyama, 2000, between civic and "cultural" or "ethno-linguistic" nationalism. Other authors discuss the distinction, but in a critical way. See Brubaker, 1998; Moore, fothcoming; and Kymlicka, 1997. My paper belongs in this second category.

4 Pfaff, 1993, sees minority nationalisms in general as ethnic. Ignatieff, 1993, argues that Quebec nationalism is ethnic. Fukuyama, 2000, sees both Quebec and Scottish nationalism as "cultural" or "ethno-linguistic."

5 The view that national and ethnic identities are malleable is especially popular among postmodernists, including many (former)Marxists who used to insist on the essentialist nature of class.

6 See R. Taylor, 2001.

7 Cited in O'Leary and McGarry, 1996, 92.

8 According to Rooney, "the divisions in Ireland are artificial ..., created and maintained by Britain to enable it to rule its last colony ... There is absolutely no natural basis for the divisions between catholics and protestants. We are the same race, speak the same language, and share the same history." (1998, 21).

9 See R. Taylor, 2001, 46.

10 See R. Taylor, 2001, 43–7. The same claim appears in Douglas, 1998, 220 and 222.

11 At the time of the Act of Union in 1801, Catholics were not allowed to sit in either the Irish or the British parliaments. Pitt's plan had been to pass the Act of Union and a bill removing the ban on Catholic MPs at Westminster simultaneously, thus associating the Union in Catholic minds with emancipation. The ban on Catholic MPs, however, was not removed until 1829.

12 Craig was responding to de Valera's boast that he had constructed a Catholic state in the south.

13 While the campaign for "equal citizenship" was publicly committed to non-sectarianism, its stress was on removing inequality between the British citizens of Northern Ireland and those in Great Britain rather than inequality within Northern Ireland.

14 See Aughey, 1989; Roberts, 1990; and Roche and Barton, 1991. O'Brien joined McCartney's United Kingdom Unionist Party and was elected under its banner to the Northern Ireland Forum in 1996. In his memoirs, he expresses support for a non-sectarian united Ireland. See O'Brien, 1998, 439–47. His position now seems to be that any civic nationalism will do as long as it is genuinely civic.

15 Roberts, 1990.

16 Bew and Patterson, 1990.

17 See Roche, 1995, 133. See also Oliver, 1988.

18 McGarry and O'Leary, 1995, 130–3. Nationalists and unionists have traditionally argued that their preferred nation-state is a bastion of enlightenment values while that of their rivals is rooted in ethnocentrism. In a recent outburst, the Northern Ireland's first minister, Nobel laureate David Trimble, contrasted Britain, which he saw as a "vibrant multi-ethnic, multi-national liberal democracy," with the Irish republic – "the pathetic sectarian, mono-ethnic, mono-cultural state to our south." *Irish Times*, 13 March 2002.

19 For more on the distinction between the aspirations of immigrants and of minority nations, see Kymlicka, 1995.

20 I have relied for these figures on the data reported on Nicholas Whyte's webpage: www.explorers.whyte.com

21 For survey data ranging from the 1960s to the 1980s, see Moxon-Browne, 1991. For data from the early 1990s, see Trew, 1996, Table 1.

22 Cochrane, 2001.

23 It may be true, as Taylor (2001, 42–8) says, that the "extent of integrated education has widened" – but it has widened only to 3 per cent of the

school-age population. Taylor cites a survey reported by Tom Hadden that indicates that "most people in Northern Ireland want to live together rather than apart," but Hadden has also argued that the "major trend" in housing since 1971 has been for both communities to "congregate in areas where they feel safer and less exposed" – see Boyle and Hadden, 1994, 33. Finally, Taylor cites an article by John Whyte in support of his claim that "there are now a number of cross-community housing projects." However, in this article, Whyte actually claims that "residential segregation is increasing." See Whyte, 1993, 115. Whyte also makes clear "the adamant opposition of unionists to any kind of united Ireland" – a conclusion that Taylor (107) overlooks or chooses to ignore.

24 The example of Bosnia in the 1990s suggests that social integration does not necessarily produce political (national) integration.

25 A 1994 republican document on the peace strategy, TUAS (reputedly an acronym for Totally Unarmed Strategy or Tactical Use of Armed Struggle), was explicit about the U.S. role: "there is potentially a very powerful Irish-American lobby not in hock to any particular party in Britain or Ireland" and that "Clinton is perhaps the first US President in decades to be influenced by such a lobby." Cited in MacGinty, 1997, 34.

26 For a more extensive analysis of the exogenous factors that led to Northern Ireland's Good Friday Agreement, see McGarry, 2001b.

27 My figures begin in 1982 because Sinn Fein did not contest elections before them. If I had contrasted the period before 1982 with the 1996–97, the growth in the nationalist vote would have been even larger. I have also used similar types of elections in each period: in both cases I picked one for the European Parliament, one for Westminster, one for local government, and one for regional council. See Nicholas Whyte's elections webpage at www.explorers.whyte.com/ The gap between the shares of the vote won by nationalists and by unionists continues to narrow. In four elections since the Agreement (again one of each type of election listed above), nationalists won an average of 42 per cent and unionists, 50.2 per cent.

28 As these figures suggest, the rise in the nationalist share of the vote is a result of the growing Catholic share of the population (as well as Sinn Fein's decision to take part in electoral politics after 1982 and a higher electoral participation rate among Catholics). See O'Leary and McGarry, 1996, 192; O'Leary and Evans, 1997. It is not a result, as an Irish civic nationalist might hope, of Protestants becoming Irish nationalists. Opinion polls clearly indicate that a Protestant Irish nationalist is a very rare animal.

29 Addressing critics of the Agreement at the UUP's annual conference in 1999, David Trimble asked if their preferred alternatives had managed to stem Sinn Fein's growing vote, or if there was an alternative plan on how to achieve this. *Irish Times*, 14 Oct. 1999.

30 Paul Bew and his colleagues, Henry Patterson and Paul Teague, called for the establishment of cross-border institutions as a "symbolic fig leaf" to nationalists. Bew, Patterson, and Teague, 1997, 214. These intellectuals deserve considerable credit for starting this shift.

31 "Shock Report Has UUP Reeling," *Irish Examiner*, 20 June 2000.

32 See McGarry, 1998.

REFERENCES

Aughey, A. (1989) *Under Siege: Ulster Unionism and the Anglo–Irish Agreement*. Belfast: Blackstaff Press.

Bew, P., and H. Patterson (1990) "Scenarios for Progress in Northern Ireland," in J. McGarry and B. O'Leary, eds., *The Future of Northern Ireland*. Oxford: Oxford University Press, 206–18.

Bew, P., H. Patterson, and P. Teague (1997) *Northern Ireland: Between War and Peace*. London: Lawrence and Wishart.

Boyle, K., and T. Hadden (1994) *Northern Ireland: The Choice*. Harmondsworth: Penguin.

Brubaker, R. (1998) "Myths and Misconceptions in the Study of Nationalism," in M. Moore, ed. *National Self-determination and Secession* (Oxford: Oxford University Press, 1998), 233–65.

Cochrane, F. (2001) "Unsung Heroes? The Role of Peace and Conflict Resolution Organizations in the Northern Ireland Conflict," in J. McGarry, ed., *Northern Ireland and the Divided World: The Northern Ireland Conflict and the Good Friday Agreement in Comparative Perspective*. Oxford: Oxford University Press, 137–58.

Douglas, N. (1998) "The Politics of Accommodation, Social Change and Conflict Resolution in Northern Ireland," *Political Geography* 17, no. 2.

Franck, Thomas (1997) "Tribe, Nation, World: Self-Identification in the Evolving International System," *Ethics and International Affairs* 11.

Fukuyama, Francis (2000) "Don't Do It Britannia," *Prospect*, May, 21–4.

Hollinger, David (1995) *Postethnic America*. New York: Basic Books.

Ignatieff, Michael (1993) *Blood and Belonging: Journeys into the New Nationalisms*. London: Viking.

Kohn, Hans (1994) "Western and Eastern Nationalisms," in J. Hutchinson and A. Smith, eds., *Nationalism.* Oxford: Oxford University Press, 162–5.

Kymlicka, W. (1995) *Multicultural Citizens.* Oxford: Oxford University Press.

– (1997) "Modernity and Minority Nationalism: Commentary on Thomas Franck," *Ethics and International Affairs* 11, 171–6.

MacGinty, R. (1997) "American Influences on the Northern Ireland Peace Process," *Journal of Conflict Studies* 43, 31–50.

McGarry, J. (1998) "Political Settlements in Northern Ireland and South Africa," *Political Studies* 46, no. 5 (Dec.), 853–70.

– (2001a) "Northern Ireland, Civic Nationalism, and the Good Friday Agreement," in J. McGarry, ed., *Northern Ireland and the Divided World: The Northern Ireland Conflict and the Good Friday Agreement in Comparative Perspective.* Oxford: Oxford University Press, 109–36.

– (2001b) "Globalization, European Integration and the Northern Ireland Conflict," in M. Keating and J. McGarry, eds., *Minority Nationalism and the Changing International Order.* Oxford: Oxford University Press, 295–324.

McGarry, J., and B. O'Leary (1995) *Explaining Northern Ireland.* Oxford: Blackwell.

Mill, J.S. (1993) *Utilitarianism; On Liberty; Considerations on Representative Government.* London: Everyman.

Miller, D. (1995) *On Nationality.* Oxford: Oxford University Press.

Moore, M. (Forthcoming) "Nationalism," in *UNESCO Encyclopedia.*

Moxon-Browne, E. (1991) "National Identity in Northern Ireland," in P. Stringer and G. Robinson, eds., *Social Attitudes in Northern Ireland: The First Report.* Belfast: Blackstaff Press.

O'Leary, B., and G. Evans (1997) "Northern Ireland: La Fin de Siècle, The Twilight of the Second Protestant Ascendancy and Sinn Fein's Second Coming," *Parliamentary Affairs* 50, 672–80.

O'Leary, B., and J. McGarry (1996) *The Politics of Antagonism: Understanding Northern Ireland.* London: Athlone Press.

Oliver, J. (1988) "Constitutional Uncertainty and the Ulster Tragedy," *Political Studies* 59, no. 4, 427–36.

Pfaff, William (1993) *The Wrath of Nations: Civilization and the Furies of Nationalism.* New York: Simon and Shuster.

Roberts, H. (1990) "Sound Stupidity: The British Party System and the Northern Ireland Question," in J. McGarry and B. O'Leary, eds., *The Future of Northern Ireland.* Oxford: Oxford University Press, 100–36.

Roche, P. (1995) "Northern Ireland and Irish Nationalism," in J. Wilson Foster, ed., *The Idea of the Union: Statements and Critiques in Support of the Union of Great Britain and Northern Ireland.* Vancouver: Belcouver Press.

Roche, P., and B. Barton, eds. (1991) *The Northern Ireland Question: Myth and Reality*. Aldershot: Avebury.

Rooney, K. (1998) "Institutionalising Division," *Fortnight*, June, 11–12.

Taylor, Charles (1997) "Nationalism and Modernity," in R. McKim and J. McMahan, eds., *The Morality of Nationalism*. New York: Oxford University Press, 31–55.

Taylor, R. (2001) "Northern Ireland: Transformation versus Consociation," in J. McGarry, ed., *Northern Ireland and the Divided World: The Northern Ireland Conflict and the Good Friday Agreement in Comparative Perspective*. Oxford: Oxford University Press, 36–52.

Trew, K. (1996) "National Identity," in R. Breen, P. Devine, and L. Dowds, eds., *Social Attitudes in Northern Ireland*. Belfast: Appletree Press.

Whyte, J. (1993) "Dynamics of Social and Political Change in Northern Ireland," in D. Keogh and M. Haltzel, eds., *Northern Ireland and the Politics of Reconciliation*. Cambridge: Cambridge University Press.

DAVID McCRONE

Understating the Nation:
The Scottish Question

Compared with those studying other social and political phenomena, students of nationalism are fairly used to addressing the legitimacy of their interests. Why, some ask, should anyone wish to study anything as nasty as nationalism? Ernest Gellner (1983) once observed that the "dark gods" theory of nationalism – the view that ethnic irrationalism might escape from its Pandora's box to infect the political world – was a stumbling block to our understanding of the phenomenon. Those who study nationalism often encounter the view that there is something dangerous in so doing, as if studying it might encourage people to believe in it. A large part of this misapprehension arises from the assumption that "real" nationalism involves deep, ethnic emotions and thus that "real" nationalism is dangerous.

This paper examines the situation in Scotland and in Britain more generally. The first section works at the complex relationships between Britain and Scotland, which defies many textbook assumptions about nation and state. The second considers Britain's history and the definition of "British." The third analyses Scottish attributes today.

BRITAIN AND SCOTLAND

Problematizing the "Nation-State" in Britain

The student of Scotland confronts such assumptions, and much more. Even the casual exploration of nationalism in Scotland raises questions.

Scottish nationalism seems unusually culture-light. It was Benedict Anderson (1996) who observed that the Union between Scotland and England in 1707, which brought into being Great Britain, was possible because the two countries were similar in religion (Protestantism) and in language (English). The feeling that nationalism in Scotland is somehow not "real" results in large part from its lack of cultural distinctiveness with England.

In comparison with, for example, Wales and Catalonia, which are much more linguistically different from their host states, Scotland has developed the most "independentist" national movement of all – namely, a strong nationalist party committed to full sovereignty within the European Union. In this respect, Scotland's comparators are Ireland and Denmark rather than Wales and Catalonia. This apparent puzzle, however, offers an opportunity for students of nationalism, not a problem. It shifts the explanation away from cultural distinctiveness to political and civic autonomy.

This paper argues that, far from being a deviant case, nationalism in Scotland allows one to go to the root of nationalism in terms of sociological explanation. In short, if Scotland has developed an advanced form of nationalism without strong differentials of language, religion, or other ostensibly cultural means, then conventional ways of explaining nationalism in terms of cultural specificities do not apply. The other, somewhat unusual approach in this paper is to argue for a less "internalist" account of nationalist movements. Nationalism in Scotland depends heavily on the nature of the British state. That, of course, is a necessary but not sufficient condition, otherwise Wales and Scotland would have very similar trajectories in their relationship with the United Kingdom, and plainly they do not.

Let us start with the key concept of the "nation-state." The term refers to virtually any "independent" state recognized by the United Nations, with "nation" and "state" being largely synonymous. Anthony Giddens, for example, defines the nation-state as "a set of institutional forms of governance maintaining an administrative monopoly over a territory with demarcated boundaries, its rule being sanctioned by law and direct control of the means of internal and external violence" (1981, 190). This is really a definition of the state, making no mention of the nation as such. Giddens sees the nation as a "bordered power-container" that exists "when a state has a unified administrative reach over the territory over which its sovereignty is claimed" (1985, 120). Giddens is not alone in redefining the nation in purely political terms and in the process losing its cultural significance.

Nevertheless, the hyphenated term nation-state aligns the strictly political realm of state with the cultural one of nation, thereby fusing two
analytically distinct spheres. Anyone who inhabits what have been
called "stateless nations" knows only too well that they are not the
same thing. There are nations – "imagined communities," in Benedict
Anderson's famous term – which are not formally independent states.
And there are political entities – states – that contain distinct territorial
cultural groupings – nations. For example, the United Kingdom is a
multinational state, despite its hitherto unitary system of governance,
and its peoples, certainly in Scotland and Wales, and increasingly in England, are willing and able to distinguish between "national" identity
(Scottish, Welsh, and English), and "state" identity (British).

Scholars are now much more willing to question the orthodoxy of
"nation-state." Famously, for students of nationalism, Walker Connor
(1990) observed that less than 10 per cent of actual states are genuine
nation-states in which nation-ness and state-ness coincide and that have
ethnic or cultural homogeneity within their boundaries. Denmark, Norway, and possibly the Republic of Ireland spring to mind, although disputed territory – Northern Ireland – lies outwith the Irish state. (That is
why I omit Northern Ireland from the non-English parts of the United
Kingdom, as it contains two unusual groupings: the majority (around
55 per cent), who make a "political" nationalist claim to be "British,"
and a minority (45 per cent), who consider themselves "Irish." Both
groups are not "nationals" in the conventional sense of having prime
allegiance to the territory in which they currently reside. Each, by and
large, wants to belong to some other place.)

Some writers such as Charles Tilly (1992) eschew the term "nation-
state" in favour of "national state" because states govern several cultural regions, and few people within their jurisdiction share cultural
identity. Others, such as Yael Tamir, observe that "the era of the homogeneous and viable nation-state is over (or rather the era of the illusion
that homogeneous and viable nation states are possible is over, since
such states never existed) and the national vision must be redefined"
(1993, 3). Again, as Benedict Anderson commented, the problem with
the nation-state is that there is a crisis of the hyphen.

In the current analytical situation, nations and states belong to different realms – the cultural and the political – and while these terms run
into each other, they are not synonyms. Above all, yoking them together
is an ideological act, conferring on states the legitimacy of culture, and
on nations the primary right to political self-determination. The world

is not made of jigsaw pieces that all fit together if only we persevere and follow the picture on the box lid. Disputed territories such as Palestine–Israel abound, and no amount of zero–sum gaming will allow them to reconcile in a neat and simple way.

This situation, of course, is to the advantage of stateless nations (or "understated nations," as I prefer to call them; few are bereft of some autonomy of governance, hence a degree of state-ness). If we now recognize in principle the ill-fit between state and nation, then we are more able to appreciate the historico-political circumstances that gave rise to the "anomalies" in the first place.

Anomalizing Scotland

Scotland is a particularly good example of such circumstances. First, it is not really convincing to argue that one of Europe's "historic nations" (with a history of political statehood going back at least to the first millennium) has generated a nationalism dependent on a sentimental time-lag. Scotland's sense of nation is wide and deep and not carried by strong cultural markers of a conventional sort such as language and religion. Its base and rationale lie elsewhere (Paterson, 1994). In key respects, Scotland has always recognized itself and been recognized by the British state as a distinctive nation. Hence there is nothing like the fraught debate that there is within Canada about Quebec's status as nation versus province. Probably as a consequence, nation-ness and national identity are poor predictors of constitutional position in Scotland. Conservatives, for example, who have long prided themselves on being "unionists" and until 1999 opposed any form of home rule for Scotland, have always taken pride in being Scottish, and some of the most quintessential Scots such as Walter Scott were Tories. Second, in Scotland, there is no simple and predictive relationship between people's constitutional preferences, their party identification, and how they construe their national identity. Thus, around one-third of voters for the Scottish National Party (SNP) do not want full independence, whereas roughly the same proportion of Labour voters do. Similarly, only one-third of SNP identifiers say that they are Scottish and not British, with the largest proportion, 44 per cent, claiming to be more Scottish than British (McCrone, 2001, chap. 7).

To some this situation looks like an attenuated form of nationalism, but it reflects strong roots in Scottish institutional experience. Scotland gave up its formal statehood to sign a Treaty of Union with England in

1707 – and one can have treaties only between sovereign states – while retaining a high measure of civil autonomy. The Union was a marriage of convenience that gave England politico-military security by breaking up the historic alliance between its two ancient enemies, Scotland and France. Scotland in return obtained access to English markets at home and abroad, having been excluded from them overseas by English mercantile power. While abrogating its national parliament, it retained and indeed developed its control over key institutions – notably law, education, local administration, and the church system. To all intents and purposes, Scotland remained autonomous in its institutional spheres until, ironically, majoritarian democracy took hold well into the 20th century.

Once that happened, the contradictions inherent in what Neil Mac-Cormick has called "the Scottish anomaly" began to surface. He pointed out in his British Academy lecture in 1997 (MacCormick, 1998) that at the heart of the British constitution lies the Scottish anomaly. England, he argued, saw the Union of 1707 as the completion and consolidation of the *soi-disant* "glorious revolution" of 1688, not a step in a quite different direction. Hence, the English legal theorist A.V. Dicey promulgated what became the conventional view that it was an "incorporating" union, not a federal or quasi-federal one. Thus, to speak of the Act of Union, rather than of a Treaty of Union as the Scots did (and do), reflects a *mentalité* that still lies at the heart of the constitutional process. Mac-Cormick observes: "In form, the Union constituted a new state with a new name. But in substance, the underlying assumption was that the larger partner [England] was a continuing entity" (1998, 139). Underlying this difference, he argues, is a more basic philosophical difference. Whereas the old English constitution was unwritten, derived from custom, convention and common law, and the absolute and sovereign authority of Parliament (the crown in Parliament), so the Scottish tradition was based on *ius regni*, the law of the realm, on popular assent authorizing and limiting monarchical power – rule by "community of the realm." MacCormick argues that we have an English constitution underpinning a British state, and within that lies a "Scottish anomaly," in which "Scotland was incorporated, but Scotland stayed different" (1998, 142).

Thus the key to the Scottish question lies less in its internalist conflicts and tensions and much more in its politico-constitutional relations with the British state. This is the sphere that explains nationalism in the British islands, and that is the next step in my argument. To anyone coming new to the study of the United Kingdom, it is a puzzle as to why it is neither a properly unitary state nor a federal one. These would seem to be the obvious and logical choices. On the one hand, England forms by far the largest element (with 85 per cent) of the British population and is the most powerful of the nations of the United Kingdom, and, as MacCormick observes, an incorporating union was the conventional view. On the other hand, the Scots had not entered that union with a view to signing away their autonomy. For them, the union amounted to "having your cake and eating it." Subsequently, they were to play a disproportionate role in the British Empire and were for a large part of union history enthusiastic and proud Brits (Fry, 2001). They did not feel any less Scottish but were content to practise nested forms of identity as – in Graeme Morton's (1999) felicitous phrase – unionist–nationalists.

BRITAIN AND THE "BRITISH"

Understanding Britain's History

It is important, then, not to run together the political histories of the non-English peoples of the Isles. While Ireland and Wales became colonies of England by the 14th century, that was not Scotland's fate, and, having asserted its political statehood in its own wars of independence in the late 13th and early 14th centuries, it remained separate from its big neighbour until, first, its king, James VI, peacefully inherited the English throne in 1603, and ultimately, Scotland threw its lot in with the English in 1707. This "Britain" that the Scots helped to create was, as Tom Nairn (1977) observed, a state made out of a pre-democratic bargain between the patrician classes of both countries. It was also a very unusual state, externally powerful and predatory, and internally weak and uncontrolling. As long as the peoples and territories of these islands did not rock the boat, they were left to their own devices. The exceptions were Catholic Ireland, which never properly became "British," and the Highland clans of Scotland in the 18th century, who sought to restore the Stewarts to the British throne, which was in the hands of Protestant Dutchman William and his wife, Mary Stewart, following the revolution of 1689, and later of the German dynasty of Hanover, descendants of James VI's granddaughter, Sophia, electress of Hanover.

The development of the United Kingdom (so-called, following the formal incorporation of Ireland in 1801) as a pre-democratic formation has led some scholars to treat it as in essence "un-modern." Writers such as David Marquand (1988) observe that there is something "un-modern" about it, in the sense not that it is socially and economically unreconstructed – Britain was, after all, the home of the industrial revolution and almost single-handedly invented market capitalism – but that in constitutional–political terms it has not (nor really tried) to resolve its inherent constitutional contradictions. Thus it has no written constitution, no formal set of citizenship rights, an unelected second chamber, a doctrine of democratic dictatorship – crown sovereignty – at its jurisprudential heart, all underpinned by a powerful social and economic elite – the "Establishment." There is much for radicals to sink their teeth into here, and the British liberal left, through organizations such as Charter 88, has sought, largely in vain, to persuade successive governments to instigate thoroughgoing constitutional reform (Barnett, 1997).

There is another important aspect to this apparently unreconstructed character of the British state. First of all, the radical historian Eric Hobsbawm has pointed out that this apparent obsession with "tradition" is frequently a front. Tradition, he observes, is not a serious obstacle to change. "Often it is merely a British way of giving a label to any moderately enduring facts, especially at the moment when these facts are themselves beginning to change. After they have been changed for a generation, they will in turn be called 'traditional'" (1969, 19). The preference for sticking old labels on new bottles, he comments, should not be confused with resistance to change. The capacity of the landed elites to reinvent themselves as a new capitalist class without the upheavals of France or Germany was a sign of this successful strategy.

Refurbishing old traditions and reinventing new ones allowed the patina of the past to overlay radical economic change. Hobsbawm observes that Britain was a state in which there had been a radical break with the past: the early destruction of its peasantry, a landed elite that survived by becoming capitalist, and its lack of severe revolutionary disruption as occurred in most other European countries. Its eventual (relative) decline was due to its early and long sustained start as the premier industrial power and, above all, to the fact that its industrialization was global, dependent on empire, and a monopoly of world trade. Its rise and fall depended on its being a "single, liberal world-economy, theoretically self-regulating but in fact requiring Britain as a semi-automatic switchboard" (1969, 14–15).

Britain's inability to hold this unusual position was partly the result of the fortunes of the pioneer, overtaken by others – notably, by the "modernizing" states such as Germany and the United States, which created state structures more in keeping with their role as pursuants of the front marker. Britain's unwillingness or inability to modernize its political institutions reflected its success in its role as a night-watchman state, with underdeveloped state structures except where, as in the case of the armed forces, they were needed to defend and extend the empire. It left civil society to its own devices, such that the British state sat lightly on it. Marquand has called it an "unprincipled" society in so far as state structures were not modernized and integrated. Thus, "Thanks to the upheavals of the 17th century – thanks in particular to the victory of the landed English classes over the Stuart kings – one cannot speak of a 'British state' in the way that one speaks of a 'French state' or in modern times a 'German state'. The UK is not a state in the continental sense. It is a bundle of islands (including such exotica as the Channel Islands and the Isle of Man which are not even represented at Westminster), acquired at different times by the English crown, and governed in different ways" (1988, 152).

The British state does not suffer from arrested political development as such, for it was a minimal state with a small state bureaucracy designed to suit market-driven adjustment in the 18th century, which, however, failed to make the transition to full modernity in the late 19th and the 20th centuries. Market liberalism was the dominant ethos and survived long after the doctrine as such was abandoned. It is hard to maintain the argument that Britain was never modern, for, as Linda Colley observes, up to the beginning of the 19th century it was the most modern and democratized in Europe. Its Protestant ethic underpinned a commitment to civil and economic liberalism, which made it the premier power until the late 19th century. It failed to make the next stage of transition and, by the final quarter of that century, was being overtaken by its continental neighbours.

We might note the (con)fusion of "British state" with "English crown" [sic] in Marquand's comments, even though England as such has not had an ethnically "English" monarchy since the middle ages: the Tudors (Welsh), the Stewarts (Scottish), William the Dutchman, the Hanoverians, the House of Saxe-Coburg-Gotha, and so on. More seriously perhaps, such a statement fails to recognize the multinational character of the United Kingdom. Possibly only a loosely structured state would suit the Scots, the junior partner in British imperialism, who were forever watchful for the erosion of national rights, be these the right of Scottish banks to issue their own notes or the power to run their own ecclesiastical affairs in their national – Presbyterian – church. In economic terms, Britain lost its lead after the 1890s, in part because Germany reinforced industry with scientific research for nationalistic reasons, but also because, in Hobsbawm's words, "Britain failed to adapt to new conditions, not because she could not, but because she did not wish to" (1969, 182).

Scotland's rise and its fall as part of this world power were closely related. On the one hand, its lowlands could take advantage of the exceptionally favourable continental and British conjuncture of the end of the 18th century. On the other hand, Scotland was so well adapted to imperial opportunities in the 19th century that the collapse of the economy after the First World War was catastrophic. The roots of Scotland's economic decline lies much more in a surfeit of, and overadaptation to, British imperialism than any failure to embrace it wholeheartedly. When the international order collapsed, Scotland was so locked into it that it suffered along with the United Kingdom as a whole (Kirby, 1981).

This, of course, is history, but it explains how the British "marriage" became less and less convenient for the Scots. The relationship between "state" and "national" interests is the key to nationalism and national identity in the British islands. The United Kingdom of Great Britain and Northern Ireland – to give the state its full title – is, in its present form, little over 80 years old, created following the secession of most of Ireland in 1921. Britain began in 1707 as a "state-nation," a union of two sovereign states, one big and one small, with the larger, England, having incorporated Wales and Ireland by conquest some three or four centuries earlier. This union-state quickly developed an empire, with the effect that Britishness grew up as an imperial identity defined by allegiance to the crown. "Civis Britannicus sum" was the equivalent of its Roman counterpart in so far as that claim could be made by those living in the far corners of the empire rather than simply by residents in the home state.

Citizenship came late to the British, and it was only after 1945 that, as a result of former colonies and dominions such as Canada asserting their right to control their own immigration, the erstwhile imperial parliament in London was forced to introduce a definition of citizenship for residence of the islands. They seem to have acquired formal citizenship by a legislative sleight of hand when the Nationality Act of 1948 made them "citizens of the UK and colonies." The preference for both Labour and Conservative parties was to consider people of the Commonwealth subjects of the crown first (made easier when the monarch remained head of state) and citizens of individual states second. In large part, the formal declaration of the independent part of Ireland – then called Eire – as a republic in 1948 was to deny that Irish citizens had any formal sovereignty under the British crown.

If British identity was externally fuzzy, so was its meaning in the United Kingdom. In Robin Cohen's words: "British identity shows a general pattern of fragmentation. Multiple axes of identification have meant that Irish, Scots, Welsh and English people, those from the white, black and brown Commonwealth, Americans, English-speakers, Europeans and even "aliens" have had their lives intersect one with another in overlapping and complex circles of identity-construction and rejection. The shape and edges of British identity are thus historically changing, often vague and, to a degree, malleable – an aspect of British identity I have called 'a fuzzy frontier'" (1994, 35).

If the United Kingdom evolved as a state-nation under imperial circumstances, how does it compare with neighbouring European states? In his study of citizenship and nationhood, Rogers Brubaker characterizes two routes: the French one, in which state preceded nation, and Germany, in which nation preceded state. This, he argues, shaped the conceptions of citizenship that each state followed. France promoted the idea of *ius soli*, the law of soil or territorial jurisdiction, such that all residents of French soil at home and abroad were citizens of the state. In Germany, *ius sanguinis*, the law of blood, was the foundation of national identity and citizenship, reflecting the late formation of the German state (in 1871), so that many "Germans" lived on the soil of another state such as Austria or Russia.

Brubaker argues that while nationality in France was thought of as state-centred and assimilationist, in Germany it was nation-centred and differentialist. "The state-centred assimilationist understanding of nationhood in France is embodied and expressed in an expansive definition of citizenship, one that automatically transforms second-generation immigrants into citizens, assimilating them – legally – to other French men and women. The ethnocultural, differentialist understanding of nationhood in Germany is embodied and expressed in a definition of citizenship that is remarkably open to ethnic immigrants from Eastern Europe and the Soviet Union, but remarkably closed to non-German immigrants" (1992, 3). While German law was changed in 1998 to give nationality to long-term immigrants such as those of Turkish origin, the historico–legal foundations were embedded in the cultural meaning of citizenship.

My purpose in citing Brubaker's ideal-types is to ask which applies to Britain. This is something of a trick question, for it does not correspond to either. While citizens of empire did not have automatic rights of citizenship, they did have some rights of settlement. Laws of "patriality," notably the Nationality Act of 1981, conferred blood rights on people with at least one grandparent born in the United Kingdom. In other words, British citizenship and rights of settlement developed as an uneasy mix of territory and blood criteria.

The United Kingdom stands awkwardly as a state in the modern world. It was created as a patrician bargain between two elites in the pre-modern era. It was a "state-nation" that contained within itself distinctive nationalities that were largely self-governing. The overlying political–cultural identity was in essence imperial and could be shared by residents, even citizens, of the former empire. It was a latecomer to concepts of citizenship, and largely by default. It was an "unprincipled" state that somehow had missed out on the process of political modernization that other states embarked on from the mid-19th to the mid-20th century. Its constitutional arrangements leapt, as it were, from pre-modern to postmodern, largely missing out the "nation-building" phase that occurred in this period and which constituted so much of modern nationalism. Its citizens call themselves "British," which at least hitherto was virtually a synonym for "English," while only the Scots and Welsh, and to differing degrees, made a distinction between "state" and "national" identity, with the Scots in particular prioritizing the latter over the former, at least since the final quarter of the 20th century.

Defining the "British"

Given this history, there grew up two parallel universes: one that focused on political–cultural relations between the different territorial peoples – the Scots, Welsh, Northern Irish, and, belatedly, English. Theirs is a debate about constitutional change and territorial representation, notably in the "devolution" of powers to the parliament of Scotland and to the assemblies of Wales and Northern Ireland. This is a universe of federating the powers of the state to recognize the distinctiveness of constituent nations, but also to buy off nationalism and prevent the break-up of Britain. The second universe is essentially an English one, framed by ethnicity and "race" and reflecting patterns of immigrant settlement in the postwar years into the major cities of England, which had substantial labour shortages.

The two discourses are largely disconnected: the territorial one concentrates on issues of nationalism in the non-English countries and on regionalism within England; the ethnic one relates to racial diversity and multiculturalism. Black or brown people in England are much more likely to describe themselves as "British," because that describes their citizenship, rather than "English," which has come to be a self-description of white people. Yet the Scots and the Welsh use "British" as a secondary, or state, identity, giving primacy to national identity. In Northern Ireland, "British" is a matter of whether or not one supports the union rather than reunification with Ireland. On the whole, the British are underdefined. Sport is a good indicator of nationality. There are very few "British" teams, apart from those at the Olympic Games, and football and rugby are "national" sports. The Conservative politician Norman Tebbit, once talked of "the cricket test": how could people of Afro-Caribbean and Asian origin be considered English if they chose to cheer on England's opposition? Tebbit's test failed to notice that the Scots and the Welsh were quite happy to cheer on the opposition to England also.

If the British state is to survive in its present form, much depends on what the Scots do. While they represent a mere 10 per cent of the population, they do constitute the largest non-English national group and are one of the two founders of the United Kingdom. There is, of course, an argument that Britain will survive even if Scotland becomes independent. "Britain" once constituted an imperial entity that has progressively lost its dominions and colonies, changing but not losing its identity. Like an iceberg that sails into warmer waters, it might become smaller, but it is still recognizable as generally the same iceberg. Compared with the angst that seems likely in Canada if and when Quebec secedes in so far as there might well be a question mark over the state's existence, there is no such feeling in England. Indeed, when asked about their preferred constitutional option for Scotland, most people in England reply much as the Scots do: a majority prefer a devolved parliament within the United Kingdom; about 25 per cent, an independent Scotland, and only one in eight, no parliament of any sort. In 1999, 40 per cent of the English said that they would be sorry if Scotland left the Union, and only 7 per cent, that they would be pleased. It is not so much a matter of geography (Scotland, unlike Quebec, is not in an awkward place), more a matter of the identity politics of the core people, the English, who represent 85 per cent of the population. The English seem much more exercised by continental Europe than by small countries on their peripheries. To the Scots, the European Union is, in Neil MacCormick's words, a theatre of opportunity rather than a threat to identity.

UNDERSTANDING THE SCOTS TODAY

And what of the Scots? Since 1999 they have had a devolved parliament with substantial powers, reflecting the fact that Scotland has always had legal autonomy within the United Kingdom. In a referendum in 1997, they voted 3 to 1 to have such a parliament and 2 to 1 that it should have tax-varying powers. In an earlier referendum, in 1979, the Scots voted narrowly for a weaker assembly, but the measure did not meet the rule that 40 per cent of the electorate had to vote in favour. The incoming Conservative government did not implement the bill, which fell when Labour was defeated at the general election the same year. During the period 1979–97, when the Conservatives were in office in London and governing the administrative apparatus of Scotland from afar, a considerable "democratic deficit" arose, whereby no matter how Scotland (and Wales, for that matter) voted, it always got a Westminster government elected by majority votes in England. By 1997, and the election of a Labour government in London, Conservative MPs were swept away in both Scotland and Wales, and by the end of 1998 devolution was on the statute book.

Support for devolution had coalesced, despite Scotland's having no elected body. Independence as an option has grown to a fairly consistent 30 per cent of constitutional opinion (Table 1). Support for independence has grown steadily over 20 years, from a low of under 10 per cent in 1979 to 30 per cent in 2000, falling back from a high of 37 per cent at the time of the 1997 referendum. Moreover, a feeling that independence was likely, regardless of personal preferences, became the common view. At the time of the referendum in 1997, 59 per cent (made up of 76 per cent of those who supported that option and 48 per cent of those who did not) thought that independence was "very likely" or "quite likely" in the ensuing two decades. In 1999, 51 per cent took this view (75 per cent of those who supported it and 43 per cent of those opposed).

Nevertheless, the modal option has long been a home rule parliament, with around half supporting it. In so far as there is a "settled will," then devolution is it, at least for the present. Over the period 1997–2000, there was a distinct falling away in people's assessment that devolution makes separation more likely (Table 2).

Those who anticipated a "slippery slope" have been confounded, at least in the short term. In like manner, the "no parliament" option has shrunk to about one in ten. Analysis of panel data shows that the strengthening of support for independence almost certainly has come as

Table 1
Support for various constitutional options, 1979–2001

	1979	1992	1997 (election)	1997 (referendum)	1999	2000	2001
Independence outwith EU*	7	6	8	9	10	11	9
Independence in EU*		17	18	28	18	19	18
Strong domestic parliament†	26	50	42	32	50	47	54
Weak domestic parliament†	28		9	9	9	8	6
No elected body	26	24	17	17	10	12	9
Sample size‡	729	957	882	676	1482	1663	1605

Sources: Scottish Election Surveys of 1979, 1992, and 1997; Scottish Referendum Survey of 1997; Scottish Social Attitudes Surveys of 1999, 2000, and 2001.
* No distinction made between the two types of independence.
† Strong domestic parliament was referred to in 1979 as "Scottish Assembly which would handle most Scottish affairs" and from 1997 onwards as "Scottish Parliament within the UK with some taxation powers." Weak domestic parliament was referred to in 1979 as "Scottish Assembly which would handle some Scottish affairs and would be responsible to Parliament at Westminster" and from 1997 onwards as "Scottish Parliament within the UK with no taxation powers." No distinction was made in 1992.
‡ "Don't know" and "Not answered" included in the base.

Table 2
Views on a Scottish parliament and independence, 1997–2000

	1997	1999	2000
Which of the following comes closest to your views? A Scottish parliament will make Scotland:	(%)	(%)	(%)
More likely to leave UK	42	37	27
More likely to stay in UK	32	30	25
No difference	19	27	43

Sources: Scottish Election Surveys of 1977; Scottish Social Attitudes Surveys of 1999 and 2000.

a result of people shifting away from supporting a strong domestic parliament, while these people were replaced by those who previously opposed any parliament, independent or devolved.

In terms of the social basis of support for independence, support rose in all social classes, although it has always been higher among the working class than the middle class (Table 3). Support for independence peaked at the time of the referendum in 1997, when about one-half of working-class people favoured it. Nevertheless, since then, around one-quarter of middle-class groups have supported independence. The gradient of

Table 3
Support for independence by class, gender, and age, 1979–2000

	1979		1992		1997 (election)		1997 (referen-dum)		1999		2000	
	%	N*	%	N	%	N	%	N	%	N	%	N
Class†												
Professional	7	45	5	22	14	34	25	28	26	57	43	59
Intermediate	8	78	19	204	22	189	25	153	20	387	22	386
Routine non-manual	8	62	19	229	24	205	30	168	25	280	28	351
Skilled manual	5	92	30	199	32	169	48	143	31	272	39	296
Semi-skilled manual	8	155	30	185	29	141	49	108	38	228	36	284
Unskilled manual	8	195	20	81	34	89	54	51	34	120	27	121
Gender												
Men	8	350	28	445	29	376	40	291	30	667	34	691
Women	6	375	18	512	24	506	34	385	24	815	27	972
Age												
18–24	11	55	30	118	36	85	46	41	44	95	44	144
25–34	7	155	27	183	35	170	50	123	31	305	44	295
35–44	10	132	27	172	30	153	38	141	30	259	31	333
45–54	6	119	27	162	25	148	36	116	27	247	23	257
55–64	4	93	12	137	19	125	32	94	22	209	28	229
65+	7	138	15	171	13	192	24	159	17	356	17	404

Sources: Scottish Election Surveys of 1979, 1992, and 1997; Scottish Referendum Survey of 1997; Scottish Social Attitudes Surveys of 1999 and 2000.
* "Don't know" and "Not answered" included in the base (N).
† Measured by Registrar General scheme, 1992–2000, and by social grade in 1979.

support in terms of social-class differences is much more pronounced for independence than in support for any kind of elected parliament, especially a devolved one, which has had fairly consistent support across the social spectrum (Paterson et al., 1999).

Nowadays, substantial minorities support independence in all class, gender, and age groups, but with the strongest support among working-class people, men, and young people, and with distinctly low levels of support only among old people. The gender difference in support is clear and stable: in all years, men have been more likely to support independence than women, usually by about five percentage points. This gender difference is not found in support for any kind of elected parliament, because women are more likely to support a domestic parliament than men.

Table 4
Support for independence by party identification, 1979–2000

	1979		1992		1997 (election)		1997 (referendum)		1999		2000	
	%	N*	%	N	%	N	%	N	%	N	%	N
Conservative[†]	3	222	4	116	7	144	11	123	9	231	13	269
Labour	4	274	21	164	22	415	37	336	22	625	25	621
Liberal Democrat	1	67	19	32	15	96	11	51	16	166	14	121
SNP	37	75	51	93	67	147	77	122	61	290	60	319

Sources: Scottish Election Surveys of 1979, 1992, and 1997; Scottish Referendum Survey of 1997; Scottish Social Attitudes Surveys of 1999 and 2000.
* "Don't know" and "Not answered" included in the base (N).
† Party identification is the reply to the question "Do you generally think of yourself as a little closer to one of the parties than the others?"

Table 5
Party identification, among independence supporters, 1979–2000

	1979	1992	1997 (election)	1997 (referendum)	1999	2000
Conservative*	13	5	5	5	6	9
Labour	22	38	42	50	36	37
Liberal Democrat	2	7	7	2	8	5
SNP	62	51	47	42	50	49
Sample size[†]	50	218	227	239	395	494

Sources: Scottish Election Surveys of 1979, 1992, and 1997; Scottish Referendum Survey of 1997; Scottish Social Attitudes Surveys of 1999 and 2000.
* Party identification is the reply to the question "Do you generally think of yourself as a little closer to one of the parties than the others?"
† "Don't know" and "Not answered" included in the base.

Certainly, adherents of the Scottish National Party (SNP) are much more likely to support independence than followers of other parties (Table 4). Since 1997, however, the SNP has consistently had about two-thirds or more of its supporters also favouring the party's core policy. Yet that leaves one-third not doing so. What is more, in the past decade, at least one half of independence supporters have not voted for the SNP, as Table 5 shows. When independence reached its recent peak of support, at the time of the referendum in 1997, a clear majority of these supporters would have voted for the Labour party, not for the SNP. Back in 1979, things were markedly different. The SNP attracted two-thirds of the small band of independence supporters but depended on opponents of independence for a much larger share of its vote than it has done recently.

The Scots seem very open to experimenting with constitutional futures. They do not see a stark divide between independence and a domestic parliament. Further analysis shows that, of those favouring independence on any occasion, at least one-third, and usually over 40 per cent, would support a domestic parliament at another occasion, but that only around 3 per cent would shift to opposing any parliament at all. Despite the apparent stability of the cross-sectional differences in earlier tables, there is no stable core group of supporters. The core group of opponents of independence is rather larger – about 55 per cent. But if we add in also the 18 per cent who, in 1997, gave independence as their second choice and cited neither type of independence as their first choice, 63 per cent of people would at least contemplate this option. Given the fluidity apparent here, that figure would almost certainly be higher if second choices had been recorded at other waves. This finding is consistent with the comment made above: the people who view independence positively tend to be much more numerous than the people who are willing to support it at any particular time.

What, however, of the view that devolution represents the "settled will" of the Scottish people? After all, devolution is by far the most popular option. Nevertheless, after two years of devolution, we find a marked contrast between which parliament, Scottish or British, is the most influential, on the one hand, and which ought to be, on the other hand. Around two-thirds say that Westminster is the most influential over the way Scotland is run, but three-quarters think that the Scottish parliament should have the most influence (Scottish Social Attitudes Survey, 2001).

In like manner, there is strong support for the Scottish parliament to be strengthened. While about two-thirds of Scots want it to have more powers, 7 of 10 "home rulers" want more powers (Table 6).

CONCLUSION

Where does Scotland stand in the scheme of things? In considering the debate about its constitutional future, it is important to take the long

Table 6
Constitutional preference and desire for more powers

Voter's constitutional preference	% wanting more powers		
	1999	2000	2001
Independent from UK and EU	82	90	93
Independent from UK within EU	85	89	89
Parliament with taxation powers	52	67	70
Parliament without taxation powers	40	42	37
No change	15	21	16

Sources: Scottish Social Attitudes, 1999 and 2000.

view. Scotland joined the Union in 1707 because it struck a bargain
with its large neighbour to the south in exchange for certain guarantees
about its institutional autonomy. For much of the subsequent two and a
half centuries this bargain held. By the second half of the 20th century,
the contradictions inherent in the Union became more manifest. A
largely self-governing society with considerable institutional autonomy
found its room for manoeuvre restricted within a state that was losing
its capacity as a world power. Three points are crucial. First, national –
i.e. Scottish – identity was always strong north of the border. The Scots
have not suddenly switched from being British to being Scottish. Second, the relationship between constitutional preferences and national
identity has never been straightforward. "Sovereignists" frequently
claimed some sense of being British. Third, people in Scotland voted for
a (devolved) parliament in 1999 for essentially instrumental reasons:
they wanted a Scotland with better and more appropriate social and
economic policies.

Will the half-way house between union and independence hold? No
one can honestly tell. To those in favour of a devolved system within the
United Kingdom, what Scotland now has is, in the parlance, the "settled will." Yet, while well over half of Scots now support devolution,
they are not averse to their parliament's acquiring more powers as and
when they are needed. In other words, they will choose the constitutional means that they judge to maximize Scotland's room for manoeuvre. Just as the Union settlement of 1707 was so flexible as to last
almost three centuries, so formal devolution may or may not remain on
the constitutional table until, as with the union-state, the Scots seek

greater autonomy. The problem with terms such as "union" and "independence" is that they imply zero–sum approaches to constitutional matters: you are either for it or against it.

What seems more the case, at least in Scotland, and more probably in the wider world, is that self-government is a continuum along which nations migrate according to their perceived self-interest. In an interdependent world, especially one in which there has been a "hollowing-out" of the conventional state, its powers being pulled up to the supra-state level and down to, in Scotland, the national level, then there is no predictable outcome. If the Scottish case has wider significance, it is that it highlights the shifting geometry of power in the modern world, without which "national" movements cannot be properly understood. Scotland may be light on the distinctive cultural markers of nationalism, but it underscores the geopolitical essence of these movements and as such is a key test-case for the 21st century.

REFERENCES

Anderson, B. (1996) *Imagined Communities: Reflections on the Origin and Spread of Nationalism*. Rev. ed. London: Verso.

Barnett A. (1997). *This Time: Our Constitutional Revolution*. London: Vintage Books.

Brubaker, R. (1996) *Nationalism Reframed: Nationhood and the National Question in the New Europe*. Cambridge: Cambridge University Press.

Cohen, R. (1994) *Frontiers of Identity: The British and Others*. London: Longman.

Connor, W. (1990) "When Is a Nation?" *Ethnic and Racial Studies* 13, 92–103.

Fry, M. (2001) *The Scottish Empire*. East Lothian: Tuckwell Press.

Gellner, E. (1983) *Nations and Nationalism*. Oxford: Blackwell.

Giddens, A. (1981) *Power, Property and the State*. London: Macmillan.

– (1985) *The Nation-state and Violence*. London: Polity Press.

Hobsbawm, E.J. (1969) *Industry and Empire*. Harmondsworth: Penguin.

Kirby, M.W. (1981) *The Decline of British Economic Power since 1870*. London: Allen & Unwin.

MacCormick, N. (1998) "The English Constitution, the British State and the Scottish Anomaly," in "Understanding Constitutional Change," special issue of *Scottish Affairs*.

Marquand, D. (1988) *The Unprincipled Society*. London: Fontana.

McCrone, D. (2001) *Understanding Scotland: The Sociology of a Nation.* London: Routledge.

Morton, G. (1999) *Unionist-Nationalism: Governing Urban Scotland, 1830–60.* East Linton: Tuckwell Press.

Nairn, T. (1977) *The Break-up of Britain.* London: New Left Books.

Paterson, L. (1994) *The Autonomy of Modern Scotland.* Edinburgh: Edinburgh University Press.

Paterson, L., et al. (1999) *New Scotland, New Politics?* Edinburgh: Polygon at Edinburgh.

Tamir, Y. (1993) *Liberal Nationalism.* Princeton, NJ: Princeton University Press.

Tilly, C. (1992) *Coercion, Capital and European States, AD 990–1992.* Oxford: Blackwell.

MONTSERRAT GUIBERNAU

Catalonia:
A Non-secessionist Nationalism?

After forty years of Franco's dictatorship, Spain's constitution of 1978 offered a new political framework within which citizens could organize their lives. One of the major issues faced by the new government was the national question, which was particularly acute in Catalonia and the Basque Country. The new constitution transformed the centralist, non-democratic government inherited from Franco and made possible the creation of autonomous communities. The lack of violence in the transition to democracy, the almost immediate acceptance of Spain by Western organizations such as the North Atlantic Treaty Organization and the European Community, together with the rapid activation of the economy, prompted the emergence of a dynamic Spain opposed to traditional patterns of backwardness and conservatism, as exemplified by the Franco regime.

How did this evolution happen, and what was at stake in it? These are the questions addressed in this paper, which has two sections. First, it sketches the historical background of Catalonia's relationship with Spain through the death of Franco in 1975. Second, it shows how, under democracy, the centralist idea put forward by Francoism gave way to the new democratic idea designed by the 1978 constitution and to a burgeoning regionalism. In doing so it analyses the national question, the creation of autonomous communities as a response to the demands of Catalan and Basque nationalism, and recent developments in Catalonia. Third, it considers possible new directions for Catalan nationalism.

CATALONIA AND SPAIN:
HISTORICAL BACKGROUND

The tension between centralization and some forms of cantonalism or federalism (Pi i Margall) has been a constant problem for Spanish rulers. The joint rule of Ferdinand and Isabella (*Reyes Católicos*) over Castile and the Crown of Aragon (which had Catalonia as its strongest member and Barcelona as its capital) from 1479 on put two very different areas under the same monarchs. As Elliott argues, the gulf between the two was made still wider by their differing political traditions and institutions. Although each possessed parliamentary institutions (*Courts*), Castile's had never attained legislating power and emerged from the Middle Ages as isolated and weak, while those of Aragon, Catalonia, and Valencia (forming the so-called Crown of Aragon) shared legislative power with the crown and were well buttressed by laws and institutions that derived from a long tradition of political liberty (Elliot, 1963, 7). Thus, apart from sharing common sovereigns, neither Castile nor the Crown of Aragon underwent any radical institutional alteration.

In practice, however, the equality between Castile and the Crown of Aragon (ruled by the count-king of Barcelona) did not long survive the death of Ferdinand the Catholic, and a widening gap between Castile and the other territories, including the states of the Crown of Aragon, began. A radical change in Castilian policy towards Catalonia took place when Philip IV appointed the Count Duke of Olivares as chief minister in March 1621. His objective was to create a powerful absolutist state, and to do so he sacrificed respect for internal diversity within the Spanish territories. The increasing tension between Castile and Catalonia had its climax in the Revolt of the Reapers in 1640, which united Catalans against the harsh treatment from Castile.

Fundamental to the history of Catalan nationalism, Catalonia became a nation without a state in 1714 after a long period beginning in the ninth century during which it had enjoyed its own political institutions and laws. Thus Catalonia maintained its rights and liberties until 1714, when, after a massive Franco–Spanish attack, Barcelona surrendered. Philip V ordered the dissolution of the Catalan institutions and subjected Catalonia to a regime of occupation. The Catalan language was forbidden, and Castilian (Spanish) was proclaimed the official language.

The industrialization of Catalonia in the nineteenth century brought major social changes along patterns similar to those in other industrialized western European countries and resulted in the creation of a sharp

contrast between Catalonia and the other peoples of the Iberian peninsula, except in the Basque Country. The most economically developed
part of the country, Catalonia, found itself politically subject to an
anachronistic and backward state, Castile. Although differences have
diminished, Catalan nationalists claim that this is still the case.[1]

By the end of the nineteenth century, the influence of Romanticism
prompted the *Renaixença* – a movement for national and cultural re-
naissance that promoted Catalan language and art. The *Renaixença*
soon encouraged Catalan nationalism, first in the form of regionalism
and later in demands for a federal state. Catalonia enjoyed a certain degree of autonomy under the administrative government of the Manco-
munitat (1913–23), suppressed in 1923 after the coup d'état of Miguel
Primo de Rivera, and under the Generalitat (1931–38), when Catalonia
enjoyed a Statute of Autonomy, which General Francisco Franco abolished by decree on 5 April 1938.

After Franco's death, Catalonia would recover its autonomous government, the Generalitat, only in 1977 and a new Statute of Autonomy
in 1979. The president of the Catalan government in exile, Josep Tar-
radellas, returned from France in 1977. Jordi Pujol, leader of the Convergence and Union coalition (Convergència i Unió, or CiU), became
the first president of the Catalan parliament in the first democratic election after Francoism (1980).

Francoist Spain: Against Difference and Modernization

Opposing conceptions of the state and the nation were at stake in the
Spanish Civil War. Franco defended a highly centralized and uniform
image of Spain, which rejected the progressive government of the
Second Spanish Republic (1931–38) and abhorred the process of decentralization initiated by it. During the Second Republic, statutes of
autonomy were sanctioned in Catalonia (1932), the Basque Country
(1933), and Galicia (1936), although only in Catalonia had the statute
been implemented at the time of Franco's rising.

The Francoist victory resulted in the suppression of all regional political institutions and laws, but also in the prohibition of the Catalan and
Basque (Euskera) languages and all sorts of symbolic elements (flags,
anthems) of the Catalan and Basque identities (see Benet, 1973). The
Francoists, "nationals," fought to impose a closed "image" of Spain,
which emphasized unity and condemned all forms of diversity. Their
nationalism emerged as a reaction against modern ideologies such as so-

cialism and anarchism, which they saw as threatening the traditional socio-political structure of Spain. Francoism developed a form of nationalism based on a conservative, centralist, and Castile-centred ideology to stop the path towards modernization initiated by republican Spain and sustained the traditional structures defended by large Conservative Catholic sectors.

The transition to democracy that began after Franco's death in 1975 can be seen as an attempt by the political class of Francoism to disentangle the problem of synchronizing Francoist institutions with the requirements of a modern society. During the 1970s, a profound dislocation between the social and the political spheres became increasingly alarming and highlighted the political system's inability to solve the many problems facing Spanish society. Yet, although Francoism endorsed significant changes in trying to adapt to the new scenario, it proved obsolete and ill-suited to run a society transformed since 1939. With one million unemployed and inflation standing at 30 per cent in 1975, the inadequacy of Francoist policies became patently clear (see Solé Tura, 1985).

Spain was no longer a rural country. Heavy industrial zones were concentrated in Catalonia and the Basque Country. A demographic explosion took place in the 1960s and, together with great internal migration, led to the growth of urban areas. A new middle class emerged, and some sectors of the bourgeoisie that had once supported Franco now pushed for reform. With the economy isolated, these new sectors pressed for the immediate integration of Spain into the European Community. Illiteracy substantially decreased from 50 per cent in 1931 to 11 per cent in 1981 (Tezanos, 1989, 106). Furthermore, the conservative Catholicism that acted as a pillar of Franco's regime from its early stages on had entered an irreversible decline that was already giving rise to a new secular society. All these changes took place in the context of a new international political scene, within which Spain could be fully accepted only if it adhered to Western democratic values. It became urgent to generate a political system based on democratic principles capable of replacing Spain's image as a backward, homogeneous, and conservative country.

Rupture and reform were the two options faced by Spaniards after Franco's death. The political establishment opted for reform, but, as Cebrián points out, the outcome was a democratic break with the past (1982, 13–24). In the light of Francoist law, the regime prompted its own historical suicide by opening the way to democratic rule. The initiative came from above. As a result, a peculiar situation arose: although the Francoist regime had disappeared, the public administration and institutions of the state remained intact. Solé Tura argues that the transition to democracy could succeed only by a combination of three factors (1985, 80). First, there was institutional stability, which arose from the leading role played by King Juan Carlos I in backing the reforms. Second, the various political factions were looking for consensus over the terms of the transition, after the Spanish people sanctioned political reform and the first democratic elections took place in 1977. Finally, large social sectors organized in favour of democratization, in contrast to the restrained attitude of the Catholic church and the army. Disentaglement of Franco's political last will reached a turning point in 1978, when Spaniards ratified the new democratic constitution. The country now needed to replace a "culture of resistance" with a "culture for democracy" (Abellán, 1982, 33).

DEMOCRATIC SPAIN AND THE REGIONS

The National Question

Probably the most dangerous legacy of Francoism was the intensification of the national minorities question, embittered by the regime's inexorable centralism. After almost forty years of division and resentment between the "winners" and the "losers" of the Civil War, there was growing pressure for what the left and some progressive Catholic groups called "national reconciliation."

The 1978 constitution was the product of consensus between the main political parties that emerged from the first democratic election. The need to obtain the support of both Francoist reformists and anti-Francoists generated endless discussions and even made for lack of precision and some incoherence in parts of the text. Nevertheless, for the first time Spain would have a constitution that was not the consequence of the opposition of one single political force against the others, and, despite some limits and deficiencies, the political model advanced by the constitution "was not exclusive or divisive, but an integration model" (Solé Tura, 1985, 84). The radically conservative character of the Spanish nationalism defended by Francoism was questioned by the new constitution. The document not only aimed to transform Spain into a democratic state, but also acknowledged the existence of national minorities within its territory.

Its preamble acknowledges the will of the "Spanish nation to protect all Spaniards and all the peoples of Spain in the exercise of human rights, their cultures and traditions, languages and institutions" (*Constitución Española*, 1979, 19). Article Two, probably the most controversial, exemplifies the tension between the unity of Spain and the social pressure to recognize historic nations such as the Basque Country, Catalonia, and Galicia: "The Constitution is founded upon the indissoluble unity of the Spanish nation, the common and indivisible *patria* of all Spaniards, and recognizes and guarantees the right to autonomy of the nationalities and regions integrated in it and the solidarity among them" (26). By emphasizing the indissoluble unity of Spain, while recognizing and guaranteeing the right to autonomy of the nationalities and regions, the constitution advanced a radically new model of the state that rejected Francoist centralism. It sought to reconcile unity and diversity within the Spanish state, described as a single nation containing "nationalities and regions";[2] however, the constitution does not define "nationalities" and "regions."

The Spanish Autonomous System

During the Francoist regime (1939–75), nationalism and democracy stood together as part and parcel of the Catalan demands for the transformation of Spain into a democratic state able to recognize diversity within itself and ready to alter its recalcitrant centralist nature. The makers of the constitution opted for a model – "coffee for everyone" (*café para todos*) – based on the symmetric decentralization. Hence, instead of directly responding to the nationalist demands of Catalonia[3] and the Basque Country as nations, they divided the territory of Spain into seventeen autonomous communities, some historically and culturally distinct – the Basque Country, Catalonia, and Galicia – others artificially created – La Rioja and Madrid, among many others.

Yet while the so-called "historical nationalities" – the Basque Country, Catalonia, and Galicia – could immediately start the process towards full autonomy, other regions would have first a five-year "restricted autonomy." Once full autonomy was achieved, however, the constitution makes no distinction among communities.

During the early stages of the system, substantially greater powers were devolved to the historical nationalities. This helped to fulfil the nationalist demands of Basques and Catalans but generated resentment among other communities enjoying fewer devolved powers.

Despite receiving varying powers, all communities are structured similarly. Each has a regional legislative assembly consisting of a single chamber. Deputies are elected on the basis of proportional representation, and usually the leader of the majority party or coalition assumes the presidency of the community. The president heads a regional executive of ministers in charge of departments, most of which follow the pattern of the Spanish state, depending on the number of powers devolved.

In many respects, the autonomous governments act as states, at least in what concerns most of their powers. The Basque and Catalan governments, for example, provide services in education, health, culture, housing, local transport, and agriculture, and they have even gained control of their autonomous police forces, which coexist with the Spanish National Police and the Guardia Civil. The Spanish government holds exclusive jurisdiction over defence, administration of justice, international relations, and general economic planning. A Compensation Fund administered by the government allocates special resources to poorer regions and is intended to promote equilibrium and solidarity among communities.

Catalonia: A Non-secessionist Nationalism?

Does regional nationalism pose a threat to the governance of Spain? Does decentralization destabilize the central government? The role played by the main Catalan nationalist party, in government since 1980, and its contribution to the governance of Spain should shed some light on these questions.

The tension between the acceptance of Catalonia as part of Spain and the desire to extend its degree of autonomy lies at the core of the nationalist discourse of the Convergence and Union coalition (Convergència i Unió, or CiU). Its leader, Jordi Pujol, has since then been re-elected six times as president. The CiU defines Catalonia as a nation but does not question Spanish unity. It supported the Socialist government (1993–95) when it lost its majority in the Spanish Parliament and supported the conservative Popular Party (PP), also short of a parliamentary majority, between 1996 and 2000. This illustrates Pujol's idea of Catalan nationalism as a non-secessionist movement. In his view, it is feasible to be a Catalan nationalist yet contribute to the governance of Spain.

Pujol granted support to the Spanish Socialist Workers Party (PSOE) in a climate fraught with constant political corruption scandals affecting socialist leaders. During this period he managed to attain a substantial development of the Catalan Statute of Autonomy. The right to retain 15 per cent of the taxes collected in Catalonia was probably his greatest achievement. Since 1997, and after negotiations with the PP, the Catalan government (Generalitat) retains 30 per cent of the taxes.

In Catalonia, so far, decentralization has not bred pro-independence nationalism. The only party standing for an independent republic to be achieved by democratic means is the Republican Left of Catalonia party (Esquerra Republicana de Catalunya, or ERC) which has generally obtained about 8.5 per cent of the vote in regional elections since 1980. Since the late 1990s, the ERC has been increasing its influence in Catalan politics because of transformations in its structure and political ideology in 1988 and a decisive leadership change in 1996.

After almost twenty years of autonomy, many Catalans and Basques are not fully satisfied with their current status and want to be recognized as nations within Spain. They demand special treatment and show increasing reluctance to accept blindly the "coffee for everyone" option set up in the 1978 constitution. They see an eventual asymmetric decentralization of Spain as an arrangement that would reflect the Spanish reality more accurately. References to the decentralization of Britain, where Scotland and Wales have received substantially different degrees of political autonomy according to the intensity of their nationalist claims and national identity, invoke a potential model. Two recent initiatives – the Declaration of Barcelona (1998) and the Catalan Self-Government Report (2001) – exemplify the growing demand for greater autonomy in Catalonia.

The Declaration of Barcelona (1998). In July 1998, the main nationalist parties in Galicia, the Basque Country, and Catalonia – the Galician Nationalist Bloc (Bloque Nacionalista Galego, or BNG), the Basque Nationalist Party (Eusko Alderdi Jeltzalea–Partido Nacionalista Vasco, or EAJ–PNV), and the CiU, respectively – signed a joint declaration demanding official recognition of Spain as a multilingual, multicultural, and multinational state. In their view, despite twenty years of democracy Spain continues to have a unitary character and has not resolved the national question. "During this period we have endured a lack of juridical and political recognition, and even social and cultural recognition of the specificity of our national realities within the Spanish state. This recognition, which if fair and democratic, is absolutely essential in the context of a Europe enmeshed in the process of political and economic restructuring which in the medium term will involve the redistribution of political power among its different layers of government. A Europe whose union should be based on respect for and the structuring of its different peoples and cultures" (*Declaració de Barcelona*, 1998, 1).

The main demand of these nationalist parties is for recognition of their regions as nations within the Spanish state. According to the 1978 constitution, Spain consists of a single nation containing some "nationalities and regions," which it never clearly defines (*Constitución Espanola*, 1978, Título Preliminar, Artículo 2). Recognition of these nations would imply a substantial change in the constitution and would recognize Spain as a "nation of nations." Representatives of the main Spanish parties – the PP and the PSOE have rejected the Declaration of Barcelona.

The Catalan Self-Government Report (2001). In December 2001, the main political parties of the Catalan left – the Catalan Socialist Party (Partit dels Socialistes de Catalunya, or PSC (PSC–PSOE)), Citizens for Change (Ciutadans pel Canvi, or CpC), the ERC, and the Initiative for Catalonia–Greens (Iniciativa per Catalunya–Verds, or ICV) – launched the Catalan Self-Government Report. The document is the first collective proposal advanced by the Catalan left in over 21 years of political autonomy. Its drafting and publication coincided with the announcement that Jordi Pujol would not stand for re-election as president in the forthcoming Catalan contest (Fall 2003). Pujol's statement triggered an already heated debate about both his successor and the future of the CiU coalition, since then turned into a federation. The report came to light amid a centralist conservative campaign launched by the Popular Party.

The report's key objective is greater autonomy. It contains over 90 specific proposals to strengthen self-government and endorses reform of the Spanish constitution and the Catalan Statute of Autonomy of 1979. Its main demands are the redefinition of Spain as a multinational state and for a Catalan institutional presence within the European Union and other international organizations.

TOWARDS A RADICAL CATALAN NATIONALISM?

Despite current criticism and increasing pressure to modify the autonomous system by conferring special status on the Basque Country, Catalonia, and Galicia, Spanish decentralization has facilitated the peaceful accommodation of regional nationalism after 40 years of dictatorship. But decentralization has not taken place without conflict and tension between regional and central governments. For instance, the demand for further resources for autonomous institutions and for greater devolved powers has characterized most of the relations between the Generalitat and Madrid. Conflict arose over the percentage of taxes collected in Catalonia to be retained by the Generalitat. It surfaced again when the central government challenged laws on the use and promotion of the Catalan language issued by the Generalitat and when the Spanish Constitutional Court subsequently examined them, although it ratified their constitutionality. Some autonomous communities, usually "non-historical," have complained about what they perceive as better treatment by the state of the "historical" communities.

For over 20 years, the majority of the Catalan population has supported the brand of Catalan nationalism represented by the CiU: a non-secessionist nationalism that defines Catalonia as a nation with a specific history, language, and culture that displays a strong desire for self-government. But could matters change in the near future? Are there any new variables that could trigger the rise of pro-independence nationalism in Catalonia?

Since 1993, Pujol's coalition has explained its support for the PSOE and later for the PP as assisting the governance of Spain and as beneficial to Catalonia. In particular, Pujol sought to appease the alienation felt by many of the CiU's supporters from the CiU–PP agreement (1996–2000) by appealing to the economic advantages for Catalonia.

On 12 March 2000, the PP obtained an overwhelming majority in the Spanish general election, which annihilated the CiU's bargaining power. When it had needed CiU support, the PP had adopted a sympathetic attitude to Catalan claims. Soon after the election, understanding gave way to a neo-centralist political discourse charged with conservative overtones. Since then, the PP has been dismissive of claims for greater autonomy for the historical nationalities and has adopted an arrogant attitude towards former political allies.

After March 2000, it became increasingly difficult for Pujol to account for the CiU's continuous support for the PP in Madrid, in return for which the PP provided needed support in the Catalan parliament. Many CiU voters were very critical of this policy and would have preferred the nationalist coalition to seek the support of a Catalanist party, such as the ERC. In 2002, CiU initiated a process that would distance it from the PP in the run-up to the November 2003 regional election.

By defending the notion of "postnationalism," based on a vulgarized version of Jürgen Habermas's "patriotism of the constitution," Spanish political pundits defend the unchanging constitution. In their view, the constitution exemplifies and guarantees civic consensus and so should remain untouched (for instance, Prime Minister José María Aznar had opposed it on nationalistic grounds when it came up for popular ratification). They see the constitution as rigid; "the problem with this representation arises when the document is not understood as a flexible frame for the evolving nature of social coexistence but as a fetish that freezes the moment of its mythical foundation" (Resina 2002). The conservative national majority – the so-called constitutionalists – defends this position. Opposed to them are the "nationalists," who are in practice neither more nationalist nor less constitutionalist. They represent national minorities and defend the idea that constitutions are adaptable. In particular, they seek amendments to the document to rectify partialities and selective constraints that are bound up with its origin.

The Spanish media have fully adopted this false dichotomy between constitutionalists and nationalists without questioning the strong Spanish nationalism of the constitutionalists. They often defend the "sentinels of a sealed constitution" and demonize advocates of reconsidering the social contract more than two decades after the uncertainty of the 1970s.

The PP is currently promoting a new brand of Spanish identity, inherited from previous socialist governments. This new identity defines Spain as a modern, industrialized, decentralized, pro-European, and secular society. Under the PP, it is also conservative and hostile to internal diversity, which it often refers to as a "nuisance," a remnant of the past, and a threat to Spain's unity.

What are the consequences for Catalonia of such radicalization of Spanish conservative and centralist nationalism? First, the centralism of the PP threatens to alienate large sectors of Spanish society, especially in the Basque Country, Catalonia, and Galicia. The delicate equilibrium among various political tendencies that enabled the transition to democracy could suffer. Restricting dialogue between constituent parts, might tarnish Spain's democracy, as might a concentration of forces so great that it might lead to a "tyranny of the majority."

Second, recent developments in Spanish politics are contributing to a re-examination of Catalan nationalism. In particular, they have fostered an open debate about whether Catalans should be content with current arrangements or should claim greater autonomy, federalism, or even independence. The Declaration of Barcelona and the Self-Government Report illustrate the desire for greater autonomy, at least within the political elite. This debate, however, also concerns the ideal status of Catalonia within an expanding European Union engaged in political integration.

Traditionally, in Catalonia only a small minority has supported secession. At present this minority is growing. According to a recent poll conducted by the Centro de Investigaciones Sociológicas (2001) of Madrid, 35.9 per cent of Catalans are in favour of independence, while 48.1 per cent are against, and the ERC stands as the party perceived as having improved its image more substantially during 2000. Such a significant change in public opinion reflects three factors – the progressive erosion of the CiU after 20 years in government and its alliance with the conservative PP, the conservative neo-centralist policies of the PP government, and the inability of the Catalan Socialists to present themselves as an autonomous party and not as an appendix of the PSOE.

In this political scenario, the ERC secessionist discourse may attract some new supporters, which could consolidate the party as Catalonia's third political force and place it in a key position, particularly if neither the CiU nor the Catalan Socialists were to achieve a majority in the 2003 election.[4]

NOTES

1 On the industrialization of Catalonia, see Vilar, 1977. On contemporary Catalonia, see Giner, 1998.

2 As Solé Tura notes (1985, 101), it is highly controversial and juridically ambiguous to stress the unity of a "nation" while recognizing "nationalities" within it.

3 On Catalan nationalism during the Spanish transition to democracy, see Guibernau, 1997 and 2004.

4 The results of the regional election of 16 November 2003 confirm my observations. The CiU lost 10 seats in the Catalan parliament (down from 56 to 46) but remains the main political force, under a new leader, Arthur Mas. The PSC (PSC–PSOE), led by Pasqual Maragall, also lost 10 seats (from 52 to 42), while the ERC obtained the larger increase, gaining 11 seats, for a total of 23. The new political landscape reflects overwhelming support for greater powers for Catalonia and confirms the rise of pro-independence nationalism, as represented by the ERC and its leader, Joseph-Lluis Carod-Rovira.

REFERENCES

Abellán, J.L. (1982) "La función del pensamiento en la transición política," in J.L. Cagigao et al., *España 1975–1980: Conflictos y logros de la democracia*. Madrid: Editorial J. Porrúa Turanzas, S.A.

Benet, J. (1973) *Catalunya sota el règim franquista*. Paris: Edicions Catalanes de París.

Cebrián, J.L. (1982) "La experiencia del período constituyente," in J.L. Cagigao et al., *España 1975–1980: Conflictos y logros de la democracia*. Madrid: Editorial J. Porrúa Turanzas, S.A.

Centro de Investigaciones Sociológicas (2001) *Situación social y política de Catalunya*. Estudio no. 2410. Madrid: CIS.

Constitución Española: edición comentada (1979) Madrid: Centro de estudios constitucionales.

Declaració de Barcelona (1998) BNG, EAJ–PNV, CiU. Barcelona: CiU.

Elliott, J.H. (1963) *The Revolt of the Catalans: A Study in the Decline of Spain (1598–1640)*. Cambridge: Cambridge University Press.

Giner, S., ed. (1998) *La societat Catalana*. Barcelona: Institut d'Estadística de Catalunya.

Guibernau, M. (1997) "Images of Catalonia," *Nations and Nationalism* 3, no. 1, 89–111.

– (1999) *Nations without States: Political Communities in the Global Age*. Cambridge: Polity Press.

– (2000a) "Nationalism and Intellectuals in Nations without States: The Catalan Case," *Political Studies* 48, no. 5, 989–1005.

– (2000b) "Spain: Catalonia and the Basque Country," *Parliamentary Affairs* 53, no. 1, 55–68.

– (2002) *Del Franquisme a la democracia: el paper del nacionalisme català*. Barcelona: Proa Press.

– (2004) *Catalan Nationalism: Francoism, Transition and Democracy*. London: Routledge.

ICPS. (1989–95) *Sondeig d'opinió Catalunya*.

Resina, J.R. (2002) "Postnational Spain? Post-Spanish Spain?" *Nations and Nationalism*.

Solé Tura, J. (1985) *Nacionalidades y nacionalismos en España: Autonomía, federalismo, autodeterminación*. Madrid: Alianza Editorial.

Tezanos, J.F. (1989) "Modernización y cambio social en España," in J.F. Tezanos et al., eds., *La transición democrática Española*. Madrid: Editorial Sistema.

Vilar, P. (1977) *La Catalogne dans l'Espagne moderne*. Paris: Flammarion.

RADHA KUMAR

Settling Partition Hostilities: Lessons Learned, Options Ahead

Since the Dayton Peace Agreement of November 1995, which brought an end to the Bosnian war, there has been increasing debate on whether or not partition can provide a solution to ethnic conflict, either in the short or in the long term.[1] Renewed hostilities in the Middle East and South Asia, precarious relations between and inside a slew of divided African nations, and the obstacle-strewn Irish and Cypriot peace processes have all made the issues of secession and/or partition critical to international policy in a post–Cold War world. As in previous postwar periods – for example, under the League of Nations after the First World War and the United Nations after the Second – international policy is once again debating the stand-off between territorial integrity and self-determination. Once again, too, the emerging doctrine of humanitarian action occupies a fuzzy middle place, even more so after the terrorist attacks on the United States on 11 September 2001 and the ensuing war on al-Qa'eda in Afghanistan and Pakistan.

There is, as well, a conceptual challenge in defining partition. In international law, any dissolution of multi-ethnic states to create mono-ethnic states can be defined as partition. If violence is the core concern in the definition, however, we can distinguish between negotiated secession and the dissolution of a federation, on the one hand, and partition, on the other. When largely mono-ethnic regions secede, the potential for violence is low because the secession does not involve the massive displacement of a people. By contrast, when conflicting ethnic groups secede from a demographically mixed region the potential for violence is high, because the attempt to create a mono-ethnic state entails the large-scale displacement of peoples.

In this paper I therefore distinguish ethnic partition from negotiated secession or a dissolved federation on two grounds – demography and borders. When an existing administrative unit leaves a state, it is secession; where new borders have to be carved out of existing units, it is partition. And where a mono-ethnic or single-religion state is created from a multi-ethnic or multi-religion state, it is ethnic partition.

What makes ethnic partition so vulnerable to conflict, even when it has been long established, as in India, Ireland, and Pakistan, or when it has been contained, as in Cyprus? Why is partition so intractable in Israel and Palestine or so unstable in Bosnia and Herzegovina? Why is it so difficult to overcome partition claims in Kosovo and Macedonia? Are there general lessons that we can learn about partition per se from a comparison of these conflicts? One aim of this essay is to draw up a checklist of lessons from older partitions for present-day policy options in ethnic conflicts; the other is to see what light the list sheds on current partition-related peace processes.

Initially, the partition debate suffered from a lack of clarity on what distinguished ethnic partition from other types of ethnic conflict, partly because ethnic conflict and resulting partition had not been studied from the standpoint of policy-making. The bulk of the literature consists of history or official reports.[2] Much of the discussion, moreover, has dealt with individual partitions rather than with comparative policy lessons. A case-by-case approach has continued dominant, and so almost every leading think tank or foreign policy school has conducted studies on India–Pakistan, Israel–Palestine, Cyprus, and Bosnia, with partition providing a context (though not, in general, the chief point of study).[3] Yet rarely, if at all, do studies on one area refer to those on another, even when borrowing models for negotiation or settlement. Proposed alternatives tend to be unvarying, despite changes in time and situation, and therefore have mixed policy impact.[4]

In the wake of the Dayton Agreement, however, a debate has sprung up on partition policy per se. Partition advocates[5] adopt British colonial arguments for partition rather than Woodrow Wilson's formulae for self-determination.[6] The colonial stance advocated the creation of ethnic states by territorial division, as a lesser evil to potential genocide. In practice, however, partition became an exit strategy ("divide and quit," in the words of the British historian and civil servant Penderel Moon) rather than a response to the needs and desires of the affected people.

Partition may not have been a lesser evil – in India it was only after partition was agreed that genocidal violence broke out – but it did serve as an exit strategy in some cases. In a post–colonial and post–Cold War period, however, it is not clear whether partition can be either a lesser evil or an exit strategy. With this question in mind, I examined the partition conflicts in Ireland, India–Pakistan, Israel–Palestine, Cyprus, and the former Yugoslavia. This paper offers a broad summary of the lessons derived in three areas – partition as a solution, post-conflict stabilization and reconstruction, and peace processes. It also presents in table forms a checklist of the best- and worst-case options available to the international community.

PARTITION AS A SOLUTION

First, far from solving ethnic conflict, partition aims have been a motivating element in the descent to war and have stimulated strife more often than ending it. Negotiations towards partition parallel, and usually foreshadow, war. Partition was considered as an alternative to devolution in Ireland in 1912 but took ten years and a civil war to achieve in 1922. The partition of India was proposed in 1940 but pushed through only in 1947, accompanied by a genocidal war in which between 500,000 and a million people died and over 15 million were displaced. Partition was first suggested for Palestine by the Peel Commission in 1937, and then again by the United Nations (UN) in 1948, but Israel and the Palestinians have yet to agree to it. In the meantime, there have been three Arab–Israeli wars and an ongoing civil war. In Cyprus, partition was threatened in 1956, avoided in 1960, and reappeared during a ten-year ethnic conflict ending with Turkey's invasion in 1974 and de facto partition of the island. The still-putative partition of Bosnia-Herzegovina took almost four years of war to arrive at and continues to simmer after seven years of peace. Kosovo's partition has spilled over into Macedonia, following over a decade of Serb–Albanian conflict that culminated with the bombing campaign by the North Atlantic Treaty Organization (NATO) in spring 1999.

Second, because demography is crucial in defining partitions, they rarely satisfy aspirations for self-determination. The attempt to draw ethnic borders around populations that are, as President Izetbegovic put it in the first year of the Bosnian war, as intermingled as corn and flour generally leads to ethnic cleansing and leaves enclaves within contested borders. In this sense, partition incites ancient hatreds rather than settling them.

Moreover, the contest over setting new borders tends to restructure the sources of ethnic conflict and burdens the international system with the permanent threat of war. Israel remains the only UN member with undeclared borders. Kashmir has been a bone of contention between India and Pakistan since partition. And the international community's attempt to evade partition in Bosnia by giving Brcko an autonomous status has turned the tiny region into a microcosm of the "now you see it, now you don't" partition of Bosnia.

By contrast, it is easier for negotiated secessions or dissolved federations to succeed. Czechoslovakia could negotiate a "velvet divorce" because the two states were relatively homogeneous, and therefore their separation did not involve the forced migration of Czechs and Slovaks. (The implications are that it ought to be easier for relatively homogeneous areas, such as East Timor and north Sudan, to separate. The fact that bitter wars have been fought over them only puts the onus more squarely on the undemocratic state.)[7]

Third, the corresponding point – that population transfers could avoid war and forced migration – begs three points: population transfers will still require force and carry the threat of conflict; they require international intervention (and what democracy would wish to be seen to be shipping people out of their native land?) and they are subject to questions of scale. Is it possible to imagine any agency – other than a genocidal one – that could transfer the roughly 16 million people who were affected by the Indian partition?

Most recently, the idea of population transfers has arisen in the Kosovo conflict: that the Albanians of southern Serbia move to northern Kosovo, and the Serbs in northern Kosovo, to southern Serbia. Despite little evidence that the two communities would move voluntarily, the proposal would appear to fetishize existing borders – why not adjust Kosovo's borders instead? And while transfers would avoid setting a precedent about changing republic borders, they could send dangerous messages to Bosnia, that population transfer can legitimize the effects of ethnic cleansing, and to Macedonia, that working towards a multi-ethnic democracy is not a winning proposition.

The proposal for transferring populations draws attention to a related problem in ethnic conflicts – that of states with contiguous diasporas. Such diasporas can extend conflict, as the Croats did in western Bosnia and the Serbs in eastern Bosnia. So did the Greeks and

Turks in Cyprus (separated though both were by the sea). Or they can prolong conflict indefinitely, as in Kashmir.

Fourth, partitioned lands tend to remain in long-term flux, with both collective and individual security sensitive to even minor irritants, and thus conflict is frequent. Whether de jure or de facto, ethnic partitions have not stabilized over time. Conflict in Northern Ireland has lasted 70 years and spawned a prolonged phase of terrorism. The 50-year-long hostility between India and Pakistan has devolved on Kashmir (along the way it also led to the creation of Bangladesh). Greece and Turkey have several times come close to threatening war over Cyprus, while the Green Line dividing the island remains a zone of tension. Conflict over Israel and Palestine continues unabated to this day.

Despite five years of peace, Bosnia remains so volatile that peacekeeping troops and contributing countries all fear that any attempt to withdraw might result in the renewal of war. The spectre hovering over discussions of partition of Kosovo includes the spread of conflict in southern Serbia and Macedonia. Most recently, India and Pakistan's nuclear tests of 1998 acquired an especially dangerous edge because of the ongoing and escalating conflict in Kashmir and Pakistan's export of jihad to the region.

Fifth, a further cause of instability is that ethnic partitions tend to usher in relatively undemocratic states or undemocratic enclaves within democracies. Pakistan has had more years under military than under civilian rule and is currently teetering under the weight of armed Islamic fundamentalists. Northern Cyprus is dominated by an alliance between the Turkish army and a local suzerain, Rauf Denktash, and Israel's occupation and reoccupation of the West Bank and Gaza made it a pariah until recently and caused innumerable fissures within Israel itself. Britain's advanced democracy lived uneasily with the fact of being a brutish presence in Northern Ireland until the Framework Agreements; India's developing democracy lives equally uneasily with its gross violations of human rights in Kashmir and has recently seen the disturbing rise of Hindu xenophobia. Xenophobia is alive in Bosnia and Kosovo, as well as in Croatia and Serbia, and is rising in Macedonia.

Sixth, the international community has so far accepted the instability of ethnic partitions because their primary purpose has been to provide an exit strategy or a means of limited containment rather than a lasting solution to an ethnic conflict. Partition worked as an exit strategy during the colonial period because it could be accepted as the price of independence. Self-determination movements in Ireland, India, and, in a skewed fashion, Palestine (the Zionists alone) swallowed the bitter pill of partition as a necessary evil for the greater good of statehood and/or decolonization. During the Cold War, partition acted as a means of containment or for the delineation of spheres of influence. Although such partitions were primarily ideological in nature, as in Germany, Korea, and Vietnam, ethnic partitions also took shelter under that rubric and were treated as a means of limited containment: the British army justified its fiat in Northern Ireland as at least keeping down the level of violence, while the de facto partition of Cyprus supposedly circumscribed the stand-off between Greece and Turkey.

A post-colonial and post–Cold War world, however, can no longer view ethnic partitions as the price of independence, and so such methods fail to provide even an exit strategy for great powers or international institutions. Kosovo is a comprehensive example of the nature of the problem. After the NATO bombing campaign, the world community could not have persuaded the Kosovo Albanians to accept partition as the price of their independence – had it favoured partition, for which there is no evidence. Independence, however, is unlikely at present, with the spectre of intensified ethnic fissures in Macedonia looming. In both Bosnia and Kosovo, local populations as well as leaders actively seek an international presence in preference to independence.

(Of the five cases under study, Palestine is perhaps the only ongoing conflict in which partition – of the West Bank – is being offered as the price of independence. It is probably not an acceptable price, given the many ambiguities that surround it. Territorial negotiations, grim as they are, are outweighed by the literally existential question of Palestinian refugees. As Israel's withdrawal from Lebanon has inadvertently shown, President Arafat is not in a position to subsume their aspirations, should he wish to do so.)

Seventh, with the end of the bloc system, the development of information technology, and the gradual integration of markets, containment is no longer a viable strategy.[8] While the Yugoslav wars are the most potent example of the dissipation of containment following the end of the Cold War, the collapse of communism has also spawned a free movement of arms and a freer, if not new, breed of cross-border and cross-continent conflicts involving chiefly non-state actors. Instead of acting as a putative exit strategy, ethnic partition more often constitutes an entry that embroils great powers and international institutions in a long-term and ever-extending program of stabilization.

As the NATO–UN–EU (European Union) presence in Bosnia, and the UN administrations in Kosovo and East Timor show, the international community is beginning to recognize that intervention can carry responsibilities for post-conflict stabilization, including state-building. Thus far, international administrations have been hampered by their own reluctance both to expand responsibilities and to provide resources. In Bosnia the world was initially unwilling to undertake state-building, and thus the immediate post-conflict phase saw a stratified, indeed anomic, division of responsibilities between often-competing institutions. The great loser was administration, particularly the rule of law. The mandates of the UN administrations of Kosovo and East Timor have partly compensated for this lacuna, despite (as in Bosnia) inadequate aid and manpower, compounded by delays in delivery.

(Note the peculiarly anomalous aspect of the Oslo process, where there was notable international commitment to state-building (security and administrative institutions) vis-à-vis the Palestinian Authority, despite the absence of a territorial state. The effort failed.)

POST-CONFLICT STABILIZATION AND RECONSTRUCTION

A major impediment to post-conflict stabilization is that attempts to implement provisions for reconstruction and development, without tackling the central dilemma of partition, can remain hostage to party rivalries. Even in the longer-term post-conflict phase, trade, infrastructure, and familial interests are unable to overcome or bypass the hostilities of partition without outside stimuli. In Northern Ireland in 1922 and India in 1947, and in the UN partition plan of 1948 for Palestine, it was assumed that over time economic interests would dissolve the partition lines; instead the lines hardened over time, hampering trade, development, and communication. Unofficial trade between India and Pakistan, for example, is conservatively estimated at $2 billion per year; official trade, in comparison, has rarely exceeded $200 million. And the two countries are, in this respect, better off than most other partitioned lands. Telephone calls between the two parts of Cyprus had to be made through Greece and Turkey, respectively.

Most attempts to use economic incentives to jump-start peace processes without tackling partition have foundered. The EU's cross-border projects for Ireland–Northern Ireland had little effect until the framework agreements began to be implemented, and key areas of the agreements, such as the power-sharing executive, have come close to foundering over decommissioning arms and police reform. The Lahore peace process between India and Pakistan came to an end before it even took off, largely because the Pakistani military feared that Prime Minister Sharif was willing to abandon Pakistan's Kashmir policy in the interests of expanding the country's exchequer.

Cross-border projects are rare in Bosnia and as yet unthinkable in Kosovo; even localized attempts to stimulate economic reconstruction have succumbed to an uncertain political future, in which accountability is one of the first victims. How to hold political representatives accountable for corruption when no one knows where their responsibility begins and the international administration leaves off – or, for that matter, when the region teeters between war and peace?

There is now a dawning recognition that trade and development will flower only after partition is addressed, either through reintegration (to differing extents, Cyprus, Bosnia, and Kosovo) or by settling its more hostile legacies (Ireland, India–Pakistan, and East Timor). How to move towards these goals, however, remains uncertain. In post Cold–War conflicts such as Bosnia and Kosovo, the key issues of demilitarization and decommissioning, state– and civil institution–building, the return of refugees, and economic reconstruction are overshadowed by the lethal combination of an uncertain political future and international fears of deepening embroilment. Thus, for example, despite recognition that security, decommissioning, and institution building are key to refugee return and reconstruction, the international community's strategy in Bosnia has focused disproportionately on elections and fiscal reform.

Admittedly, neither security nor nation-building is easy in societies that have suffered widespread destruction of their infrastructure and polity. By contrast, in the decolonization periods that followed the First and Second World Wars, partition conflicts caused relatively little destruction. For example, infrastructure was not devastated in Ireland, India–Pakistan, or Israel–Palestine, and a legitimate party could take power and deal with nation–building and all that it entailed.

In terms of reconstruction and nation-building, there are key differences between colonial and post–Cold War conflicts over partition. Historically, where partitions occurred as part of the transfer of power, there were usually legitimate political parties to hand power to – for example, the nationalists in the Irish Free State, the Indian National Congress in India, and the Muslim League in Pakistan. This allowed greater flexibility: for example, paramilitaries disappeared as lawful armies emerged, and aid and resources could arrive from diaspora communities, "parent" nations, or sympathetic governments, which might have been less generous to an interim international administration.

Demilitarization and decommissioning, police and administration, the establishment of the rule of law, and the development of civil institutions could thus proceed (with hiccoughs) in Ireland, India, Pakistan, and Cyprus. (Where there were no legitimate parties, as in Northern Ireland or in cases of de facto partition, such as northern Cyprus or Pakistan-held Azad Kashmir, state and civil institution–building remained in abeyance, and the areas remained relatively underdeveloped. See Table 1 for five key issues – demilitarization and decommissioning, refugees, nation-building, economic development, and freedom of movement.)

In post–Cold War ethnic conflicts, however, the descent to partition goes hand in hand with widespread delegitimizing of political parties – through the negotiating process itself – leaving a vacuum that armed and criminalized gangs generally fill. The world community is supposed to step into the breach through transitional administrations, ranging from protectorates to trusteeships. Historically, however, such stop-gaps have worked only when administering countries have had a stake in the people's welfare. The stake generally translates into benefit for the ruling countries, as under colonial and imperial rule. Disinterested international administrations, especially when they are time-bound, run the risks of being hollow at the core, as were the mandates of the League of Nations, which had all the trappings of colonialism without its occasional liberal obligations.[9]

But there are also other attendant dangers in prescribing such administrations for regions devastated by ethnic conflict, without seeking to figure out appropriate responses. This problem is especially acute when there is a failure to distinguish between decolonization conflicts and new wars. Ironically, the principle of neutrality, or non-collaboration with any one side, that informs transitional international administrations applies even when a conflict involves decolonization rather than a new war. In East Timor, for example, a legitimate party waited in the wings almost a year after the humanitarian intervention, even though it had few challengers and reconstruction aid might have flown more readily if it were in power.

Table 1
Key issues of post-conflict stabilization, five conflicts

Key issues	Ireland	India–Pakistan	Israel–Palestine	Cyprus	Former Yugoslavia	
					Bosnia	Kosovo
Demilitarization and decommissioning	Lawful army, Ireland paramilitaries, gradually taking to terror, Northern Ireland Cease-fire holds, but decommissioning major stumbling block for peace process. IRA ties decommissioning to troops reduction, Britain refuses link. Little significant reduction in British troops in Northern Ireland, but their presence considerably muted and no major human rights violations by British troops	Lawful armies, India, Pakistan. Uprising, East Pakistan, paramilitaries absorbed into lawful army with creation of Bangladesh, 1972 Paramilitaries in India's northeast, till today, in Bangladesh hill tracts (on Indian border) until 1998, peace pact, decommissioning 1989; rise of armed insurgency in Indian-held Kashmir, Pakistan's response to turn "Afghan policy" into "Kashmir policy."	Paramilitaries absorbed into Israeli army, though extremist Zionist paramilitaries remain Palestinian armed groups develop in exile Peace process: more extremist Zionist paramilitaries gradually phased out, although armed settler groups remain Palestinian Liberation Army absorbed into Palestinian security forces, with slightly compromised	Greek paramilitaries gradually phased out after military rule ended in Greece Turkish paramilitaries absorbed into security forces in Turkish, held northern Cyprus, but Grey Wolves still remain Turkish troop reduction still key issue for peace talks	Still not one lawful army, absorption of paramilitaries into local Serb and Croat security forces keeping high level of tension in peace process	Kosovo Liberation Army partly absorbed into Kosovo security forces, but new formations (such as Liberation Army of Kosovo, Medveda, and Presevo) threaten fragile peace Serb security forces' infiltration in northern Kosovo continues.

Table 1 (continued)

Key issues	Ireland	India–Pakistan	Israel–Palestine	Cyprus	Former Yugoslavia — Bosnia	Former Yugoslavia — Kosovo
		Pakistani religious schools training, arming, and infiltrating Pakistani and Afghani militants into Kashmir valley and Jammu. High risk of war between nuclear-armed neighbours	legitimacy as they are expected to guarantee Israeli security. Hamas and Hezbollah remain, but outside the peace process, and no moves to bring them in. Aim of decommissioning distant			
Refugees	Semi-voluntary migration Continuing semi-voluntary migration within Northern Ireland, mainly Protestants fleeing anticipated Catholic rule	Almost complete ethnic cleansing in Punjab, Bengal, large scale in Sind. Refugees at forefront of nation-building India and Pakistan, but are called *mohajir* (foreigner) in Pakistan	Two major waves of ethnic cleansing, 1948 and 1967 Palestinian diaspora now close to 7 million Israel refuses to accept right to return, seeks regional solution	Turkish Cypriot refugees absorbed into northern Cyprus Northern Cyprus authorities arrogate to themselves refugee rights, claim to barber both their rights to	Right to return still largely accepted only in principle, hotly contested on ground Under Dayton agreement UNHCR actually given charge of commission on refugee	NATO intervention to guarantee right to return might prove to be limited to Kosovo Albanians Large question mark over Serb right to return

Table 1 (continued)

Key issues	Ireland	India–Pakistan	Israel–Palestine	Cyprus	Former Yugoslavia	
					Bosnia	Kosovo
		and in both countries are key intensifiers of hostility. About 50,000 stateless in India from 1948 Kashmir war, about 200,000 Hindus expelled from the valley during 1990s	along Jordan model (i.e., host countries to grant citizenship) Also seeks to limit Palestinian authority's decision-making capacity on the issue	return and property rights 200,000 Greek Cypriot refugees in republic	return, but largely unable to fulfil mandate Croatia still to accept refugee rights, though beginning to make right noises	
Nation-building	*Then:* Relatively low level of infrastructure destruction, Irish republic inherited colonial institutions. No state-building in Northern Ireland, though higher level of infrastructure development under British	Relatively low level of infrastructure destruction Both countries inherited colonial institutions India had edge as only country to emerge from ethnic conflict as multi-ethnic state, also all central	*Then:* Against the odds, a triumph in Israel, but with unstinting U.S. aid, which continues Nevertheless, a state based on expropriation – i.e., invisiblization of Palestinians and "strategic depth" offered by occupation	Initially major problems, given Greece's implicit refusal to recognize an independent Cyprus – to the extent that Cyprus had to partition After partition, newly democratic Greek aid and support to republic,	Very high level of systemic destruction, which makes clear that social and political destruction much more serious than infrastructure destruction International community not willing to privilege one party above others	*Then:* Oddly, problem in reverse to Bosnia's. International community first hoped that KLA would be the legitimate party to aid in state-building, then had to deal with problem that they were not.

Table 1 *(continued)*

					Former Yugoslavia	
	Ireland	*India–Pakistan*	*Israel–Palestine*	*Cyprus*	*Bosnia*	*Kosovo*
Key issues	*Now:* Nation-building in process, with key issues being police reform and local government	institutions in India Crisis-ridden in Pakistan, partly because first builders semi-feudal landed gentry who opted out of colonial modernization process Kashmir: virtually no local administration in Pakistan-held Kashmir, illegitimate administration in Indian-held Kashmir Direct rule by Pakistan in northern areas Continuing conflict, little prospect of nation-building in near term	*Now:* Rise of suicide bombings and reoccupation of West Bank and Gaza threat to both Israeli and Palestinian nation-building Disintegration of fragile Palestinian Authority, no rule of law Little potential for Palestinian nation-building	relatively successful state-building Turkish-held northern Cyprus: almost no state-building, Turkish aid mainly to maintain Denktash's rule Potentially a major problem for peace process, currently not a problem since aim is to reach a formal together–but–separate agreement	as legitimate, therefore peculiarly notional form of state-building (i.e., much talk of securing borders so customs can be collected, but, without unified civil service, whose coffers will it go into?) Waiting game: hope that over time non-ethnic parties will be voted in so state-building can begin	*Now:* A halfway house of attempts to create local administrations without any clarity on which communities will be administered – i.e., will there come a time when Serbs will be permitted to opt out?

Table I (continued)

					Former Yugoslavia	
Key issues	Ireland	India–Pakistan	Israel–Palestine	Cyprus	Bosnia	Kosovo
Economic development	*Then:* Ireland mired in poverty, having lost two major trading centres. Change comes about with membership in EU, which brings economic development to the Irish Republic – incidentally also helps Ireland relinquish sovereignty claims over north *Now:* If peace process can be made to work possible prosperity for Northern Ireland, but this depends on whether current	Sheer size could ensure some level of economic development in India and Pakistan, but the former does manage a significant degree of self-sustainment, which is marred by an inability to adjust to the post-heavy industry era. Despite its relative wealth, Pakistan opts for a dependent economy – most intensely felt in Bangladesh – and is now in serious crisis. *Now:* India has the promise of	In contrast, Israel develops precisely because it is a created Jewish homeland; however, its economy remains dependent on U.S. aid and Arab expropriation. If expropriation is a variable, U.S. aid is likely to be the constant that will see israel through to the next stage of sustainable development. Palestine suffers even further hardship as Israeli punishment for decolonization, and its economic	"Parent nation" aid has ensured that neither the republic nor Turkish-held Cyprus suffers serious hardship, but inflation is high in the republic, while Turkish-held northern Cyprus is relatively poor. *Now:* the potential prosperity anticipated by the republic's membership of the EU is a disincentive to reunification, while the Turkish, held area does not have the luxury of making a Denktash-free choice.	The many phases of reluctant aid. (a) late fulfilment of pledges; (b) funneling aid through a delegitimized government; (c) dumping them because of corruption; (d) small-time aid to civil society *Now:* having given up on serious reconstruction aid, pegging the currency, talking borders and customs, looking to the EU to pick up the slack. Introducing conditionality in the shape of	Smaller in scale, no real impetus for multi-ethnicity, but same problems as Bosnia, of lag between pledge and aid, compounded by a throwback problem: Albanians are good at cross-border smuggling and little else.

Table 1 (continued)

Key issues	Ireland	India–Pakistan	Israel–Palestine	Cyprus	Former Yugoslavia	
					Bosnia	Kosovo
	demographic instability changes	stratified prosperity with its eastern neighbours, but without a trade relationship with Pakistan the north-west of the subcontinent is becoming a basket case	prospects remain dim in the current Arab situation of unwillingness to offer preferential economic deals.	Prospects: depend on the extent to which Turkey can influence Denktash	cross-border projects, when there is little hope of dissolving the dividing lines. Only hope: micro-credit	
Freedom of movement	Possible, but not used	Not across borders	–	–	–	–

Table 2
Best- and worst-case options, five conflicts, then and now

Options	Ireland	India–Pakistan	Israel–Palestine	Cyprus	Former Yugoslavia	
					Bosnia	Kosovo
Best-case option (Then)	Home Rule in 1912, resulting either in the marginalization of extreme nationalists and unionists or in a later disintegrative war of partition	Decentralized federation of secular states/unitary state with Jinnah as Prime Minister	UN Partition Plan with economic union/bi-communal, binational state	Unitary state with explicit rejection of enosis and full minority rights protected	UN/NATO troops on borders/ Protectorate Dayton: single army, joint police training Constituent assembly rather than final constitution	NATO troops close by during Rambouillet, to prevent ethnic cleansing should talks fail Demilitarization agreement with KLA after war ended
Worst-case option (Then)	Continuing civil war, enforced British rule	Decentralized federation of religious-majority states with the likelihood of a later disintegrative war of partition	Unilateral British withdrawal, non-intervention by UN	Cyprus to Greeks/ de jure partition	Non-intervention, appeasement of Serb and Croat war aims De jure partition	Non-intervention Mass expulsion of Kosovo Albanians
Best-case option (Now)	Implementing framework agreements and gradual demilitarization, including phased	Renewal of Lahore process, Pakistan shutting down training and support of mujahe-	Israeli withdrawal from Gaza, West Bank, Golan and Lebanon, security and water-sharing	Bi-communal, binational state, with countervailing force of EU membership (freedom	Substantial investment in South-East European Stability Pact Unified civil service	Demilitarization decommissioning of border control Resources for policing, economic

Table 2 (continued)

Options	Ireland	India–Pakistan	Israel–Palestine	Cyprus	Former Yugoslavia	
					Bosnia	Kosovo
	withdrawal of British troops IRA participation in decommissioning, restoration of government, police reform Northern Ireland as part of "Europe of the Regions"	deen/fidayeen, all-party talks towards autonomy for Kashmir. Settling Siachen, Sir Creek, disputes over Wullar, opening trade routes, over time giving substance to SAARC	agreements with Syria, shared soveregnty for settlements, right to return, but not implemented Partition to create Palestinian state with open borders Regional guarantees by Arab states	of movement), dissipation of partition	and police training, decommissioning and arrest of war criminals and profiteers, unconditional civil society investment Return and/or compensation for Serb refugees from Croatia	reconstruction Increased aid for Macedonia and Montenegro Support for nation-building in Macedonia
Worst-case option (Now)	Definite return to direct British rule as against current indefinite return	Indian refusal to talk, Pakistan's renewal of Kashmir Jihad, everpresent, threat of wider war, increasing Pakistan crisis, leading to increasing instability spiral from Kashmir into rest of India	Reoccupation of West Bank and Gaza by Israel Partition, with closed borders	Endless proximity talks without results, unilateral accession of Cyprus to EU, strengthening partition and estranging Turkey from Europe	Continuing pusillanimity leading to hardening of partition, growing disintegration of state and society	Spread of cross-border conflict in southern Serbia Hardening of criminalization in Kosovo Expulsion of remaining Serbs in enclave Renewal of ethnic conflict in Macedonia

The complex problem of political delegitimization appears most sharply in Kosovo. Policing – at least in the majority Albanian areas – would be much easier if the international administration could use the 5,000-strong police force that existed under the parallel government of Ibrahim Rugova (maintained though a decade of repression). But Rugova lost stature during the Rambouillet negotiations, where the KLA emerged as a major force. Although the international administration has attempted to bring the two parties together, it has failed to do so. While moves are afoot to transform the KLA into a kind of armed police/security force, civilian policing remains restricted to a woefully small international force and an internationally constituted academy, which has thus far recruited a few hundred trainees. These gaps in the rule of law allowed Kosovo to become a base for Albanian insurgency in Macedonia.

PEACE PROCESSES

Table 2 lays out the best- and worst-case options that were available during decolonization negotiations at the time of partition and those that are available in peace processes now. The conflicts devolved then, and now, on contested scales of devolution, from limited autonomy to independence.[10] Ironically, in many cases sustained devolution – allowing the local people to develop democratic institutions – might have worked better than independence (the exit option). The League of Nations intended mandates to help local communities build institutions that would facilitate creation of independent states. (The mandates did not work in that way; they were given to colonial powers Britain and France, neither of them well placed to nurture societies to independence.) The principle underlying Woodrow Wilson's Fourteen Points was that colonialism was unacceptable, irrespective of its "civilizing mission": it took another world war to bring the point home.

In a similar way, since the end of the Cold War a new principle has been emerging: sovereignty is not an end that justifies all means. At present, this principle cuts both ways. Intervention against genocide is now acceptable, although what constitutes genocide continues to be debated, and in the near future this principle will probably be acted on selectively and rarely.

Meanwhile, if state fiat against self-determination movements is becoming a matter of international rather than of internal concern alone, armed groups seeking self-determination, such as the Irish Republican

Army (IRA), Islamic Jihad, and the Kashmir militants, are increasingly seen as impediments to peace, especially at a time when the world community is more supportive of devolution than it was either under colonialism or during the Cold War. The increasing consensus that violence is not an acceptable route to self-determination, however, is complicated by the war on terrorism following the attacks on the United States of 11 September 2001. Growing numbers in the Muslim world believe incorrectly that the war against terrorism targets only Muslim self-determination movements, which puts the onus on the international community either to show "even-handedness" or to support Muslim self-determination.

Whether ethnic or religious states are the chief goals of self-determination movements is a moot point. As the history of partition shows, in each case the decision to partition has been a close call. Alternatives were proposed in India: for example, in 1945–46 the Unionist governments in Bengal, Punjab, and Sindh suggested a decentralized federation of secular states, which represented a serious (as against wishful) alternative and could have pre-empted prolonged ethnic conflict. Irish Home Rule in 1912 could have yielded Catholic support for the British in the First World War. This would have loosened the tie of guilt and loyalty that bound the British government to the Ulster Unionists – which the latter used to telling effect after the war – and might have allowed a gradual transfer of power with devolution instead of partition.

A similar tale holds in India and in Cyprus: nationalists in both cases would have supported the Allies in the Second World War had the British promised self-determination, which might have paved the way for a phased exit. The histories of our five partition conflicts show that ethnic constituencies (and, during war, ethno-territories) consolidate themselves during third party–led negotiations. This consolidation has been generally contested, but the negotiating process pushes secular or pluralist contestants to the margin.

Yet, as the contemporary peace processes in the five cases show, marginal parties often achieve breakthroughs. Arguably, the process in Northern Ireland has been the most successful. Since its inception in the late 1980s, it has progressed by fits and starts, but always incrementally. As a result, although it might appear fragile – dismantling a couple of police stations and an army base could bring down the executive – its roots are strong. Three key elements in its success present yardsticks for the other conflicts.

First, there can be a change of heart in the parent nation/diaspora support. The big breakthrough for Northern Ireland occurred only when the Irish–American diaspora stopped supporting paramilitary groups, chiefly because of the efforts of the U.S.-based Friends of Ireland. This shift expanded U.S. influence on the British government aimed at starting an all-party peace process. Similar hopes have surfaced vis-à-vis Bosnia now that there is a democratic rather than a nationalist government in Croatia, although Serbia remains incalculable; and for Cyprus, given cautious rapprochement between Greece and Turkey. For Kashmir, following the cease-fire initiatives of 2000, and especially after 11 September 2001, the U.S. and British diaspora has had a change of heart, which could generate key support for a breakthrough, if the escalating hostility between India and Pakistan can be defused. A similar change of attitude among Sri Lankan Tamils in Canada and Britain, and possibly more so in the Indian state of Tamil Nadu, could make all the difference to that island's partition-related conflict. In contrast, breakthrough in the highly complicated Israeli–Palestinian conflict frequently stumbles over the plethora of contesting regional and diaspora supporters.

Second, at the local level, the big shifts are more likely to come from marginal rather than from dominant parties. At the political level, the first visible breakthroughs in Northern Ireland came from the Social Democratic and Labour Party of John Hume, long regarded as swept aside by history. In other words, it is crucial to distinguish between a cease-fire, which only the dominant parties can deliver, and a settlement, which will put in place building blocks for long-term stability.[11]

As Britain recognized, for the framework agreements in Northern Ireland to achieve substance, all parties had to be involved. This is a lesson that has not yet taken hold in our other peace processes, although in each of them track two and track three are encouraged, to varying degrees. This is where the differences kick in: in Cyprus, for example, it is possible to conceive of a long time frame, whose first step might be a formal agreement to coexist, with the understanding that membership in the EU would in time restore freedom of movement of goods, services, and people. Nevertheless, local talks will be necessary to work through problems such as the Green Line through Nicosia, property returns and/or compensation for refugees, and the fate of Anatolian settlers. Greek Cypriot social-democratic parties and the Turkish Cypriot diaspora could conceivably aid at this level.

From opposite points of departure, both India and Pakistan fear all-party talks because of ensuing domestic confrontations, yet most people realize that without such talks the spiral of conflict will continue.

In Bosnia and Kosovo, where peace rests on still-precarious agreements, all-party talks are feared because they might reopen old wounds. Nevertheless, all-party involvement in social, political, and economic reconstruction is essential if the international community is to have any prospect of an exit.

A debate continues over whether the Madrid talks might not have yielded a firmer Middle East peace process than the Oslo negotiations did. While the question might seem academic, it is difficult to see how to resolve some of the more complex issues – for example, of refugees – without all-party talks.

Third, a regional framework is essential to underpin peace and move participants towards long-term stability. Membership in the EU helped push the Irish Republic to relinquish claims of sovereignty over Northern Ireland; as Northern Ireland moves towards stabilization under the framework agreements, the EU might now help to dissolve the lines of partition. A South-East European Stability Pact could play a similar role in the former Yugoslavia; however, such an association of weak states would need a formal alliance with the EU. In South Asia, there is a crying need for the South Asian Association for Regional Cooperation (SAARC) to be strengthened and its mandate expanded. Cross-border conflicts plague every country in the region, but paradoxically its governments are so deeply suspicious of each other that freedom of movement appears to be available only to militants. Yet these countries are better placed, by reasons of geography, markets, culture, and politics, to form a strong regional alliance than many others are. Regional acceptance has been a long-term dream of the Israelis; the problem has been in coming to terms with the Palestinians. Whether and what kind of a regional association can be built there remains an open but very much present question.

CONCLUSION

In brief, I derive five overall lessons from my comparative analysis of five partition-related conflicts.

First, partitions do not work as a solution to ethnic conflict; rather they restructure the sources of conflict around borders, refugees, and diasporas. Nor, in a post-colonial and globalizing world, can they serve either as an exit strategy or as a means of containment.

Second, in most cases, third-party negotiators force partition through as a way of separating the warring parties. However, because partition restructures the sources of conflict, the separation of forces tends to be temporary. How to turn an agreement on partition into a separation-of-forces agreement remains the great challenge for peacemakers, and perhaps we need to turn the question on its head: i.e., to look for ways to prevent separation of forces from turning into partition.

Third, the historical examples – proposed alternatives based on a combination of human rights and devolution at various stages of partition-related conflicts – can be useful. Where there is a high level of commitment at international and regional levels, third-party negotiations would do well to draw on the Irish model; where commitment may be partial or weaker, alternative proposals are criminal.

Fourth, in post-conflict reconstruction, the process will be slow unless it involves local communities in both planning and implementation. When potential governments exist, as in East Timor, the role of an international administration is limited in both time and scope. When putative governments might need to be nursed along, international commitment should vary according to the amount of input into stabilization in the immediate post-conflict phase.

Fifth, the evolving formula of "evolution with devolution" – in other words, of providing a regional underpinning for post-conflict stabilization and peace processes – which has proved so important to the Irish peace process and is being developed with the South-East European Stability Pact, has enormous potential. The fact that this formula is still largely limited to the EU should not be a deterrent. Cautious as the Association of South East Asian Nations (ASEAN) is, and as weak as the Organization of African Unity (OAU) and SAARC are, long-term stability can be best served by prodding them into growth.

NOTES

1 Revised draft of a paper presented to both the Council on Foreign Relations Study Group on Ethnic Conflicts, Partitions and Post Conflict Stabilization and the Association for the Study of Nationalities convention on 6 April 2001.

2 For example, see Nicolson, 1921, Coupland, 1937, and *The Transfer of Power* volumes. A rare exception is Elon, 1972, who advocates Israeli acceptance of partition. For a devastating critique of partition as an exit policy by a former civil servant, see Moon, 1961, on the partition of India in 1947–48.

3 Northern Ireland has not received the same wide foreign interest; Bosnia, which might be the most widely written-about conflict, alongside Vietnam, is only now being looked at in terms of partition.

4 For example, bi-national and bi-communal solutions have been advanced in both the Israel–Palestine and the Cyprus conflicts, but no one has examined why the formula has become ascendant vis-à-vis Cyprus and negligible for Israel–Palestine, even though the answers might clarify when and how to apply such a model. For an example of this lack, see Tutunji and Khaldi, 1996.

5 See Mearsheimer and Pape, 1993; Mearsheimer and Van Evera, 1995; Kaufmann, 1996; Weiner, 1996; Mearsheimer, 1997; and Mearsheimer and Van Evera, 1999.

6 I have dealt with these arguments at length in Kumar, 1997.

7 The fact that Czechoslovakia's "velvet divorce" remains exceptional testifies to another point – that sovereignty/devolution remains one of the most fiercely contested processes. In other words, it is at least theoretically possible to negotiate a peaceful secession.

8 As the U.S.-Department of Defense warned in 1991, and as former Vice-President Al Gore recently noted, ethnic conflicts now involve proliferation of weapons, terrorism, and ethnic cleansing, none of which are amenable to containment.

9 See Kumar, 2000.

10 If this point seems trite, it gains in value from a comparison with conflicts that do not concern devolution, such as the diamond wars in Africa.

11 In this sense, Bosnia is still in the cease-fire period. A five-year holding period – whose greatest achievement, apart from holding the cease-fire, has been the gradual push to arrest war criminals – is gradually beginning to marginalize some of the most rabid extremists.

REFERENCES

Coupland, Reginald (1937) *Palestine Royal Commission Report.*

Elon, Amos (1972) *The Israelis: Founders and Sons.* (New York: Holt, Rinehart and Winston).

Kaufmann, Chaim (1996) "Possible and Impossible Solutions to Ethnic Civil Wars," *International Security* 20, no. 4.

Kumar, Radha (1997) "The Troubled History of Partition," *Foreign Affairs* 76, no. 1.

– (2000) "The Partition Debate: Colonialism Revisited or New Policies?" *Brown Journal of International Affairs* 7, no. 1 (winter–spring).

Mearsheimer, John J. (1997) "An Exit Strategy for Bosnia," *New York Times*, 7 Oct.

Mearsheimer, John J., and Robert A. Pape (1993) "The Answer: A Three-Way Partition Plan for Bosnia and How the US Can Enforce It," *New Republic*, June.

Mearsheimer, John J., and Stephen Van Evera (1995) "When Peace Means War," *New Republic*, Dec.

– (1999) "Redraw the Map, Stop the Killing," *New York Times*, 19 April.

Moon, Penderel (1961) *Divide and Quit*. London; reprinted in Mark Tully and Tapan Raychaudhuri, eds., Delhi: Oxford University Press, 1998.

Nicolson, Harold (1919) *Peace-Making*. London; reprinted Simon Publication, 2001.

Tutunji, Jemal, and Kemal Khaldi (1996) "A Binational State in Palestine: The Rational Choice for Palestinians and the Moral Choice for Israelis," *International Affairs* 27, no. 1.

Weiner, Myron (1996) "Bad Neighbors, Bad Neighborhoods: An Enquiry into the Causes of Refugee Flows," *International Security* 21, no. 1.

MICHAEL MURPHY

Understanding Indigenous Nationalism

Indigenous peoples around the world are increasingly adopting the language of nationalism to describe their claims to self-determination and to challenge the authority of the settler states that have asserted sovereignty in and over their traditional territories (G. Alfred, 1995; Reynolds, 1996; Durie, 1998). Whereas the discourse of stateless nationalism has attracted a fair amount of attention from theorists of multiculturalism or multinational diversity (Tamir, 1993; Kymlicka, 1995; Carens, 2000), relatively few works focus on indigenous nationalism as a distinctive phenomenon. Even fewer investigate the relationship between the normative dimensions of indigenous nationalism and the distinctive challenges associated with its implementation. These challenges include the relatively small size and capacity of indigenous communities; the mixing of indigenous and non-indigenous populations; the internal cultural diversity of country-wide indigenous populations; and the persistence of local political identities and allegiances. This combination of factors means that, despite its normative similarity to more conventional claims to national self-determination, indigenous nationalism requires a wider variety of territorial, non-territorial, and hybrid institutional designs.

This essay attempts to fill some of these gaps in our understanding of indigenous nationalism, drawing on examples from Australia, Canada, and New Zealand. I divide the discussion into three sections. The first develops a theoretical, or normative understanding of indigenous nationalism in terms of three interrelated dimensions of democratic self-determination: external, internal, and shared-rule democracy. The second responds to some common criticisms of indigenous nationalism by making a clearer distinction between its normative and its empirical–institutional dimensions. The third section explores the implications of this normative framework in concrete political terms – specifically, the kinds of indigenous communities that will exercise the right to self-determination and what sorts of institutions are possible and/or already exist.

INDIGENOUS NATIONALISM: THEORETICAL DIMENSIONS

There is no shortage of theoretical literature on indigenous rights and governance. These works present a broad spectrum of theoretical standpoints, including appeals to the concept of citizenship (Dodds, 1998; Requejo, 1999; Carens, 2000), multiculturalism (B. Walker, 1997; Levy, 2000), decolonization (Green, 1995; R.J. Walker, 1999), and equality of peoples (Dodson, 1996; Macklem, 2001). Others have studied indigenous self-determination from within an explicitly nationalist frame of analysis, though generally as part of a broader discussion of multiculturalism (Kymlicka, 1995) or liberal nationalism (Tamir, 1993). While there is much of value in this literature, studies of indigenous nationalism as a phenomenon in its own right are rare (Alfred, 1995; Ramos, 2000). Rarer yet are studies that systematically investigate the link between indigenous nationalism and the theory and practice of democracy. Granted, there are approaches that invoke key democratic principles such as sovereignty, consent, and equality (Tully, 1995; Macklem, 2001) and others that speak the language of self-government and collective autonomy (Kymlicka, 1995; Reynolds, 1996; Durie, 1998), but the democratic dimensions of indigenous self-determination have not received the rigorous and sustained attention that they deserve. This oversight is surprising – democracy seems such a crucial element in contemporary political development and is so central to the theory and practice of indigenous nationalism.

At the heart of indigenous nationalism lies the claim to self-determination. This is a democratic claim, an expression of indigenous peoples' desire to regain control over their individual and collective futures in the socio-economic and geopolitical contexts of today. The broader claim to self-determination contains three more specific dimensions of democracy that require elucidation – external democracy and intergovernmental relations; internal democratic principles and governing practices; and shared-rule democracy in state institutions. In the following subsections I explore each of these in turn.

External Democracy

The external dimension of democratic self-determination refers to a people's right to decide its own future as free as possible from external interference or domination (Philpott, 1995, 352; De-Shalit, 1996, 911; Murphy, 2001, 373–7). External self-determination can be elusive in practice, and many states that claim to be implementing such a policy continue to insist on significant powers of control and oversight, sometimes to the extent that the institutions in question seem to have less to do with indigenous self-determination than with a reconfiguration of government control. These sorts of issues continue to be central to debates over the implementation of policies of indigenous self-determination in countries such as Canada and Australia (Bennett, 1999, 197; Rynard, 1999; Tully, 1999; Sanders, 2002). Indigenous peoples view their right to self-determination as neither derivative of nor subordinate to that of any other political community. It is a right that can be recognized and protected by the statutory and constitutional law of settler states, but whose source is viewed as prior to and more fundamental than those legal instruments, anchored as it is in the historic independence of self-governing indigenous societies. Unlike other identity groups, indigenous peoples challenge the state's right to assert and exercise its jurisdiction over them. As such, indigenous nationalism expresses more than simply a demand for toleration or limited forbearance of indigenous cultural differences, but is instead a demand for a rightful recognition of political status and for a share of political power. Contrary to the opinion of some theorists, this does not constitute an appeal for special consideration or a special right to self-determination (Buchanan, 1998) but is instead an appeal to the same democratic right to freedom from alien rule that is comfortably assumed by nations that control states. For indigenous nationalists, the basic political question is not why or to what degree the state should accede to their demands for autonomy, but how indigenous peoples and the state can mutually accommodate their equal entitlements to self-determination.

The demand for external self-determination is sometimes interpreted as a desire for separation or for parallel indigenous and non-indigenous societies and governments that will have little to do with one another

(Cairns, 2000, 91–115). However, indigenous nationalism does not represent an absolute rejection of the state's authority, and it is rarely, if ever, an expression of a desire for secession. Indigenous nationalists mean it as a rejection of intergovernmental relationships based on unilateralism and domination in favour of those based on mutual recognition and consent and protected by secure and binding guarantees. This concept finds overwhelming confirmation in the statements of indigenous leaders and intellectuals, who recognize that the socio-economic, cultural, and political development of their communities depends on the cultivation of stronger but mutually beneficial relationships with the state (Henderson, 1994; Reynolds, 1996; Durie, 1998; Borrows, 2000). As representatives of the James Bay Cree stated before the United Nations Commission on Human Rights, their goal is not to secede from Canada but "to *join* Canada ... in a manner that fully respects the principles of equality and mutual respect" (GCC, 1992, 180). In summary, indigenous nationalism contemplates a relationship between indigenous peoples and the state, but one not predicated on their comprehensive legal and political subordination.

Internal Democracy

Theoretical accounts of indigenous self-determination tend to emphasize the external element of autonomy and non-interference, but two additional dimensions – internal democracy and shared rule – are of equal importance. Internal democracy refers broadly to the right to choose how and by whom one will be governed. This includes the right to choose one's own political representatives and to design the institutions in terms of which those representatives are to be selected and held accountable. It further involves the freedom to decide what will be governed – particular populations, territories, resources, policy jurisdictions, and programs and services. It is also implicated in debates regarding the degree to which forms of indigenous governance should adhere to traditional customs, practices, and values. Whereas some observers see the revival of more traditional governance models as essential to indigenous cultural preservation and independence from the state, others point out that many indigenous peoples no longer identify with traditional forms of governance and feel that more contemporary forms of self-rule and administration will better meet their needs (Alfred, 1999; Barcham, 2000). An example from New Zealand is the ongoing debate as to whether only traditional *iwi* (tribes) should receive and administer benefits derived from Treaty of Waitangi settlements or whether contemporary forms of Māori political association, such as urban *iwi*, should share this right (Barcham, 1998; Durie, 1998; Mahuika, 1998). Whatever forms their governments are to take, indigenous peoples are entitled to make these decisions as part of the internal process of democratic self-government. These governments are therefore accountable first and foremost to the people who consent to live under their authority.

Shared Rule

The third democratic dimension of self-determination involves shared rule in state institutions. Indigenous self-determination may seem to imply little more than separate and autonomous self-government, but it is frequently both necessary and advantageous that self-rule be combined with participation in shared-rule institutions such as national parliaments and co-management regimes (Henderson, 1994; Borrows, 2000; Catt and Murphy, 2002). Forms of shared rule are often essential where indigenous and non-indigenous populations are intermixed and seek access to the same territories and resources. Land and resource co-management regimes in Canada's Nunavut and Yukon were designed with this sort of arrangement in mind (Hicks and White, 2000; White, 2003). Indigenous representation in state institutions – for example, the guaranteed seats for Māori representatives in New Zealand's national parliament – can introduce indigenous peoples' concerns into national forums and debates. Moreover, shared rule may also be essential when state institutions enjoy the capacity to modify or revoke the self-governing powers of indigenous governments; representation in those institutions may help prevent this without those communities' consent (Schouls, 1996). Other commentators have argued that representation in central institutions may help ease the marginalization or ghettoization of indigenous peoples, promoting instead co-operative and mutually beneficial relationships with non-indigenous peoples and governments, which in turn may increase intercommunal trust and solidarity (Henderson, 1994; Borrows, 2000).

One of the keys to the success of indigenous participation in shared-rule institutions is to conceive of them as complementary rather than as alternatives to institutions of internal self-government. This may not be as much of a challenge in a country such as New Zealand, with a long history of relatively positive experiences with shared-rule institutions for Māori, but it will be more difficult in Canada and Australia, which originally intended enfranchisement and legislative representation to undermine autonomous self-government and to assimilate the indigenous populations. In such cases it may be crucial to proceed first with institutions of self-rule as a means of building the trust essential to the element of shared rule contemplated by representation in institutions at the centre.

DISTINGUISHING THEORETICAL
AND EMPIRICAL DIMENSIONS

Whereas the language of indigenous nationalism is gaining currency among political theorists and even government officials, others feel that this conceptual framework is inappropriate and counterproductive in the symbolic and practical reconciliation of indigenous–state interests. This objection is motivated by a number of concerns. First, some critics argue that the language of nationalism is empirically misleading when applied to indigenous peoples (Cairns, 2000; Flanagan, 2000). Most indigenous communities are relatively small in comparison to stateless nations such as the Kurds or the Catalans, sometimes numbering in the low hundreds. For example, Yukon has approximately 7,000 indigenous inhabitants distributed among 14 First Nations, the smallest with just over 100 members (Catt and Murphy, 2002, 56). "National" self-determination for communities of this size, critics charge, will produce a nation of government, with virtually every member of the community necessarily occupying some position in the public service. Moreover, the critics continue, many indigenous communities lack the necessary capacity and training to run a large, complex, and multi-jurisdictional national government. As well, they will remain highly dependent on cash transfers from the central government in order to provide even the most basic programs and services – a situation that belies the independence promised by the term "nation" (Cairns, 2000; Flanagan, 2000).[1]

Second, many indigenous people are not even a part of a territorially concentrated indigenous community, large or small. Large portions of indigenous populations around the world are territorially dispersed and often highly intermixed with non-indigenous populations. In 1998 in Australia, for example, approximately 30 per cent of the indigenous population resided in major urban centres, and in Canada in 2001 the figure was closer to 50 per cent (Australia, 2002; Canada, 2003). In

New Zealand in 1996 approximately 80 per cent of Māori resided away from a traditional land base in urban centres (New Zealand, 2002). Urban indigenous populations are also highly internally diverse in terms of such factors as language, culture, kinship ties, and communal or political identification and solidarity and thus cannot be said to constitute a single unified or viable national community. In summary, the critics contend, the conceptual framework of nationalism inaccurately describes the life situations of large percentages of the world's indigenous population and unnecessarily raises the expectations of indigenous communities with respect to the size, capabilities, and independence of indigenous governments. As such it should be rejected in favour of a more appropriate conceptual framework or metaphor (Cairns, 2000, 6–12).

The empirical circumstances of indigenous peoples are more complex than these critics allow. For example, although the Māori population in New Zealand lives overwhelmingly in urban areas, large portions of these urbanites are *iwi* (tribal) in terms of both descent and self-identification, a crucial factor for developing appropriate forms of Māori representation and governance (Durie, 1998, 192; Maaka, 1998, 202). Similarly, in Canada, despite a general assumption of a steady and increasing movement of indigenous peoples from rural areas and reserves to urban centres, this diaspora moves back and forth between reserves and urban centres, with some years a net migration back to reserves (Norris, Cooke, and Clatworthy, 2002; Peters, 2002). Hence, although governance solutions for urban populations are an increasingly urgent priority, solutions are essential for indigenous peoples who continue to reside on a land base or who migrate back and forth between the land and the city. These caveats aside, one cannot simply dismiss these challenges relating to the size, capacity, and geographical distribution of indigenous communities. My intention in the remainder of this chapter is to demonstrate why these challenges can and should be faced within an indigenous nationalist framework.

The first step in this task is to draw a clearer distinction between the empirical and the normative dimensions of indigenous nationalism. For critics who focus on the empirical shortcomings of indigenous nationalism, the normative dimensions of the claim often simply drop out of the equation (Flanagan, 2000). Some analysts appear to conclude that notions of indigenous nationalism, sovereignty, and nation-to-nation relationships of equality have been superseded by the facts: by the state's effective assertion of its own sovereignty, by the relative weakness and dependence of indigenous peoples, and by the increasing interpenetration of indigenous and non-indigenous societies and cultures (Cairns, 2000, 142–3). This is a particularly difficult conclusion for indigenous peoples to accept, for not only are they asked to live with the realities of dispossession, depopulation, and societal fragmentation brought on by colonization and processes of modern state formation, they are expected to give up their right to challenge the justifiability of this assault on their freedom and well-being.

The normative dimension of indigenous nationalism challenges states to confront this issue. It asks them to defend the legitimacy of their unilateral assertions of sovereignty and to justify their denial of an equal right to self-determination to the indigenous inhabitants whose territory they now occupy. Despite the sometimes very different empirical needs, characteristics, and circumstances of indigenous and non-indigenous populations, the normative basis of each claim is identical. Each appeals to the basic democratic right to determine freely their individual and collective futures and to negotiate relationships with other societies and governments predicated on equality and consent. Indigenous nationalists may agree that the disruption of their traditional economies, societies, and forms of governance as a result of colonization will affect how they exercise self-determination but refuse to agree that these disruptions have altered their entitlement to the right per se. States may refuse to confront this challenge, but in doing so they cast a shadow on their own democratic credentials.

Retaining the normative dimension of indigenous nationalism also helps distinguish the claims of indigenous peoples from those of cultural or religious minorities (Kymlicka, 1995, 26–33). Using a nationalist framework to understand indigenous claims allows us to appreciate that what indigenous people seek is not only toleration of their cultural distinctiveness or equal access to the social and economic benefits of citizenship but also a degree of legal and political independence from state institutions and a measure of real power over their territories, peoples, and resources. This applies no differently to landless and dispersed populations than it does to geographically concentrated indigenous communities on a land base. For example, redressing urban poverty and powerlessness for indigenous and non-indigenous peoples could be justified simply on the basis of need and treated like any other public policy initiative for the population at large. However, the normative dimension of indigenous nationalism helps us see why indigenous peoples, unlike other members of the urban underclass, feel justified in demanding not simply equal treatment and greater access to resources but also control over decision-making and implementation processes relating to programs and services for indigenous peoples in urban centres. Whatever their circumstances, the state should not assume an automatic right to act on their behalf, treating them as passive objects rather than as active authors of governance initiatives relating to their interests.

FROM THEORY TO PRACTICE

Squarely facing these normative questions should not make us neglect the complex empirical reality of indigenous–state relations. On the contrary, the normative dimension of indigenous nationalism explains why the indigenous claim to a right of self-determination is worthy of respect but does not indicate who should exercise this right and how. Once a nationalist claim is deemed worthy of respect and redress, the next question involves the best way to implement it under a given set of circumstances. For most indigenous peoples, what can feasibly be done will differ quite significantly from the situation of larger and more powerful stateless nations, such as the Québécois, but the institutional possibilities may be quite varied, even for very small and dispersed communities. Accepting that the principle of national self-determination applies to a group such as the Sechelt of British Columbia, with just over 1,000 people, might suggest that indigenous nationalism can exist without indigenous nations, but there are many ways of "being a nation in practice" (Seymour, 2000, 228–30; Pearson, 2001, 6–7). Conventional nationalist thinking envisions a fairly narrow range of ideas about the types of communities capable of self-determination and the institutional means to exercise the right in practice. I discuss each of these two issues – which communities? and institutional design – in turn.

Which Communities?

A common criticism of indigenous nationalism is that it implies a country-wide pan-indigenism that ignores internal linguistic and cultural diversity, which tends to produce more localized identities, political loyalties, and sites of governance. As one observer concludes in the Australian case, even though indigenous spokespersons tend increasingly to appeal to nationalist imagery, in reality local and regional affiliations still predominate (Pearson, 2001, 8–9). Similarly, in New Zealand one prominent theorist cautions that attempts to address Māori demands justly and effectively should work not from an idealized notion of what Māori as a group are or ought to be but from the associations and identifications of their daily lives. Although the Māori language could serve as the basis for a country-wide Māori national identity, allegiances to *whanau* (extended family), *hapu* (clans), and iwi (confederation of hapu) and more contemporary forms of Māori political association dominate everyday life (Maaka, 1994, 329–30; Sharp, 2002, 36–7). Experience suggests that political initiatives must account for the internal cultural and political diversity of indigenous communities. In Canada for example, local indigenous communities' perception that national-level indigenous organizations did not adequately represent their voices and concerns in the negotiations leading up to the Charlottetown Accord of 1992 played a large part in their rejection of that document, despite its recognition of an Aboriginal third order of government in the Canadian federation (Turpel, 1993).

Although this more universal and homogenizing formulation of indigenous nationalism would appear to have at least qualified support in the literature (Reynolds, 1996; Walker, 1999), it bears little resemblance to mine. Indigenous nationalism as I understand it does not require the dissolution of local allegiances, communities, and cultures in favour of some overarching pan-indigenous community. Instead, it assumes that indigenous communities at the local, regional, and national levels can and should exercise self-determination. It denies that these groups or communities are necessarily competing or mutually exclusive sites of governance and self-determination. On the contrary, co-operative initiatives should engage indigenous communities at local, regional, cross-regional, and national levels. Such a multi-communal understanding of indigenous nationalism is itself sometimes mistakenly taken for a form of pan-indigenous nationalism. This charge has been laid against P.G. McHugh's discussion of New Zealand Māori, when in fact he argues for Māori regional and/or national communities that would complement local communities in political influence and governing capacity.[2]

Such a complementarity of self-determining communities at several levels may be difficult to achieve, but such initiatives are not alien to current practice. In Canada, the Assembly of First Nations (AFN) is a national-level representative body comprising a national grand chief, regional chiefs representing indigenous constituencies from each of the Canadian provinces, and chiefs representing local First Nations (AFN, 2002). The Council for Yukon First Nations (formerly the Council of

Yukon Indians) was formed in the 1970s by the territory's 14 First Nations as their central representative political body. It later negotiated the Umbrella Final Agreement with the Yukon and Canadian governments – a land-claims and self-government template that serves as the model for negotiating specific agreements with individual Yukon First Nations.[3] In Australia, although the Aboriginal and Torres Strait Islander Commission (ATSIC) has been criticized for not being able to represent the full spectrum of indigenous diversity there (Sullivan, 1996, 122), it has made significant strides towards the co-ordinated representation of local, regional, and national indigenous interests (Sanders, 2002, 6–8). The Waipareira Trust, a Māori controlled organization in Auckland, delivers social programs and services to a pan-Māori community comprising individuals from different iwi and hapu across the country. Though not an organ of self-government per se, it illustrates how to organize governance of an internally diverse, pan-indigenous urban community.[4] In international forums such as the United Nations Working Group on Indigenous Peoples, indigenous representatives work for the interests of their more localized communities but just as often for their world-wide community, for which they seek recognition in international law (Feldman, 2001).

I argue not for the strengths or weaknesses of any of these initiatives but only that it is both possible and desirable to locate sites of self-determination at several levels.[5] The success and legitimacy of such initiatives are crucially connected to the representation and co-ordination of these sites as complementary rather than mutually exclusive alternatives. For example, the Māori seats in New Zealand's parliament may not be the best possible means of representing the interests of particular iwi and hapu across the country, but they are a valuable symbolic expression of a unique constitutional position and a means of keeping Māori concerns before government and the public and of representing country-wide Māori concerns, such as language attrition and socio-economic deprivation. Similarly, whereas few observers would agree that the efforts of indigenous representatives in the international sphere are a good means of addressing the specific concerns of indigenous peoples in rural areas of Australia's Northern Territory or in urban centres in the Canadian province of Manitoba, achieving full and fair recognition of indigenous rights to self-determination in international law may increase pressure on domestic governments to negotiate detailed arrangements with their indigenous populations. As such, these efforts may help indigenous peoples world-wide.

Institutional Design

The tremendous variety of indigenous communities means that institutional design for self-government is difficult. In this subsection I seek to demonstrate that such innovation is both a possibility and an emerging reality.[6] As in the previous subsection, I do not delve into the merits and demerits of any of these designs. My primary intention is to show the range of potentially viable options. There is a strong temptation to assume that national communities will exercise self-determination almost exclusively via control of large representative assemblies with a comprehensive range of exclusive legislative jurisdictions and competences, exercising authority over a territorially concentrated population residing within established political borders. In practice, this is not always true even of more familiar examples of sub-state nationalism. For example, prior to 1990, majorities in Scotland and Wales were content to have their national interests represented through various access points at Westminster, such as MPs and representation on parliamentary committees. Moreover, these access points still help to represent these interests, even after the creation of the Assembly of Wales and the Scottish Parliament (Jones and Wilford, 1986, 6; Bogdanor, 1999). In similar fashion, Québécois not only compete with each other for control of the Quebec National Assembly but also have representation in the Supreme Court and the Parliament of Canada. In 1991 the Bloc Québécois, a federal political party committed to Quebec's independence, sent 54 MPs to the federal Parliament – enough to form the official opposition. In summary, national self-determination does not always require full-blown territorial assemblies, and in many cases a combination of self-rule and shared-rule institutions may be the best prescription. Below I consider institutional arrangements for geographically concentrated, urban, and dispersed indigenous populations.

For geographically concentrated indigenous populations a more familiar range of institutional options is possible. One of the best-known examples is Nunavut, Canada's most recent territory, created in tandem with the settlement of a massive land claim with the Inuit – the traditional indigenous occupants of the territory. Though created specifically to satisfy the political aspirations of the Inuit, the government of Nunavut was designed not only for Inuit but all of the territory's residents. In the negotiations leading up to the creation of Nunavut in 1999, the Inuit did not press for guaranteed control of the legislature, because they recognized both that the rest of Canada would more readily accept public government and that non-Inuit needed access to the democratic process (Abele and Dickerson, 1985, 12). Nevertheless, in practice the Inuit are virtually guaranteed a majority in the legislature – they comprise 85 per cent of the population. Elected in 1999, the first legislature had 19 members, 15 of whom were Inuit, including the first premier, Paul Okalik. The legislature enjoys a broad range of powers, comparable to those exercised by Canadian provinces (Hicks and White, 2000), and governs a territory of roughly 2 million square kilometres (approximately 20 per cent of Canada's landmass) and a population of some 22,000. The Inuit have indicated that their long-term goal is provincial status and have also maintained that they may choose an Inuit-exclusive form of self-government should the demographics shift in favour of non-Inuit (Ittinuar, 1985, 52; Légaré, 1997, 423).

The Nisga'a Final Agreement was the first modern treaty with an indigenous First Nation in Canada's province of British Columbia. The resulting system of government is not public like Nunavut, and only citizens of the Nisga'a Nation can vote or hold public office. The government has three levels: a *Lisims* government to make decisions affecting the nation as a whole; four village governments with authority primarily over local matters; and three urban locals to serve citizens living temporarily in urban centres outside the territory (see discussion below). The Nisga'a govern a territory of approximately 2,000 square kilometres in northwestern British Columbia and roughly 6,000 citizens (Catt and Murphy, 2002, 56). The treaty provides them with a range of legislative powers encompassing both provincial- and federal-type jurisdictions, including language, culture, citizenship, education, and natural resources.[7] These powers are exercised in terms set out by the treaty and by the Nisga'a constitution, ratified in a community-wide referendum in 2000. The treaty is also the first self-government agreement in Canada to receive explicit constitutional protection under section 35 of the Constitution Act of 1982 (Canada, 1998, 17–18).[8]

Territorial self-governance initiatives such as Nunavut and the Nisga'a Treaty are far more advanced in Canada, but there are a few interesting initiatives in Australia. These include the Torres Strait Regional Authority, a form of local or municipal public government for the Torres Strait Islanders, and community-of-interest governments for indigenous-majority communities in the Northern Territory and Queensland (Sanders, 1996; Arthur, 1997). Although no such initiatives exist in New Zealand, one hypothetical option is to expand the role of tribal *Runanga* (councils) from management and distribution of crown settlement assets to making and/or implementating policy at the local level. In the decade after 1900, local Māori governing councils had limited jurisdiction, but they were later abolished (Ward and Hayward, 1999, 388–90).

Institutional options for urban and geographically dispersed indigenous populations are less developed on the whole, but promising possibilities are in varying stages of proposal and implementation. An example from Australia is the Aboriginal and Torres Strait Islander Commission (ATSIC), an elected body whose members are drawn from and represent indigenous peoples throughout the country. ATSIC is not a legislature but an institution that provides policy advice to the Commonwealth government and allocates part of the government budget earmarked for indigenous Australians. It also plays a role in policy development and implementation, working closely with the Ministry of Aboriginal Affairs. In an attempt to represent some measure of the regional diversity of the indigenous population, ATSIC forms one of two layers of administration. The bottom layer comprises 36 regional councils, whose members are chosen by indigenous voters resident in the region. These councils play an active role in budget allocation for community projects and are empowered to formulate regional plans to improve the socio-economic and cultural well-being of their indigenous constituents. The regions are themselves grouped into 16 zones, each of which, along with the Torres Strait region, elects one member to ATSIC. The members in turn elect the chair of ATSIC (Catt and Murphy, 2002, 103–5). Despite serious concerns expressed regarding ATSIC's independence from government, it remains the primary expression of indigenous self-determination in Australia, and a number of innovative proposals have been advanced that would see marked increases in its fiscal and political autonomy and its potential emergence as a third order of indigenous government in Australia (Sanders, 2002).

In all three countries, urban populations are also being served by an increasing number of indigenous-controlled program and service-delivery organizations. While some of these bodies are linked to land-based indigenous communities and political organizations, most are independent of any particular indigenous community and instead are run by and serve a multi-tribal or pan-indigenous urban population (Maaka, 1994, 330; Peters, 2002, 7–9). Examples include in New

Zealand multi-tribal iwi such as the Waipareira Trust and the Manukau Urban Authority in Auckland, which many observers feel should be recognized alongside traditional kinship-based iwi as full partners with the crown in the Treaty of Waitangi (Makaa, 1994; Barcham, 1998; 2000). Similar examples can be found in Canada, probably in their most developed form in cities with larger indigenous populations, such as Winnipeg and Edmonton (Hanselmann, 2002; Peters, 2002). Like their New Zealand counterparts, they deliver programs and services only within the parameters of policy designed exclusively by non-indigenous governments, a situation that impedes the design of effective urban indigenous policy (Gibbins and Hanselmann, 2002; Peters, 2002). Despite models contemplating the direct involvement of urban indigenous political organizations in the policy process – for example, those proposed by Canada's Royal Commission on Aboriginal Peoples – to date no such initiatives exist in the three countries examined in this chapter.[9]

There are also at least three interesting hybrid initiatives for urban and dispersed populations. First, the urban local serves as a democratic bridge between the Nisga'a territorial government and citizens residing temporarily in urban areas. Citizens of each urban local are entitled to elect an individual to serve as their representative to the Nisga'a *Lisims* government (Canada, 1998, 162; Nisga'a Nation, 2000, 14–15). Second, a land-based indigenous nation may extend its jurisdiction into an adjacent urban area where enough of its citizens reside. In the Canadian province of Saskatchewan, the Touchwood File Hills Qu'Appelle Tribal Council represents 16 First Nations and provides numerous programs and services to its members in the nearby city of Regina (Anaquod, 1993). Third, a more comprehensive hybrid initiative is currently being negotiated among representatives of the Federation of Saskatchewan Indian Nations, Canada, and the province of Saskatchewan. The negotiations contemplate an integrated and layered system of First Nations governance comprising a single province-wide government, an intermediate layer of regional governments based on tribal or treaty areas, and a third layer of over 70 First Nations governments. The idea is to preserve the independence and autonomy of local governments, while enabling them to delegate authority upwards to take advantage of increased capacity and economies of scale. This system would provide for First Nations jurisdiction both on and off reserve. For example, the province-wide government could design and administer its own system of primary education, which would be available to indigenous (and non-indigenous) children on reserves and in off-reserve rural and urban settings (Hawkes, 2002).[10] The initial negotiations will deal with First Nations jurisdiction in education and child and family services, and subsequent negotiations are anticipated on justice, lands and resources, hunting, fishing, trapping and gathering, health, and housing.

Shared-rule initiatives are the final set of institutional options to be surveyed. One of the more familiar examples is the Māori electorates in New Zealand. Created in 1867 as a temporary measure to facilitate Māori assimilation (Fleras, 1985, 555–8), they have survived and evolved into one of the primary expressions of the crown–Māori treaty partnership, and Māori support for their retention remains relatively strong (New Zealand, 1986; Ward and Hayward, 1999, 386).[11] Under this system there are separate electoral rolls for Māori and non-Māori, and self-identifying Māori can choose the particular roll on which they wish to cast their vote. Only Māori can stand for election in the Māori electorates, but they are also free to stand in the general electorates and have been regularly elected to parliament in this manner. As in the general roll, the number of Māori electorates is pegged to population numbers, and there were seven in the 2002 election (Catt and Murphy, 2002, 95–9). In Canada, the Committee for Aboriginal Electoral Reform (CAER), created as part of the Royal Commission for Electoral Reform and Party Financing in 1991, proposed a similar system of Aboriginal Electoral Districts, but it was never implemented (Canada, 1991; Schouls, 1996). Indigenous academics in Canada have also been showing increasing interest in this form of representation and have floated a number of interesting proposals, but guaranteed representation in either provincial or federal legislatures remains very much at a theoretical stage of development (Henderson, 1994; Borrows, 2000).

An example of a shared-rule institution that exists in all three countries studied is the functional co-management board. These boards are used extensively in Canada, and to a somewhat lesser extent in New Zealand, to facilitate equal participation of indigenous peoples in the co-management of land, water, wildlife, and natural resources (Catt and Murphy, 2002, 89–94; White, 2003). In Australia, another interesting variation allows for co-management of national parks on indigenous lands. A 1985 amendment to the National Parks and Wildlife Conservation Act of 1975 stipulates that wherever a national park falls within indigenous territory a co-management board must be established, including an indigenous majority nominated by the territory's traditional owners (Altman and Allen, 1992, 128–34). The first of these, the Cobourg Peninsula Sanctuary Board, was created in 1981 to manage Gurig National Park on the Cobourg Peninsula in the Northern Territory. It has eight members, four nominated from among the traditional indigenous landowners and four by the minister for conservation. The chair must be a traditional owner and holds a casting vote. The board's primary responsibility is to develop a management plan for the park, which must be approved by the territorial legislative assembly. The broad aims of the management plan are to facilitate the principle of conservation and the sustainable development of the economic potential of the park and to help realize the needs and interests of the traditional owners (Foster, 1997).

Like any of the examples mentioned in this subsection, co-management boards are not perfect, but they can give indigenous peoples a significant degree of decision-making authority over key resources or jurisdictions (White, 2003, 98–100, 108–9). They are also highly flexible, capable of managing either a specific resource such as forest or fisheries or a specific jurisdiction such as education or the environment; moreover, their authority can extend either to territorially concentrated or to territorially dispersed and intermixed populations.

CONCLUSION

This paper set out to accomplish several objectives. The first was to uncover the normative foundations of indigenous nationalism in basic principles of democracy. A key part of this objective involved the disaggregation of the external, internal, and shared-rule dimensions of indigenous nationalism that are essential to meeting the needs of indigenous communities whose distinctive characteristics frequently set them apart from the more familiar stateless nations.

A second objective was to distinguish between the normative and the empirical elements of indigenous nationalism. Appreciating this distinction helps us understand that, despite their distinctive empirical characteristics and circumstances, indigenous nationalists appeal to the same democratic right to self-determination taken for granted by the nations that control the states within which they reside. The normative dimension of indigenous nationalism tells us why the indigenous claim to self-determination is worthy of respect and why it is different from the claims of other minorities with which they coexist. Moreover, it places the onus on the state to justify its de facto assertion of sovereignty over indigenous peoples and to explain why they are not entitled to an equal right to self-determination.

A third and final objective was to demonstrate that these normative questions must not ignore the vastly different empirical characteristics and circumstances of indigenous communities. One reading of nationalism may lead to the conclusion that indigenous nationalism implies indigenous nation-states, but theories of nationalism can be extraordinarily conservative in this regard, and, as I hope to have demonstrated in this essay, there are a variety of ways of being a nation in practice. The examples considered in the final section indicate that a host of institutional designs can serve the needs and circumstances of a variety of indigenous communities. In most cases, an integrated layering of mutually supporting institutions is essential – they can address issues such as economy of scale and governing capacity, the internal diversity of indigenous populations, and the need to combine self-rule and shared-rule institutions. Understanding indigenous nationalism in the way described in this paper helps allay charges of empirical inaccuracy and irrelevance while preserving a normative insight that is crucial to the negotiation of just and sustainable indigenous–state relations.

NOTES

1 Even Canada's Royal Commission on Aboriginal Peoples (RCAP), which threw its weight firmly behind the right of self-determination for Aboriginal peoples, articulates a fairly conservative understanding of what constitutes an Aboriginal nation that can be said to enjoy this right (RCAP, 1995, vol. 2, part 1, 177–81). For a critique of this position, see Ladner, 2001.

2 McHugh prefers the term "ethnicity" over "nationality," but his call for a New Zealand–wide ethnic Māori identification resembles the nationalist framework described in this paragraph (McHugh, 1998). Compare Durie, 1998, 228–33.

3 For additional discussion of the Yukon model and a list of additional sources on the agreement and related initiatives, see Hogg and Turpel, 1995; Catt and Murphy, 2002, 75–7.

4 For a similar discussion of pan-indigenous urban identities and governance in a Canadian context, see Anderson, 2002.

5 Ultimately, these determinations must be made on a case- and context-specific basis, predicated on considerations such as economies of scale,

governing capacity, and, most important, the identities and consent of the communities in question.

6 The institutionalization of indigenous governance is far more advanced in Canada than in either Australia or New Zealand. This explains why so many of the cases discussed below come from the Canadian experience. Parts of my discussion draw on Catt and Murphy, 2002; more detailed description and analysis of these cases appear there in chapters 3–7.

7 Most indigenous governments in Canada exercise their legislative powers concurrently with federal and provincial governments. This means that two levels of government can both legislate in the same jurisdiction so long as the laws are not incompatible with one another. In cases of incompatibility, rules of paramountcy come into play. Questions of paramountcy in the Nisga'a case are very complex, with federal, provincial, and Nisga'a laws prevailing at different times depending on the jurisdiction in question. See Canada, 1998, 159–83 and throughout.

8 Some constitutional experts argue that all modern self-government agreements in Canada receive such protection, regardless of whether this measure was explicitly contemplated by the negotiating parties. See Hogg and Turpel, 1995, 211–12.

9 See the community-of-interest model developed in RCAP, 1995, vol. 2, 273.

10 See Hawkes, 2002. The Saskatchewan strategy of negotiating an integrated layering of institutions to implement indigenous self-determination is gaining increasing attention in both Australia (Smith, 2002, 25–7) and Canada (IOG, 2000).

11 A recent article in the *Dominion Post* (Wellington, New Zealand) notes that Māori participation rates in the special electorates are on the rise and are very high among newly eligible Māori voters (24 Jan. 2003, A4). I thank Simon Hope of Auckland University for drawing my attention to this reference.

REFERENCES

Abele, F., and M.O. Dickerson (1985) "The 1982 Plebiscite on Division of the Northwest Territories: Regional Government and Federal Policy," *Canadian Public Policy* 11, 1–15.

Alfred, G. (1995) *Heeding the Voices of Our Ancestors: Kahnawake Mohawk Politics and the Rise of Native Nationalism in Canada*. Oxford: Oxford University Press.

Alfred, T. (1999) *Peace, Power, Righteousness: An Indigenous Manifesto*. Toronto: Oxford University Press.

Altman, J., and L. Allen (1992) "Living Off the Land in National Parks: Issues for Aboriginal Australians," in J. Birckhead, T.D. Lacy, and L. Smith, eds., *Aboriginal Involvement in Parks and Protected Areas.* Canberra: Aboriginal Studies Press.

Anaquod, D.C. (1997) "Urban Institutional Case Study – Regina," in Canada, RCAP, *For Seven Generations: An Information Legacy of the Royal Commission on Aboriginal Peoples.* CD-ROM.

Andersen, C. (2002) "Courting Colonialism: Contemporary Métis Communities and the Canadian Judicial Imagination." Paper presented to the conference "Reconfiguring Aboriginal–State Relations in Canada," Institute of Intergovernmental Relations, Queen's University, Kingston, Ont.

Arthur, W.S. (1997) *Towards a Comprehensive Regional Agreement: Torres Strait.* Canberra: Centre for Aboriginal Economic Policy Research.

Assembly of First Nations (AFN) (2002) "Charter of the Assembly of First Nations." www.afn.ca/About%20AFN/charter_of_the_assembly_of_first.htm

Australia (2002) Australian Bureau of Statistics. www.abs.gov.au/

Barcham, M. (1998) "The Challenge of Urban Māori: Reconciling Conceptions of Indigeneity and Social Change," *Asia Pacific Viewpoint* 39, 303–14.

– (2000) "(De)constructing the Politics of Indigeneity," in Duncan Ivison, ed., *Political Theory and the Rights of Indigenous Peoples.* Cambridge: Cambridge University Press, 137–51.

Bennett, S. (1999) *White Politics and Black Australians.* St Leonards: Allen & Unwin.

Bogdanor, Vernon (1999) "Devolution: Decentralisation or Disintegration?" *Political Quarterly* 70, 185–94.

Buchanan, A. (1998) "What's So Special about Nations?" in Jocelyne Couture, Kai Neilson, and Michel Seymour, eds., *Rethinking Nationalism.* Calgary: University of Calgary Press, 283–309.

Cairns, A. (2000) *Citizens Plus: Aboriginal Peoples and the Canadian State.* Vancouver: University of British Columbia Press.

Canada (1991) *The Path to Electoral Equality: Committee for Aboriginal Electoral Reform. Royal Commission on Electoral Reform and Party Financing.* Ottawa: Minister of Supply and Services.

– (1998) *Nisga'a Final Agreement.* Ottawa: Queen's Printer.

– (2003) 2001 Census Data on Aboriginal Peoples. www.statcan.ca/start.html

Canada, Royal Commission on Aboriginal Peoples (RCAP) (1995) *Final Report.* 5 vols. Ottawa: Minister of Supply and Services.

Carens, J. (2000) *Culture, Citizenship and Community: A Contextual Exploration of Justice as Evenhandedness.* Oxford: Oxford University Press.

Catt, H., and M. Murphy (2002) *Sub-state Nationalism: A Comparative Analysis of Institutional Design*. London: Routledge.

Coates, K., and P.G. McHugh (1998) *Living Relationships: Kākiri Ngātahi. The Treaty of Waitangi in the New Millennium*. Wellington: Victoria University Press.

Council of Yukon First Nations (CYFN) (2002) www.cyfn.ca/index.html

De-Shalit, A. (1996) "National Self-determination: Political, not Cultural," *Political Studies* 44, 906–20.

Dodds, S. (1998) "Citizenship, Justice and Indigenous Group-specific Rights – Citizenship and Indigenous Australia," *Citizenship Studies*, 2, 105–20.

Dodson, M. (1996) "Equity and Social Justice: A Dysfunctional Relationship between Government and Indigenous Peoples," in C. Fletcher, ed., *Equity and Development across Nations*. St Leonards: Allen and Unwin.

Durie, M. (1998) *Te Mana, te kawanatanga: The Politics of Māori Self-determination*. Auckland: Oxford University Press.

Feldman, A. (2001) "Transforming Peoples and Subverting States: Developing a Pedagogical Approach to the Study of Indigenous Peoples and Ethnocultural Movements," *Ethnicities* 1, 147–78.

Flanagan, T. (2000) *First Nations? Second Thoughts*. Montreal: McGill-Queen's University Press.

Fleras, A. (1985) "From Social Control towards Political Self-Determination? Māori Seats and the Politics of Separate Māori Representation in New Zealand," *Canadian Journal of Political Science* 18, 551–76.

Foster, D. (1997) "Gurig National Park: The First Ten Years of Joint Management." Australian Institute of Aboriginal and Torres Strait Islander Studies. Canberra.

Gibbins, R., and C. Hanselmann (2002) "Another Voice Is Needed: Intergovernmentalism in the Urban Aboriginal Context." Paper presented at the conference "Reconfiguring Aboriginal–State Relations in Canada," Institute of Intergovernmental Relations, Queen's University, Kingston, Ont.

Grand Council of the Crees (GCC) (1992) *Status and Rights of the James Bay Crees in the Context of Quebec's Secession from Canada*. Submitted by the Grand Council of the Crees (of Quebec) to the United Nations Commission on Human Rights, Forty-eighth Session, 27 Jan.–6 March.

Green, J. (1995) "Towards a Détente with History: Confronting Canada's Colonial Legacy," *International Journal of Canadian Studies* 12, 85–104.

Hanselmann, C. (2002) "Uncommon Sense: Promising Practices in Urban Aboriginal Policy-Making and Programming." Calgary: Canada West Foundation.

Hawkes, D. (2002) "Re-building the Relationship: The 'Made in Saskatchewan' Approach to First Nations Governance." Paper presented at the conference "Reconfiguring Aboriginal–State Relations in Canada," Institute of Intergovernmental Relations, Queen's University, Kingston, Ont.

Henderson, J.S.Y. (1994) "Empowering Treaty Federalism," *Saskatchewan Law Review* 58, 241–329.

Hicks, Jack, and Graham White (2000) "Nunavut: Inuit Self-determination through a Land Claim and Public Government?" in Jens Dahl, Jack Hicks, and Peter Jull, eds., *Nunavut: Inuit Regain Control of Their Lands and Their Lives*. Copenhagen: International Work Group for Indigenous Affairs, 30–115.

Hogg, P., and M.E. Turpel (1995) "Implementing Aboriginal Self-Government: Constitutional and Jurisdictional Issues," *Canadian Bar Review* 74, 187–224.

Institute on Governance (IOG) (2000) "Governance Models to Achieve Higher Levels of Aggregation: Literature Review." Institute on Governance. www.iog.ca/

Ittinuar, P. (1985) "The Inuit Perspective on Aboriginal Rights," in M. Boldt and J.A. Long, eds., *The Quest for Justice: Aboriginal Peoples and Aboriginal Rights*. Toronto: University of Toronto Press, 47–53.

Jones, J., and R. Wilford (1986) *Parliament and Territoriality*. Cardiff: University of Wales Press.

Kymlicka, W. (1995) *Multicultural Citizenship: A Liberal Theory of Minority Rights*. Oxford: Clarendon Press.

Ladner, K. (2001) "Negotiated Inferiority: The Royal Commission on Aboriginal People's Vision of a Renewed Relationship," *American Review of Canadian Studies* 31, 241–64.

Légaré, A. (1997) "The Government of Nunavut (1999): A Prospective Analysis," in J.R. Ponting, ed., *First Nations in Canada: Perspectives on Opportunity, Empowerment, and Self-Determination*. Toronto: McGraw-Hill Ryerson, 404–31.

Levy, J. (2000) *The Multiculturalism of Fear*. Oxford: Oxford University Press.

Maaka, R.C.A. (1994) "The New Tribe: Conflicts and Continuities in the Social Organization of Urban Māori," *Contemporary Pacific* 6, 311–36.

– (1998) "A Relationship, Not a Problem." In Coates and McHugh, eds., 1998, 201–5.

Macklem, P. (2001) *Indigenous Difference and the Constitution of Canada*. Toronto: University of Torono Press.

Mahuika, A. (1998) "Whakapapa Is the Heart," in Coates and McHugh, 1998, 214–21.

McHugh, P.G. (1998) "Aboriginal Identity and Relations in North America and Australasia," in Coates and McHugh, 1998, 107–86.

Murphy, M. (2001) "The Limits of Culture in the Politics of Self-Determination," *Ethnicities* 1, 367–91.

New Zealand (1986) *Report of the Royal Commission on the Electoral System: Towards a Better Democracy.* Wellington: New Zealand Government Press.

– (2002) *Te Puni Kokiri.* Ministry of Māori Development. www.tpk.govt.nz/default.asp

Nisga'a Nation (2000) "The Constitution of the Nisga'a Nation." Document on file with the author.

Norris, M.J., M. Cooke, and S. Clatworthy (2002) "Aboriginal Mobility and Migration Patterns and Policy Implications," in J. Taylor and M. Bell, eds., *Population Mobility and Indigenous Peoples in Australasia and North America.* London: Routledge.

Pearson, David (2001) "Divergent Nationalisms: Some Comparative Thoughts on Australia, Canada, and New Zealand," *Political Science* 53, 3–16.

Peters, E. (2002) "Geographies of Urban Aboriginal People in Canada." Paper presented at the conference "Reconfiguring Aboriginal–State Relations in Canada," Institute of Intergovernmental Relations, Queen's University, Kingston, Ont.

Philpott, D. (1995) "In Defence of National Self-Determination," *Ethics* 105, 352–85.

Ramos, H. (2000) "National Recognition without a State: Cree Nationalism within Canada," *Nationalism and Ethnic Politics* 6, no. 2, 95–115.

Requejo, F. (1999) "Cultural Pluralism, Nationalism and Federalism: A Revision of Democratic Citizenship in Plurinational States," *European Journal of Political Research* 35, 255–86.

Reynolds, H. (1996) *Aboriginal Sovereignty: Three Nations, One Australia?* St. Leonard's: Allen and Unwin.

Rynard, P. (1999) " 'Welcome In, But Check Your Rights at the Door': The James Bay and Nisga'a Agreements in Canada," *Canadian Journal of Political Science* 33, 211–43.

Sanders, W. (1996) "Local Governments and Indigenous Australians: Developments and Dilemmas in Contrasting Circumstances," *Australian Journal of Political Science* 31, 153–74.

Sanders, Will (2002) "Towards an Indigenous Order of Australian Government: Rethinking Self-Determination as Indigenous Affairs Policy." Discussion Paper No. 230. Centre for Aboriginal Economic Policy Research, Australian National University, Canberra.

Schouls, T. (1996) "Aboriginal Peoples and Electoral Reform in Canada: Differentiated Representation versus Voter Equality," *Canadian Journal of Political Science* 29, 729–49.

Seymour, M. (2000) "Quebec and Canada at the Crossroads: A Nation within a Nation," *Nations and Nationalism* 6, 227–55.

Sharp, A. (1997) *Justice and the Māori: The Philosophy and Practice of Māori Claims since the 1970s.* Auckland: Oxford University Press.

– (2002) "Blood, Custom and Consent: Three Kinds of Māori Groups in New Zealand and the Challenges They Present to Government and the Constitution," *University of Toronto Law Journal* 52, 9–37.

Smith, D.E. (2002) "Jurisdictional Devolution: Towards an Effective Model for Indigenous Community Self-determination." Discussion Paper No. 233, Centre for Aboriginal Economic Policy Research, Australian National University, Canberra.

Sullivan, P., ed. (1996) *Shooting the Banker: Essays on ATSIC and Self-Determination.* North Australia Research Unit, Australian National University, Darwin.

Tamir, Y. (1993) *Liberal Nationalism.* Princeton, NJ: Princeton University Press.

Tully, J. (1995) *Strange Multiplicity: Constitutionalism in an Age of Diversity.* Cambridge: Cambridge University Press.

– (1999) "Two Visions of Aboriginal Title and Reconciliation," in Frank Cassidy, ed., *Delgamuukw – One Year Later.* Victoria: University of Victoria Publications.

Turpel, M.E. (1993) "The Charlottetown Discord and Aboriginal Peoples' Struggle for Fundamental Political Change," in K. McRoberts and Patrick Monahan, eds., *The Charlottetown Accord, the Referendum and the Future of Canada.* Toronto: University of Toronto Press, 117–51.

Walker, B. (1997) "Plural Cultures, Contested Territories: A Critique of Kymlicka," *Canadian Journal of Political Science* 30, 211–34.

Walker, R.J. (1999) "Māori Sovereignty, Colonial and Post-Colonial Discourses," in P. Havemann, ed., *Indigenous Peoples' Rights in Australia, Canada and New Zealand.* Auckland: Oxford University Press, 108–22.

Ward, A., and J. Hayward (1999) "Tino Rangatiratanga: Māori in the Political and Administrative System," in P. Havemann, ed., *Indigenous Peoples' Rights in Australia, Canada and New Zealand.* Auckland: Oxford University Press, 378–99.

White, G. (1991) "Westminster in the Arctic: The Adaptation of British Parliamentarianism in the Northwest Territories," *Canadian Journal of Political Science* 24, 499–523.

– (2003) "Treaty Federalism in Northern Canada: Aboriginal–Government Land Claims Boards," *Publius* 32, no. 3, 89–114.

THOMAS W. POGGE

Linguistic Rights for U.S. Hispanics

English is the predominant language in the United States.[1] However, Spanish is the native language of some 35 million U.S. citizens and residents, whom I refer to as "Hispanics."[2] Many of them do not speak English well. Clearly, the position of English carries with it significant advantages for native speakers ("Anglos") and substantial impediments to at least those Hispanics who do not speak it well. Does justice require special protection or support for U.S. Hispanics and their language, and, if so, what measures?

One might expect the answer to depend heavily on historical facts. Opponents of accommodation can argue that the United States has been English-speaking from its beginning some 200 years ago. People who move there or choose to stay there certainly have fair warning of this fact. If they have not learned to speak English well, or have not ensured that their children would be fluent, then any resulting disadvantages are surely their own fault. Supporters of accommodation can argue that many current U.S. native speakers of Spanish are descendants of people who were incorporated into the United States without their consent when Spain ceded Florida to Britain in 1763 or when Mexico ceded the lands of Texas, California, Nevada, Arizona, Utah, and New Mexico to the United States in the 1830s and 1840s, under morally questionable circumstances.

I do not believe such historical arguments very relevant. Our question concerns accommodations among people today, and the two historical arguments have little bearing. I reject in particular the great

moral weight that Will Kymlicka places on the distinction between national and ethnic minorities. Hispanics draw no such distinction, and
anyway too many of them have mixed ancestry and too many intermediate cases of other sorts.[3] Moreover, the moral significance of such
a distinction is doubtful even in pure cases. Why should Carmen,
whose distant ancestors fell to the United States through annexation,
have more extensive rights than Letitia, whose distant ancestors immi-
grated there?

KYMLICKA AND EQUAL CITIZENSHIP

If the historical arguments are largely irrelevant, the issue would seem
to turn on the value of equality, or of equal citizenship – the value that
Kymlicka primarily invokes in his discussion of various kinds of accommodation rights.[4] Both sides can appeal to equality. Kymlicka sketches
the egalitarian position against accommodation rights as follows: "Ethnocultural groups, like religious groups, should be protected from discrimination, but the maintenance and reproduction of these groups
should be left to the free choices of individuals in the private sphere,
neither helped nor hindered by the state."[5] Or, one might rather substitute, "*equally* helped or hindered by the state." If the state were to help
or hinder such groups differentially, it would implicitly express a judgment on their relative worth – a judgment that a liberal theory and a
liberal state should scrupulously avoid.

Kymlicka argues that liberalism so understood delivers a kind of
formal equality that amounts to substantive inequality. An early version
of this argument modifies a thought experiment introduced by Ronald
Dworkin.[6] This experiment involves an island about to be settled by
newcomers. Since no newcomer has a better claim to its natural resources than any other, Dworkin suggests an original auction in which
the newcomers, each equipped with an equal number of clamshells, can
bid for particular resources. These bids may be indefinitely revised in
light of the bids entered by others until at long last a stable distribution
of resources emerges. In this final distribution, each item goes to the
highest bidder, who pays at least as much for it as any other person was
prepared to bid. Because this is so, Dworkin reasons, the emerging personal bundles of resources necessarily pass a no-envy test. Immediately
after the auction ends, none of the newcomers will prefer any other
newcomer's bundle to his or her own.[7]

Kymlicka stipulates that the newcomers arrive simultaneously on two vessels of very different sizes, on which different languages are spoken. We may suppose that the vast majority of the newcomers, arriving on the larger vessel, speak English, and the others, Spanish. If this fact is known, the Hispanics are likely to want to live near one another, and their bids will reflect this preference. Kymlicka concludes: "In order to ensure that they can also live and work in their own culture, the minority members may decide, prior to the rerun of the auction, to buy resources in one area of the island, which would involve outbidding the present majority owners for resources which *qua* resources are less useful to their chosen way of life. They must incur this additional cost in order to secure the existence of their cultural community. This is a cost which the members of the majority culture do not incur, but which in no way reflects different choices about the good life (or about the importance of cultural membership within it)."[8]

This argument does not go through. Suppose that, in early runs of the auction, the northern part of the island happens to receive a disproportionate number of Hispanic bids. This fact may incline other Hispanics to shift their bids towards the north. But any resulting increase in the price of northern resources would be negated by Anglos shifting their bids southwards. Anglos have no reason to pay a premium for northern real estate (on the contrary, many of them may prefer to avoid the more heavily Hispanic north). Even though Hispanics may be prepared to pay a considerable premium for resources in the north, no such premium will actually emerge, so long as the Anglos do not share the same preference. To see this clearly, consider an analogous scenario in which phone numbers are auctioned off in Montreal. One tenth of available numbers begin with a "6," and a superstitious 8 per cent of the city's people are willing to pay a fat premium for such a "lucky" number, while the remaining 92 per cent do not care. In this scenario, the superstitious would get their "lucky" numbers for free, because the slightest premium would induce those who do not care to switch their bids to a number that does not begin with a "6."[9]

Kymlicka's conclusion is not borne out in the real world either. Resources in heavily Hispanic areas are actually, if anything, cheaper than intrinsically similar resources in predominantly Anglo areas. This follows partly from the fact that Anglos are, on the whole, more affluent than Hispanics. Yet Hispanics find it cheaper than Anglos do to live among their own.

Rectifying Unchosen Inequalities?

None the less, ordinarily "the members of minority cultures [do] not have the same ability to live and work in their own language and culture that the members of majority cultures take for granted" (Kymlicka, 1995, 107, cf. 109). And this disadvantage is unchosen. Kymlicka argues that society ought to even out such unchosen disadvantages. It follows that the United States owes compensating accommodation to Hispanics.

In an earlier book, Kymlicka (1989) expresses this point as follows: "No one chooses to be born into a disadvantaged social group, or with natural disabilities, and so no one should have to pay for the costs imposed by those disadvantageous circumstances. Hence liberals favour compensating people who suffer from disadvantages in social environment or natural endowment. ... Someone who cultivates a taste for expensive wine has no legitimate claim to special public subsidy, since she is responsible for the cost of her choice. Someone who needs expensive medicine due to a natural disability has a legitimate claim to special public subsidy, since she is not responsible for the costs of her disadvantageous circumstances" (186).

But do we really believe in state compensation to rectify unchosen natural differentials – in looks, height, talent, or cheerfulness, for example? This is certainly not a position widely endorsed among liberals, not even by the two whom Kymlicka cites so frequently in this context. Through his device of a hypothetical insurance market, Dworkin provides a general approach to this issue. This stance would support Kymlicka's point if and only if people would, if this were possible, buy pre-birth insurance against linguistic minority status, homely looks, or a melancholy temperament. Only in this case would Dworkin want the state to mandate compensatory side payments in the amount of the hypothetical insurance premiums and benefits.[10] Rawls explicitly rejects any such compensation, insisting that "the natural distribution is neither just nor unjust" and that social positions should thus be defined in terms of social primary goods alone, without regard to the distribution of natural primary goods such as "health and vigor, intelligence and imagination." "A hypothetical initial arrangement in which all the social primary goods are equally distributed ... provides a benchmark for judging improvements."[11] Rawls's difference principle permits (unchosen) inequalities in income and wealth caused by differential talents, in so far as they raise the lowest socio-economic position. Rawls allows higher pay for the more demanding leadership positions even though they will typically also require special talents and will thus be closed to those who, through no choice of their own, lack these gifts. Thus he permits unchosen inequalities.

The discussion above has shown, I believe, that Kymlicka's strategy of defending accommodation rights for Hispanics as one instance under a general principle of rectifying unchosen inequalities is not promising. The principle does support the desired conclusion; but it supports a lot of other demands as well – demands that for most of his liberal and non-liberal readers constitute a reductio ad absurdum of the principle.[12]

A FUNDAMENTAL PRINCIPLE
OF PUBLIC EDUCATION

"In his new book, Kymlicka (1995) also presents a new and far more believable argument for rectification. This argument turns on how the government – funded by and responsible to all citizens – treats various linguistic groups: "Many liberals say that just as the state should not recognize, endorse, or support any particular church, so it should not recognize, endorse, or support any particular cultural group or identity ... But the analogy does not work. It is quite possible for a state not to have an established church. But the state cannot help but give at least partial establishment to a culture when it decides which language is to be used in public schooling, or in the provision of state services. The state can (and should) replace religious oaths in courts with secular oaths, but it cannot replace the use of English in courts with no language" (111).[13] Further, "Government decisions on languages, internal boundaries, public holidays, and state symbols unavoidably involve recognizing, accommodating, and supporting the needs and identities of particular ethnic and national groups. The state unavoidably promotes certain cultural identities, and thereby disadvantages others" (108). At least the state cannot help doing so in certain respects. If this is so, and if the state ought to treat all of its citizens equally, then it is incumbent upon it to rectify the unequal treatment that it unavoidably metes out in some respects through inversely unequal treatment in others. If the state gives preference to the Anglos by maintaining English as the official public language, then it must somehow make it up to those of its citizens who are native speakers of another language.

This line of argument is far more convincing than its predecessor and has been invoked in many other contexts, often to widespread acclaim.

Thus it has been proposed that it is unjust for the state to subsidize some kinds of art but not others, to recognize some kinds of domestic partnership but not others, to construct public facilities without compensating those who cannot use them, and so forth.

Let us apply this line of reasoning to a society whose government finances a public school system and also requires that children attend school – either a public institution free of charge or else a private one. I assume that there is a plausible justification for requiring all children to attend school and for requiring all taxpayers to contribute to the public system. The difficult question is then what the language(s) of instruction ought to be.

Consider this further quote by Kymlicka (1989): "In a society where the members of minority cultures (e.g. Indians, francophones) could get their fair share of resources within their own cultural community, it's not clear what would justify denying people access to publicly funded education in English. If some of the members of a minority culture choose to learn in that language, the notion of protecting the cultural context provides no ground for denying them that opportunity. On the other hand it's not clear why there should be rights to publicly funded education in any given language other than that of the community. Why should the members of minority cultures have a right to a public education in English, but not, say, in Greek? They should of course be free to run a school system in whatever language they choose at their own expense, but why a right to it at public expense?" (194f).

This passage is not entirely transparent. The first two sentences suggest one quite radical claim. *Claim 1. In a society where the members of a minority culture cannot get their fair share of resources within their own cultural community, denying the members of this community access to publicly funded education in English is justifiable by the purpose of protecting the cultural context of this community.* I cannot be sure that Kymlicka would in fact endorse claim 1. It would be a very surprising one for an avowed liberal to make. Claim 1 denies minority families – and only them – the right to avail themselves of an opportunity for their children on the grounds that this restriction on their liberty helps protect an endangered minority culture. It allows the state to press minority children into the service of perpetuating a cultural community irrespective of whether this benefits the children concerned and irrespective also of whether the children themselves, or their parents, support this purpose.[14] This is a clear violation of Kymlicka's own liberal principle, because it would introduce an unchosen inequality (Anglo children are offered public schooling in English, minority children are not). It is precisely for this egalitarian reason that the U.S. Supreme Court unanimously declared the San Francisco School District to be in violation of Title VI of the Civil Rights Act for failing to make accessible a public education in English to students of Chinese ancestry who do not speak English.[15] One might respond here with a separate-but-equal argument: Anglos and Chinese were treated equally, as both received a public education in their respective native language. But this argument holds little promise: a public education in a minority language – and one that, by assumption, is endangered in the United States – is not equal, because it does not give children the same opportunities to participate in the social, economic, and political life of their society.

Another radical claim, again not clearly endorsed in the passage, appears in its third and fourth sentences: *Claim 2. There is no more reason to entitle the members of a minority culture to a public education in English than there is to entitle them to a public education in any other (for them) foreign language, such as Greek.* This claim too is highly problematic. Hispanic or Chinese or Navajo children derive very much more benefit from receiving an education in English than from an otherwise equivalent education in Greek. Does Kymlicka propose to count the greater benefit to these children as no reason at all? Moreover, offering Navajos a less useful public education in Greek and Anglos a more useful public education in English would discriminate against the former on the basis of their national origin. Offering both Navajos and Anglos a public education in English would at least greatly reduce, if not eliminate, this unchosen inequality.[16]

I conclude that claims 1 and 2 must be rejected. They give entirely unacceptable reasons for denying members of minority cultures access to a publicly funded education in English on a par with the education available to members of the dominant Anglo culture. More acceptable reasons for such a denial are considered below.

Kymlicka clearly is endorsing a less radical claim. *Claim 3. Members of minority cultures should have the right to send their children to a public school where their instruction is entirely in the minority language.* Kymlicka does little to support this claim, simply writing that "people should have, as part of the respect owed them as members of a cultural community, the opportunity to have a public education in the language of their community" (1995, 195). But this appeal to respect is somewhat problematic. It is certainly desirable to show persons respect by allowing them to make decisions about their own life. Yet, in the case at hand, we would be showing parents respect by allowing them to make decisions about how their children will be educated at public expense. In this case, there is a countervailing reason – a reason against allowing parents to make decisions that would be worse for their children.[17] To see whether and how this countervailing reason might come into play, let us examine claim 3 against its most prominent alternative – the thesis that it is permissible for a government in the United States to run its public education system in English. (In 1998, California voters, passing Proposition 227 with a 61 per cent to 39 per cent margin, obliged their government to do just that.) How might we settle the conflict between such an English public education system and a multilingual one in which parents may choose the language of their children's instruction?

I propose that we resolve this conflict in three steps. First, Kymlicka is right to stress that a government has a fundamental duty of equal treatment. A liberal outlook, however, casts this duty in terms of individual citizens, rather than of various groups and cultures. Thus it is by reference to the interests of individual citizens that the conflict is to be resolved.

Second, among the individual interests bearing on the design of a public education system, the interests of children are to be of paramount importance. Many other individual interests may bear on the question – the interest of adult minority members that their language should continue to be spoken; their interest to communicate easily with their children and grandchildren; the interest of some corporations and government agencies in prospective employees with native foreign-language skills; and so forth. I am suggesting not that all these interests are minor and should be ignored – only that they should not override the interests of the children themselves.

I propose a fundamental principle of public education: the best education for each child is that which is best for this child. Of course, public education does not have the resources to provide each child with the best possible education for him or her. But it should spend whatever resources it has on providing children with whatever affordable education is best for them. My hope is that, if this fundamental principle can be agreed on, the remaining differences will be much less divisive and probably resolvable through empirical research on whose design experts now in conflict can agree in advance.

Given the principle that I propose, the fundamental duty of a just public education system is to promote the best interests of each and every child and to do so equally. This duty must trump any desire to increase or decrease the prominence of this or that language or culture in the United States.[18] It is in the light of this duty that a legislature must decide whether to mandate that minority children be offered a public education in their native language only, to mandate that all children be offered a public education only in English, or to make available an education in various languages from among which parents can choose for their children.

This brings us to the third and most difficult step – deciding which of these options is, under given empirical circumstances, favoured by the test that I propose. My discussion here is illustrative only, because much depends on complex empirical assessments with regard to which I can claim no expertise. These assessments may well be different in different contexts (for example, California versus Florida) and for different languages in the same context (Navajo versus Spanish in New Mexico). I do not propose any particular settlement, but merely sketch what the pre-settlement debate might look like.

Given the constraints that I have imposed, each option would have to be defended by appeal to the best interests of the children. Thus one might argue for option B – for example, by claiming that it best enables all students to participate fully in U.S. society, socially, economically, and politically. Here is a straightforward way of filling in this kind of argument: One postulates a principle of English-first. *The most important linguistic competence for children now growing up in the United States is the ability to communicate in English; the language of instruction in public schools should therefore be chosen by reference to the goal of effectively helping pupils develop fluency in English.* And one tries then to support the empirical claim that choosing English as the universal language of instruction is part of the most effective method for helping students develop fluency in English.

Let us consider two ways of attacking this argument.[19] One line would deny the empirical claim, asserting that option B does not provide the most effective method for helping students become fluent in English – that minority students will reach higher levels of English proficiency if they first develop full literacy in their native tongue. If this approach were fully successful, it might provide an acceptable argument for option A. The other line of attack would appeal to goals other than that of effectively helping pupils develop fluency in English, arguing that, once we consider their bearing on the question, option B will not come out ahead.

Though formally distinct, both lines of reasoning are likely to appeal to similar empirical considerations. They would seek to show that being abruptly exposed to a foreign-language environment for several hours per day constitutes a significant shock for many young children – a shock that makes it difficult for them to relate well to their teachers and fellow pupils[20] and (partly for this reason) difficult also to progress in English, as well as in other subjects.

Now one might counter that these problems, however real, do not alter the fact that children's important long-term interest in being fully literate in English is best served by early immersion and that this interest is stronger than the interest in avoiding those temporary problems. But one should also think of various ways of revising option B to accommodate the stated concerns. Thus one might support programs that facilitate parents' affording pre-school exposure to English for their children and programs that help them to achieve fluency in English themselves. One might further support the availability of special foreign-language tutors whom pupils could turn to outside regular hours if they find it difficult to follow lessons in English during their first few school years. In addition, one might also support the early introduction of sufficiently prominent minority languages as academic subjects in order to allow students to develop full literacy also in their native language and to see that their native language is valued rather than viewed as dispensable and to-be-displaced. Such instruction should continue through all grades, so that native speakers of Spanish, for example, as well as other students after they have learned basic Spanish in more elementary courses, can study the literature and culture of the Spanish-speaking world and perfect their competence in this language. Such course offerings would make clear that the public school system is endeavouring not merely to give every student full competence in English, but also to let students develop an equal competence in the native tongues of any minorities that (locally) are numerically significant.[21]

Enriched by complementary programs of these four kinds, option B may well become widely accepted among those willing to put the interests of the children before all else. To be sure, acceptance of the English-first principle would tend to reduce the prominence of other languages in the United States below what it would be if they were also used, alongside English, as languages of school instruction. In this sense, English-first privileges English at the expense of these other tongues. But this unfairness[22] does not here reflect an unfairness towards the various speakers of different languages. The choice of English as the universal language of instruction is justified by reference to the best interests of children with other native languages, for whom speaking good English (in addition to their native language) will be an enormous advantage in their future social and professional lives. As supplemented, English-first would not then, I believe, disadvantage children who are native speakers of other languages vis-à-vis Anglo children. Such children are, in a sense, initially disadvantaged by getting a somewhat later start towards English competence (although they also have a significant and permanent advantage through their head start in their native language). But this disadvantage exists before these children enter the public education system, and it is one that this system is designed to erase.

The English-first principle is not of a piece with the English-only initiatives that have been cropping up for 20 years in federal and state legislatures. Endorsement of English-first is fully consistent with the view that it is highly desirable that Spanish and other minority languages survive as native languages.[23] This goal is well served by giving native speakers of Spanish, and other children as well, the opportunity to develop full competence in Spanish through the public school system.

CONCLUSION

My rather cautious stance is motivated by a concern for the moral costs of accommodation rights. Moral costs include particularly "liberal" costs in terms of freedom and equality, which arise when individuals are used to promote some group interest. We should be especially alert to such costs when they would be imposed on children, who have so very little influence on the social environment that will shape them so profoundly. Claim 1, discussed above, asserted that access to publicly funded education in English may be withheld from minority children if this helps to protect the cultural context of their community, whose members cannot get their fair share of resources within it. Moral costs also include the costs to other ethnic, linguistic, religious, or "lifestyle" groups. These costs are especially obvious in the case of language. Even if we agree that U.S. residents should speak more languages than they now do, each of them might speak fluently very few. And the promotion of one additional language through the public education system will thus inevitably take place at the expense of other languages, such as French, some of which may then not survive in the United States at all.

To be sensitive to such potential costs, those who demand accommodation rights for some group(s) should take care to base these demands on principles by which they would be prepared to judge the demands of any other groups as well.

NOTES

1 This lecture is adapted from Pogge, 2000. It is informed by the more general theoretical framework developed in Pogge, 1997.

2 "Latinos" is also frequently used. I prefer "Hispanics" because of its etymological connection to the Spanish language – a main theme of this essay.

3 Such as Puerto Ricans within the 50 states, who might count as members of a national minority in so far as ancestors of theirs were incorporated into the United States together with their homeland and who might also count as members of an ethnic minority in so far as ancestors of theirs voluntarily left Puerto Rico. For more detail, see Pogge, 2000, 182–4.

4 He considers various additional and complementary arguments for accommodation rights in chapter 6 of Kymlicka, 1995.

5 Kymlicka, 1997, 72.

6 Dworkin, 1981a; 1981b. See also Ackerman, 1980, featuring the denizens of a spacecraft about to touch down on a virgin planet.

7 If any newcomer did prefer another's bundle to his or her own, he or she would rationally have asked for another round of bidding in which he or she would then have bid for some or all of the resources in the other bundle. Some complication is required to cope with ties (two or more exactly equal bids for the same item).

8 Kymlicka, 1989, 188–9.

9 Kymlicka's modification of Dworkin's thought experiment will make a difference to individuals. Some Hispanics will be hurt by their linguistic preference in conjunction with their other preferences. A hilltop lover may face a hard choice between living in the north, where hilltops are scarce or highly coveted and therefore expensive, and living among Anglos in the south, where hilltops are more plentiful or less coveted and therefore cheaper. But then, individual Anglos may face similar hard choices – for example, between a cheaper beachfront site among Hispanics and a more expensive one in the south. Moreover, the prevailing linguistic preferences may also benefit individuals. If mainly Hispanics covet hilltops, Anglo hilltop lovers will benefit from Hispanic bids shifting north. And if mainly Anglos covet beachfront, Hispanic hilltop lovers will benefit from Anglo bids shifting south.

10 Cf. Dworkin, 1981b, 297–9.

11 Rawls, 1971, 102, 62. See also Pogge, 1989, especially sections 3.5, 4.4, and 10.4, where I argue at some length that Rawls's criterion of justice does not take account of natural inequalities and is therefore a "semiconsequentialist" criterion. Kymlicka overlooks this important departure by Rawls from the liberalism advocated by himself and (to some extent) Dworkin.

12 Is there perhaps an even narrower principle that would be more reasonable and still entail Kymlicka's desired conclusion? One may think that what entitles those disadvantaged by an inequality to compensation (or rectification) is not the mere fact that their disadvantage is the result of no choice of their own, but rather this fact in conjunction with the further fact that this disadvantage flows from the choices of others. It is unchosen social inequalities that call for compensation; unchosen natural inequalities do not. This proposal runs into two difficulties. First, the boundary between these two inequalities is often unclear, as when both natural and social factors are necessary to explain why someone has a melancholy temperament or is considered homely looking. Second, the proposal does not fully capture common intuitions, as it is generally believed that serious natural handicaps (such as blindness) should be compensated and that certain social disadvantages (unpopularity) should not be. Kymlicka's view is basically that Hispanics should be compensated for the bad luck that they encounter with regard to the distribution of language skills in the society into which they were born. It is unfortunate for them that their native language is spoken only by a minority while almost everyone speaks English.

But life is full of bad luck of this kind. I have unchosen talents whose market value greatly depends on what capacities are in demand in my society – for example, on what kinds of music, sports, and other entertainment my compatriots cherish. I have unchosen desires for things whose market price depends heavily on how strongly others desire them. And I have unchosen desires for social activities whose possibility depends importantly on whether others have similar or complementary interests and preferences. I may find myself strongly drawn to a certain research topic, for example, only to discover that this topic is of interest to barely a dozen people or so. In all these cases, demands for compensation or rectification would be laughed out of public debate. So why should we take seriously the demand, so justified, to compensate native speakers of minority languages?

13 For extensive discussion and refinement of this argument, see also Lagerspetz, 1998.

14 The word "coercively" is not out of place. Most minority families cannot legally avoid sending their children to public school. Only the affluent fami-

lies can, by enrolling their children in private school – an option that Kymlicka graciously concedes in the final sentence of the passage quoted.

15 *Lau v. Nichols*, 414 U.S. 563 (1974).

16 I use "Navajo" here as a stand-in for all minorities. I do so because I am not sure how broadly Kymlicka intends his term "minority culture" here. We can be sure, however, that this term covers the national-minority Navajo culture, so I use this culture to illustrate how claim 2 is untenable.

17 This reason is recognized in many other contexts. Parents' choices are constrained by child labour laws, for example, and parents are required to send their children to school up to a certain age and forbidden from withholding modern medical care from them. In all these cases, we do not allow parents to make certain choices for their children – even when we recognize that such choices would be conscientiously based on deeply held (for example, religious) values that deserve recognition and respect.

18 It is frustratingly unclear whether Kymlicka agrees on this point, or whether he would think it permissible, under certain circumstances, to sacrifice the best interests of children to the political goal of preserving an existing culture for the benefit of those for whom it provides their context of choice.

19 I do not consider a third kind of attack, which would deny that the ability to communicate in English is the most important linguistic competence for children now growing up in the United States. This denial can be made plausible by emphasizing that what matters here is the value of English proficiency in the future, for which public education is supposed to prepare the children in its care. But then the future importance of English and Spanish proficiencies cannot straightforwardly inform the design of the present education system, because it also depends on this very design. The more children now receive their education in Spanish, the more important Spanish proficiency will be during their adult lives (Linda Alcoff made this point forcefully in discussion). And yet, under any foreseeable realistic scenario, during the lifespan of the children raised today, English proficiency will continue to be more useful than Spanish proficiency for almost all U.S. residents (most Puerto Ricans excepted).

20 And even to their parents, who, if they have little command of the universal language of public education, may come to appear to their own children as existing at the margins of society.

21 I would like to express this point as a demand for (the availability of) bilingual education. But this expression is now used mainly not for an education system that helps students become bilingual but rather for one that teaches them in one language and others in another.

22 Which cannot be completely avoided in any case, assuming that we reject the goal of making all languages equally prominent in the United States and lack the resources to provide even the sole Kazakh child in Putnam County with a public education in her native language.

23 For Spanish, there is little doubt that it will survive and even thrive as a native language. Through high birth rates as well as legal and illegal immigration, Hispanics are the fastest-growing U.S. group, expected to reach 100 million in about 2015. It is not inconceivable that the Spanish language will one day become coequal with English. There are many obvious reasons to welcome such a development. But there are also reasons to regret it: If it were as important for U.S. residents to know both Spanish and English as it now is to know English, then it would probably become even harder for other languages to survive.

REFERENCES

Ackerman, Bruce (1980) *Social Justice and the Liberal State.* New Haven, Conn.: Yale University Press.

Dworkin, Ronald (1981a) "What Is Equality? Part I: Equality of Welfare," *Philosophy and Public Affairs* 10, no. 3 (summer), 185–246.

– (1981b) "What Is Equality? Part II: Equality of Resources," *Philosophy and Public Affairs* 10, no. 4, 283–345.

Kymlicka, Will (1989) *Liberalism, Community and Culture.* Oxford: Clarendon Press.

– (1995) *Multicultural Citizenship: A Liberal Theory of Minority Rights.* Oxford: Oxford University Press.

– (1997) "Do We Need a Liberal Theory of Minority Rights?" *Constellations* 4, no. 1 (April), 72–87.

Lagerspetz, Eerik (1998) "On Language Rights," *Ethical Theory and Moral Practice* 2, no. 1, 181–99.

Pogge, Thomas W. (1989) *Realizing Rawls.* Ithaca, NY: Cornell University Press.

– (1997) "Group Rights and Ethnicity," in Will Kymlicka and Ian Shapiro, eds., *Ethnicity and Group Rights,* NOMOS vol. 39. New York: New York University Press, 187–221.

– (2000) "Accommodation Rights for Hispanics in the US," in Jorge J.E. Gracia and Pablo de Greiff, eds., *Hispanics/Latinos in the United States: Ethnicity, Race, and Rights.* New York: Routledge, 181–200.

Rawls, John (1971) *A Theory of Justice.* Cambridge, Mass.: Harvard University Press.

HENRY MILNER

The Status of Finland's Swedish National Minority: Exemplary – but for Whom?

In this paper, I look at the relationship between the Finnish majority and the Swedish national minority in Finland. I speak of "Swedish Finns" – a less cumbersome term than "Swedish-speaking Finns." It does not imply any identification on their part with the Swedish state. The Swedish Finns are Finns as a matter of citizenship and history, and they share with the Finnish-speaking majority the Lutheran religion: it is their language that constitutes the foremost aspect of their specific identity. The population of Finland is 5.1 million, of which the Swedish Finns make up roughly 6 per cent. They are concentrated on the Åland islands, in the region of Ostrabothnia (in the northwest), and in certain communities along the west and south coasts. In the last section of the paper, I set this relationship into comparative context, especially vis-à-vis Quebec and Canada.

I do not examine the Finns in Sweden, since their situation has been quite different – three waves of late-arriving settlers rather than a constituent national minority. Assimilation has left no real trace of the first group of Finnish speakers, who moved to Sweden in the 16th century. The second group found itself on the wrong side of the border after Finland was separated from Sweden in 1809. Concentrated in the northern border region of Norrbotten, their communities have survived despite pressure to assimilate (their descendants were estimated to number 33,000 in 1951), although many speak a kind of creole that they call Meankiele, rather than Finnish. The third and largest group settled in the two decades after 1945 essentially to find work. Some returned after the Finnish economy began to catch up at the end of the 1960s; many of those who remained assimilated. Those who moved to Norr-botten, especially to the Haparanda area near the border, have retained a strong identity.[1] Unlike the situation for Swedish Finns, Swedish national authorities largely ignored Finnish Swedes until recently[2] (although some localities provided Finnish-language education).

Institutional arrangements for the Swedish minority in Finland, I argue, provide some valuable insights into the relationship of national minorities, national majorities, and the state. On matters of economic and social policy, many experts look to the Nordic countries – but not on relations within and among nation-states. Most people assume that these are pure nation-states, where boundaries coincide with those of historical nations. Yet national minorities are part of the Nordic region. Moreover, globalization and the European Union (EU) have brought this dimension to the fore.

The EU question in the Nordic countries has heightened divisions between an increasingly Europeanized south and a northern, more nationalist hinterland. The EU link has sharpened concerns over protection for the national minorities. In Denmark, the Faroe Islanders have chosen not to be part of the EU and are moving towards even greater autonomy. In Finland, something similar is happening in Åland (on which more below), which chose, independently of Finland, to join the EU.

While EU membership is a relatively new issue, the underlying identity question relates intimately to Finland's own geopolitical reality. Moreover, geopolitics makes Finland a possible model of majority–minority relations. Its location in eastern Europe – on the boundary between Russia and the West – makes it an especially useful comparison for national minorities in central and eastern Europe and in the former Soviet Union – for example, Hungarians in Slovakia, Turks in Bulgaria, Romanians in Hungary, and Russians in the Baltic states.

Finland's un-Nordic lack of ambiguity over EU membership reflects geopolitics,[3] which also underlies the relationship between its Swedes and its Finns, but to see it we have to go back into history. A brief historical journey below reveals an exemplary relationship between a national majority and minority. First, I examine its history, indicating its basis in the constitution and in political organization. Second, I consider demographics and everyday reality – that is, in the language-related choices of the people. Third, I sketch in the special case of Åland, and, fourth, I consider the applicability of the "Finnish model" elsewhere.

HISTORY

There are records of Finnish tribes in Finland going back to the 12th century, although clear evidence of a written Finnish language goes back only to the 16th century. Well before then, the area had come under the domination of an expanding Swedish empire, which reached its peak during the Thirty Years War (1618–48), extending well into the European mainland. For many centuries, Finland was part of Sweden, and the Swedish language dominated public life. At the end of the 17th century, the Russian empire emerged, contesting Swedish domination of the eastern Baltic region. The Russian army advanced through Finland during the Napoleonic Wars and into northern Sweden in 1808. The Treaty of Vienna confirmed Russia's annexation of Finland, with its population of about one million (compared to 2.5 million for Sweden and 40 million for Russia). Sweden in return received Norway. In 1812, Tsar Alexander I moved the capital from Turku, in the southwest – the Finnish city closest to Stockholm – to the small town of Helsinki on the south coast.

Under Alexander I, Russia gave the Finns autonomy as a Duchy. Finland remained more traditional, with a more autocratic government and theocratic society than Sweden, which modernized more rapidly in the 19th century. (A useful comparison here is the British conquest of New France.) The conquest soon spurred national aspirations: the mostly Swedish-speaking intellectuals in Finland concluded that they would never be Swedes or Russians, so they might as well be Finnish. Not only did they learn the Finnish language, but a number of them fostered Finnish literature. Out of these efforts came a comprehensive, high-quality Finnish language system of education: while in 1890, the majority of secondary school students were still studying in Swedish, by 1900 only 38 percent were doing so.[4]

The Russians initially recognized Finnish and Swedish as the official languages of the duchy. But, over the years, they increasingly demanded "Russification," spurred on later in the century by the rise of Russian nationalism. In response, Finnish nationalism intensified. As the only basis of unified opposition to "Russification," the movement won support from the Swedish-speaking minority, which soon found its privileges threatened by democratization, which came to Russia – and thus to Finland – in 1905. Democratization affected relations between the two groups. The Swedish minority lost its effective veto when, in 1905, the four-chamber diet, where each group effectively controlled two chambers, became a single-chamber assembly.

This was the situation in 1917, when, in the aftermath of the First World War and the Russian Revolution, Finland became independent. The new diet would have to regulate the language question. In 1919, after long and hard negotiations, it adopted a new constitution, which proved remarkably advanced and durable, even through Finland soon plunged into civil war. The conflicting Reds and Whites represented social classes rather than regions or national groups, but virtually all the former spoke Finnish.[5]

After the civil war, the primary task was to rebuild this highly divided society. Language tensions were high in the 1930s. The most bitter disagreement (reminiscent of Quebec in the late 1960s and 1970s) was over education. Friction concerned second-language teaching, the many small and thus expensive second-language (i.e., usually Swedish) public schools, and the language used in the (formerly Swedish-speaking) national university, which had been moved to Helsinki from Turku in 1828 and changed its name from Imperial Alexander University to the University of Helsinki in 1919. Only in 1937 did Finnish become the nation's working language (although services and courses in Swedish for Swedish students were guaranteed). Nevertheless, the number of "Swedish chairs," fixed at 15 in 1937, remained unresolved until after the Second World War, when new Swedish- and Finnish-language universities were founded. (There are now 27 such chairs for about 150 Swedish-speaking students out of 2,500.)

Finland suffered greatly during the Second World War, in two protracted battles with the Soviet Union. The second, the "Continuation War," ended with an armistice that included reparations to be paid by Finland and further human losses as Germany decided to punish the Finns. The immense social costs of the world wars, like those of the civil war, placed the linguistic issues in perspective and no doubt made their resolution easier.

The Constitution

The 1919 election returned a Social Democratic plurality, which, with Agrarian support, formed a government. In May 1919 the Swedish party organized a congress of representative Swedish speakers from all parties and interest groups through a community-wide unofficial election that attracted a large majority (some 111,000) of the Swedish-speaking voters. The elected representatives to the new Svenska Finlands folkting, or Swedish People's Assembly, articulated the aspirations of Swedish Finns and put pressure on the Finnish parliament as it drafted a constitution. The new republican constitution guaranteed minority linguistic rights and set up a strong presidency. The Swedish People's Party (SFP) and the conservatives had sought a strong executive, and the Conservatives were thus amenable to concessions on language, as were the Social Democrats, who were supported by workers of both language groups.

Hence the constitution of 1919 enshrined the linguistic rights of the minority. Finnish and Swedish were "national languages," and citizens could use either one in the courts or with administrative authorities. The state was to provide for the "cultural and economic needs" of both groups. Linguistic rights were "guaranteed by law," with the rights of both language groups protected "on an equal basis." A 1922 law specified that laws, decrees, and various forms of communication between the government and parliament, such as bills, motions, replies, and other documents, were to be in both languages. Military units were to be organized and trained according to mother tongue, but the language of command of the forces would be Finnish.

The constitution was revised at the end of the 1990s (the six relevant passages appear in the Appendix). In language, as in other areas concerning rights, the constitution merely spells out the principles and refers to laws that specify the modalities. The new constitution more explicitly specifies the powers and prerogatives of the municipalities and regions where the aboriginal Sami languages have official status. A 1991 law guarantees the right to use Sami in local administration and the courts in 13 per cent of Finnish territory. Section 121 specifies that the Sami have linguistic and cultural self-government there.

The 1919 constitution organized administrative services territorially such that that the Finnish- and Swedish-speaking populations can receive services in their own language on equal terms.[6] Each municipality or commune is officially unilingual (either Finnish- or Swedish-speaking) if the minority makes up less than 10 per cent of the population, and bilingual if it reaches or exceeds that level. Helsinki, Turku, and Vaasa, as capitals of the three bilingual provinces, were to remain bilingual even if the language minority fell below 10 per cent.[7] This basic classification then became the basis for larger judicial and administrative districts of all kinds. Such districts were to be bilingual if they contained either one or more bilingual communes or unilingual communes of both languages. There were to be reviews every ten years, although a minority had to reach 12 (now revised to 10) per cent for a unilingual commune to become bilingual or to drop below 8 per cent (now revised to 6 per cent) for a bilingual commune to become unilingual. In Finland, as elsewhere in Scandinavia, governments provide services mainly through local government within the framework of laws voted on by parliament. Hence application of linguistic rights relates very much to the activities of local government.

Initially, this was not seen as a victory for the minority. Leaders of the majority community sought during the 1920s and 1930s to reduce the "privileges" of Swedish Finns through municipality-based language guarantees. Concretely, Swedish-speaking residents of some key medium-sized cities – the most important being Tampere – effectively lost their right to administrative services in Swedish. However, over the years, as Swedish speakers concentrated increasingly in the bilingual cities, this principle became a means of accommodation and adjustment to their needs.

Political Organization

As we saw above, the SFP depended on the Swedish minority. It evolved from a very conservative force to a pragmatic organization, supported by the highly representative Swedish People's Assembly, able and willing to secure guarantees from coalition governments.[8] One example was the creation of separate Swedish-speaking dioceses of the Lutheran church in 1923, with separate congregations in most communities.

Over the years, the SFP has proven highly effective. It receives the support typically of at least two-thirds of Swedish Finns; only among organized workers does it share votes with other parties (mainly the Social Democrats). The SFP can call on 50,000 active members, or roughly one third of those who vote for it – a remarkably high proportion. McRae, 1999, shows how strategic voting under proportional representation gave the Swedish Finns overrepresentation in parliament and, even more so, in the (quasi-permanent coalition) government.[9] With almost continual representation in cabinet (in 43 of 63 governments between 1917 and 1995), the SFP altogether held 8 per cent of the 1,100 ministerial positions. (This does not include those Swedish Finns elected for other parties, most frequently Social Democrats.[10])

DEMOGRAPHICS AND EVERYDAY REALITY

While, as we see below, not all differences have been conclusively resolved, apparent demographic stability produced a period of linguistic consensus beginning in the early 1970s. The data (Liebkind, Broo, and Finnäs, 1995) show that the Swedish-speaking minority has declined gradually from 14 per cent to 6 per cent since 1880. The sharpest change has been in Helsinki. In a process reminiscent of Montreal in a similar period, Helsinki went from being 55 per cent Swedish in 1880 to 90 per cent Finnish a century later. While the Swedish population remained relatively stable, except during heavy postwar migration to Sweden, the Finnish-speaking one was growing. Hence constitutional protection of the Swedish language and follow-up legislation did no more than slow the decline of the Swedish Finns. In the 1970s, the Swedish population stabilized at just fewer than 300,000. Given that the Samis and other minorities combined have never totalled more than 1 percent of the population (McRae, 1999, Table 2.1), the Swedish Finns have always been the only real minority. Unlike French Canadians, they never had to share that role with immigrant groups.

Many factors, as we see in this section, contributed to the demographic stability that made generous compromise possible. Hence, when the proportion of Swedish speakers in Turku (Åbo) declined to below 8 per cent in 1961, parliament set 5,000 minority-speaking residents as the minimum, a number reduced to 3,000 in 1975. Similarly, minority-language schools in Finnish unilingual districts were maintained. Such an accommodation was possible because changes in recent decades have seen the end to the overall disparity in educational attainment among those under 40 – a situation similar to Quebec since the Quiet Revolution.

How has the relative stability been maintained over the past 30 years? Overall, the language of children in mixed-marriage households – by the 1970s, a staggering 50 per cent of Swedish Finns had intermarried – closely corresponds to the language of the surrounding milieu. Assimilation cost Swedish Finns perhaps 8 per cent of their numbers. In addition, the Swedish-speaking population is ageing – roughly 500 more die than are born each year – although their fertility rate has been catching up somewhat (Finnäs, 1997; 1998).

It would seem that the main compensating mechanism allowing for the stability of the Swedish Finn population is the attractiveness of Swedish-language schools. About 60 per cent of the children of mixed marriages are registered as Swedish: in Finland, each citizen is registered on birth by (only one) mother tongue. Linguistic status has no effect on individual linguistic rights (although the linguistic status of the municipality and district is based on the number registered). Still, children registered as Swedish are probably more likely to be educated in that language.

Despite a scarcity of national statistics, this effect of school choice is reflected in numbers for Vaasa, the biggest city in Ostrabothnia, historically a commercial centre for Swedish Finns.[11] While the overall population is 26 per cent Swedish speaking, one-third of the students are studying in Swedish-language schools. While Vaasa probably does not represent overall trends, these figures suggest that access to schools may become a point of contention – as it remains in Quebec, which has limited access to English schools. The absence of a third "allophone" group in Finland has diminished the political salience of this issue, but the situation could change if this trend intensifies.[12]

More than 75 per cent of Finnish speakers now live in unilingual municipalities, and less than 50 per cent of Swedish Finns live in majority Swedish municipalities (compared to over 75 per cent in 1920). In 1993, there were 21 unilingual Swedish and 43 bilingual municipalities (of which 22 had a Swedish majority) among the 460 total. By the 1980s, Swedish unilingualism had essentially died out outside Åland and the isolated coastal villages in the northwest. On the mainland, it is virtually non-existent – something that cannot be said about English in Quebec.

Constitutional and demographic factors shape the relations between the majority and minority, but there is also a subjective dimension. Observers agree that the key to the complementarity of the two lies in the attitude towards the exercise of rights. Swedish speakers generally apply a rule of reasonableness when demanding use of their language in public communications. The guarantees can be maintained because it is understood that they will not be pushed to their fullest technical possibility. For example, the published Swedish versions of laws are generally limited to essentials, with the Finnish version complete and comprehensive. And Swedish services are far less than universal in the provinces containing metropolitan Helsinki, Espoo, Vantaa, and Turku, where some 160,000 Swedish Finns (i.e., the majority) are dispersed among the 2 million residents. In Helsinki, Swedish speakers account for about 7 per cent of the population. Although the legal requirements for Swedish public services remain, they could not be put into practice given the linguistic abilities of city employees. But most Swedish-speaking Finns living in the capital are bilingual.

In effect the majority accepts the principle of the two languages being formally equal while knowing that practice will differ; the minority agrees that its language is not equal in practice because its legitimacy is respected. Mutual respect has many dimensions. The existence of the Swedish Finnish minority is recognized in its assembly, by its national day (6 November) and by Runeberg day (5 February) celebrating its great writer, and by cultural institutions such as Helsinki's Swedish Theatre, located prominently at the end of the Esplanade. Its two scientific academies, one working primarily in Finnish, the other in Swedish, collaborate in their publication series (McRae, 2002).

For its part, the minority community takes on the burden of linguistic accommodation. In bilingual as well as in Finnish cities and towns – i.e., effectively throughout the mainland – Swedish Finns switch to Finnish when even one Finnish-speaking person joins the conversation. Swedish children are taught to be unobtrusive in using their language. And institutions are permitted to evolve to accommodate the new reality. The state's funding of the assembly's extensive translation services has gradually replaced the more traditional guarantee of equal services that the state itself can no longer deliver. "Swedish speakers in general accept these changes. Realistically, they have no alternative" (McRae, 2002) .

Ståhlberg's (1995) survey well captures the cultural reality for numbers of the minority. Wherever they live, they speak Swedish[13] but are unreservedly Finns; they are bilingual, but their identity as Swedish Finns is clearly secure. Networks of cultural associations, schools, and media support this identity. A respected national Swedish-language daily newspaper, *Hufvudstadsbladet*, has a daily circulation of 55,000 copies, and there are several regional dailies and many weeklies.[14] The minority population also supports its own radio and television programs. Via a chain of FM transmitters along the south and west coasts, completed in 1963, a full schedule is broadcast in Swedish. Television broadcasting was initially an area of tension. Channels from Sweden could be received along Finland's west coast, but not in the Helsinki area, while the Finnish public TV channels, YLE 1 and 2, transmitted Swedish programs only for a certain number of hours and only on certain days.[15] A settlement came in the 1990s with the inauguration of Swedish-language TV4, which fills out its schedule with rebroadcasts of programs from Swedish television.[16] And recently a youth radio network and digital television channel in Swedish were inaugurated.

In October 2000, I lectured to a public administration class at the Vaasa campus of the Swedish-language university, Åbo Academy.[17] I asked the students how many watched the news in Finnish on YLE. All said that they did, along with the TV4 Finnish Swedish news, as well as, for most, the Swedish national news (which they could pick up from across the Bay of Bothnia). This level of interest struck me as surprisingly high (in comparison to students in Canada),[18] but they explained that it was necessary to watch both (or, indeed, all three) to cover the different aspects of their world. They all took for granted that watching YLE news in Finnish, or reading *Helsinkin Sanomat* (the major Finnish-language newspaper) was the best way to get needed information about Finland. Yet I see nothing comparable among francophones in Canada vis-à-vis the *Globe and Mail* and CBC news or among anglophones vis-à-vis *La Presse* and Radio Canada.

Finland's considerable investment in bilingual statutes and public documents helped it integrate into Scandinavia (and thus strengthen its connection with the West). Hence the Nordic connection has strengthened the position of the Swedish minority.[19] This has become less important as EU membership has solidified Finland's European identity. Of late, educated Finns have come increasingly to prefer English to Swedish in conversations with Swedish Finns and other Scandinavians. The process of European integration weakened the role of Swedish as the second language. Membership in the EU has placed great pressure on the Finns to learn one of its working languages – almost always English.

ÅLAND

The Åland Islands lie in the Baltic between Sweden and Finland, with not much more than 25,000 people – just under 1 per cent of Finland's population – 94 per cent Swedish speaking. Following proposals of the League of Nations, in 1920 Åland was granted institutions of provincial self-government – its own elected assembly (Landsting, now Lagting), executive council, and governor (appointed by the Finnish president, with the agreement of the Landsting. Åland is demilitarized, and so its residents are exempt from military service. Its official language for state and communal administration,[20] as well as its language of correspondence with central authorities, is Swedish. Schools are Swedish only. Mainland Finns must wait five years – as well as demonstrating satisfactory knowledge of Swedish – to acquire Åland regional citizenship, i.e., municipal and state voting rights, the right to own real property, and exemption from military service. Sale of Åland land is subject to a right of repurchase or redemption at current market price by the state, municipality, or a legally domiciled private individual. In a number of areas of jurisdiction, such as fishing, shipping, agriculture, and broadcasting, approval of regional authorities is required.

The Åland flag is flown on ships, and passports have an additional Åland designation; there are Åland postage stamps. Like the Faroe Islands and Greenland, Åland is independently represented on the Nordic Council. Åland's special status was manifested, and enhanced, during negotiations over EU membership. Finland's terms of entry were agreed on in March 1994 (along with those for Austria and Sweden). Those terms recognized Åland's autonomy in the form of a separate accession procedure and a special protocol in the treaty itself that recognized the existing legal privileges of regional citizenship in Åland as permanent derogations from the EU treaties, provided only that there be no discrimination in their application between non-Åland citizens of Finland and other EU citizens. The protocol also provided customs exemptions for ferry traffic – and hence the right to sell cheap alcoholic beverages to travellers – to and from Åland in order to preserve a "viable local economy."

When the results of the negotiations were submitted to popular referenda in Finland, on 16 October 1994, 57 per cent of citizens voted for membership. Ålanders took part, supporting Finland's entry (by a narrow 52 per cent majority), and then voted again on 20 November (after Sweden had narrowly opted for entry) on whether Åland should join under the special protocol. This time they voted yes by a decisive 74 per cent.

THE "FINNISH MODEL"

Finland's economy, which floundered with the sudden loss of Soviet markets with the demise of the USSR, recovered in the 1990s. The land of Nokia is becoming an IT model.[21] Helsinki is becoming a European and a world city as Finland takes a major place, relative to its size, in the EU and thus the world. The Finnish-speaking majority, no longer the more introspective of the two language communities, is increasingly sophisticated and outward looking. It is coming to resemble the Swedish-speaking minority, with its deep historical links to the surrounding world.[22] The same could be said of Montreal and the French and English speakers of Quebec.

This is what makes Finland's treatment of its minority community especially interesting – namely, that the minority consists of the descendants of the once-dominant group, and its culture, of the once-dominant culture – similar in that way to the English-speaking minority in Quebec. In addition, Åland is clearly recognized as a "distinct society." On the mainland, the minority receives the fullest – technically equal – formal rights and legitimacy in return for its exercising those rights only to a reasonable extent, accepting the individual costs of bilingualism and maintaining unquestioned loyalty to, and identity with, Finland. In return, the majority accepts asymmetry in the case of Åland.

Can these principles apply to Canada and Quebec? Had the Canadian constitution early on given the same recognition to the French Canadians that Finland gave to the Swedish Finns in 1919, Canada would now be very different. Even today, Canada could learn much from Åland. Given differences in population and the importance of the non-francophone minority in Quebec, the specifics would differ. But the principle would be similar: recognition of autonomy not applicable elsewhere in Canada. True, unlike Finland, Canada is already federal, but, given the diverse forms that federalism is taking today, in Belgium, Spain, and the United Kingdom, for example, there is no objective reason why Finnish-style asymmetry could not be incorporated into a federal system. Of course, as long as Canadian public opinion insists that all provinces must be equal, this path remains closed.

I close by addressing a comparison sometimes drawn by Swedish Finns: why should Quebec restrict the use of English when Finland accepts Swedish as equal to Finnish? From what we have seen, there are several reasons why this analogy is inappropriate. Finland each year receives hundreds of immigrants; Quebec, several tens of thousands, for whom English has far more attraction than does Swedish in northeastern Europe. Would the Finnish majority have stood by if tens of thousands of immigrants every year adopted Swedish? Moreover, although it has evolved in the past 25 years, as long as Quebec remains a province of an 80-per-cent English-speaking country, anglophones will not take on individual bilingualism to the same extent as have the Swedish Finns. Conversely, Quebec as a province has neither the constitutional powers nor the international recognition to afford it the security to be as generous to its minority as a sovereign state such as Finland.

Although the overall Finnish approach is thus inapplicable to Quebec – at least a Quebec with only the powers of a Canadian province – there is still one major lesson directly applicable. English Quebec needs the equivalent of the Swedish People's Party, which, combined with proportional representation, would guarantee it fair political representation. Such a mobilized population would perhaps seek to create its own assembly along the lines of the Swedish Finns' *folkting*. If so, this should be welcomed by the majority. Finnish experience suggests that English Quebec, with truly representative institutions, could over time reject the uncompromising approach of the Equality Party and Alliance Quebec and, learning from Finland, develop leaders and policies that could contribute to creative compromises reflecting the needs and interests of both minority and majority.

APPENDIX: EXCERPTS FROM THE NEW FINNISH CONSTITUTION

Section 17: *Right to one's language and culture*

The national languages of Finland are Finnish and Swedish.

The right of everyone to use his or her own language, either Finnish or Swedish, before courts of law and other authorities, and to receive official documents in that language, shall be guaranteed by an Act. The public authorities shall provide for the cultural and societal needs of the Finnish-speaking and Swedish-speaking populations of the country on an equal basis.

The Sami, as an indigenous people, as well as the Roma and other groups, have the right to maintain and develop their own language and culture. Provisions on the right of the Sami to use the Sami language before the authorities are laid down by an Act. The rights of persons using sign language and of persons in need of interpretation or translation aid owing to disability shall be guaranteed by an Act.

Section 51: *Languages used in parliamentary work*

The Finnish or Swedish language is used in parliamentary work.

The Government and the other authorities shall submit the documents necessary for a matter to be taken up for consideration in the Parliament both in Finnish and Swedish. Likewise, the parliamentary replies and communications, the reports and statements of the Committees, as well as the written proposals of the Speaker's Council, shall be written in Finnish and Swedish.

Section 79: Publication and entry into force of Acts

If an Act has been enacted in accordance with the procedure for constitutional enactment, this is indicated in the Act.

An Act which has been confirmed or which enters into force without confirmation shall be signed by the President of the Republic and countersigned by the appropriate Minister. The Government shall thereafter without delay publish the Act in the Statute Book of Finland.

The Act shall indicate the date when it enters into force. For a special reason, it may be stated in an Act that it is to enter into force by means of a Decree. If the Act has not been published by the date provided for its entry into force, it shall enter into force on the date of its publication.

Acts are enacted and published in Finnish and Swedish.

Section 120: Special Status of the Åland Islands

The Åland Islands have self-government in accordance with what is specifically stipulated in the Act on the Autonomy of the Åland Islands.

Section 121: Municipal and other regional self-government

Finland is divided into municipalities, whose administration shall be based on the self-government of their residents.

Provisions on the general principles governing municipal administration and the duties of the municipalities are laid down by an Act.

The municipalities have the right to levy municipal tax. Provisions on the general principles governing tax liability and the grounds for the tax as well as on the legal remedies available to the persons or entities liable to taxation are laid down by an Act.

Provisions on self-government in administrative areas larger than a municipality are laid down by an Act. In their native region, the Sami have linguistic and cultural self-government, as provided by an Act.

Section 122: Administrative divisions

In the organisation of administration, the objective shall be suitable territorial divisions, so that the Finnish-speaking and Swedish-speaking populations have an opportunity to receive services in their own language on equal terms.

The principles governing the municipal divisions are laid down by an Act.

NOTES

1 They have here benefited from Finnish-language services provided from Tornio, inside the Finnish border.

2 Recently the Swedish government acted in response to a report recommending that the state provide some Finnish-language services, notably in day care and broadcasting.

3 European integration holds the least danger to Finnish identity: only 1 per cent of Finns identified themselves as exclusively European (rather than either Finnish or both European and Finnish) in *Eurobarometer* no. 50, below even Sweden, Denmark, and the United Kingdom. Moreover, non-membership – i.e., a form of neutrality – is no real option for Finland. The experience of Sweden, where neutrality works, contrasts very much with that of Finland. EU membership has provided Finland a measure of economic and political security after decades in an imposed neutrality in the form of a "special relationship" with the Soviet Union. Finland can now affirm its identity as a European, Western country – something that the other Nordic countries never lacked (Novack, 2000).

4 This number continued to decline, to 15 per cent in 1940. By the late 1950s, Finnish speakers' representation in the educational system was approaching proportionality, reflecting the democratization of the school system.

5 The Reds stronghold, and scene of major battles, was Tampere (which has a Lenin Museum) – Finland's second-largest (and largest unilingual) city.

6 University-educated civil servants were expected to have "complete command" (no use of dictionary) of the second language. Others needed only working knowledge. The emphasis is clearly on the public administrative sector. Finland has seen far less recourse to courts than Canada (or Switzerland or Belgium), as well as far fewer efforts to regulate language use in the private sector.

7 Technically, I should write – as I do elsewhere – Helsinki/Helsingfors, Turku/Abo, and Vaasa/Vasa, since bilingual cities have two names, one in each language.

8 The members of the Swedish People's Assembly are elected at the time of municipal elections from lists provided by the SFP and the Swedish-language organizations within the other parties.

9 For Swedish-speaking political leaders, the sine qua non of participating in government is working effectively in Finnish.

10 There is a monolingual Swedish Finn federation inside the Social Democratic Party and a new similar organization inside the National Coalition (Conservative) Party.

11 If there is any difference in the school-age proportion, it would favour Finnish speakers.

12 Finland is seeing a different kind of development, because of the strength of English. Provisions of the education act require the second national language and an international language, but local authorities choose the priority. In reality, while Finnish remains the second language in Swedish schools, English is becoming the second language in Finnish schools (English is much closer to Swedish than to Finnish and so easier for Swedish speakers to learn outside school).

13 Linguists have noted that the Swedish language in Finland – traditionally different from that used in Sweden and comparable to British versus American English – is now becoming even more Finnishized. In a development comparable to "franglais" in Quebec, Swedish Finnish is increasingly using Finnish words and constructions.

14 As late as 1890, there were more Swedish- than Finnish-language papers. In 1917, 10 per cent of newspapers appeared in Swedish, with circulation of daily papers more or less proportional to the population of the linguistic groups. Contemporary Finland is a country with proportionately many papers and many newspaper readers.

15 Not only were these hours relatively few, but they sometimes coincided, since they operated autonomously. This provoked tensions that would have been greater except for the fact that a good proportion of Swedish Finns could pick up Swedish TV.

16 In return, it was agreed with Swedish authorities that Finnish programming from Finland would be carried in the Stockholm region.

17 Abo Akademi University, located in Turku and Vaasa, offers instruction is Swedish. In 2000, it had 7,000 students, 78 per cent of them Swedish speakers. Helsinki also has separate Swedish and Finnish business schools, the former with about 2,200 students (McRae, 2002).

18 The disparity is even greater in newspaper reading, where the Finns – and other Nordics – read them far more than do North Americans (see Milner, 2001).

19 The council for many decades urged more Swedish television programming in Finland (and Finnish-language programming in Sweden) and helped attain improvements in Finland's Swedish-language television, described above.

20 Finnish citizens who are residents can request Finnish translations in dealing with state and local officials.

21 See Milner, 2002, chap. 9.

22 Most symbolic perhaps is the triumph of Nokia in its intense competition with Ericsson for the cellular phone market.

REFERENCES

Allardt, Eric (1977) *Finland's Swedish-speaking Minority*. Research Reports No. 17. Helsinki: University Press.

City Planning/City Strategies (1999) *A Place in the Sun: Vasa in Brief*. Vaasa, Finland: Vaasa City Council.

Finnäs, Fjalar (1997) "Social Integration, Heterogeneity, and Divorce: The Case of the Swedish-speaking Population in Finland," *Acta Sociologica* 40, 263–77.

– (1998) *Finlandsvenskarna 1996 – en statistisk Oversikt*. Folktinget: Helsingfors.

Finnish National Commission for UNESCO No. 66 (1995) *Cultural Minorities in Finland: An Overview towards Cultural Policy*. Helsinki: Finnish National Commision.

Liebkind, Karmela, Roger Broo, and Fjalar Finnäs (1995) "The Swedish-speaking Minority in Finland: A Case Study," in *Cultural Minorities in Finland: An Overview towards Cultural Policy*. Helsinki: Finnish National Commission.

McRae, Kenneth D. (1999) *Conflict and Compromise in Multilingual Societies*. Conflict and Compromise in Multilingual Societies: Finland, vol. 3. Waterloo, Ont.: Finnish Academy of Science and Letters and Wilfrid Laurier University Press.

Milner, Henry (2002) *Civic Literacy: How Informed Citizens Make Democracy Work*. Dartmouth, NH: University Press of New England.

Modeen, Torre (1989) "The Linguistic Situation of the Cities in Finland in a Historical Perspective," in Kjell Herberts and Joseph G. Turi, eds., *Multilingual Cities and Language Policies/Villes plurilingues et politiques linguistiques*. Turku, Finland: Åbo Akademis.

Novack, Jennifer (2000) "The Politics of Identity in Finland and Sweden during the First Five Years of European Union Membership: Pushing toward or away from the European Core?" Paper presented at the PSA, London, April 2000.

Ståhlberg, Krister, ed. (1995) *Finlandssvensk Identitet och Kultur*. Åbo: Åbo Akademis.

Swedish Assembly of Finland (1997) *Swedish in Finland: An Introduction*. Helsinki: Miktor.

RAJEEV BHARGAVA

The Majority–minority Syndrome and Muslim Personal Law in India

The sweep of Hindu–Muslim relations after the rise of nationalism in the Indian subcontinent is not the concern of this paper. Nor is it a theoretical essay on nationalism or community rights. Moving uninhibitedly between normative theory and micro-historical explanation, it deals with one aspect of the contemporary status of Muslims, who constitute a little over 11 per cent of India's one billion people. In particular, it focuses on their demand for the right to live by their own culture – specifically, by their religiously coded personal laws. Exercise of this right raises profound worries concerning the violation of individual liberty and gender justice, however. This has led some activists in India to demand the abolition of those laws. Many other citizens, including ordinary Hindus, have also demanded that the entire discourse of minority rights be jettisoned and replaced by a uniform discourse of individual rights. Predictably, Muslim orthodoxy has reacted obdurately and pressed for not just the retention of minority rights but an even more stringent application of personal laws in exactly the morally objectionable form in which they currently exist.

In the second section of this paper, after outlining the relevant history and describing individual and group rights, I offer what I take to be a contextually reasonable position that reconciles the redeemable features in the best interpretation of both individual rights and stronger group rights. I argue for retention of the discourse of minority rights, accommodating even personal laws though not in their present form. Sadly, as we see in the third section, even this reasonable position appears unfeasible in the current context, in which a historically transmitted majority–minority syndrome pits the two groups against each other. I begin the first section, however, by delineating two key ideas – the majority–minority syndrome and framework – that frame the discussion that follows.

FRAMEWORK AND SYNDROME

The terms "majority" and "minority" are ambiguous and evoke two different conceptions. The first is linked to conceptions of procedural equality and individualist agency, wherein every agent, regardless of substantive identity – for example, gender, religion, ethnicity, language, or race – is given one vote per issue that is meant to embody his or her preference. Majority and minority emerge when such preferences are aggregated. This may be called preference-based majority–minority. Such blocs are inevitable in democracies so conceived and, because preferences change or vary from issue to issue, are usually temporary.

It is, however, the identity-dependent majority–minority that forms focus of my paper. To understand this conception, first consider a set of individuals who define themselves and others not in terms of preferences (i.e., the desires that people choose to have) but rather by their more or less permanent attributes (such as colour, ethnicity, religion, and language), widely believed to constitute the very identity of individuals. Individuals with an identical set of any of these features can be grouped together and be seen as communities. Now consider two such diverse communities with differing numerical strengths. A majority and a minority then exist on the basis of identity-constituting features. In a large society where people do not share the same identity-constituting features, majorities and minorities are more or less permanent (for example, Tamils in Sri Lanka, Québécois in Canada, non-Hindu religious groups within India, non-Anglican religious groups in England). Here we may speak even of (relatively) permanent majorities or minorities.

However, enumeration, though necessary, is not sufficient to constitute a minority and majority. Three other features enter its current understanding. First, groups must view themselves as a minority or a majority. Self-identification or persistent identification by others in these terms, simultaneously or subsequently recognized by the relevant group, is central to majority–minority formations. Given this self-awareness, members of such groups are likely to display a fairly high degree of solidarity. Second, the group must believe that it has or should have the power to preserve its attribute-related culture and traditions and, under certain conditions, to shape or alter, in accordance with its traditions and culture, the structure of the social and political order in which it lives. Third, when this belief is accompanied or followed by the inability to exercise power, the resulting sense of impotence breeds a sense of disadvantage and the group believes itself to be in a non-dominant position. Usually, particularly within representative democracies, the numerically larger group is also dominant and numerically smaller groups are non-dominant. However, sometimes the group in numerical majority feels that its power is thwarted by minorities. Whatever the case, when either one or both groups believe that they are unable to exercise power and blame the other for this real or perceived disadvantage, a majority–minority syndrome begins to set in.

The term "syndrome" suggests something strongly pejorative. When a deep malaise creeps into a system, causing, for some reason, a spiralling estrangement between the minority and the majority, then a majority–minority syndrome develops. Typically, in such a situation mutual animosities circulate freely, adding layer on layer of grievances. Over time, chronic mutual paranoia develops, inter-group relations are perverted, and both groups begin to play antagonistic games, fighting over nothing at all. Rightly or wrongly, everyone feels continually humiliated. The majority–minority syndrome must be distinguished from a majority–minority framework, within which groups have distinct identity, some distance, but none of the snowballing alienation or chronic malaise that typifies a syndrome.

The presence of the syndrome means that the basic trust, mutual confidence, and perhaps common understanding between the majority and the minority has broken down. The framework, in contrast, suggests a common understanding and mutually binding moral rules that ensure that all citizens may live with security, self-confidence, and self-respect. The framework is entirely compatible with groups making demands on one another in a reasonable manner. It allows even for occasional conflict of interests or values between the majority and minority. A polity with such a framework is not a state of utopian harmony realized on earth!

A majority–minority syndrome is not something that is always "out there." It is an agent-dependent process. It is set in motion by a long chain of closely nested, mutually interlocking actions between small sections within the majority and minority, but it gradually engulfs almost everyone. It can disappear if certain types of agents stop interacting in particular ways. The primary responsibility for the syndrome may lie with the majority, with the minority, or sometimes even with a third, contextually relevant political actor (as in empire- and colonial states). Sometimes it may be set off simply by the will of any one group. For instance, a minority group may wish to shape the structure exclusively or disproportionately but not be allowed to. When this happens it cannot really complain of injustice. Yet, unflinchingly and unmindful of others, a powerful minority may persist with its own exaggerated demands and precipitate a majority–minority syndrome, with disastrous consequences for everyone. Usually, however, it develops when a minority group tries merely to co-determine the social and political structure but is not permitted by the majority to do so. In such instances, partly because the terms of engagement of the two groups are grossly unequal, a syndrome is accompanied by and results in persistent and very real discrimination against and/or humiliation, marginalization, exclusion, or subordination of minorities. In extreme cases, it threatens the very survival of the minority community.

Such a syndrome may be removed or alleviated by the introduction of the majority–minority framework. Of the two types of frameworks – hierarchical and egalitarian – the hierarchical is irrelevant in this context because it tries to bind the majority and minority in a relation of domination. However, if subordination is itself the primary problem and the initial cause of the syndrome, then only an egalitarian framework, usually with constitutionally protected minority rights, can be of use. The entire point of such rights is to eliminate hidden inequalities and injustice and to give minorities some power to shape the social and political structure so that they too are able to do or obtain what the majority group routinely procures by virtue of the structural conditions in that society. Such rights may be purely political, as when a minority is granted self-government or special representation rights. An arrangement with such political rights may be called a political majority–minority framework. Alternatively, there may be non-political rights, such as the right for a group to maintain its own educational institutions or to protect its language, script, religion, or culture. Such socio-cultural rights may generate a social majority–minority framework. In what follows, I speak of this egalitarian version in both its political and its social forms.

The claim that the majority–minority framework helps remove the syndrome must be read with care and nuance. First, the framework and syndrome exist on the qualitatively different existential fields of collective psychology and legality. Law by itself cannot cure a perverted collective psyche. Yet, in the long run, a legally secure discourse of rights can shape preferences and change attitudes. Therefore a framework of rights, though not sufficient, is necessary for the eventual alleviation of the syndrome, particularly in contemporary democracies. Second, a framework must be suitable for its political and socio-cultural context. If the framework does not have the proper form or is introduced wrongfully, by the wrong people at the wrong time, it may exacerbate the syndrome.

Anyhow, the majority–minority framework is not the only conceivable solution to the syndrome. Sometimes the syndrome is resolved by the secession of the minority group. Secession is feasible only when the minority group has the will to separate and is concentrated within a particular territory. But even then, secession may overshoot its point and exact enormous costs all round. Its feasibility does not entail its moral desirability, and a political majority–minority framework might be preferable. Nor is the majority–minority framework the only possible arrangement that gets rid of the syndrome. For example, some people believe that the best way to jettison the syndrome is to install an individualist liberal-democratic framework with a uniform charter of individual rights.[1] Other ways of dissolving the syndrome include the imposition of the majoritarian framework – for example, by the covert assimilation of minorities into an overweening majority. Even more obnoxious methods of eliminating the syndrome exist, such as pushing the minority beyond the borders of the nation-state or even liquidating it. For all such situations, the majority–minority framework itself is a problem, and the framework *is* the syndrome.

In my view, a perspective that identifies the framework with the syndrome unashamedly ignores morality altogether or at least glosses over the complex strands within it. But does not insistence on the majority–minority framework underestimate the problems generated by it? Why must one put up with a permanent state of radically distinct groups that see themselves only numerically and remain divided and distanced from one another? Why not aspire to a political society that recognizes the equal standing of all viable groups and simply jettison talk of minorities and majorities?[2] Why take refuge in a divisive discourse of rights at all? My straightforward response is that the best available option is not always realizable. Enabling conditions may be present, but, once the opportunity thrown up by the historical process is missed, a society may lose even the chance of securing other morally defensible but second-best options.

Let me explain this point. A pervasive myth within modernist self-understanding is that modern conditions destroy every collective formation and unleash different forms of individualisms. On this view, collective identities and commitments cannot survive the modernist onslaught. Even a cursory glance at the process of modernity reveals, however, that while it undermines some kinds of groups, it simultaneously generates and bolsters others.[3] The most obvious example of a group made possible and supported by modern processes is the nation (and other sub-national groups). Now, the same processes that generate national identity also usher in a sense of equality and intense competitiveness – ingredients that may foster a majority–minority syndrome. A syndrome is not inevitable. A mechanism ensuring equality and mutual respect may well be introduced before competitiveness among groups goes too far. If this happens, society secures dignified and peaceful coexistence of groups, perhaps without resorting even to a framework of rights. However, in most instances, the very formation of groups is dependent on and accompanied by a sense of equality and radical competitiveness. Groups are formed within the very same process that produces the conditions of the syndrome. One possible solution to contain it, to foster institutionalized toleration, is a context-sensitive system of group-rights. However, if these are not granted at the appropriate time by the right type of agents, complex feelings of disadvantage and marginalization may grow and a majority–minority syndrome may set in, and once it is entrenched – this is my argument – a necessary though not sufficient solution is to adopt a suitable majority–minority framework. To insist then on the futility or irrelevance of the framework when in fact the syndrome is already entrenched is at best to belie a shallow utopianism and at worst to shamelessly disguise inequalities between groups.

RECONCILING THE REDEEMABLE: HISTORY, RIGHTS, REFORM?

History

The partition of the Indian subcontinent in 1947–48 left an even smaller (though in absolute terms still huge) Muslim minority in India, composed largely of illiterate poor scattered all over the country, a rather beleaguered rump in a state of confusion, guilt, and fear. Its members felt guilty that they may have had or would be seen to have a hand in partition, confused about their status, and fearful and uncertain about their future in a new Hindu-dominated nation-state. Clearly, unlike those who made it across the border, Muslims who chose to stay back or were left behind had become extremely vulnerable. The Constituent Assembly, set up in December 1946, six months before partition, but which finished its three-year-long deliberations on the new constitution well after it, rejected the political majority–minority framework. This rejection was justified on the ground that special representation rights in India had begun the awful habit of treating Hindus and Muslims as distinct political entities. A system of separate electorates freed majority representatives from the obligation of securing support from the minority, strengthened the resolve of every community to care for only its own interests, bolstered sectarianism, ghettoized minorities, and forced considerations of general welfare out of politics. But most of all, it was seen to be single-handedly responsible for India's partition and "had sharpened communal difference *to a dangerous extent* and had proved one of the main stumbling blocks to the development of a *healthy and (unified)* national life."[4]

The rejection of such a framework was, however, entirely consistent with the acceptance of a social majority–minority framework. Members of the Constituant Assembly believed that the majority–minority framework might eventually go, but "the minorities must be dissolved into the majority by *justice*." As one member put it, "if this elementary justice is not given to minorities, we may open up the dangerous path of fanatical nationalism." For Ambedkar, one of the main architects of the constitution, such minority rights had an absolute status: "No matter what others do, he urged, we ought to do what is right in our own judgement and, therefore, every minority, irrespective of any other consideration, is entitled to the right to use their language, script and culture and the right not to be precluded from establishing any educational institution that they wish to establish." Muslims were recognized as a distinct cultural and religious group and received constitutionally guaranteed rights to the survival and renewal of their own cultural resources, to their languages and its scripts, to maintain and administer their own educational institutions, and to freedom of worship. Many today believe that they also have a right to their own personal laws – i.e. laws pertaining to family, marriage, divorce, maintenance, inheritance, child custody, and adoption.

Group Rights versus Individual Rights

Of these rights, that to personal laws, though not explicitly guaranteed by the Indian constitution, has become more significant. For a number of reasons into which I cannot go in this paper, Muslim identity in India is identified with personal laws, and the right to the maintenance of cultural resources has come to mean the right to the maintenance of existing personal laws. The entire majority–minority framework has been identified with the right to personal laws.

For my limited purposes, I refer to only four aspects of these laws. The first has to do with inheritance. Muslim personal law requires that women receive a share of the parent's property, albeit roughly half the amount granted to male descendants. The other three relate to marriage, divorce, and maintenance. Polygamy is much talked about, and I say nothing about it. The position on *Talaq* (divorce) is familiar too. If convinced that the marriage has broken down, the man can quietly pronounce divorce, which becomes effective only after the period of *Iddat* (roughly three months). If the man has not retracted the pronouncement during this period, the marriage is dissolved, although this situation need not be permanent; provided that the woman agrees, the man can revive the marriage. This renewal can occur twice in the lifetimes of the couple, however. With the third pronouncement of Talaq, the marriage is irrevocably dissolved. If divorced, the woman must be paid her *mehar* (her share in matrimonial property). She also gets alimony but only until she is re-eligible for marriage, which, once again is in roughly three months.[5]

Should Muslims have a right to these laws?[6] Opinion on this matter has long been sharply divided. Modernists in India, Muslims as well as Hindus, Sikhs, and Christians, have firmly demanded the abolition of separate personal laws for religious minorities and the institution of a uniform civil code on liberal grounds of justice for women as individuals. In the current context, this amounts to a demand that the majority–minority framework be abandoned. Let us call this anti-communitarian stance the radical individualist position, or simply position A. Pitted against it is B, the conservative communitarian position that seeks strict preservation of separate personal laws on grounds of religious integrity and community identity. It desires further extension of personal laws in order to replace the diverse customary practices that indulge freely in inter-cultural borrowing. This position advocates the retention of the majority–minority framework as it interprets it.

I believe that neither of the two positions is satisfactory. There are many reasons why this is so, and I hope to identify them below. Despite their opposition, A and B share a number of assumptions. First, an ontological assumption that to treat groups as irreducible is to view them as organisms, of which individuals are functional parts, and that therefore they necessarily subsume individuals within it. Second, there is the normative assumption that if groups have value then it must always be greater than the value of the individuals who make it up – that group interests always override individuals' interests, including, when necessary, their material interests. Advocates of A associate these assumptions with a defence of group rights and counter it. One objection is that groups cannot have rights, simply because they have no irreducible existence. Since minority rights form a species of group rights, there can be no irreducible minority rights and, it follows, no separate right to personal laws. The second objection is grounded in normative considerations. Whatever the truth or falsity of ontological individualism, groups have no moral worth (value) independent of the individuals who compose them. Since only entities with moral worth have rights, groups and therefore minorities have no rights. Proponents of B, working within the same framework, affirm the two assumptions. So despite sharing at some level the same framework, A and B conflict because A denies these assumptions and B affirms them. I believe that, by challenging the very framework embodying these assumptions, we can reject both A and B. We can then show that a proper understanding of some of the basic feature of groups, ignored by both positions, enables us to arrive at an alternative, reformist position C that reconciles A and B and seeks reform, not abolition, of these laws. I support one version of C below and try to demonstrate why A and B are mistaken and in particular to show how some crucial issues elude both positions and how they misunderstand the precise character of threats to the survival of individuals and groups.

Individual Rights. Ontological individualism is the view that only human individuals exist and that groups are mere aggregations of individuals. This view is false. First, it gets the specific ontology of groups all wrong. Human groups are neither sets nor aggregates but distinct wholes with individuals as their parts. Unlike aggregates, wholes are extremely sensitive to the relationships between their parts, and, unlike sets, they tolerate changes without losing their identity. A human collectivity is individuated by the relations among individual members. When these relations are destroyed, an aggregate of individuals remains, but the group has ceased to exist. Likewise, the identity of a human group, – for example, a university – is not changed when the current lot of students, teachers, and staff members leave and is replaced by different individuals. It would change if the university were merely a set of these individuals. Second, at least some attributes of individuals already presuppose the presence of group-constituting social relations and in particular the existence of groups to which individuals belong. This does not mean that all attributes of human individuals depend on groups and certainly not that they depend exclusively on specific groups. For example, human beings have sentient life without groups; many of their bodily needs and their felt pains and pleasures inhere in them without their belonging to groups.

Value individualism is the view that (a) only lives of individuals have ultimate value and (b) that (all) collective entities derive their value from their contribution to the lives of individual human beings.[7] Let me first remove an unhelpful vagueness that plagues this view. (a) is ambiguous between lives of individuals understood aggregatively (taken one by one) and holistically (taken together) and between lives understood purely materially and also socially. If value-individualism is the claim that only lives of individuals aggregatively understood have ultimate value and that all collective entities derive their value from the contribution that they make to the material life of each individual taken separately, then it is false. The value of many dimensions of our lives is irreducibly holistic (group-related/collectivist): either their value is a value for all relevant individuals taken together (solidarity, a way of life), or, when enjoyed singly, it makes ineliminable reference to what can only be valued together (speaking a language, appreciating art, praying). Many collective entities (family, nation, university, institutions of a free press) derive their value from the contribution that they make not to lives understood purely materially (biological needs, absence of physical pain) but also socially (collective meaning).

This claim defending group-related values does not deny a partial truth in value individualism appropriately understood – namely, that the material lives of individuals understood aggregatively have basic value and that (some) collective entities also derive value from their contribution to such lives. Some very powerful moral claims emerge from this recognition: many of our absolute prohibitions such as not to kill, not to maim, and not to cause suffering to others, as well as positive moral claims derived from the basic needs of others, such as helping the destitute, have this individualist basis. The presence or fulfilment of certain kinds of pleasures – primitive comforts and basic needs (for food, drink, sleep, sex, warmth, and ease) and the absence of certain kinds of pain (of injury, sickness, hunger, thirst, excessive cold, and heat and exhaustion) have not only agent-neutral but group-neutral value. All these values can help ground the value of collective entities (for example, hospitals and welfare states). If the value of collective entities derives partly from these basic individualist values, such collective values never constitute a sufficient reason for overriding basic individualist values.

Nor must a defence of collective values be conflated with what I call the subsumption thesis. According to that thesis, everything of value in the life of an individual derives from his or her membership in any one group. That I do not subscribe to this view is evident from my claim that the value of the material life of individuals is independent of membership in any group. Additionally, the value of the social life of an individual is unlikely to be exhausted by membership in any one group. Individuals interact with different individuals and at any given time are members of different groups, and therefore the overall value of their social life is conditional on their membership in many groups.

Group Rights. I hope to have becalmed some fears of individualists. But a crucial issue between value-individualists and non-individualists still needs examining. The issue between value-individualists and non-individualists is ancient: the individualist must ask of everything: what is in it for me? And he or she asks the same of membership in a group, because ultimately all he or she wants is protection and preservation. The non-individualist claims that at least sometimes we must ask: what am I required to do for the group, for the sake of collective values? Under some conditions it is worthwhile to desire and value the protection or preservation of groups.

But what do groups need protection from? What threatens group values? Now, I believe, group values can be threatened in at least three different ways that may lead to demands for their protection. (a) When the structural conditions in a society favour the values of one group but are inimical to the growth and survival of values of the other, or when another, more dominant group may seek to destroy the values of one group, here a real, external threat obtains. (b) When members of a group, out of *akrasia* (weakness of will), wilful or unwitting neglect (self-interest or laziness), ignorance, confusion, or delusion, may cease to care for group values, this might be called an internal threat.[8] (c) A third "threat" occurs when members deliberating over these values realize their inadequacy or limitation and find better formulations thereof (as when a poor conception of freedom gives way to a richer one) or discover still better values (as when hierarchy is replaced by equality) and seek to realize this change with or without the help of relatively independent agencies such as the state.

Notice that (c) threatens existing formulations of values but rarely the values themselves. Even when some values are genuinely threatened, the purported threat comes from new values that sublate (cancel and preserve) older ones. So (c) never entails an insensitive rejection of group values and therefore need not be counted as a real threat to the existence of the group. This is not to say that it not perceived or imagined as one. But threats that are merely perceived or imagined do not legitimate special protection for groups. Some collectivists mistakenly or deliberately subsume (c) under (a) or (b). Individualists quite rightly emphasize the importance of (c) but generally tend to think of all changes in value as instantiating it. And, although the less optimistic among them have begun to see the danger of external threats, they hardly ever recognize internal threats. Anyone pointing these dangers out is instantly suspected of harbouring authoritarian intentions, willing to sacrifice an individual for the sake of the group, an enemy of (c), of advocating the subsumption thesis.

So, one contentious issue on which individualists and non-individualists stand divided is internal threats to group values. Generally, four possibilities exist in face of internal threats. First, let group values die. Second, coerce or manipulate some individuals into protecting them. Third, rely on the heroism of individuals. Fourth, ensure that no one "free rides" – that each member sacrifices some of his or her desires and does his or her fair bit in sustaining them. Individualists rightly oppose the exercise of the second option. They grudgingly accept the third – heroism is voluntary – but, because they do not see the full force of group values, they are unable to grant validity to the fourth. Nor do conservative communitarians, who also meet internal threats by cementing what can be called an unfair division of moral labour.[9] Thus most societies live by the second and third options: group values are preserved by the moral hard work of some (who sacrifice much more of their desires for the sake of groups), while others free ride.

A basic feature of the ontology of groups allows this. A group can survive without all its members working for it all the time. This enables its members, first of all, to lead their material lives. (They can sleep, eat, and so on.) Second, they can belong to other groups, both over time and at any given time. Third, they can leave one group and join another. Groups can frequently bear costs of departure of some members – a feature that adds to the richness of human existence. (All these show why a commitment to irreducible groups does not entail the subsumption thesis.) But the same attribute of groups that yields positive benefits also creates a disadvantage. It encourages moral inequalities. Generally, groups become internally asymmetric, so that some persons or types of persons bear unfair costs of nurturing goods that benefit all members. Let me give an obvious example. Most of us value family life for the enduring relations that it makes possible. Both men and women equally share the joys of family, but the burdens generally are unfairly distributed. Many women selflessly sacrifice their desires by indirect strategies such as the internalization of their role as glorified mothers or wives. Such asymmetries within the family make it a repressive group. This is the truth in individualist claims. But it does not follow that the family has no independent value and therefore that the non-individualist claim is false.

To sum up: It is a truism that groups in all societies perpetually face internal threats. It is equally true that many individuals within the group are often engaged in the critical examination and the revision of its values. Thus a subterranean tension exists between free riders in the group and its committed reformers. It is also true that reform often seems to many members of a group – particularly to those who benefit from its firmly entrenched power relations – a threat to its very survival. In this very complex situation, the mere presence of the dominant majority may have the following negative consequence. The tension between the ultra-individualists' tendency to free ride, the critical collectivists' to reform the group, and the conservative communitarians' to preserve the status quo may sometimes be circumvented, first, by public proclamations that even the slightest challenge to an existing interpretation of values jeopardizes their survival, emboldens the majority, and thereby magnifies the external threat, and, second, by the curtailment of internal debate and the forging of a united front against outsiders. The most striking consequence of failure to reform is the active preservation of unfairness in the division of moral labour.

Some members continue to carry the task of sustaining the group by upholding all its values, including ones that are palpably disintegrating or crying for ethical sublation.

Reform of Muslim Personal Law

If what I have said is reasonable, then position A, which denies for one reason or another the value of groups or denies that they need protection and therefore collective labour for sustenance, is indefensible. Both ontological and value individualism are implausible or false. But B is not justifiable either; it also misunderstands the nature of groups and their relations to individuals. Groups do not hover over and above individuals, and although they have irreducible value, it does not follow that the value of some properties of individuals is any less and can be overridden. In short, A does not recognize any group rights. B recognizes them but in the wrong way, endorsing the subsumption thesis that has no place for the needs and desires of individuals. B rejects the necessity or desirability of justice-based reforms.

The implication of this abstract philosophical discussion is this. Muslims as a group have rights, and, given the importance of law within Islam and the contextual significance in India of the domain of the private, they may even have a right to their personal laws. It does not follow, however, that Muslims have a right to the protection of existing interpretations of laws grossly unjust to women. The social majority–minority framework has a justifiable place in India, but not in its present form. For a start, my account rules out, in an unabashedly individualist vein, the violation of basic individual rights in the name of group values. Freedom from domestic violence, a right to share in inheritance, and the right to maintenance for divorced and destitute women (flowing from the agent and group-neutral reason of fulfilment of basic needs) must be legally enforceable, irrespective of the group to which women belong. The state has simply to enforce the exercise of such rights, no matter how incompatible this is with the personal laws or customary practices of any group. Any custom or law of Muslim orthodoxy that violates these basic rights must be set aside.[10] Thus, a section of a Muslim personal law that decrees that a husband is liable to provide maintenance to his divorced wife only during the period of iddat and not thereafter must be brushed aside. Section 125 of the Indian Criminal Procedure Code provides for the husband's maintenance of his divorced wife until she remarries and is applicable to all women regardless of their religious affiliation. (This was precisely the issue at the heart of the famous *Shahbano* case; see below).[11]

Other reforms in personal laws can be introduced without violating community identity. For example, marriages can be legally registered, the permissible age of marriage for women can be raised, women can be given the unconditional right to reside in their matrimonial homes, a married women need not be treated as the property of her husband, cruelty or the irretrievable breakdown of marriage can be made a legitimate ground of divorce. No Muslim can reasonably argue that these reforms constitute an internal threat to his culture. More controversially perhaps, the "offence of adultery" by women can be dropped as a ground for divorce, and the mother can be recognized as one of the guardians of the child.

But – and this is the crux of the problem – a prima facie incompatibility exists between Muslim personal laws and the best available standards of equality and autonomy. These standards dictate that polygamy be abolished, that women have a right to equal share in inheritance, and that divorce be effected by mutual consent rather than by the punitive exercise of an exclusive male prerogative. Does this straight away lead to a uniform civil code? There is need for caution here. In the absence of a clear perspective on where Islam stands on the values of gender equality and autonomy, without proper discussion at all levels on these issues and under conditions where there anyway exists an external threat, it is not entirely unreasonable to claim that any such tampering with Muslim personal laws might be viewed as a threat to the culture of Muslims and, if a group of Muslims is behind such moves, which it is, even as an internal threat. I believe that there is something to be said in favour of this view and that we might therefore support a reconciliatory position, C, for which the answer is reform, not outright rejection of personal laws.

However, this position is, morally speaking, still too simple. To be sensitive to the complex moral dimensions of this issue, we need a better specification of how this reform is to come about. So C, the reformist position, bifurcates further. C1, which I awkwardly call direct paternalist reformism, argues that reforms for the good of the community can be imposed on it from above, with the exclusive initiative of the state. The other view claims that such reforms must come from within the community. The latter view is subject to further division. The first, anti-paternalist reformism, or C2, argues that the argument of reform from within entails that the state adopt a strict policy of non-interference in the personal matters of the Muslim community. The second, C3, which I call indirect paternalist reformism, argues for a distinction between paternalistic coercion and parentalistic interference and claims further that the rejection of paternalistic coercion is compatible with an obligation on the state to provide conditions that facilitate reform within the community. A combination of C with A in a contrasting system of priorities completes the picture.

In India, citizens have the option of complying with the uniform civil code rather than with the personal laws of the community into which they are born. Before independence, this option was conditional on the complete renunciation of one's religion and therefore of one's cultural identity. This pre-condition virtually blocked the right of individuals to exit from their respective personal laws. Since independence, it has been possible both to keep one's religious identity and to opt for the common civil code. This means D, a policy of optional civil code: combining B or C with A. Finally, there may exist automatic compliance (E) with a common civil code, but citizens may have the option to be governed by personal laws. (A is more basic, but an option exists for B or C.)[12] The two policies D and E differ in the relative weight that they place on secular-individual and religious-group identity. The identity made optional in the policy is also judged to be relatively less important for the relevant agents.

I plum for the solution that advocates a version of D – i.e., that combines C3 with A.[13] A commitment to C3 entails a rejection of B, C1, and C2 and is consistent with what in my view is the best interpretation of liberal and democratic principles. (This version of D I less adventurously call the liberal-democratic option). I believe that reforms within Muslim personal law must come from within but that a liberal and democratic state is committed to the provision of conditions that facilitate a full and free deliberation over the entire issue, a pre-condition of any reform. I also believe that Muslim women must be given the right to exit the system of personal laws. Since there are no advocates for the removal of the option to be regulated by a common code (a sign, surely, that the Muslim orthodoxy does not view it as threatening and a sign too that Muslim women do not see it as a reasonable option), on the question of deciding which of the two – a uniform civil code or separate personal laws – is paramount, I currently place more importance on separate personal laws not on the ground that they are sacred but on the more general ground that Muslims have a right to a separate cultural identity. Since it is this more general reason that grounds the right and entails duties on individuals, groups, and the state, it would be wholly consistent with my position if, on the more specific grounds of justice, personal laws were eventually overhauled and replaced by something else that better protects their separate identity. However, whatever replaces personal law is not likely to and perhaps should not entail an entirely culture-insensitive, homogenizing civil code.

Let me try and put this point differently. Suppose that egalitarians were to overhaul the personal laws of all cultural communities, giving full consideration to concerns of gender justice. I can bet that a residual cultural difference will abide in the new, reformed set of laws. Let me take an example: all religious codes includes some legal criteria that make a marriage valid. For example, the Hindu marriage is solemnized according to *saptapadi*, which by all accounts is a male chauvinist tradition. Its removal does not mean, however, that all Hindu marriages be solemnized in the civil court; other progressive traditions exists within the religion that are not male chauvinist. Similarly, in Hindu personal law, men, not women, have at birth unequivocal rights to coparcenary property (joint share in inheritance). Such rights presuppose an undivided joint family governed by Mitakshara law. Now it is not clear why giving equal rights to coparcenary property to women must entail dissolution of the joint family. Muslims too have many traditions of solemnizing marriage, even different legal traditions that do not accord the same status to women. It is not clear why more progressive legal traditions within Islam cannot be relied on to improve the status of women. Cultural differences may remain even when all personal laws are made egalitarian.

What is my defence of this position? Everything hinges on how Muslim women view their own situation. Do most of them see themselves as under a bell jar, as surely must be assumed by those who advocate swift imposition of uniform civil code on liberal-emancipatory grounds? Is this purely a gender issue, with nothing to do with cultural identity? Or do Muslim women entirely accept their current role within Muslim culture as dictated by the *shariat*? Do they see the division of moral labour as legitimate or as unfair? Rather than forcing the situation of women into one or the other pigeonhole, surely it is better – certainly more in keeping with their status as full moral agents – to view their situation as riven with an internal conflict. Despite all the inequalities of their condition, many of them can see the importance of their cultural identity just as much as Muslim men do. They realize the value of their group. (Position A denies this, and position E does not give it enough stress, at least not in the current context.) But they can also imagine themselves independent of their current status within the group, as bearers of interests that grant them greater moral worth than they currently enjoy as members. Such interests become central when they think of themselves either as equal interlocutors deliberating over the values of their group or as potential members of other groups. Its better to see Muslim women, and to some extent Muslim men, as playing out this internal struggle. A Muslim cultural identity matters to (the relevant) women. But, unlike for Muslim orthodoxy, which wants it to be so, it is not the only thing that matters to them. This is an internal struggle within the Muslim community, between status-quoists and pro-change Muslims.

In the *Shahbano* case, an elderly Muslim woman sought maintenance from her husband after he divorced her and obtained a favourable judgment from all Indian courts but earned the wrath of Muslim orthodoxy and brought India's secular laws in conflict with Muslim personal law. We can surely read the case in this manner. Recall my discussion above of sources of value change.[14] Muslims in India can be seen to undergo all three processes at once (a, b, and c). Muslims face an external threat (structural conditions favour the Hindu majority, surely the reason that grounds minority rights). There is also some evidence of an internal threat (the reason why orthodoxy plays a hegemonic role among Muslims today). But there are also persistent attempts within the Muslim community to reinterpret their tradition (as examples, see the valiant attempts of both modernist and traditional Muslims).[15] True, it is always in the interest of Muslim orthodoxy to blur the line between (b) and (c), but the pervasive presence of (a) nevertheless creates a perpetual dilemma, above all for Muslim women such as Shahbano, who reason probably in the following way. All Muslims value their group-identity. They also face internal and external threats. Such a context blurs the line between real and perceived threats. Although the division of moral labour seems grossly unjust to Muslim women, the burden that they largely carry helps sustain the group in the face of continuing external threat. Therefore, no matter how costly it is to them, they should not press now for justice.

Now, I believe that it is futile to deny this impasse. I see D as a solution precisely because it points to a way out. Positions A, B, C1, C2, and E do not properly see this impasse. B, C1, and C2 deny claims of gender justice. A and E deny the value of groups. D not only takes serious note of the dilemma mentioned above but also takes it by the horns.

It seeks reforms of existing personal laws of Muslims and sympathetically understands the tremendous costs of exercising the right to exit. But it gives Muslim women the right to opt for the common civil code, and it enjoins the state to create conditions for deliberation on the reforms of all personal laws, for the free exercise of the right to opt for the common civil code, and for full protection for those who make this choice and in addition to create more opportunities for minority groups to reinterpret their identities.

No proponent of group rights committed also to gender justice would dare propose setting up a deliberative body of Muslims were he or she convinced that reform from within was in principle impossible. The proposal of a deliberative body is predicated on at least some grounds for hope of change. Is this hope justified? I believe that partial reform of Muslim personal laws is possible. This brings me to a discussion of substantive policy issues. Let me begin with polygamy. First, the incidence of polygamous relations is very small among Muslims, much less than in many other groups in India. Second, the Quran neither enjoins nor prohibits polygamy. I think that it is pretty futile to bring in the Quran in support of such practices, because, generally speaking, for every verse or statement enlisted in support, there is another that takes it away.

However, widespread prejudice against Islam compels me to quote the relevant verse, "Marry of the women, who seem good to you, two or three or four, and if ye fear that ye cannot do justice then one only."[16] This rules polygamy out for all practical purposes, for I cannot see how patterns of perfect reciprocity, surely required by justice, within emotionally charged relations can be maintained under conditions of polygamy.[17] As for justice within interpersonal and sexual relations, no society has yet properly devised standards of fairness in this domain. The Muslims are not uniquely responsible for what must surely be a deep-rooted but common human failing.

Strictly speaking, then, justice requires not a ban on polygamy but the availability of this option for women too! I am not being frivolous here, although this is obviously an even more hopeless demand. Under the circumstances, the best approach would be to build into the law financial disincentives to polygamy.[18] The main concern, remember, is the maltreatment of women, not sexual promiscuity. The emotional suffering that another relationship causes cannot be handled legally, but the law can control the financial hardships that polygamous marriages usually bring. In short, polygamy can be regulated.

On Talaq, the prospects are even better! First of all, the very fact that divorce is acceptable within Islam speaks of its partial liberal premises.[19] Marriage, though a repository of a semi-sacred relation, is also a contract. It is a dissoluble union. Moreover, the identity of a Muslim women is not wholly exhausted by her marital status. She continues to have an identity outside her marriage. Her consent to marriage and to its continuance is necessary – unlike the case in other traditional systems of marriage. Second, in addition to her share of inheritance from her own parents, a woman has a right to *Maher* – i.e., to her proper share in matrimonial property. Gender equality is more prevalent in Islam than in many other traditional systems. The Muslim wife can legally retain her name, her property, her independent legal status, and even the school of law that is part of her faith.

This provides the general context for the Islamic understanding of divorce. Excessive attention has been bestowed on the notion of triple Talaq, and very little on other parts of Islamic law. For example, Islam also recognizes, Khul – divorce purely at the behest of the woman. In other words, no man can force his wife to cohabit with him, if she refuses to. Khul within Islamic law is as important as Talaq. Besides, Talaq and Khul, there also exists Mubaraat, whereby a couple can jointly, on mutual agreement, dissolve the marriage. It appears that if the position of Muslim women within their community is deplorable, it is on account not of Islamic law but of extra-legal malpractices.

I mention this not because I believe that traditional Islam has all this and much more to offer for the emancipation of women. I do not believe that traditional systems are fully equipped with such resources. But stereotypes, far as usual from truth, have it that the deplorable condition of Muslim women is incomparable and is sanctioned by Islamic law. This is not true. The point in favour of partial reform of Islamic law is that some resources within traditional Islamic law can help bring about gender-just laws. Surely, this is demonstrated by what I have mentioned above.

THE MAJORITY–MINORITY SYNDROME IN INDIA: HISTORY AND RESOLUTION?

Alas, conditions in India are not propitious for even the realization of position D. Why cannot a policy be implemented that is based on a contextually reasonable and reconciliatory stand such as the one I defend? Why is reform not possible? Because a propensity to stall reform is built into the majority–minority syndrome that continues to infect Indian politics. To explain this situation – the dilemmas and paradoxes, the frustrating impasse in Indian politics and society, and the acute vulnerability that this creates for Indian Muslims, – I offer a brief excursus into recent Indian history.

There was much in common between Hindus and Muslims in pre-independence India.[20] A majority of Muslims belong to the same ethnic group as Hindus. Urdu, widely thought to be a language of Muslims, was actually spoken by only about 30 per cent of Muslims and by a large number of Hindus in the north. Certain social customs were common to both communities. Many Muslims retained Hindu names. Hindu rites were sufficient in many parts of the country to solemnize Muslim marriages. Many Muslims continued to follow Hindu law in matters of marriage, guardianship, and inheritance. Muslim Pirs had Hindu disciples, and Hindu Yogis had Muslim Chelas. The caste system remained integral to both communities. Except in Bengal, Hindus and Muslims were not divided along class lines or along the rural–urban divide. There is then strong evidence to support the contention of several historians that, "objectively speaking," differences between Muslims and Hindus were not large enough to justify separation.[21]

Yet a successful separatist movement emerged in India. It underwent four stages. First, there emerged heightened use of religion as an identity marker in public spaces and the consolidation of community identities based on religion. By the end of the nineteenth century, powerful revivalist movements had sprung up among Hindus, along with a sense of the need to be unified and recognized as one homogeneous group. This growing self-awareness was often accompanied by the feeling that Hindus had been a subject group, subordinated first to Muslims and later to the British. Revivalist movements therefore frequently assumed a strident anti-Muslim character. This factor was to cause great consternation among Muslim elites, which now sought new strategies to create a social and political space for a hardened religious identity.

Second, majority–minority self-identifications developed, and a demand for a social and political majority–minority framework. Introduction of modern census and representative institutions, particularly of separate representation for Muslims, ushered in this second phase. This opened up space to use religion for political mobilization, to launch a majority–minority discourse, to form a communal party such as the Muslim League, and to sow the seeds that would transform a community into a nation.

Third, there was a public proclamation that religious communities are nations. Henceforth there was a qualitatively different kind of majority–minority framework, with elites demanding self-government rights for statutory majorities in existing and newly carved out provinces that had a Muslim majority. Once these elites began to believe that Muslims too were a nation, they also started to dream of complete economic and political power for themselves and to demand finally that these self-government rights be exercised only within an independent, politically sovereign nation-state.[22]

However – and this has much relevance to what I claim below – these demands were laced with a long list of exaggerated or imagined grievances conjured up by them. Muslim elites were really not backward, but they feared being left behind in a predominantly Hindu regime, so they created the myth of the backward Muslim. They were not really oppressed but feared political domination in a Hindu-majority India, so they spun tales of Hindu tyranny. They were neither historically disadvantaged nor unable to voice their demands but still manufactured the fiction of marginalization. Perhaps it is inappropriate to identify the term "imaginary" with "unreal." As the historian Beni Prasad, writing in the thick of the demand for partition, said, "in politics there is a profound significance in Adler's thesis that complexes are due not to the past but to the fear of the future."[23] But by the 1940s this fear has turned into paranoia, which helped generate the majority–minority syndrome.

Nor was fear of the future the only ingredient in the syndrome. A deeply divided memory of the past also played a key role in its development. Against the dominant current of anti-colonial ideology, Ambedkar made this point with cold-blooded clarity. He agreed that large groups of Hindus and Muslims shared a common way of life but insisted that this commonness should not be exaggerated.[24] Using Renan's arguments that, to qualify as a nation, a people must share a common heritage and cherish a common memory and noting that Hindus and Muslims had divided memories, he concluded that they constituted two nations. "Even when both referred to the same events, one remembered it with shame and sorrow and the other with great pride. Thus there was no common cycle of participation for a common achievement. Their political and religious past was one of mutual destruction and mutual animosities. It is embedded in their religion, and for each to give up its past is to give up its religion. To hope for this is to hope in vain."

According to Ambedkar, political and religious antagonisms divided the two groups more deeply than the so-called common things bound them. On the period in which Gandhi was tirelessly advocating Hindu–Muslim unity, Ambedkar claimed that it is "no exaggeration to say that it is a record of 20 years of civil war between Hindus and Muslims ... The acts of barbarism against women, committed without remorse ... show the depth of antagonism between two communities ... The tempers on both sides are like tempers of two warring nations ... What is astonishing is that these cold and deliberate acts of rank cruelty were not regarded as atrocities to be condemned but were treated as legitimate acts of warfare for which no apology was necessary."[25]

Even though he does not use the term, Ambedkar is alluding here to what I have called the majority–minority syndrome – a diseased network of relations so completely poisoned and accompanied by such a vertiginous assortment of negative emotions (envy, malice, jealousy, spite, and hatred) that collective delirium leads to cold-blooded acts of revenge, sending groups on a downward path of deeper and still deeper estrangement. Each group makes demands on the other that can rarely be fulfilled, conjures up imaginary grievances, insists precisely on that which hurts the other most, and at one time obsessively desires the very same thing that the other wants and at another asks for the exact opposite, always with the sole purpose of negating the claims of the other. Ambedkar provides several examples: "Hindus and Muslims make preparations against each other," he tells us, "without abatement reminding one of a 'race in armaments' between two hostile nations. If the Hindus have the Banaras University, the Muslims must have the Aligarh University. If the Hindus start the *Shuddhi* movement, the Muslims must launch the *Tablig* movement. If the Hindus start sangathan, the Muslims must have the *Tanjim*. If the Hindus have the R.S.S., the Muslims must reply by organising the *Khaksars*."[26] Again, "the Muslims (read extremist Muslims) agitated fiercely to introduce representative government in Kashmir but elsewhere they opposed it. Why? Because in all matters their determining attitude is how will it affect the Muslims vis-à-vis the Hindus. In Kashmir it would have meant transfer of power from a Hindu king to Muslim masses; elsewhere where the ruler is Muslim and subjects Hindus, it means Hindu masses will be victorious." He adds, "The determining and dominating consideration is not democracy but how democracy with majority rule will affect the Muslims in their struggle against the Hindus."[27] Ambedkar was wrong about Kashmiri Muslims, but he had grasped the mindset of extremists more generally. As he himself recognized, extremist Hindu politics was similarly perverted. In different circumstances, a political majority–minority framework for Muslims within a united India should have been a satisfactory solution to all sides. But, given the majority–minority syndrome, "in which a hostile majority is forever pitted against a hostile minority," Ambedkar concluded, only a separate state seemed viable.

The development of the syndrome prevented a reasonable and accommodating solution to the Muslim question in India. It also stopped reform, particularly for Muslims. Anti-reform tendencies within a group are severely intensified if a society is in the grip of a majority–minority syndrome. Ambedkar was quick to grasp this point. When groups regard each other as a menace, he argued, they spend all their energies on preparing to meet "the menace." The exigencies of a common front of the majority against a powerful minority and the minority against the majority generate a "conspiracy of silence over social evils."[28] Neither party attends to them "even though they are running sores and requiring immediate attention, for the simple reason that they view every measure of social reform as bound to create dissension and division and thereby weaken the ranks when they ought to be closed to meet the menace of the other community." This ensures social stagnation, and a spirit of conservatism continues to dominate the thoughts and actions of both sides.

In a passage that anticipates the dilemma faced many decades later over the *Shahbano* case, Ambedkar laments the passing of the Dissolution of Muslim Marriage Act VIII of 1939. This act annulled the previous law, under which the apostasy of a male or a female married under the Muslim law ipso facto dissolved the marriage, so that if a married Muslim woman changed her religion, she was free to marry a person professing her new religion. The new retrograde law bound a married Muslim woman to her husband even if his religious faith was repugnant to her. Conversion of a woman and her subsequent marriage were seen to be undertaken solely with a view to changing the relative numerical strength of communities and therefore as a depredation by one community against the other. Thus the real motive, Ambedkar claimed, was to prevent the illicit conversion of women to alien faiths in order to ensure that the numerical balance between the two communities remains undisturbed. Ambedkar concluded that the law was changed and the rights of women sacrificed purely in order to maintain a certain numerical balance between the two communities. Such reasoning, which turned a social issue requiring urgent reform into a contentious matter between warring communities, epitomizes a majority–minority syndrome.

David Hume says somewhere that enmity between hostile groups endures even though the original cause of animosity has disappeared and even when it goes against their current interests.[29] Resentments, hatred, and grudges are sometimes bequeathed from generation to generation. In India, Hindu extremists and Muslim orthodoxy and, by default, large sections of ordinary Hindus and Muslims appear to have inherited features of the majority–minority syndrome, with particularly disastrous consequences for the smaller group. The original situation of conflict may have disappeared, but extremists from the majority Hindu community and, foolishly, sections of Muslim orthodoxy talk and behave in a manner that resuscitates the syndrome.

In the *Shahbano* case, a slight error on the part of the Supreme Court – the judge took it on himself to interpret the Quran – was sufficient for Muslim orthodoxy to press panic buttons about Hindu majoritarianism, to paint alarmist scenarios of great danger to Islam, and to manufacture, à la the pre-independence Muslim League, an unending list of imaginary grievances. Internal debate was stifled, the government succumbed to pressure and passed a new law favouring the status quo on Muslim personal law, and poor Shahbano was forced to retract. The slogan of Islam in danger soon turned into a self-fulfilling prophecy, as Hindu chauvinists first began to harangue Muslims on how they should shed backwardness, then charged successive Congress governments of Muslim appeasement, and eventually began to consolidate a fiercely anti-Muslim, political Hindu identity. Old Hindu grievances, mostly imaginary, were reinvented: the destruction of Hindu temples by Mughals, the temerity of supporters of partition to ask for a framework respecting minority rights, the disloyalty induced by pan-Islamicism, the alleged Muslim propensity to flout family-planning norms solely to increase their numerical strength, and the alleged role that polygamy and therefore Muslim personal law play in their march to outpopulate Hindus. Unwittingly, thanks largely to its orthodox leadership, a much weakened Muslim community had helped trigger the majority–minority syndrome. With the syndrome in full swing (for example, recent events in Gujarat, where the ghastly killing of 58 Hindus by a provoked Muslim crowd led to a state-abetted pogrom of over two thousand innocent Muslims by organized Hindu mobs – the closest that independent India has come to localized ethnic cleansing), anti-reform tendencies are likely to congeal and the already unjust division of moral labour is bound to be further aggravated. Now that the external threat is real, chronic, and pervasive, the Shahbanos within the Muslim community are even more likely to tell themselves that, despite all the unfairness, they must, in these difficult times, shoulder the burden of community values entirely on their own. The majority–minority syndrome makes reform within Muslim personal law virtually impossible.

The deadlock over reforms within Muslim personal law aggravates the quite unreasonable misgivings among otherwise reasonable Hindus about the very framework of minority rights in India. The offensive discourse of Hindu militants and the violence that frequently accompanies it leave Muslims wondering whether their citizenship in India is based on the sufferance of the majority. What then is the future of the Indian nation-state? Its durability depends on the dissolution of the majority–minority syndrome. The syndrome can be cured, first of all, when those who exacerbate it are legally curtailed and made politically powerless. In the current context this largely means curbing the power of Hindu extremists, who, ironically, perpetuate the syndrome in trying to implement their own radical solution. In the long run, however, it can be eliminated only when large sections of Hindus begin to value the idea of equal citizenship and to uncouple equality from sameness when Muslim leaders and those who blindly follow them, having fatefully embraced conservative communitarianism, begin to value individual rights and adopt a somewhat less instrumentalist attitude to liberal and democratic institutions. None of this is possible, however, unless the syndrome is treated and cast off. Alas, here, as in many other places, things move in vicious circles. Tragically, no one in India appears to have the vision or the skill to resolve the conundrum.

NOTES

1 I deal with this framework in greater detail below.
2 See Raz, 1994, 159.
3 Likewise it is mistaken to believe that pre-modern social processes undermine every version of individualism and uphold every form of collectivism. These processes also support individualist tendencies.
4 Patel, 1999, 197–251. The historian Beni Prasad also linked separate electorates to acute civil strife and claimed that if " separate electorates were introduced for Catholics, Protestants, Presbyterians and Nonconformists in England, they would take not more than a generation to arouse acute antag-

onisms. Introduce the system into the United States and the greatest of republics would soon resound with the battle cries of all the races and nationalities of Europe" (1944, 54).

5 Under the old Criminal Procedure Code (CPC) of 1898, any neglected wife, including a Muslim woman, had rights of maintenance. Confined to the privacy of her home, with few opportunities for employment, she could survive only with maintenance. This right therefore was grounded in her basic material needs. But frequently, when a Muslim woman sought the help of the court to secure maintenance, the husband divorced her, thus freeing himself from payment of maintenance beyond the required three months. To check this malpractice, the CPC of 1973 amended the relevant act to include divorced women in this category. Muslim orthodoxy mischievously objected to this amendment, complaining that it violated its religious laws. Viewed thus, the conflict between group and individual rights appears irreconcilable, heading for collision between the rival world-views of modernity and Islam. I deal with this conflict at greater length below.

6 A more detailed treatment appears in Bhargava, 1999, 169–205.

7 Hartney, 1991, 297.

8 Tocqueville comes immediately to mind as one who warned of internal threats. A retreat from the public good consequent on overprivatization seemed to him a serious threat to liberty. See Taylor, 1985, 310.

9 The division of moral labour means different things to different people. For example, Nagel uses it to refer to the internal division between the personal and the impersonal standpoints. Others link it to role morality and to how society divides moral labour into institutions and roles. I mean something related, but the core idea is dependent on how the protection of group values requires that members set aside self-interest or claims of autonomy and how the costs of setting them aside are distributed among members.

10 My use of the term "basic" does not imply that, relative to other rights, they matter more to all individuals. It does mean, however, that other rights supervene on them.

11 For a brief discussion of the case, see Bharghava 1996, 37–8.

12 The two policies differ in the relative weight that they place on secular-individual and religious-group identity. The one optional in the policy also receives less stress. Position E is proposed by the Shetkari Sanghatan. See Omvedt, 1996, 9–13.

13 Other versions of position D could combine A with B or C1 or C2.

14 See above, p. 12.

15 This struggle is waged not only by a large number of liberal-secular women and men but also by a section of Muslim theologians; by organizations such as the Anjuman Taraqqi Pasand; the Kerala Islamic Shariat Boad; the Muslim Satyashodak Mandal, and Muslimeen; and by exemplary Muslim intellectuals such as Asghar Ali Engineer. For details, see Singh, 1994, 102, and Keshwaar, 1996, 88–94.

16 Quran IV:3, quoted in Mahmood, 1975, 36.

17 It was roughly this interpretation of the Quran that legitimated the decision of the Tunisian president to ban polygamy.

18 I have the impression that the noted scholar of jurisprudence Upendra Baxi makes a similar point somewhere.

19 It is often said that Islam is egalitarian, and it is remarkably liberal for its times, especially if one compares its laws with laws on offer by Hindu or Christian scriptures.

20 For example, in Karla, until at least 1865, Muslim peasants were worshipping old village deities. In Altar and Bharatpur, the Meos continued to have Hindu names and celebrated, not just joined in, festivals such as Janamashtami, and the Parihar Minar forbade the consumption of beef. Muslim cultivators near Ratlam followed Hindu customs in marriage. The sect of Mehadawis near Ahmedabad, steeped in Muslin orthodoxy in appearance, were known for concealing their real, un-Islamic beliefs. In Sind, Sunni Memans freely practised ancient cults of the worship of trees and rivers and revered both living and dead saints. The list of sects and communities that, despite their formal adoption of Islam, retained their pre-Islamic beliefs and practices is almost endless. For a good account, see Mujeeb, 1985.

21 Muslims anyway began to feel insecure because of the pressure of change put on them by the "rise of monied men and resurgence of Hindu landholding communities and by some colonial government policies such as making it mandatory on Indian officials to be able to read both the Devnagri and the Persian script." See Hasan, 1993, 36.

22 The installation of a Congress government in Uttar Pradesh started this phase. While keen to have a large Muslim representation within the government, Congress, believing itself to be the party of all Indians, refused to induct the largest group of Muslims in the legislature, members of the Muslim League, into the ministry, unless that body disbanded as a party. This was unacceptable to the League. As a result, Muslim elites were deprived of a share in power. Soon they lost some of their privileges. Even more important, they came to realize that, to obtain any more political favours, they would now have to lean not on the British but on Congress – a political or-

ganization that also relied on Hindu support. This generated in them recep-
tivity to the mobilizing strategy of the Muslim League and eventually to
espousal of separatism. See Hasan, 1993, 1–43. For Hindu communalism in
Bengal, see Chatterjee, 1995.

23 Beni Prasad, 1944, 59.

24 Many of these common features were a result not of choice, of a "conscious
attempt," but of "mechanical causes" such as incomplete conversions, the
mere facts of living on common land and in a common climate, and vestiges
of a brief period during Akbar's rule when religious amalgamation did genuinely take place. See Ambedkar, 1990, 33–7.

25 Ambedkar, 1990, 184–6.

26 Ambedkar, 1990, 246.

27 Ambedkar, 1990, 236.

28 See Ambedkar, 1990, 247.

29 See Holmes, 1995, 50–1.

REFERENCES

Ambedkar, B.R. (1990) *Writings and Speeches, Vol. 8: Pakistan or the Partition
of India*. Education Department, Government of Maharashtra.

Bhargava, Rajeev (1996) "Conflict of Penal and Personal Law," in Jaising, 1996.

– (1999) "Should We Abandon the Majority–Minority Framework?" in D.L.
Sheth and Gurpreet Mahajan, eds., *Minority Identities and the Nation-state*.
Delhi: Oxford University Press.

Chatterjee, Joya (1995) *Bengal Divided, Hindu Communalism and Partition
1932–1947*. Cambridge: Cambridge University Press.

Hartney, Michael (1991) "Some Confusion Concerning Collective Rights," *Canadian Journal of Law and Jurisprudence* 4, no. 2 (July).

Hasan, Mushirul (1993) *India's Partition: Process, Strategy and Mobilization*.
Oxford: Oxford University Press.

Holmes, Stephen (1995) *Passion and Constraint*. Chicago: University of Chicago Press.

Jaising, I., ed. (1996) *Justice for Women*. Goa: Other India Press.

Keshwaar, Sanober (1996) "The Triple Talaq: Unjust, Untenable, Un-Islamic,"
in Jaising, 1996.

Mahmood, T., ed. (1975) *Family Law and Social Change*. Bombay: N.M. Trip-
athi Ltd.

Mujeeb, M. (1985) *Indian Muslims Munshi Ram Manoharlal*. Delhi:

Omvedt, Gail (1996) "Towards a Non-Sexist 'Civil Code,' " in Jaising, 1996.

Patel, Sardar (1999) "India's first Home Minister," in *The Constituent Assembly Debates, Book I, Vol. V*, Lok Sabha Secretariat.

Prasad, Beni (1944) *India's Hindu–Muslim Questions*. Lahore: Book Traders.

Raz, Joseph (1994) "Liberal Multiculturalism," in *Ethics in the Public Domain*. Oxford: Clarendon Press.

Singh, Kirti (1994) "The Constitution and Muslim Personal Law," in Zoya Hasan, ed., *Forging Identities, Gender, Communities and the State in India*. Westview Press.

Taylor, Charles (1985) *Philosophical Papers*, vol. 2. Cambridge: Cambridge University Press.

ROGERS BRUBAKER

Ethnicity, Migration, and Statehood in Post–Cold War Europe

Among the most salient and politically charged issues of the last two decades in Europe have been questions of ethnicity, migration, and statehood. These closely interlinked issues have figured centrally in political, cultural, and social transformations throughout the continent. In eastern Europe, they are often understood to be linked in a vicious circle. States founded on ethnicity – and understood as the states *of* and *for* particular ethnocultural nations – are seen as engendering violent conflict and forced migration. Ethnic cleansing has come to epitomize this diabolical intertwining of ethnicity, migration, and statehood. In western Europe, by contrast, some observers have seen a more benign intertwining. The post-national erosion of sovereign statehood, on this view, has produced a continent-wide space for free migration and has allowed previously suppressed ethnoregional cultures to flourish. Darker accounts, to be sure, stress migration from outside Europe, which is seen as generating unwanted ethnic pluralism, reactively ethnicized understandings of nationhood, and pressures for a renationalization of the state (or for a state-like – and perhaps nation-like – "fortress Europe" that would keep outsiders at bay). While none of these accounts is particularly nuanced, each points to the importance of the intertwined themes of ethnicity, migration, and statehood, and together they suggest that these issues can be configured in quite different ways. In this essay, I seek to specify persisting differences in the way these questions are posed in different parts of Europe, yet to avoid the often caricaturally oversimplified east–west contrasts that inform many accounts of contemporary Europe.

ETHNICITY

Almost all European societies, like most societies world-wide, are ethnically heterogeneous, but that heterogeneity takes sharply differing forms. In order to reveal crucial differences in the configuration – the genesis, form, and political consequences – of ethnic heterogeneity in Europe, I distinguish two ways in which ethnic heterogeneity can be socially organized and politically expressed. The first I call "immigrant ethnicity," and the second, "territorial nationality."[1]

On the first model, characteristic mainly of western Europe, ethnic groups arise through migration and are generally territorially dispersed.[2] On the second model, characteristic of east-central and eastern Europe, ethnic groups are indigenous (or at least make claims to be so); they are in many cases generated by the movement of borders across people, rather than that of people across borders; and they are generally territorially concentrated. Their members are ordinarily citizens of the country in which they reside, yet they often identify culturally and sometimes politically with a neighbouring "kin" or "homeland" state, to which they see themselves as "belonging" by shared ethnicity or culture but not by legal citizenship (Brubaker, 1996). Lastly, and crucially, they define themselves in national terms. They see themselves as belonging not simply to a distinct ethnic group but to a distinct nation or nationality that differs from the nation or nationality of their fellow-citizens. In this second model, then, ethnicity takes the form of nationality, and ethnic heterogeneity is "coded" as national heterogeneity. This territorial ethnicity-cum-nationality is very different from immigration-engendered polyethnicity. Using the same term – "ethnicity" or "ethnic minorities" – to designate both can be misleading.

The political claims that can be made in the name of ethnicity differ sharply in the two cases. Immigrant ethnicity evokes a politics of anti-discrimination, civic inclusion, and "soft multiculturalism" (claims to recognition, resources, and sometimes special immunities and exemptions). Territorial nationality involves claims for national self-determination, for symbolic recognition as a state-bearing nation rather than as a mere "minority," for extensive language rights, for territorial autonomy or even full independence, and sometimes for rapprochement with a neighbouring "kin" or "homeland" state.

Clearly, the claims of territorial nationality can threaten the basic nature of the state in a way that the claims of immigrant ethnicity generally do not. When ethnic claims become national claims, based on putative territorial nationhood and nationality, they become more fundamental, and potentially more threatening, precisely because they raise what Linz and Stepan (1996) have called the "stateness" problem – the problem of the integrity and boundaries of the state.[3]

In east-central Europe, ethnicity speaks this potentially explosive language of nationality. Nationality or nationhood, in turn, is understood as based on ethnicity (language, culture, a vague sense of shared descent, and so on), rather than – as in the putatively civic model of nationhood – on political citizenship. One might say that ethnicity is nationalized, while nationality and nationhood are ethnicized. In western Europe, in contrast, after decades of heavy labour migration and subsequent family reunification, public attention has focused on immigrant ethnicity, while ethnic claims have not generally been framed as national claims.

There are, of course, important exceptions to this pattern on both sides. In much of east-central Europe, there are fundamental issues associated with the large, socially stigmatized, spatially segregated, and in part economically marginalized Gypsy or Roma population. These issues are *sui generis* and cannot be neatly subsumed under our usual conceptual rubrics. Depending on how Roma are represented by others, and how they represent themselves, they can be conceived as an ethnic group, a national group, a caste, or a social underclass (Vermeersch, 2003).[4]

In western Europe, in contrast, ethnicity sometimes involves claims to territorial nationality or nationhood, and the politics of ethnicity then becomes a politics of national autonomy and self-determination. This is true above all in Spain, Belgium, and Britain, all of them multinational (and not simply multi-ethnic) polities. There is also the interestingly ambiguous case of Italy, where the Northern League sometimes claims that northern Italy, or Padania, is a distinct nation. Only in the case of Northern Ireland – the western European case most similar to the classic national conflicts of central and eastern Europe – is a cross-border "kin" state or ethnic homeland involved in any significant way. As a result – and notwithstanding the political violence associated with Irish, Basque, and Corsican nationalist movements – this type of ethnonationalist politics is less threatening to states than the characteristic eastern European configuration.

A further crossover, blurring the sharp outlines of the east–west distinction, is that just as ethnicity is nationalized – understood as nationality – in some western European as well as in most east-central

European cases, so too nationality and nationhood may be ethnicized in western as well as in eastern Europe. And this is true not only for ethno-regional nationalisms. In response to growing Muslim and non-European immigrant populations, national self-understandings have also been ethnicized, to some degree, even in the so-called state-nations of northern and western Europe, in countries with traditionally state-framed understandings of nationhood.

Ethnicity in east-central Europe, I have suggested, often takes a specifically national – and nationalist – form. Yet despite this potentially explosive configuration, and despite the resurgence of nationalism that accompanied the collapse of communist regimes, ethnic violence has been less widespread, ethnic mobilization less strong, and ethnic identity less pervasively significant than is ordinarily assumed. Having made a good part of my professional living recently off ethnicity and nationalism in eastern Europe, I have no interest in minimizing their significance. In general, however, I think that discussions of the region are overly ethnicized and that an exaggerated focus on ethnicity and nationalism risks crowding out other, often more important theoretical and practical perspectives.

Of the ghastly violence in Yugoslavia and parts of the former Soviet Union we need no reminder. But as Tom Nairn (1995, 91–2) put it, even though one would certainly not want to make light of these terrible conflicts, one should also beware of "making dark" of them. One should resist the temptation to see eastern Europe as a whole as a seething cauldron of nationalist politics and ethnic conflict, on the verge of boiling over into violence and ethnic cleansing; and one should keep the violence that has occurred in perspective.

Ethnonationalist violence has been limited to a relatively small part of eastern Europe and the former Soviet Union – overwhelmingly concentrated in Yugoslavia, Transcaucasia, and the North Caucasus. One should remember, moreover, the violence that has not occurred, the dogs that have not barked. In this perspective, what is striking is the relatively peaceful character of the disintegration of the Soviet Union. Consider, for example, the 25 million Russians stranded as minorities in nationalizing successor states by the breakup of the Soviet Union. Many analysts – myself included, in the early 1990s – thought that at least some of these Russians would be the flashpoints of ethnonational conflict and violence. Yet outside the self-proclaimed "Dniester Republic" in Moldova, successor-state Russians have been neither the objects nor the perpetrators of nationalist violence (Laitin, 1998, chap. 12; Melvin, 1998; Braun, 2000).

What about ethnic and nationalist mobilization? Here too there is a case-selection bias at work. We pay attention to the spectacular moments of high mobilization – the human chain across the Baltic republics, the great crowds that filled the main squares of Yerevan, Tbilisi, Berlin, Prague, and other cities in 1988–90. But these have been the exception, not the rule. Moments of high mobilization have been few and ephemeral. Even where "nation" was a galvanizing category at one moment, it was not at the next. On the whole, especially since 1990, people have remained in their homes, not taken to the streets. In conspicuous contrast to interwar east-central Europe, demobilization and political passivity, rather than fevered mobilization, have prevailed. Much has been written on the strength of nationalist movements in the former Soviet Union; not enough on their comparative *weakness*.[5]

There is, moreover, a kind of optical illusion involved in the view from afar. From a distance, one risks taking too seriously the claims made by ethnonational entrepreneurs – who have indeed proliferated as ethnic modes of claims-making have become more legitimate – and not asking to what extent they really speak for those in whose name they claim to speak. One should not forget that people do not necessarily respond particularly energetically or warmly to the nationalist utterances of politicians who claim to speak for them.

Since the mid-1990s, I have been conducting fieldwork in the Transylvanian town of Cluj, where a bitterly nationalist local politics pits majority Romanian against minority Hungarian claims. Yet there has been virtually no nationalist mobilization by ordinary people, and most remain indifferent to the endless cycles of nationalist talk. This has made palpable for me the loose coupling, or lack of congruence, between nationalist politics – which seems to run in a sphere of its own, unmoored from its putative constituencies – and everyday life. And there are many parallels elsewhere in the region. The general political passivity of Russians in Soviet successor states, for example, has been striking, despite various attempts to mobilize them.

Forty years ago, sociologist Dennis Wrong (1961) criticized Parsonian functionalism for its "oversocialized conception of man." Much social analysis today is informed by what might be called an *overethnicized* conception of history, politics, and social interaction. This comes from treating ethnicity and nationality in substantialist terms, as entities, as substantial, enduring, internally homogeneous and externally bounded collectivities. Despite theoretical work stressing the constructed, imagined, even invented nature of ethnic and national "communities,"[6] groupist language maintains a tenacious hold in the study of ethnicity and nationalism, curiously mirroring its tenacious hold in the practice of ethnic and nationalist politics. Ethnicity and nationalism need to be understood as particular ways of talking about and experiencing the social world and as particular ways of framing political claims, not as real boundaries inscribed in the nature of things. At some places and times, these ways of talking about the social world and of making political claims have deep resonance and powerfully shape how people think and talk and act in everyday life, as well as how they understand and act on their political interests. At other times and places, the language of ethnicity and nationalism deployed by political entrepreneurs falls on deaf or simply indifferent ears. Ethnic and national groupness is a variable, emergent property that may "happen" – as E.P. Thompson (1963) famously said of class – at particular moments. Or it may not happen – and often does not happen – even when and where political rhetoric places great weight on ethnicity and nationality.[7]

This is not a merely theoretical point. The unreflectively groupist language that prevails in journalism, politics, and much social research – the habit of speaking without qualification of Hungarians and Romanians, or Serbs and Albanians, or Russians and Estonians as if they were sharply bounded, internally homogeneous "groups" – not only weakens social analysis but undermines the possibilities for liberal politics in the region.

MIGRATION

Like ethnicity – and in part, of course, in connection with ethnicity – migration too has become a central issue throughout Europe. But just as patterns of politicized ethnicity differ, so too do patterns of migration. First, and most obviously, the problematics of migration in western Europe have focused on immigration, especially from outside the region,[8] while in eastern Europe questions of migration have been, in the first instance, about emigration – seen both as a problem (for the state, in so far as it involves the disproportionate outmigration of highly educated or skilled younger people) and as a solution (for individuals, in so far as temporary work abroad or permanent emigration offers a means of coping with economic dislocation or getting ahead;

for the state, in that it generates remittances; or for nationalists, if it removes or weakens "unwanted" communities).

As a corollary of this basic difference, migration has been experientially marginal in western Europe. After long years of invisibility, migrants – and their distinctive cultural practices – have become conspicuously visible and central to everyday experience in many western European cities and towns. But migration itself – even in former countries of emigration such as Greece, Italy, Portugal, and Spain – is something that *others* do. In eastern Europe, by contrast, migration has become experientially central, figuring pervasively in the way ordinary people think and talk about their plans, strategies, dreams, and hopes.

Within western Europe, migration has of course become more free with the enlargement of the European Union (EU), the (delayed) introduction of free movement for citizens of new EU member states, the abolition of internal frontiers within the Schengen zone, and the general weakening of national citizenship as an instrument of social closure. In much of eastern Europe, migration has become less free, in certain respects, as political space has contracted; as borders, visas, and new citizenships have been introduced; and as the initially open door with which Western countries welcomed migrants fleeing collapsing communist regimes quickly closed. In other respects, to be sure, migration possibilities there have expanded. Notably, citizens of most east-central European countries no longer require visas to travel to EU/Schengen countries. This does not, of course, grant them the right to work, and even after the eastward enlargement of the EU in 2004, existing member states will be permitted to limit labour migration from new member states for a transitional period of up to seven years. But the ability to travel without the hurdles and indignities of having to seek a visa nonetheless marks a significant improvement for citizens of these countries (and also, of course, makes it easier to work without documents).

In western Europe – to highlight a final stark dimension of difference – migration involves mixing and generates new forms and degrees of ethnic, racial, linguistic, and religious heterogeneity, together with the new challenges to national self understanding, and the new forms of politicized ethnicity sketched above. In eastern Europe, much migration – not only in the last fifteen years, but over the last century – has involved *unmixing*, reducing rather than increasing heterogeneity (Brubaker, 1995). This is notoriously the case, of course, for the infamous instances of forced migration – starting with the Balkan wars at beginning of the

20th century, via the massive displacements during and after the Second World War, to the Balkan wars at century's close – that have come to be known as "ethnic cleansing" (Naimark, 2001; Mann, forthcoming). But it is also the case for quieter, less dramatic forms of ethnic unmixing, involving, for example, the migration of Germans from Poland, Russia, and the former Soviet Union to Germany; of Hungarians from Romania, Yugoslavia, Ukraine, and Slovakia to Hungary; of Russians from various Soviet successor states to Russia; and of Jews from the former Soviet Union to Israel (Brubaker, 1998; Joppke, forthcoming).[9]

Of course, patterns of migration are a great deal more complicated than this. "Western Europe" and "Eastern Europe" are not single places but differentiated series of places, differently positioned – for economic, political, and geographic reasons – with respect to migration flows. Consider just one example. In the more prosperous east-central European countries – especially Poland,[10] the Czech Republic,[11] Hungary,[12] and Slovenia – emigration pressures are weaker, while labour migration from points further east, and requests for political asylum from Asian and African as well as eastern European countries, have emerged as significant issues. In this respect, these countries may be following in the path of Spain, Portugal, Italy, and Greece, which made the transition from emigration to immigration countries during the last quarter-century.

More than a decade after the collapse of the Soviet Union, it is worth keeping in mind the migration that has *not* occurred from – and within – eastern Europe. In 1990, experts warned of an "exodus," a "human deluge,"[13] an "invasion" of "hungry hordes," a "mass migration on a scale unseen since World War II,"[14] a "flood of desperate people," amounting to a modern-day *Völkerwanderung*, akin, in the words of Peter Jankowitsch, chair of the Foreign Relations Committee of the Austrian parliament, to that in which "the Germanic people[s] moved west and destroyed the Roman Empire." "How many Poles will stay in Poland?" Jankowitsch asked rhetorically. "How many Romanians will stay in Romania?"[15] Plenty, it turned out. Sizeable though westward migration has undoubtedly been in the experience and – even more so – in the social imagination of ordinary citizens of eastern Europe, its magnitude, for western countries, has remained modest. In the "frontline" states of Germany and Austria, such migration has been much more significant, but even there its rhythms have been measured, not cataclysmic.

Around the same time, haunted by the Yugoslav refugee crisis, analysts envisioned convulsive episodes of forced or politically induced migration on a much vaster scale, pointing with special concern, in this context too, to the 25 million Russians outside Russia. Yet while many Russians have left Central Asia and Kazakhstan, the migration has been comparatively orderly, and the large majority of Kazakhstani Russians have chosen so far to remain in Kazakhstan.

STATEHOOD

My final cluster of themes concerns the state. The restructuring of the state has been a major issue throughout Europe. But in this domain, too, questions have been posed in very different ways in different parts of Europe.

The most striking difference would seem to be this: while the reorganization of political space in western Europe has pointed – at least in anticipation – *beyond* the nation-state, the spectacular post–Cold War reconfiguration of central and eastern Europe has involved a move *back to* the nation-state. Apart from unified Germany, of the twenty-two successor states to the multinational Soviet Union and Yugoslavia and binational Czechoslovakia, all but three expressly understand themselves as nation-states – i.e., as the states of and for the particular nations whose names they bear (and the three exceptions – the Russian Federation, rump Yugoslavia, and Bosnia-Herzegovina – are themselves closely linked to particular nations). If western Europe is entering a post-national age, the political context for much of eastern Europe is *post-multinational*. Just as the great Habsburg, Romanov, and Ottoman empires crumbled at the beginning of the "short 20th-century," leaving an array of nationally defined successor states, so too, at the close of the century, multinational states have again fragmented into sets of *soi-disant* nation-states.

Yet this view requires qualification, and not only because the massive eastern enlargement of the EU that will officially occur on 1 May 2004 blurs the west–east distinction. More fundamentally, the EU does not represent a linear or unambiguous move "beyond the nation-state" to a supranational form of political authority. As Milward (1992) argues, the initially limited moves towards supranational authority worked – and were intended – to restore and strengthen the authority of the nation-state. What has been occurring is a complex unbundling and redistribution – upwards, downwards, and in various oblique directions – of previously tightly bundled powers and competencies. The resultant "multi-level" or even "neo-medieval" polity does not look much like a supranational super-state: an oft-quoted remark describes the EU as an "economic giant, a political dwarf, and a military worm."[16] Events of the last decade, notwithstanding the Treaty of Maastricht and the announced formation of a common security and defence policy, have done little to undermine that view.[17]

Although there is no clear move beyond the nation-state, the classical model of unitary, centralized, sovereign statehood, in which all authority derives from a single central point, no longer describes political reality. Authority has been reconfigured, and competencies have been unbundled and redistributed – not only to the EU (itself a set of institutions and authorities, not a single entity), but also to other international organizations and to sub-national polities and jurisdictions. This raises fundamental questions about the changing nature of statehood and political authority.

Granted that the EU is not very state-like at present, how might it become more state-like in the future? What attributes historically associated with statehood might it come to acquire? What does its development imply about the statehood – or, following J.P. Nettl (1968), the "stateness" – of existing states? Are they becoming less state-like as they give up conventional sovereign powers, such as control over borders and over monetary and fiscal policy?

Once we revise our understanding of statehood to allow for the unbundling and sharing of powers and competencies previously monopolized by a single sovereign centre of authority, then questions of stateness also arise for lower-level polities emerging within federalizing or otherwise decentralizing states. To what extent do more or less autonomous but non-sovereign polities such as Catalonia, Flanders, and Scotland take on attributes of stateness as they gain new and often quite considerable powers and competencies,[18] even while remaining parts of larger, more embracing states? This is a familiar issue in the literature on federalism, but that literature has been quite separate from the historical and political sociological literature on the development of the modern state. The latter has defined the modern state as centralized and sovereign – as monopolizing the means of coercion within a particular territory, in Weber's classic formulation – and has cast the story of its development in teleological form, involving the progressive appropriation of previously dispersed powers by a single centre. This perspective has marginalized the experience of federal states. Their very existence is something of an anomaly; they are by definition not very state-like.

The complex unbundling and redistribution of powers and competencies, in short, are forcing a fundamental rethinking of the very notion of "the state." The notion may prove too heavily encumbered by the political theory of sovereignty and its monist, unitarist connotations to be of much analytical use in conceptualizing the complex, multi-level polity that is emerging.

In eastern Europe, questions of statehood and stateness are posed in quite different terms. There is, in the first place, the sheer proliferation of new states in the region. Almost all of them, as noted above, have defined and constituted themselves as sovereign nation-states, drawing on highly institutionalized – if outdated – rhetorics and models of sovereignty and nationhood (Meyer, 1987). These institutionalized "performances" of sovereign nation-statehood do not represent an unambiguous move "back to the nation-state." Almost all the new states are involved, in one way or another, in processes of regional integration, notably as members or candidate members of the North Atlantic Treaty Organization and/or the EU on the one hand and the Commonwealth of Independent States on the other. Yet the invocations of sovereignty and nationhood are not mere rhetoric. There is a real tension between the model of sovereign nation-statehood and that of supranational integration; the latter does not automatically trump the former. The model of sovereign nation-statehood remains normatively more robust in eastern than in western Europe and has its attractions not only for newly constituted states but also for those newly freed from the Soviet economic and security embrace. Although referenda have shown overwhelming support for EU membership in most candidate states, the outcome remains in doubt, as of this writing, in Estonia, where a June 2003 poll showed voters evenly divided. As the leader of the Estonian anti-EU movement put it, to join the EU would be to move "from one union to another" (Smith, 2001).

Second, there are the special "stateness" problems – in Linz and Stepan's sense, not Nettl's – posed by politicized ethnicity in eastern Europe. As I indicated above, the ethnically framed challenges – or perceived challenges[19] – to the territorial integrity and boundaries of existing states are particularly delicate in eastern Europe, because they often involve cross-border links connecting ethnonational claimants within particular states and a patron state abroad that represents the same ethnocultural nationality.

Third, and most important, although the initially prevailing understanding of post-communist "transition" posited the need to liberate economy and society from the grip of an overly strong state, more recent analyses have made almost the opposite argument.[20] The post–Cold War moment of triumphant anti-statism has passed. As Stephen Holmes and others have argued with respect to Russia – although the point has broader relevance for the region – it is not the strength of the state, but its weakness, that threatens the basic rights and well-being of citizens.[21] The "withering away of the state" in Russia and elsewhere in the 1990s destroyed the capacity to provide the most elementary public goods and services. Neoliberals increasingly concede what palaeoliberals knew all along: a strong, even powerful state is a pre-condition for everything that they hold dear, including the orderly workings of markets, the protection of citizens against violence, and the enforcement of human rights. Hence the calls to strengthen and build up the state, to liberate what are in theory the distinctively public powers of the state from the clutches of those who have expropriated and in effect privatized them.

The force of renewed calls for a "strong" or "powerful" state depends of course on how we understand these terms. Here Michael Mann's (1993, 59–60) distinction between "despotic" and "infrastructural" power is helpful, the former denoting arbitrary power *over* civil society, the latter the power of state institutions to co-ordinate and regulate social life by penetrating and working *through* civil society. Despotically "strong" states may be infrastructurally "weak," and vice versa. What is urgently needed in much of eastern Europe – and throughout the Third World – is an infrastructurally strong state, one that can keep the peace, punish force and fraud, enforce contracts, collect taxes, provide basic services, protect public health, implement legislation, and prevent wholesale plundering by criminal and quasi-criminal networks.

State-building, then, is still very much on the agenda in eastern Europe. While western and parts of east-central Europe move towards the unbundling and redistribution of previously concentrated powers, in much of eastern Europe we see (or at least hear about the need for) moves in the opposite direction, towards the rebundling and reconcentration of previously dispersed – and in considerable part privately appropriated – powers.[22] Whether such changes will succeed – whether an effective, infrastructurally strong state can be built – is by no means certain. Over the long sweep of European history in the last millennium, sustained military competition eventually led to the weeding out of the most blatant forms of patrimonial administration.[23] Today, however, pressures to reform conspicuously corrupt, grossly inefficient state administrations are much weaker. States (and other actors) continue to make war, but war no longer makes states the way it used to.[24] The world-wide club of states includes a large and perhaps increasing number of "quasi-states" (Jackson, 1990) – organizations that are officially recognized and certified internationally as "states" yet fail to do the most elementary things that states are supposed to do, such as maintaining order throughout a given territory. Today, thanks to the reification and sacralization of existing state borders in prevailing international discourse and practice,[25] such quasi-states can continue to exist, irrespective of their abysmal performance, with little threat that they will go out of business. Eastern Europe may not harbour the worst specimens of this lamentable genre, and of course there are great differences within the region. In much of the region, however, the making of the modern state, far from being a completed chapter of history, is a matter of great contemporary urgency.

NOTES

1 As the rich comparative literature on ethnicity makes clear (see, for example, Akzin, 1966; Schermerhorn, 1970; Francis, 1976; Rothschild, 1981; van den Berghe, 1981; and Horowitz, 1985), these are not the only ways in which ethnic heterogeneity can be socially organized and politically expressed. But this distinction does capture a key dimension of variation in the organization and expression of ethnicity in Europe. A broadly similar distinction has been introduced into political theory – especially into discussions of multiculturalism – by Kymlicka, 1995. For an attempt to bring Western political theory to bear on ethnicity in eastern Europe, see Kymlicka, 2001.

2 Even when ethnic groups are concentrated in immigrant neighbourhoods or enclaves, the nature and consequences of such territorial concentration are quite different for immigrant ethnicity and for territorial nationality.

3 Some ethnopolitical or ethnoreligious claims can threaten the state even without involving claims to territorial nationhood – for example, radical Islamist claims.

4 And just as Gypsies straddle conceptual boundaries, they cross state borders as well. Some of the ugliest episodes of immigration control in the 1990s were driven by efforts to control their unwanted movement.

5 A similar point could be made about western Europe. Substantial literatures address the rise of xenophobic, radical-right, or national-populist parties (for overviews, see Betz, 1994; Betz and Immerfall, 1998) and of anti-immigrant violence (Björgo and Witte, 1993). Again, without minimizing the significance of the new right parties, or still less that of the appalling attacks on asylum seekers and other foreigners in Germany and elsewhere, one should not overestimate the strength of xenophobic nationalism in western Europe.

6 From a large literature, see Barth, 1969; Hobsbawm and Ranger, 1983; Anderson, 1991; and Jenkins, 1997.

7 For an elaboration of this argument, see Brubaker, 2002.

8 There has been a good deal of concern with intra-EU migration, but mainly in terms of how it articulates with immigration from outside the region, given the need – since abolition of internal frontiers within the Schengen zone – for EU states to harmonize external admissions policies.

9 Even as it involves a reduction in ethnic heterogeneity in the countries of origin, such migrations of ethnic unmixing generate new forms of ethnic or quasi-ethnic heterogeneity in the putative national homelands: ethnic Hungarians from Romania are treated as "Romanians" in Hungary, while Germans and Jews from the former Soviet Union are treated as "Russians" in Germany and Israel. On the ambiguous and contested national identity of ethnic Hungarian migrants to Hungary, see Fox, 2003.

10 www.drc.dk/dk/publikationer/boegerogpjec/boeger/safe3rd/poland.html

11 popin.natur.cuni.cz/html/policy/migration.html

12 These three countries (and Slovenia) are "buffers" or "transit" countries between eastern and western Europe.

13 *Independent*, 29 Nov. 1990.

14 *Los Angeles Times*, 3 Dec. 1990.

15 *Boston Globe*, 1 Nov. 1990.

16 Mark Eyskens, former Belgian foreign minister, quoted in William Drozdiak, "Once Again, Europe Follows American Lead," *Washington Post*, 26 March 1999.

17 Leading European intellectuals critical of the war in Iraq have called for a "core Europe" capable of serving as a counterweight to American hegemony (Derrida and Habermas, 2003), but as Paul Kennedy (2003) pointed out in reply, there are substantial political and institutional obstacles to this occurring.

18 In certain respects these powers and competencies may be more substantial, and more state-like, than those of the EU.

19 What constitutes a challenge to the territorial integrity of a state is open to dispute. In Romania, for example, the demands made by the ethnic Hungarian party for autonomy are perceived (or at least publicly represented) by much of the Romanian political elite as a threat to the territorial integrity of the state, even though Hungarian minority politicians insist that, while they are challenging the internal structure of the Romanian state (and its constitutional definition as a unitary nation-state), they pose no threat to its territorial integrity.

20 See Stark and Bruszt, 1998, chap. 4, for an analysis and critique of this swing in the intellecutal pendulum.

21 Holmes, 1997, was writing before Putin's accession to the presidency in 2000. Putin has sought to strengthen and recentralize the state, notably by recovering powers previously appropriated by regions (Orttung, 2001).

22 Note that powers may be dispersed in two senses: through the formally acknowledged decentralization of power (as in the various agreements that ethnofederal polities within Russia made with Moscow during the 1990s); and through the de facto appropriation by regional or local officials (or even by persons with no official standing, such as some warlords and criminal bosses) of powers formally held by the central state. On the concept of appropriation, Weber's discussion of patrimonial authority remains pertinent and richly suggestive (1968, 231ff).

23 For the most recent and comprehensive treatment of this theme, see Ertman, 1997.

24 Much warfare in the ex-Second and Third Worlds is carried out not by states, but by an array of quasi- and non-state forces (Fairbanks, 1995). Another, more fundamental reason, as Tilly himself admits, is that, with the gradual "filling-in of the state system," states have increasingly been made – literally created, and allowed to exist, regardless of their infrastructural strength – chiefly by other states (Tilly, 1975a, 636; 1975b, 46).

25 Much has been made, in the last decade, about the weakening of this tendency; but this confuses the weakening of the model of sovereignty (which has indeed occurred) with the desacralization and de-reification of state borders, which has not. Borders are normatively more permeable, but they remain, in principle, "inviolable," in the sense of unalterable. Thus in Kosovo, the United States and NATO could claim to be respecting the borders of Yugoslavia even when they challenged Yugoslav sovereignty within those borders. Note that the new states that did emerge from the Soviet Union, Yugoslavia, and Czechoslovakia already existed as states within formally federal states and already possessed their own borders, territories, and even (in principle) the right to secede from the wider federal state.

REFERENCES

Akzin, Benjamin (1966) *States and Nations*. Garden City, NY: Doubleday.

Anderson, Benedict (1991) *Imagined Communities: Reflections on the Origin and Spread of Nationalism*. Rev. ed. London: Verso

Barth, Fredrik, ed. (1969) *Ethnic Groups and Boundaries: The Social Organization of Cultural Difference*. Boston: Little, Brown and Company.

Betz, Hans-Georg (1994) *Radical Right-Wing Populism in Western Europe*. New York: St. Martin's Press.

Betz, Hans-Georg, and Stefan Immerfall, eds. (1998) *The New Politics of the Right: Neo-populist Parties and Movements in Established Democracies*. New York: St Martin's Press.

Björgo, Tore, and Rob Witte, eds. (1993) *Racist Violence in Europe*. New York: St Martin's Press.

Braun, Aurel (2000) "All Quiet on the Russian Front? Russia, Its Neighbors, and the Russian Diaspora," in Michael Mandelbaum, ed., *The New European Diasporas: National Minorities and Conflict in Eastern Europe*. New York: Council on Foreign Relations Press, 81–158.

Brown, A. (2001) "Vladimir Putin and the Reaffirmation of Central State Power," *Post-Soviet Affairs* 17, no. 1, 45–55.

Brubaker, Rogers (1995) "Aftermaths of Empire and the Unmixing of Peoples: Historical and Comparative Perspectives," *Ethnic and Racial Studies* 18, no. 2, 189–218.

– (1996) *Nationalism Reframed: Nationhood and the National Question in the New Europe*. New York: Cambridge University Press.

– (1998) "Migrations of Ethnic Unmixing in the 'New Europe,' " *International Migration Review* 32, no. 4, 1047–65.

– (2002) "Ethnicity without Groups," *Archives européennes de sociologie* 43, no. 2, 163–89.

Derrida, Jacques, and Jürgen Habermas (2003) "Nach dem Krieg: Die Wiedergeburt Europas," Frankfurter Allgemeine Zeitung, 31 May.

Ertman, Thomas (1997) *Birth of the Leviathan: Building States and Regimes in Medieval and Early Modern Europe*. Cambridge: Cambridge University Press.

Fairbanks, Charles H. Jr. (1995) "The Postcommunist Wars," *Journal of Democracy* 6 no. 4, 18–34.

Fox, Jon (2003) "National Identities on the Move: Transylvanian Hungarian Labour Migrants in Hungary," *Journal of Ethnic and Migration Studies* 29, no. 2.

Francis, E.K. (1976) *Interethnic Relations*. New York: Elsevier.

Hobsbawm, Eric J., and Terence Ranger, eds (1993) *The Invention of Tradition*. Cambridge: Cambridge University Press.

Holmes, Stephen (1997) "What Russia Teaches Us Now: How Weak States Threaten Freedom." *American Prospect* 33, 30–9.

Horowitz, Donald L. (1985) *Ethnic Groups in Conflict*. Berkeley: University of California Press.

Jackson, Robert H. (1990) *Quasi-States: Sovereignty, International Relations and the Third World*. New York: Cambridge University Press.

Jenkins, Richard (1997) *Rethinking Ethnicity: Arguments and Explorations*. London: Sage.

Joppke, Christian (forthcoming) *Ethnic Migration in the Liberal State*.

Kennedy, Paul (2003) "Europe's Old Laggards Will Never Balance US Power," *Guardian*, 24 June. www.guardian.co.uk/eu/story/0,7369,983804,00.html

Kymlicka, Will (1995) *Multicultural Citizenship: A Liberal Theory of Minority Rights*. Oxford: Oxford University Press.

Kymlicka, Will, and Magda Opalski (2001) *Can Liberal Pluralism Be Exported? Western Political Theory and Ethnic Relations in Eastern Europe*. Oxford: Oxford University Press.

Laitin, David (1998) *Identity in Formation*. Ithaca, NY: Cornell University Press.

Linz, Juan J., and Alfred Stepan (1996) *Problems of Democratic Transition and Consolidation: Southern Europe, South America, and Post-Communist Europe*. Baltimore: Johns Hopkins University Press.

Mann, Michael (1993) *The Sources of Social Power: The Rise of Classes and Nation-States, 1760–1914*. Cambridge: Cambridge University Press.

– (forthcoming) *The Dark Side of Democracy: Explaining Ethnic Cleansing*.

McFaul, M. (2000) "Putin in Power," *Current History* 99, no. 639, 307–14.

Melvin, Neil J. (1998) "The Russians: Diaspora and the End of Empire," in Charles King and Neil J. Melvin, eds., *Nations Abroad: Diaspora Politics and International Relation in the Former Soviet Union*. Boulder, Col.: Westview Press, 27–57.

Meyer, John W. (1987) "The World Polity and the Authority of the Nation-State," in George M. Thomas, John W. Meyer, and Francisco O. Ramirez, eds., *Institutional Structure: Constituting State, Society, and the Individual*. Newbury Park: Sage, 41–70.

Milward, Alan S. (1992) *The European Rescue of the Nation-State*. Berkeley: University of California Press.

Naimark, Norman M. (2001) *Fires of Hatred: Ethnic Cleansing in Twentieth-Century Europe*. Cambridge, Mass.: Harvard University Press.

Nairn, Tom (1995) "Breakwaters of 2000: From Ethnic to Civic Nationalism," *New Left Review* 214, 91–103.

Nettl, J.P. (1968) "The State As a Conceptual Variable," *World Politics* 20, no. 4, 559–92.

Orttung, Robert (2001) "Putin's Federal Reform Package: A Recipe for Unchecked Kremlin Power," *Demokratizatsiya* 9, no. 3, 341–9.

Reddaway, P. (2000) "Will Putin Be Able to Consolidate Power?" *Post-Soviet Affairs* 17, no. 1, 23–44.

Rothschild, Joseph (1981) *Ethnopolitics: A Conceptual Framework*. New York: Columbia University Press.

Schermerhorn, R.A. (1970) *Comparative Ethnic Relations: A Framework for Theory and Research*. New York: Random House.

Smith, Benjamin (2001) "Tallinn Dispatch: Western Union (Growing Opposition to Membership in the European Union in Estonia)," *New Republic*, 16.

Stark, David, and László Bruszt (1998) *Postsocialist Pathways: Transforming Politics and Property in East Central Europe*. Cambridge: Cambridge University Press.

Thompson, E.P. (1963) *The Making of the English Working Class*. New York: Vintage.

Tilly, Charles (1975a) "Western State-Making and Theories of Political Transformation," in Charles Tilly, ed., *The Formation of National States in Western Europe*. Princeton, NJ: Princeton University Press, 601–38.

– (1975b) "Reflections on the History of European State-Making," in Charles Tilly, ed., *The Formation of National States in Western Europe*. Princeton, NJ: Princeton University Press, 3–83.

van den Berghe, Pierre L. (1981) *The Ethnic Phenomenon*. New York: Elsevier.

Vermeersch, Peter (2003) "Ethnic Minority Identity and Movement Politics: The Case of the Roma in the Czech Republic and Slovakia," *Ethnic and Racial Studies* 26, no. 5, 580–602.

Weber, Max (1978) *Economy and Society: An Outline of Interpretive Sociology*. Ed. Guenther Roth and Claus Wittich. First pub. 1922. Berkeley: University of California Press.

Wrong, Dennis (1961) "The Oversocialized Conception of Man in Modern Society," *American Sociological Review* 23, no. 2, 183–93.

BENEDICT ANDERSON

The Future of Indonesia

As late as the beginning of 1997, what is often comically called "international opinion" generally viewed Indonesia as a "success story," making sustained, even spectacular economic strides under the durable dictatorship of General Suharto. Today, almost four years later, that same international opinion, without missing a step, has largely decided that Indonesia is virtually ungovernable and on the edge of catastrophe. The spectres haunting this opinion are economic collapse, ethnic and religious violence, a totally corrupt judiciary and bureaucratic apparatus, serious separatist movements, an incompetent political class, and a brutalized and internally divided military. In Indonesia itself, the initial euphoria unleashed by the fall of the ageing tyrant in May 1998 and by the holding of remarkably free, fair, and unviolent elections in the summer of 1999, has largely disappeared, and the number of middle-class and intellectual doomsday-prophets has been steadily increasing. For them – rightly, if mostly for the wrong reasons – the central question is the future of their (even the) postcolonial nation-state in the new century. We consider this question by first looking at the more sophisticated arguments of the best-intentioned pessimistic patriots. Then we examine the reasons for optimism. The final section outlines possible parallels with Canada.

THE PESSIMISTS' ARGUMENTS

Crisis of the State

The pessimists argue that globalizing forces have undermined, and will continue to undermine, the authority and integrity of the old-fashioned nation-state. Proponents claim that for decades the Suharto regime was kept afloat by vast external injections of capital – the huge annual subventions of the Inter-Governmental Group for Indonesia (IGGI) since the late 1960s, the interventions of the World Bank, which helped turn Indonesia's technocrats into some of its most notorious kleptocrats; the caprices of the world financial markets, and investments by transnational companies to exploit the country's quite finite natural resources in timber, minerals, petroleum, and natural gas. A vast amount of this capital was squandered and stolen with the complicity of external capital. This process profoundly corrupted the Indonesian state itself, which increasingly treated the country's natural and financial resources in an entirely predatory ("foreign") manner. A recent court case nicely illustrates this process. At the time of the final crisis in East Timor, the head of military intelligence, who was bankrolling the atrocious pro-Indonesian militias there, ran out of money and arranged for a substantial counterfeiting operation. To ensure the quality and credibility of the forged currency – for his own "boys"! – he required the help of the governor of the Bank of Indonesia, who for substantial sums sold him as-yet-unused serial banknote numbers.

Second, the pessimists argue that with the collapse of the Cold War's bipolar world, the Indonesian state faces increasing difficulties in resisting the arrogant and opportunistic political interventions of an "international community," which is essentially a mask for American and western European interests. They often cite East Timor to make this case. They note that the initial brazen invasion by Suharto, on Pearl Harbor Day 1975, had the clear support of U.S. President Gerald Ford and U.S. Secretary of State Henry Kissinger, who were in Jakarta the day before the invasion began, and that Presidents Jimmy Carter and Ronald Reagan later provided covert military assistance to the occupiers. Daniel Moynihan, U.S. ambassador to the United Nations (UN) at the time of the invasion, later boasted publicly of his success in thwarting any effective UN action on behalf of the Timorese. Britain and France were major suppliers of Suharto's military all along, at a time when Indonesia faced no serious external threats. Yet in 1999, these powers turned around and, in the name of human rights and self-determination, forced the Indonesian government to accept a UN-controlled referendum on independence in East Timor. East Timor is now the first place in the world where the UN actually exercises, on its own and in its own name, temporary sovereignty. The same UN has demanded that key officers involved in the post-referendum atrocities be put on trial in Indonesia or, failing that, by an international tribunal.

Third, education and communications are a matter of serious national concern. In the 1950s and 1960s Indonesians largely educated themselves and took real pride in their educational institutions. But in the 1970s and 1980s, the Suharto regime sent many young bureaucrats overseas for advanced degrees, and elite and middle-class families had money to send their children to the West for high school and college. This situation left "national education" for second-class citizens; unsurprisingly, its quality then steeply deteriorated. Furthermore, the regime's abiding fear of student opposition required near-totalitarian political control of campuses and high schools. Many of the products of foreign education who did return were contemptuous of their fellow-countrymen and eager to be co-opted by foreign capital and other institutions. Transnational communications and entertainment conglomerates have destroyed the national film industry and "satellitized" national television. The rise of electronic communications has largely put an end to the state's traditional role as a central site for the dissemination of political and other information. This is why the Ministry of Information has effectively been disbanded.

Fourth and finally, there is the disastrous condition of the Indonesian military. It was once high in the national esteem. Forged as a guerrilla force in the mid-1940s, it fought to an effective standstill the quarter-million Dutch troops sent to reimpose colonial rule after the Japanese occupation. In the 1950s Indonesians were proud to have fought for four bitter years, without any foreign support, to achieve independence. Their military was still close to the population and rarely guilty of atrocities. But by the late 1950s the army was sending more and more young officers abroad for training, mostly in the United States. They later became key personnel for the construction of the Suharto dictatorship (although Suharto himself never trained overseas). They increasingly applied American-style counter-insurgency doctrines and methods to regional and other dissidence. The elite Red Berets, responsible for most of the worst atrocities committed by the military in the last thirty years – including leadership of the vast massacres of the left in 1965–66 – modelled themselves on the U.S. Green Berets and were the pride and joy of their American trainers.

Crisis of the Nation

Pessimism about globalization from "above" the nation-state is matched by gloom about the growth of powerful forces "below." This anxiety is not entirely new but is now changing its character. The 1950s saw the integrity of the new nation threatened by a small separatist rebellion in the Protestant South Moluccas, which certainly had the covert support of angry departing Dutch military personnel, and by the PRRI-Permesta regional (but not at all separatist) rebellion in West and North Sumatra and in North Sulawesi, supported extensively by the U.S. Central Intelligence Agency (CIA), as well as by Generalissimo Chiang Kai-shek's Taiwan and by Ramon Magsaysay and Carlos Garcia's Philippines.

But today, in its condition of grave weakness, it faces a well-armed Acehnese Independence Movement; increasingly bold, if mostly peaceful, demands for the independence of West Papua; and bloody religious conflict in the Moluccas. Patriotic pessimists know that these crises are the direct product of brutal misrule by Suharto, but whether and how to resolve them are newly complicated.

Aceh is a perfect case in point. The Acehnese were finally incorporated into the Netherlands Indies only in the decade after 1900, following an exceptionally savage 25-year war. Aceh was the only province that the Dutch, returning after the Japanese occupation, never attempted to resubdue. The Acehnese made major military and financial sacrifices for and contributions to the armed struggle for independence. In the 1950s, a low-intensity rebellion was resolved by negotiations; but it was not separatist in nature – it was aimed against the composition and certain policies of the government in power in Jakarta – and no one doubted the national commitment of the people. As late as the early 1980s, the province was peaceful and orderly and under civilian rule. This calm was destroyed with the discovery and exploitation of vast fields of natural gas, developed mainly by American corporations. Around these fields an enclave economy grew up that largely excluded Acehnese, and its profits went almost entirely into greedy hands in Jakarta. A non-Acehnese military ruthlessly suppressed protests and new militants turned to Malaysia for asylum and covert sympathy and to Libya for arms and military training. By the 1990s, something un-known before – a Movement for Acehnese Independence – had substan-tial support at home and increasing sympathy overseas.

The story of West Papua is no less striking, if very different. This re-mote, vast, underpopulated region was, like Aceh, among the last addi-tions to the Dutch colonial empire. When transferring sovereignty to the Republic of Indonesia in 1949, the Dutch refused to include West Papua, imagining it as a useful place to move the colony's Dutch-loyal Eurasians and to maintain an imperial presence in the Far East. In doing so, they had the backing of the powerful American "mediator," diplo-mat Merle Cochran. After a decade of increasing acrimony between Jakarta and The Hague, marked by the nationalization of all Dutch en-terprises in 1957 and military threats by President Sukarno, the Ameri-cans again intervened, this time on Indonesia's side. The territory was turned over first to a temporary UN authority and then, despite the ob-jections of the local people, to Indonesia.

But things did not start too badly. Elderly pro-independence Papuans still speak with affection of the dedicated young teachers who arrived in 1963–64 from Java and Sumatra to spread literacy in the region's far-flung, scattered villages. Unluckily, however, Sukarno fell from power in the winter of 1965–66 and was replaced by Suharto. For the new re-gime, eager for Western support and investment, Papua was simply a vast resource of copper ready to be exploited. The U.S. mining con-glomerate Freeport made its initial investment in 1967 and remains the major source of profit in the province. The Organisasi Papua Merdeka (OPM) – a small insurgency in the name of Papuan independence – be-gan in the late 1960s in the face of military repression, assassinations, and torture, and it has continued desultorily ever since. The Indonesian rulers were not only keen to protect Freeport and to gain financially from it; they also worried about the presence next door of the new state of Papua–Niugini and did their best to intimidate it into avoiding any overt displays of sympathy for the OPM.

For 30 years, for Papuan separatists, Freeport was the prime symbol of the collusion of transnational capital with Jakarta in military oppres-sion and the theft of Papuan national resources. These days, however, the Papuan Independence Movement is on the point of opening a sub-stantial office attached to the UN Headquarters in New York. Who is paying for this mission? None other than Freeport. One can scarcely doubt that Freeport's change of "heart" has caused anger and anxiety among nationalists in Indonesia. But it seems that they can do nothing.

Freeport is too powerful in the United States (Henry Kissinger is among its highly paid lobbyists) to confront.

In the Moluccas, there is no separatist movement as yet, and probably none will emerge. But the scale of quasi-religious communal violence is terrifying and without precedent in Indonesia's history. (The anti-communist massacres of 1965–66 were far more extensive and even more brutal, but they were organized by the military high command.) How do patriotic pessimists explain it? Its origins, they say, lie in the dictatorship's early decisions to require all Indonesians to be affiliated with one of the officially recognized religions and to suppress almost all forms of autonomous social and political life. Only religious institutions managed to retain a certain independence. Thus all kinds of social and economic interests came to be channelled into them, if not through the state's corrupt electoral machine, known as Golkar. In this way every sort of social conflict came to be expressed through religious organizations and their affiliates – hence the hostility between Muslims and Christians became increasingly open and widespread. Yet the election of the summer of 1999 produced in the Moluccas a defeat of Golkar in favour of Megawati Sukarnoputri's nationalist party, which strikingly drew support from both Muslims and Christians. The losers struck back by manipulating communal anxieties on both sides.

The onset of the violence was precipitated, however, by another malign residue of the old regime – the practice of employing gangsters for political intimidation, economic extortion, and protection of rackets, especially gambling, prostitution, and drugs. A group of well-established Protestant Moluccan gangsters in Jakarta was forcibly extruded by Muslim militants from its control of certain gambling halls and then sought refuge and revenge by returning to the Moluccas and starting communal war through local massacres. Inevitably there came a reaction from Muslim militants as well as Muslim gangsters, in a process that increasingly involved Christians and Muslims from outside the Moluccas. Efforts by the military and police to contain the violence proved ineffective, as members of their forces were drawn by religious sympathies to one side or the other, wrecking the ordinary chain of command. For the pessimists, therefore, the uncontrolled spread of communal violence shows the current weakness of national solidarity as well as of the national state in the face of political identifications, locally held but attached to the supranational aspirations and affiliations of Islam and Christianity.

In conclusion, the pessimistic nationalists see nothing good emerging from the crisis of Indonesian nationalism and the Indonesian state. If religious antagonisms continue to increase, uncontained and ruinous violence will spread. Religious affiliation is often correlated, especially outside Java, with ethnicity. In the Moluccas so far the violence has taken place within a single ethnic group, but the group is very unusual in its even division between Muslims and Christians. The possibility of ethnic conflict fusing with religious antagonism is quite real. Furthermore, most members of the country's small but economically powerful Chinese minority are at least nominally Christian, and the country has an 80-year-old tradition of anti-Chinese violence. Parcellization of the country – along Yugoslav lines, so to speak – offers no salvation. The pessimists see local gangsters taking over from national-level gangsters, local warlords succeeding national-level warlords; and the parcellized localities being even more subject to the destructive forces of globalization than Indonesia itself now is.

THE OPTIMISTS' ARGUMENTS

The pessimists obviously have plenty going for them, but by no means everything. The Indonesian nationalist project still possesses some powerful and unexhausted assets. First, the country has a long and honourable nationalist tradition stretching back almost a century, and all the major ethnic and religious groups have played a historic role. It is striking that since the fall of Suharto, and despite the economic crisis, there has been a large-scale republication of banned or out-of-print books dealing with the national independence struggle, its various heroes, and its variegated participants.

Second, the country lacks any overriding ethnic or religious majority. The Javanese, who form the largest ethnic group, still amount to substantially less than half the population, and they are deeply divided among themselves. All governments from 1949 onward have been based on ethnic coalitions. This feature makes unlikely the extreme ethnic tension visible in bi-ethnic states such as Sri Lanka and Sudan. Formally speaking, Muslims represent 90 per cent of the population, but they range from militant fundamentalists to "statistical Muslims" whose beliefs are built on Hindu–Buddhist and animist foundations. In neither of Indonesia's two free elections, held in 1955 and 1999, did Muslim parties, even aggregated together, win a majority of the vote.

Third, the country has, for reasons too complex to detail here, an un-equivocally accepted national language – *bahasa Indonesia* – which be-longs to no one ethno-linguistic group. Its power and appeal are particularly notable in peripheral regions. In Papua, the name of the in-dependence movement, Organisasi Papua Merdeka (OPM), is in the In-donesian language, and its militants communicate among themselves in that language. Even in East Timor, the most widely understood lan-guage today is Indonesian.

Fourth, there is a curious residue of the colonial past that plays its own role. The Dutch have long ceased to play any major role in Indone-sian life, but they have left behind a certain sense of uniqueness. Many former British, Portuguese, Spanish, and French colonies understand themselves as affiliated culturally and linguistically with other former colonies of the imperial centres. Indonesia, in contrast, was the only sig-nificant colony of tiny Holland. This factor may help to explain the re-markably low level of emigration of Indonesians to Europe and to North America.

Fifth, the behaviour of Indonesia's voters in their only two free elec-tions (1955 and 1999) is remarkable. Though held almost 45 years apart, both showed that only "national" parties were successful, while regional or ethnic parties failed.

If these resources exist and can be effectively harnessed, what govern-mental transformations could mitigate the present deep crisis? I now look at four possible areas of profound change. First, *orderly civilianiza-tion and decentralization* have two interrelated dimensions. To start with – and this is already partly under way – the military will have to be with-drawn from regional political life, since hostility to army brutality and exploitation is the major source of popular anger. For the duration of the Suharto regime, the military's power rested not on its combat battalions, but on its territorial apparatus, which paralleled (and overrode) the civil-ian territorial bureaucracy right down to the village level. For his own reasons, Suharto devoted only a small share of the national budget to the military, leaving officers at every level to seek their own resources – mo-nopolies, extortion of local businesses, and rackets (marijuana, gam-bling, and so on). Withdrawal of the military from regional life is essential for any decentralization that does not lead to warlordism and petty gangsterism. This will require a major change in current national budgetary allocations – something under intensive current discussion.

In addition, decentralization will have to involve devolution of sub-stantial political and economic decision-making power to the provinces.

But the factoral endowments of the provinces differ very widely, and the central state's task is to create the necessary transfers to poor regions. This requires transparency, extensive national-level consultation, and the ending of the capital city's greedy absorption of most regionally generated revenues.

Second, the "separatist" provinces Aceh and Papua will have to be treated in a special way. "Autonomy" in itself is unlikely to work, for Aceh, at least on paper, has for 40 years been a "special province" with an unusual degree of self-governance. In practice, the central government, especially after the gas discoveries, ignored this autonomy. One idea being discussed in limited circles is "internationally guaranteed autonomy." What this would mean is still rather obscure, but it would probably involve a formal protocol between Indonesia and the UN, entitling Aceh and Papua to inform the UN when they felt their autonomy threatened. Many Indonesian nationalists would find such a protocol repugnant, an irreversible diminution of national sovereignty. But the seriousness of the crisis may change some minds, particularly if it is made clear that the guarantees mean only that the state must live up to its own commitments and if it becomes apparent that this is the only realistic alternative to endless violence. It would also probably obviate the present situation where a U.S. conglomerate funds Papua-at-the-UN.

Third, *inclusion and reconciliation* are under way. The present political system in Indonesia is profoundly lopsided in one central respect. All the main political parties are conservative, in a country with huge numbers of extremely poor people. The massacres of 1965–66 killed between 600,000 and 2 million Indonesians and destroyed the Indonesian Communist Party, then the largest in the world outside the Communist bloc and also the oldest in Asia (founded 1920). Afterwards, hundreds of thousands of people were imprisoned without trial for as long as 14 years and on their release lost normal political rights, were prohibited from taking jobs in the civil bureaucracy or in vital economic sectors, and were kept under intense, intimidating surveillance. The official doctrine of "dirty environment" imposed the same penalties on the wives, widows, children, grandchildren, and other close relatives of the prisoners.

In the post-Suharto era, representatives of this vast ostracized group have gradually been making themselves heard in the press and the mass media, but most of the officially imposed stigmata remain in effect. Many conservative military men and Islamic leaders have expressed a fear that the old Communist Party will revive if the controls and ostracism are lifted, but there is no chance of such a revival. "Normalization" would begin the growth of the democratic left-wing party that the country seriously needs. It would also bring democratization of political life, an organized voice for the have-nots, and a nationalist weapon against the ravages of neoliberalism. President Abdurrahman Wahid has proposed to parliament exactly such normalization, as well as an end to the dictatorship's ban on Marxism in any form. He has also suggested the creation of a South African–style Truth Commission to investigate all aspects of the bloody events of 1965–66. So far a conservative parliament has failed to accept these proposals, but at least they are in the public domain. It is particularly significant that Wahid has made these proposals, since members of his organization's youth group, the Barisan Ansor, played a major part in the massacres.

One other major aspect of normalization and reconciliation is now under discussion: the future of citizens of Chinese descent. Suharto's policies towards these people involved cultural and political repression. Culturally, the government forced most Chinese to change their names to something looking "Indonesian," prohibited all publications in Chinese characters, closed all schools teaching Chinese and Chinese classics, and outlawed all Chinese associations except one run by the state. Politically, there was systematic discrimination in employment. No Chinese ever became a cabinet minister under Suharto until his last month in office, when he finally appointed one of his most notorious cronies. Chinese were also effectively excluded from the officer corps, from the higher civil service, from key academic management positions, and so on, while young Chinese faced narrow quotas for entry into the state's universities. The effect of all this was to drive young Chinese into the one world open to them – business enterprise – thereby reinforcing the old resentful perception of them as merely "economic animals." In addition, Suharto, fearful of enriching "real Indonesians" outside his family who could aspire to political power, systematically favoured a small group of Chinese tycoons who developed a maze of monopolies, crooked banks, natural-resource exploitations, and rackets. The rise of these robber barons naturally only accentuated popular hatred of the Chinese and, in the end, of their patron, Suharto.

With the support of President Wahid, serious discussions are now going on to dismantle the legal and informal barricades to normal Chinese participation in Indonesian life. The president also showed the way by appointing the widely respected and famously nationalist Chinese economost Kwik Gian Gie as his first co-ordinating minister for economic affairs (although he soon kicked him out). Furthermore, newly published books are showing the cultural and political roles of Chinese citizens in the past and the present – making it clear that some of the most courageous and patriotic figures in modern Indonesian life have come from this minority.

In all these instances, there is room for cautious optimism. A successful nationalist project can not live by systematic exclusion of key elements of the population. Inclusion of survivors from the old left and of ordinary Chinese would "bring on stage" people who were the least corrupted by the Suharto regime and the most willing to seek further change.

Fourth, there is the dynamism of youths. Except in 1965–66, Indonesian students and high school youths have a long and honourable tradition of nationalist political participation. The nationalist movement had its origins in student organizations in the Netherlands Indies and in Holland; young people launched the Revolution of 1945–49 and carried much of the real fight for independence. In 1974, again more widely in 1978, and finally in 1998, students formed the vanguard of protest against Suharto. Students have been active in the struggle against militarism, in creating the possibility of free elections, and in helping peasants peacefully overthrow dozens of corrupt Suharto-beholden village chiefs. They are very aware of their "tradition" and proud of it. They are too young yet to be seriously entangled in their elders' webs of corruption and duplicity. They are a major source of optimism for the future: provided, of course, that they receive courageous and farsighted national leadership.

My own inclination is perhaps theirs too. We need. I think, some of Gramsci's famous political medicine: "Pessimism of the intellect, optimism of the will."

COMPARISONS WITH CANADA

One central purpose of the conference for which I prepared this essay was to bring to bear comparative data on the complex questions surrounding the future of Canada and of Quebec. At first, and even at second, sight, nothing seems more remote from the rich, generally peaceful, northern neighbours of the Americans than impoverished, violence-racked Indonesia on the other side of our little globe. Canada has no modern history of racist external domination, of foreign military occupation, of a prolonged and costly physical revolution for independence, or of a 30-year savage, greedy military dictatorship. Canada's modern politics has been grounded in a binary conflict between two large ethnolinguistic groups, both founded by settlers from northwestern Europe and both retaining substantial contacts with their countries of origin. Indonesia is a hugely populous nation-state containing dozens of significant ethnic groups, of which even the largest, the Javanese, remain a minority. It has never been ruled by one ethnic group, and there is no possibility there of anything like Anglo domination in Canada. All successful political parties have been "national" and multi-ethnic. Historically the deep lines of conflict have been not ethnic, but between left and right and between pious and less-pious Muslims along with assorted kinds of Christians.

It is on the cards, however, that both Canada and Indonesia as we know them will not exist 20 years from now, because of significant separatist movements within their internationally recognized borders. Do we find here at least a useful point of departure for comparison? I have my doubts on this score. First, the accidents of history blessed Indonesia with a genuinely popular national language, which "belongs" to no significant ethnic group, and this language completely dominates the mass media, the educational system, and everyday life in the big multi-ethnic cities. For the most part the other (and older) ethnic languages are used for informal speech, although several have distinguished classical literatures. Furthermore, this national language does not come from "somewhere else," especially from the former colonial master, and it is shared only with the small neighbouring country of Malaysia and the minuscule "oil-sheikdom" of Brunei. This is a condition in radical contrast to Canada, where both Anglos and Québécois speak and write their own languages in private and in public, where both languages have vast, separate cultural resources available to them in the anglophone and francophone worlds, and where there really is no consensual "national language."

Second, Indonesians have been through a lot together since the dawning of the nationalist movement about a century ago. People from all major groups participated in the struggle for independence between 1908 and 1942 (when Japanese armies destroyed Dutch rule) and in the great Revolution of 1945–49, which ended in international recognition of that independence. Even during the civil war of the late 1950s, which had territorial bases in Sumatra and northern Sulawesi, the object of the struggle was control of the capital and of a unified state. Until the late 1980s, there were no significant separatist movements except in West Papua (and even there the movement was not by any means dominant).

Unitary nationalism still runs very deep. In Canada – luckily or unluckily – it is hard to find much that looks like any of this: no strong,
unifying nationalist movement against Britain; substantial military contributions in the First World War, which many francophones resisted;
and no unifying neighbouring national enemy.

It is not at all difficult to imagine a reasonably prosperous and peaceful independent Quebec, but would there be a unified Anglo Canada if
the francophones departed? The Québécois have a modern society,
stable political and legal institutions, a variegated economic base, and,
at least in the last half-century, a democratic tradition. Such expectations are difficult to harbour for Aceh and for West Papua. Both regions
have been heavily militarized in the last 15 years. The major revenue
sources of both are controlled by gigantic foreign conglomerates. There
is little urban life, and next to no industry. The Papuans comprise many
often-rival ethnic groups speaking often-unrelated languages; Aceh contains a substantial minority of local Gayonese, who have little good to
expect from an independent Aceh and are therefore open to external
manipulation. Independence in both cases might result in rule by predatory warlords and racketeers in collusion with foreign capital. (The fate
of independent Papua–Niugini is not encouraging.) In both Aceh and
West Papua separatism seems to be a reaction to savage misrule, and a
better (much better) Indonesian government might bring both territories back into the national fold. Such possibilities are, paradoxically
enough, less plausible in the case of Canada, even though "misrule" has
been far less violent and exploitative.

But then there is the case of tiny East Timor, which, against all the
odds, after almost a quarter-century of ruthless Indonesian colonialism,
has actually beaten its giant oppressor and will soon join the UN. Here,
perhaps, we have something much more resonant with Quebec. In East
Timor, unlike anywhere else in Indonesia, the Indonesian language was
violently imposed, and the local lingua franca (Tetun) and Portuguese
were systematically suppressed. Under Suharto's rule it was the one region in which Indonesian was never accepted consensually as the national language. Nor, beneath the state rhetoric of bringing the
Timorese into the big Indonesian family from which the Portuguese had
separated them, was there ever a real sense of national brotherhood.
Indonesian officials frequently complained publicly and privately about
the "ingratitude" of the East Timorese – a typically colonial terminology that they would never have applied to the Madurese or Balinese.
(Citizens of a true nation-state are never thought to owe "gratitude" to

each other or to their government.) One can find some echoes of this language among Canadian Anglos, some of whom also loudly complain about Québécois "ingratitude." The imaginative failure was even more strikingly evident in the complete inability of the Suharto regime to produce, for high schools and universities in Indonesia and East Timor, history textbooks that managed to make East Timor's history a believable part of Indonesia's. Of such inability there are perhaps some echoes in Canada.

BIBLIOGRAPHICAL NOTE

There is much good published work on modern Indonesia written in a variety of languages, with Indonesian and English predominant. For the topics covered by this essay, a continuing stream of minutely researched publications by Amnesty International (London) and Asiawatch (New York) are indispensable resources. The most useful, up-to-date account of many aspects of Indonesia's current crisis, particularly its ethnic and separatist components, is Benedict Anderson, ed., *Violence and the State in Suharto's Indonesia* (Ithaca, NY: Cornell University, Southeast Asia Program, Studies on Southeast Asia, 2001), especially the chapters on East Timor by Douglas Kammen, on Aceh by Geoffrey Robinson, and on West Papua by Danilyn Rutherford. Other useful texts include:

Carey, Peter, and G. Carter Bentley, eds. (1995) *East Timor at the Crossroads: The Forging of a Nation*. London: Cassell.

Dayan Dawood and Sjafrizal (1989) "Aceh: The LNG Boom and Enclave Development," in Hal Hill, ed., *Unity and Diversity: Regional Economic Development in Indonesia since 1970*. Singapore: Oxford University Press.

Kell, Tim (1995) *The Roots of Acehnese Rebellion*. Ithaca, NY: Cornell University, Cornell Modern Indonesia Project.

Kohen, Arnold (1999) *From the Place of the Dead: Bishop Belo and the Struggle for East Timor*. Oxford: Lion.

Osborne, Robin (1985) *Indonesia's Secret War: The Guerrilla Struggle in Irian Jaya*. Sydney: Allen and Unwin.

Schwarz, Adam (1994) *A Nation in Waiting: Indonesia in the 1990s*. Boulder, Col.: Westview.

Sharp, Nonie, with Markus Wonggor Kaisiepo (1994) *The Morning Star in Papua Barat*. North Carlton, Australia: Arena.

Siegel, James T. (1998) *A New Criminal Type in Jakarta: Counterrevolution Today*. Durham, NC: Duke University Press.

Shiraishi Takashi (1997) "Anti-Sinicism in Java's New Order," in Daniel Chirot
    and Anthony Reid, eds., *Essential Outsiders: Chinese and Jews in the Mod-
    ern Transformation of Southeast Asia and Central Europe*. Seattle: University
    of Washington Press.

Tanter, Richard (1990) "The Totalitarian Ambition: Intelligence Organisations
    in the Indonesian State," in Arief Budiman, ed., *State and Civil Society in In-
    donesia*. Clayton: Monash University, Asia Institute.

Taylor, John G. (1991) *Indonesia's Forgotten War: The Hidden History of East
    Timor*. London: Zed.

KENNETH McROBERTS

The Future of the Nation-state and Quebec–Canada Relations

There is an assumption in many quarters that the nation-state is "finished" or at least on the way out. In both Europe and North America the established nation-states do seem to be losing some of their prerogatives. In Europe, they are losing them to new supranational institutions, based largely in Brussels. In North America, they are surrendering them in new arrangements, such as the North American Free Trade Agreement (NAFTA), which prevent them from taking actions that they took in the past, such as subsidies, non-tariff barriers to goods and capital, and resource-marketing policies. Yet what follows for the "state" component of the "nation-state" couplet may not follow for the "nation" component. This paper explores the fate of both the "nation" created by the state and the "nations" that can be found within many states. It does so with particular reference to the Canadian and Quebec nations.

EUROPE AND NORTH AMERICA

"Internal Nations" and the State

What about the nations *within* the nation-states? In other words, what about the many "internal nations" or "nations without states" that have continued to persist despite the best efforts of the nation-states to absorb them? One thinks perhaps of Catalonia, the Basque Country, Scotland, and Quebec. Firmly rooted in such social conditions as language, culture, and communication patterns, these nations often trace a long historical existence. They command a loyalty among their members that transcends any deference or attachment to purely political structures (McRoberts, 2002). What about the many regions that do not claim the status of nation but have been seeking autonomy? It is not at all clear that the processes of integration among nation-states also entail movement of powers and responsibilities downward to the nations and regions within them.

In Europe, the situation seems to vary greatly from one nation-state to another. But it is instructive to look at the case of Catalonia. Not only is it one of the better known "nations without states," but over the last few decades it has assiduously sought to establish a presence beyond the borders of Spain. Catalonia has set up a network of trade offices in various countries in Europe and beyond and signed many agreements with regions elsewhere in Europe. But it has failed to secure any meaningful role within the supranational organizations of the new Europe. Like many other of Europe's regions and "states without nations" it enjoys membership in the advisory Committee of the Regions of the European Union (EU). But cities comprise most of the committee's 222 members. The Spanish state continues to block the demand of Catalonia, and the sixteen other Autonomous Communities, that one of their members be able to attend meetings of the EU's Council of Ministers when matters involving the Communities are under discussion (McRoberts 2001, chap. 4). The European states may have lost some of their prerogatives to the EU, but they can still block the international aspirations of their nations within.

In North America, states and provinces have been able to sign agreements with their counterparts in other nation-states and to maintain offices beyond their borders (Frye, 1991). But the issue of representation in supranational bodies does not even arise: North America has none. The continent's three major nation-states may have lost some of their prerogatives to new agreements, but it is not clear that the states and provinces have gained new ones. Some analysts (Robinson, 1995) argue that the states and provinces have been the real losers.

At the same time, any notion that the United States, unlike Canada or Mexico, should have lost effective power as a nation-state through NAFTA defies credibility. Both its continuing status as world superpower and the differences in the size of the three national economies make North American integration asymmetrical to a degree not experienced in Europe. Typically, the measures that NAFTA precludes are those that the United States would not have taken anyway. It is Canada that, back in the 1970s, pursued a scheme to restrict energy exports; NAFTA was in part designed to ensure that Canada would not do so again. Similarly, proposals for a common North American currency invariably presume that Americans would occupy the overwhelming majority of seats within any regulatory body. Ultimately, integration is less about the construction of a new North America than about the economic and cultural absorption of Canada, and even Mexico, within the United States. The context of continental integration is radically different in Europe and in North America.

The "Nation" of the Nation-State

However much most of the states of Europe, as well as Canada and Mexico in North America, may have lost prerogatives and powers, they retain the form of the nation-state. But what about the nation? By this I mean not the "minority nations" or "states without nations" but the nations that these nation-states had sought to create.

These ideas of a common nation were always a bit contrived. Typically, they involved projecting onto the population as a whole characteristics associated with the dominant or majority nation within the state. These processes were never quite completed. In a good number of instances, minority nations simply survived the state's efforts to absorb them in its idea of a nation.

Still, will these nations suffer the same fate as the states that tried to will them into being and decline as they do? Will citizens who saw themselves as members of these nations be less inclined to see themselves this way once their states lose powers and prerogatives? As these states give way to continent-wide institutions or agreements will citizens within them tend more to see themselves as Europeans or North Americans? Will they more readily identify with nations or regions within the state? There is every reason to believe that these processes would be much slower. It's one thing to change institutions; it's something quite different to change how people see themselves and to modify their collective identities.

These processes are at work in Europe: a collective identity as Europeans is beginning to emerge just as identification with some internal nations may be reinforced. But what about North America? There, the conditions for developing a collective identity would seem to be much less favourable. As citizens of a superpower, Americans would have little incentive to abandon their identity for one that transcended the

United States. For the same reason Canadians, and even Mexicans, are more likely to see a North American identity as fundamentally American rather than as one that transcended their powerful neighbour. There are no supranational institutions with which they might identify.

Conversely, however, conditions might be favourable for heightened identification with regions and nations within the states of North America. Once again, this would not apply to the United States, but it might to Canada. Economic links between individual provinces and neighbouring American states have grown dramatically in recent years (Fry, 1997). And NAFTA and similar arrangements have eroded the capacity of the Canadian state.

For Quebec, the proportion of residents identifying with the province rather than with Canada as a whole has grown dramatically over recent decades (Pinard, 1995). Yet such a process is no mere function of integration. After all, the emergence of a distinct Québécois identity can be traced back to the 1960s. The Quiet Revolution was itself largely a consequence of social and political change within Quebec itself. Urbanization and industrialization there, which started about 1900, created space for a new francophone middle class, which by the 1950s was sufficiently strong to seek leadership of the provincial government. It secured its objective through the 1960 election of the Liberal Party. With the active support of labour, the new middle class rapidly expanded the roles and powers of the Quebec state at the expense of both the church and the anglophone business class. Quebec nationalism provided legitimacy for this new Quebec state. These processes of political modernization firmly implanted a distinctly Québécois political identity among young francophones. Links with the United States, and more specifically with American capital, may have facilitated this expansion of the Quebec state, as happened with financing for the nationalization of English-Canadian hydro firms. But the dynamic for the Quiet Revolution and the concomitant rise of a Quebec national identity was essentially internal to Quebec itself.[1]

CANADA

The Rise of the Canadian Nation, 1945–

In the rest of Canada, there simply does not seem to have been comparable growth in identification with the provinces. There, the sense of being Canadian has been surprisingly resilient, in face of the ongoing integration of most provincial economies with their American counterparts. As recently as 1999, overwhelming majorities declared that they saw themselves as Canadians rather than as residents of their province. The proportion was highest in Ontario (87 per cent), followed by British Columbia (82 per cent), the Prairie provinces (80 per cent), and Atlantic Canada (65 per cent). Yet in Quebec only 42 per cent declared themselves Canadian first (the proportion would almost certainly be lower within the francophone majority); 49 per cent said that they were Quebecers first. Similarly, overwhelming majorities outside Quebec strongly agreed that they were "proud to be Canadian." This sentiment was strongest on the Prairies (92 per cent), followed by Ontario (90 per cent), Atlantic Canada (89 per cent), and British Columbia (88 per cent). In Quebec, the figure was only 50 per cent (CIPO, 1999).

The Canadian state was a latecomer to the process of nation-building. It was only after the Second World War that it began to instill the idea of Canada as a distinct nation. The Canadian Citizenship Act was passed in 1946, and a Royal Commission on National Development in the Arts, Letters and Sciences (the Massey Commission) was established in 1949 on the premise that "[i]t is in the national interest to give encouragement to institutions which express national feeling" (as quoted in Simeon and Robinson, 1990, 142). Even so, during the 1960s this Canadian nationalism was coupled with attempts to recognize the very different notion of a "binational" Canada, as Lester Pearson's Liberal government (1963–68) attempted to accommodate the new Quebec nationalism. The government may have adopted the new Maple Leaf flag in 1965, but it also created a Royal Commission on Bilingualism and Biculturalism, charged with recommending "what steps should be taken to develop the Canadian Confederation on the basis of an equal partnership between the two founding races" (Canada, 1995, 151), and Pearson himself referred on occasion to Quebec as "a nation within a nation" (McRoberts, 1997, chap. 2). With the arrival of Pierre Elliott Trudeau as prime minister in 1968, the attempt to build a single Canadian nation, centred in the Canadian state, finally took full flight. Through both policies and constitutional change, Trudeau succeeded in entrenching a quite coherent notion of a Canadian nation, rooted in pan-Canadian bilingualism, multiculturalism, a charter of rights, equality of the provinces, and a strong national government in Ottawa. For Trudeau, all these ideas had been part of his effort to lead Quebec's francophones to see Canada, rather than Quebec, as their nation, yet he had relatively few takers among them. But his vision has been widely embraced outside Quebec. In effect, his nation-building strategy worked, but with the "wrong" population.

Outside Quebec, the Charter of Rights and Freedoms (1982) stands as a leading, perhaps the leading, element of Canadian nationhood. Thus any attempt to use the "notwithstanding" clause to avoid application of the charter is treated as heresy, as with the Quebec's government's use of the clause in 1989 to reinstate a component of Bill 101, Quebec's Charte de la langue française. Outside Quebec, the formal equality of the provinces has become a basic principle of the new Canadian nation; multiculturalism, the prevailing way of conceiving Canadian society; and Ottawa, more important than the provincial governments and the state of the Canadian nation. And reinforcing support for these principles is strong identification with Canada itself.[2]

A variety of factors help explain the impact of this new Canadian nationalism outside Quebec. With the postwar decline of Britain and the British connection, many anglophone Canadians were looking for a new identity to replace an essentially British conception of Canadian nationality. Reinforcing this desire was the rise of the United States to world hegemony. The definition of Canada as a bilingual and multicultural nation seemed to offer the perfect contrast to the American sense of nationhood – especially as perceived by Canadians.

Beyond that, the new nationalism emerged in an unusual and compelling manner. Unlike many state nationalisms, it was not simply the projection of the traits of the national majority. Spanish nationalism denies national status to Spain's minority nations and treats their languages, such as Catalan, as simple dialects of the true national language, Spanish. French nationalism reserves national status for French, excluding such languages as Breton and Corsican. The new Canadian nationalism actually embraces the language of the national minority, French, and places it on the same formal level as English, while rejecting the claims of the minority itself to national status. The Canadian nation is explicitly constructed to include both francophones and anglophones, not as members of distinct linguistic, let alone national, communities, but as undifferentiated members of the Canadian nation, some of whom happen to speak French and some of whom happen to speak English

The "bilingual nation" may be problematic on sociological grounds. By its nature, the concept of nation stresses commonality and shared experience. Yet differences in language imply quite the opposite. Conceivably, languages can embody different values and assumptions, with the result that common events are experienced differently. Even if they are not, languages can hinder any sharing of common reactions. Beyond that, as Canadian experience has shown, two or more languages within the same state will tend to be concentrated in territorially defined centres of dominance. Their survival depends on such segregation. Yet this requirement of territorial division is bound to pose problems for national unity, especially when the state is federal. As well as fostering attachment to regions rather than to the nation as a whole, it can hinder mobility within the nation. None the less, whatever its sociological complications, the idea of a "bilingual nation" serves to give the Canadian nation a real distinctiveness, especially in North America.

By the same token, the new nationalism carefully eschews any notion of a national culture that is based on the national majority, let alone on the national minority. The past notions of a Canadian "Britishness" are steadfastly rejected, as are those of a "bicultural" Canada pioneered in the 1960s by the Royal Commission on Bilingualism and Biculturalism. Instead, Canada is to be "multicultural." As Pierre Trudeau declared in promulgating the new multiculturalism policy in 1971, "there are no official cultures in Canada" (Canada, 1971, 8546).

Finally, given its unorthodox method of construction, the new Canadian nationalism can even make a reasonable claim that it is not nationalism at all. Canada is deemed to have transcended nationalism and to have become a "non-nation." As such, Canadian nationalism can escape many of the conventional critiques of nationalism as "narrow" and "reactionary." Quite the contrary, Canada stands as the vanguard of history; the world's first "postmodern"nation. By the same token, if the Canadian nation transcends the limitations of common notions of the nation, and of nationalism, then it is easy to dismiss as narrow, and inevitably ethnic, the competing nationalism of a Quebec nation. It's a case not of majority nationalism versus minority nationalism but of universalism as opposed to nationalism per se.

This is of course a state nationalism – and a quite conventional one at that. The flags and other symbolic paraphernalia of a national state are combined with distinctive political institutions, such as a Charter of Rights and Freedoms and parliamentary federalism, and all is sealed with the boosterism (now discredited) of being "Number One" in UN rankings.

The clearest expression of this state nationalism came during the years of Pierre Trudeau. Trudeau explicitly adopted the discourse of "nation-building," as in a November 1981 statement in which he declared that the time had come "to reassert in our national policies that Canada is one country which must be capable of moving with unity of spirit and purpose towards shared goals. If Canada is indeed to be a nation, there must be a national will which is something more than the lowest common denominator among the desires of the provincial governments" (Mulgrew, 1981).

On this basis, Trudeau vigorously pursued an explicit and ambitious "nation-building" strategy. Not only did the strategy entail the pursuit of major policy initiatives, such as official bilingualism and multiculturalism, but it remade political institutions through constitutional repatriation and the adoption of the Charter of Rights and Freedoms. The charter's components served to entrench the key principles of official bilingualism (sections 16–22), multiculturalism (section 27), and equality of the provinces (the amendment procedure).

So deeply rooted has the new Canadian nationalism become outside Quebec that attempts to further modify the constitution, in ways that do not accord with new premises, have aroused vociferous opposition. The Meech Lake Accord of the late 1980s constituted a modest set of measures; some simply entrenched established practice, others had been under discussion for years. Initially, the accord was generally acceptable to the public outside Quebec, just as it was within Quebec. However, opposition rapidly mobilized in anglophone Canada, focusing first and foremost on the clause recognizing Quebec as "a distinct society." It was no more than an interpretive clause that would have had limited concrete effect. None the less, the notion managed to violate all the premises of the new Canadian nationalism. Trudeau led the campaign against the accord, rallying the majority of Canadian anglophones (but not francophone Quebec) to his position that the clause constituted an affront to the idea of one Canadian nation.[3]

The Canadian Nation and Quebec

But what about the nation that was supposed to be displaced by this new idea of a Canadian nation, articulated by the Canadian state: the Quebec nation? Support for this nation continued to grow all through this period. Thus the proportion of Quebec francophones declaring themselves "Québécois" rather than "Canadian" or "French Canadian" grew from 34 per cent in 1970 to 59 per cent in 1990; the proportion declaring themselves "Canadian" fell from 34 per cent to 9 per cent (Pinard, 1992, Table 3).

This relative failure of the idea of a Canadian nation to take hold in francophone Quebec relates to the characteristics ascribed to this nation, especially when presented to Quebecers. First, for Quebec, was the argument that the Canadian nation is bilingual. French enjoys a status equal to English not simply within the federal government but throughout Canada. More fundamentally, the Canadian state's argument went, francophone society exists not just in Quebec, as many Quebec nationalists were wont to declare, but throughout the Canadian nation. Thus, in linguistic terms, Quebec was not unique. Moreover, the federal government was acting vigorously, through a variety of measures, to reinforce this francophone presence outside Quebec. Yet Quebec francophones were quite aware that that the French presence in Quebec is fundamentally different. Only in Quebec did francophones constitute the overwhelming majority, and only in Quebec could the provincial government be counted on to protect and strengthen this presence. In terms of association with the French language, the Quebec nation had a distinct advantage over the Canadian one.

Beyond bilingualism and language equality, advocates of the Canadian nation placed great emphasis on the Charter of Rights and Freedoms. To Quebecers, the charter was presented as a powerful instrument for protecting the position of francophone minorities outside Quebec, especially through obliging provincial governments to provide them with French-language education. Indeed, Pierre Trudeau used to declare that these provisions were the primary reason for his fierce struggle to adopt the charter. Yet for many of Quebec's francophones the charter's appeal in these terms was countered by the extent to which it also imposed obligations on Quebec, protecting access by anglophones to English-language schools in Quebec. And Quebec nationalists would stress that the charter, with its restriction on the Quebec government's jurisdiction over education, was adopted without the consent of the Quebec government.

Multiculturalism as a defining characteristic tended to meet with an ambivalent response in francophone Quebec. If Canada is to be composed of a multitude of cultures, where does that leave francophone culture? Back in the 1960s, federal leaders had celebrated the notion of a "bicultural" Canada and even a Canada composed of two linguistically defined "nations." Quebec nationalists could readily present multiculturalism as a major setback for Quebec francophones.

Similarly, the stress on a federalism in which all provinces have equal status could mean only that Quebec was "a province like the others."

This too was bound to have little appeal to Quebec francophones. For many decades, Quebec's political leadership had championed the notion that its government had a distinct mission of protecting Quebec's francophone society and culture. From the early 1960s onward, it had sought a "special status," or *statut particulier*, under which Quebec would assume responsibilities that would remain with the federal government for the rest of Canada. Moreover, during the 1960s this idea had enjoyed widespread support in federal circles. It may have fallen out of favour in Ottawa with the accession of Pierre Trudeau. But the notion had become deeply entrenched in Quebec. By the same token, the new Canadian nationalism's emphasis on strengthening the role of the federal government as the nation-state of Canada was bound to have little appeal.

In short, in francophone Quebec the new Canadian nationalism was unable to dislodge a counter-nationalism that had deep historical roots. Quebec nationalism offered much more powerful arguments about the relationship between language, the state, and the nation. To the extent that Canadian nationalism appeared to be challenging the postulates of Quebec nationalism, as indeed it was, then it became a provocation to many Quebec francophones. In effect, it rendered illegitimate what remained the predominant understanding of nationhood among Quebec francophones. It seemed to imply that there was no place in Canada for such beliefs, nor perhaps for those who believed them.

For these reasons, the Meech Lake Accord met with widespread sympathy in francophone Quebec. The specific constitutional changes fell well short of the type of revision that had been sought by many Quebec nationalists. Yet at least the "distinct society" clause flew in the face of Canadian nationalism's vision of Quebec and its place in Canada. Quebec francophone support solidified as opposition to the accord built among anglophone Canadians.

The failure of the Meech Lake Accord therefore had a profound effect in Quebec. Many francophones saw rejection of the accord, especially of its "distinct society" clause, as a rejection of Quebec itself. Out of this sense of "rejection"and "humiliation," support for sovereignty soared. By November 1990, it had reached as high as 64 per cent among Quebec residents (*L'Actualité*, 1991).[4] In 1995, a referendum held by the Quebec government came breathtakingly close to a "Yes" vote for its question of whether Quebec should become sovereign, after proposing a new economic and political partnership with Canada: 49.4 per cent voted "Yes," with 50.6 per cent saying "No." Close to 60 per cent of Quebec's francophones had voted "Yes."

Yet it is important to recognize the basis of this ostensible surge in support for Quebec independence. For many voters, the surge reflected less a conversion to sovereignty, and to the idea of a fully independent Quebec state, than a sense of being rejected by the rest of Canada and anger over this rejection. Thus, a month before the referendum, 34 per cent of respondents intending to vote "Yes" declared that they were attached to Canada; four months after the referendum, 78 per cent of Quebecers agreed that francophones and anglophones should be proud of what they "have accomplished together in Canada." Most who voted "Yes" clearly expected that Quebec would be linked to Canada through an economic and political partnership. In one survey, 22 per cent of "Yes" voters thought that with sovereignty Quebec would remain a province of Canada (McRoberts, 1997, 229–30).

Over recent years, the momentum to Quebec sovereignty has declined significantly. Many federal officials ascribe this change to federal actions – most notably, "Plan B," which has sought to persuade Quebecers that sovereignty could be politically difficult and economically disastrous. The heart of the strategy has been Parliament's "Clarity Act," which would entitle Ottawa to set conditions for the negotiation of sovereignty that are far more stringent than those generally presumed at the time of the 1995 referendum.

Yet other factors may have been far more influential in producing this effect. The passage of years has allowed for dissipation of the profound reaction to the collapse of the Meech Lake Accord. Bitterness over Meech may also have been attenuated by the 1998 decision of the Canadian Supreme Court on Quebec's right to declare independence. The decision stated that the federal government had a constitutional obligation to enter into negotiations over Quebec sovereignty, should a "clear majority" of Quebecers support a "clear question" on sovereignty. Beyond that, it asserted federalism as one of Canada's constitutional principles and declared that an essential reason for federalism was to permit French Canadians to pursue their collective interests in Quebec, where they constitute a majority (par. 59). Finally, disaffection with the Parti Québécois (PQ) government – the perhaps-inevitable result of its eight years in power – has further weakened support for the PQ's option of sovereignty.

If the sovereignty movement has lost momentum, collective identification with Quebec is still intact. With Canada, as with other would-be nation-states, the challenge still remains: the presence of "internal nations" that continue to resist the nation-building strategies of the central state. Just as in Scotland and Catalonia, so in Quebec, most citizens are also loath to embrace sovereignty as an alternative. In Quebec, the preferred arrangement remains some sort of common structure, perhaps an asymmetrical federalism, that can accommodate Quebec's national distinctiveness. Canada has yet to come to terms with its multinational character. By some criteria, it has lost ground over recent decades.[5]

CONCLUSION

So, the state component of the nation-state couplet may be under siege, but we should not exaggerate its decline. Of course, the state is not at all in decline if it happens to be the world's superpower. In contrast, the nation of the nation-state seems to be faring quite well, even though it was the creation of particular states and remains very much focused on those states. Even if it was unable to supplant the minority nations within the state, it may well prove to be much more resilient than the state itself. The case of Canada outside Quebec suggests that the nation may be especially resilient if it seems – at least at the level of national myth – to transcend the normal structures of a nation with more than one language and a multitude of cultures. It then can claim to transcend the state from which it emerged. Rather than being a residue of a previous age, threatened by the forces of globalization, it may appear to be on the forefront of globalization.

The other notion of the nation, however, is also holding up well. Within many states, Canada included, where strong majorities are firmly attached to the nations constructed by the states, significant minorities remain deeply tied to socially constructed "internal nations," which continue to have a life of their own. There is every indication that these states will continue to be sites of competition between very different conceptions of nationhood.

NOTES

1 This at least is the stance of McRoberts, 1993, chap. 5.
2 I develop this argument in McRoberts, 1997.
3 This interpretation of the Meech Lake Accord debate comes from McRoberts, 1997, 190–207.

4 Using the term "independence" or "sovereignty," Pinard found that support stood at 56 per cent in November–December 1990 (Pinard, 1992, 480).
5 This is the reasoning of McRoberts, 2002.

REFERENCES

L'Actualité (1991) "Portrait des Québécois," 13–16 Jan.
Canada (1971) House of Commons. *Debates*, 8 Oct.
– (1995) Royal Commission on Bilingualism and Biculturalism. *Preliminary Report*. Ottawa: Queen's Printer.
Canadian Institute of Public Opinion (CIPO) (1999) *Reports*.
Frye, Earl H. (1997) "Regional Economic Development Strategies in Canada and the United States: Linkages between the Subnational, National and Global Settings," *International Journal of Canadian Studies*, no. 16, 69–92.
McRoberts, Kenneth (1993) *Quebec: Social Change and Political Crisis*. Toronto: Oxford University press.
– (1997) *Misconceiving Canada: The Struggle for National Unity*. Toronto: Oxford University Press.
– (2001) *Catalonia: Nation Building without a State*. Toronto: Oxford University Press.
– (2002) "Canada and the Multinational State," *Canadian Journal of Political Science* 34, no. 4 (Dec. 2001), 683–13.
Mulgrew, Ian (1981) "Provinces Using Federal Money but Ottawa Is Not Credited: PM," *Globe and Mail*, 25 Nov.
Pinard, Maurice (1992) "The Dramatic Resurgence of the Quebec Independence Movement," *Journal of International Affairs* 45, no. 2 (winter), Table 3.
Robinson, Ian (1995) "Trade Policy, Globalization, and the Future of Canadian Federalism," in François Rocher and Miriam Smith, eds., *New Trends in Canadian Federalism*. Peterborough: Broadview, 234–69.
Simeon, Richard, and Ian Robinson (1990) *State, Society and the Development of Canadian Federalism*. Collected Research Studies of the Royal Commission on the Economic Union and Development Prospects for Canada, vol. 71. Toronto: University of Toronto Press.

MICHEL SEYMOUR

Conclusion:
The Rights and Obligations
of Persons and Nations

COMMON THEMES

In conclusion, I would like to highlight common themes developed in the essays in this book and then draw from them some normative implications. Several authors have concentrated on the nature of the nation-state, while others considered the viability of multi-nation states. These methodological choices sometimes led to normative judgments regarding nation-states, multinational states, or supranational organizations. But what fascinates me is how respectful everyone has been towards nations and nationalism. No one seems to condemn without nuances nationalism as such. No one wants to treat it as intrinsically repulsive or repugnant. No one forcefully announces its future disappearance, as Eric Hobsbawm would have done not too long ago. Of course, Margaret Canovan reminds us of the dangers of defending very liberal theories of secession, but she dismisses an individualistic, cosmopolitan approach that chooses to ignore the very existence of nations. Liah Greenfeld forcefully argues that nations, nationalisms, and nation-states are still the driving forces behind modern liberal societies. Brubaker emphasizes the value of the liberal civic nation-state for central and eastern Europe, and he suggests that countries there should still look to such a model.

All the authors seem aware of the insidious manifestations of nationalism. Everyone seems to realize that very often its apparent absence in a society can be explained only by its determinant omnipresence. No one would endorse, for instance, the view that the United States has achieved Jürgen Habermas's ideal of "constitutional patriotism" – a post-national republic in which the only "ties that bind" are those of a constitution. Contrary to what Alan Ryan wrote in a piece on Habermas,[1] the United States does not rest merely on constitutional patriotism and does not form a post-national constellation. On the contrary, it is perhaps the clearest manifestation of the traditional nation-state.

Thomas Pogge shows this when he notes the importance for young Hispanic Americans of learning English – the common public language. No one could claim that the United States is just a republic of individual citizens. There is an American nation held together not only by a constitution but also by a national consciousness: the ties that bind are a common language, a common institutional culture, and a common historical heritage. If Americans were ready to engage in a purely constitutional patriotism similar to the one that is now emerging in Europe, they might be willing, for example, to accept the creation of a supranational currency in North America as a whole. But everyone knows that Americans would do so only if all the countries involved accepted the U.S. dollar. For that reason, among many others, the United States presents a very clear case of a nationalistic society.

Every writer in the book seems to agree on the need to build institutions to accommodate nations. Contrary to authors such as Brian Barry, no contributor here denounces the political recognition of cultural diversity in a multi-nation state. Furthermore, no one seems to think that only one political format can accommodate nations. All are sensitive to the particular geopolitical and historical context in which linguistic national minorities or minority nations evolve. For instance, Daniel Weinstock adumbrates different sorts of nation-building, whether top–down or bottom–up. Jocelyne Couture remarks on the historic changes taking place within nation-states in the context of globalization, and she proposes a new definition of the nation appropriate for that context. Kai Nielsen re-examines the old models of political organization in an era of global economic markets.

Most of the authors, if not all, are willing to acknowledge many viable models of political organization, depending on the circumstances. Benedict Anderson, for instance, notices the differences between Indonesia and Canada. John McGarry writes about the different sorts of conflicts in the Balkans and in Ireland. David McCrone outlines the differences between Scotland and Quebec.

In short, there appears to be a core of values entertained by all the contributors. They all seem sensitive to the importance of nations and nationalism and to political diversity and cultural pluralism. But is that the only conclusion that one can draw? How can this respectful critical assessment of nations and nationalism be understood from a moral point of view? It could be argued that no unified moral account is possible, given the irreducible existence of a very wide diversity of cases. So we perhaps cannot link these essays together in a seamless moral web. But it does not mean that we can say nothing, for we can draw at least some specific conclusions. These concern precisely the preservation of diversity and pluralism.

THREE LESSONS

It seems to me that the lessons that one can extract from these papers are three-fold. First, the nation-state can no longer count as the only model of political organization. In addition, we must find ways to consolidate multi-nation states and supranational organizations. Nations no longer need to become politically sovereign. There is no teleology involved, no historical necessity for nations to have their sovereign state.

Of course, this does not mean that the nation-state model is obsolete or that there cannot be new ways to understand nation-states. We can imagine politics of recognition designed to accommodate component nations in the context of a newly understood form of nation-state. As Ross Poole points out, there can be "multi-nation nation-states." Nobel Peace Prize winner Lester B. Pearson used to talk about "nations within nations." Loyalty to an encompassing state must perhaps be mediated by loyalty to an encompassing nation. Even if a nation can be less than fully sovereign, and can thus be part of a multi-nation state, perhaps the encompassing state must often also be national in some way. Even if Europe comes to provide a good illustration of constitutional patriotism, there may never be a European state – perhaps because there may never be a European nation. In short, even if there have to be stateless nations, we need not allow for post-national multinational states. We can accept stateless nations, yet find a way to keep the nation-state model, whose value Greenfeld underlines. It may be possible to modify the traditional version to accommodate stateless nations.

Be that as it may, the first lesson remains relevant. The nationalist principle must be abandoned and buried once and for all.

Second, alternatives to the traditional nation-state will not be viable unless the encompassing states conduct themselves properly vis-à-vis their component minority nations. Multi-nation (nation)-states must give political recognition to their component nations. The reason should be obvious. Trust cannot arise among nations without mutual political recognition. No invokable form of nation-building, not even one that stems from a civic variant, could prevent us from having to deal with the recognition of component nations. A bottom–up variety of nation-building could never emerge in a multinational society without political recognition. In a multinational nation-state, members belonging to a component nation will feel allegiance towards the encompassing state only if they are recognized as a distinct nation. It is precisely the reference to the component nations that creates the possibility of treating the constitution as our constitution and allows for minority nations to identify with an encompassing nationality. So if nation-building implies non-recognition of minority nations, then it becomes morally problematic.[2]

All this amounts to recognizing a primary right to self-determination for nations in general and for stateless nations in particular. But there can be many ways to interpret that right. First, it can be understood as the right that a sovereign state may enjoy in the international arena. Second, it may be seen as a right to secede (external right to self-determination) or as a right that a nation can enjoy within an encompassing state (internal right to self-determination). The latter version can then be interpreted in the very weak and purely formal sense: individuals may decide on their own institutions. This happens as soon as consultations are made, negotiations take place, royal commissions are instituted, or referenda are introduced and the population is invited to adopt some kind of reform for its political institutions. There can be internal self-determination in this sense even if no constitutional reform ever occurs.

But in a stronger sense, the internal right to self-determination is the right of a nation as a whole to have its own specific institutional organization within the encompassing state. In this case, a nation as such is able to build an adequate institutional arrangement, with institutions that reflect the presence of nations within the state. It is in this sense that I conceive of a primary right to self-determination for nations.

Here, I am thinking of such notions as devolution, subsidiarity, particular status (for a province), or asymmetric federalism. Matthew Evangelista, Radha Kumar, and Ken McRoberts allude to those approaches in their papers. John McGarry describes the specific, complex arrangements of the Good Friday Agreement for Northern Ireland. David McCrone outlines the solutions adopted by the British government for Scotland, and Montserrat Guibernau shows us how Spain has dealt historically with the issue of Catalonian autonomy. The idea is that in order to achieve full internal self-determination, a nation must be entitled to find its own specific administrative arrangements, as when a province acquires a special status or when a federal system becomes asymmetrical. It is only this approach that allows for opting-out measures and specific vetoes, and this is the only way that stateless peoples can achieve adequate administrative autonomy.

Such administrative arrangements would not be stable without political recognition of the component nations. A formal entrenchment in the constitution asserting the political recognition of component nations is thus a necessary condition for the viability of the arrangements themselves. It provides the basic symbolic framework that serves as a justification for these arrangements. A social contract between nations in a "federation of peoples" thus requires mutual recognition and the acceptance of the institutional consequences of such recognition. In other words, asymmetric federalism and special status, opting-out proposals, and vetoes must themselves also formally be present in the constitution. The instability of Spain noted by Guibernau should be an incentive for constitutional reform that would formally recognize administrative arrangements. Instead of remaining a de facto multinational federation, Spain could thus become a truly de jure multinational federation. In Canada, where Quebec as a province enjoys much more fiscal and political autonomy than Scotland, Wales, Catalonia, or Galicia, there remains no formal recognition of the Quebec people. This problem has opened up the door for the "Framework on Social Union," which allows the Canadian government to use its spending power in exclusive provincial jurisdictions, and it has led to a fiscal imbalance between the federal government and the provinces. In Canada, all provinces are not equal in treatment but they are all equal in status, and so there is no recognition of the Quebec people as such and a fortiori no acceptance of the institutional consequences that would follow from such recognition. So, in the context of a Canadian nation-building that is still under way, Quebec's political and/or fiscal autonomy is in constant jeopardy. Even if the 1867 constitution distinguishes precisely the powers of the federal and provincial levels, the federal government constantly invokes a so-called spending power apparently contained in the constitution to violate the constitution. Without formal political recognition of component nations, the most basic underlying principles of a federation such as the separation of powers, subsidiarity, and fiscal responsibility may be threatened in the name of nation-building.

Thus, in the stronger sense, internal self-determination is a right of nations to get the appropriate arrangements within the encompassing state, and it is not merely a formal, individual right to vote on a particular constitutional reform. The formal ability to vote on constitutional reforms is compatible with the violation of internal self-determination in the strong sense, for it is compatible with a status quo that never meets the demands for recognition. The stronger right to internal self-determination can be fully exercised and respected only when constitutional reform actually takes place and when the component nations as well as their accommodating institutional arrangements are fully recognized by all. Internal self-determination, under this account, is the establishment of effective room to manoeuvre for a nation within a multi-nation state.

Stateless nations have a right to determine themselves within the encompassing state. This is a collective right – perhaps the most basic form of such a right. There is no need to evoke the ontology of nations or to provide a strict definition of nationality in order to acknowledge formally their existence in the public sphere. After all, there is now a growing international consensus concerning fundamental individual rights and liberties, despite lack of agreement on the difficult ontological issue of personal identity. So why should we think otherwise in the case of nations? In many of the essays in this book, authors recognize collective rights for groups – especially Rajeev Bhargava, David Ingram, Henry Milner, Ross Poole, and Michel Seymour. Michael Murphy has also forcefully argued for the Aboriginal right to self-determination. This open-mindedness towards the collective rights of nations and national linguistic minorities is perhaps the only way to acknowledge the internal self-determination of nations in a multinational society.

Third, if truly liberal and democratic minority nations are unable to gain political recognition within the multi-nation state, they will be morally justified in seeking such recognition by achieving full sovereignty (or, if they cannot afford that option, by performing peacefully some kind of collective civil disobedience). Just as one should not adopt the nation-state as the unique model of political organization, one should admit that there are circumstances in which the multi-nation state is no longer viable and when the creation of a new nation-state is morally justified. I am not thinking simply about cases where fundamental human rights of the members of the component nation are being threatened by the encompassing state. I do not need to invoke only ex-

treme violations of human rights in order to find a moral justification
for secession. I am thinking rather of the violation of the internal right to
self-determination. Such a right could after all be considered a matter of
global decency – Avishai Margalit's happy phrase. Without political recognition, a nation is humiliated in some way or other. We can grasp the
connection that holds between lack of recognition for a nation and its
humiliation if we realize the close relationship between its identity and
its political recognition, as Charles Taylor has argued.[3]

International law already acknowledges such a connection, for it recognizes that the violation of internal self-determination is itself already a
strong moral justification for secession. Unfortunately, the theories of secession that grant some moral legitimacy to the act of secession often impose very restrictive constraints. One can think here of very sophisticated
accounts such as those of Allen Buchanan,[4] not only of popularized versions such as those of Michael Ignatieff.[5] Even if Buchanan is perhaps
right to reduce the right of secession to a remedial right, we should perhaps enlarge the class of violations that can justify the exercise of such a
right. We could, for instance, grant that the absence of formally recognized institutional arrangements for nations constitutes a violation of a
fundamental right that calls for remedial solutions, including secession. If
a state cannot respect the internal self-determination of its nations, then
they are entitled to secede.

Some will think that the remedy is radical and disproportionate when
compared with the harm created. Why should the failure of political
recognition be a sufficient justification for such an "extreme" solution?
But there are different ways to secede, just as there are different ways to
get a divorce. The seceding process can itself be morally constrained
and can be conceived in accordance with the maintenance of different
partnership relations (economic and political union) between the successor states. Secession in a globalized economy does not necessarily
imply the same thing as it would have in the 19th century. It can now
take place in regions with free trade, common markets, and economic
unions. The seceding state may still be part of different supranational
organizations. Those observers who consider secession an extreme solution often have in mind an outdated form. Imagine, for example, an independent Quebec in an economic and political union with Canada,
sharing the Canadian dollar with Canada, involved in the North American Free Trade Agreement (NAFTA) with Canada, the United States,
and Mexico, and also closely related to the United States by 272 treaties. Imagine that Quebec would keep federative links with Canada in

certain areas such as defence (the North Atlantic Treaty Organization and North American Air Defence)[6] and confederative ties with Canadians for participation in certain supranational bodies (the World Trade Organization and the G8). If the accommodation of a Quebec nation within the Canadian federation is no longer a serious alternative because many Canadians do not even want to consider this possibility, why should we completely rule out such imaginative solutions?[7]

Moreover, one should refrain from applying different standards depending on whether the nation to be recognized should be the encompassing nation or the component nation itself. One cannot have it both ways. We cannot minimize the gravity of failing to afford political recognition for the component nation and react violently against secession for the harm that it creates to the encompassing nation, for it amounts to differential treatment concerning the importance of political recognition in both cases. If nations need not be politically recognized, why should we then complain against the harm created to the encompassing nation when one of its component nations decides to become politically sovereign? If the encompassing nation does not recognize the existence of the component nation, why should it suddenly believe that something important has been lost when the component nation chooses to secede? Finally, as Kumar emphasizes in her paper, one must not confuse the partition of a population within a single nation-state with the negotiated secession of a province from an encompassing state. This distinction is not often made in the literature. We often think of secession as a particular instance of partition.

So the third lesson that one can draw is that without political recognition a nation could morally be entitled to achieve secession.[8] Note that this approach is not vulnerable to the three paradoxes that affect political theory according to Margaret Canovan. I am not claiming that we should "let sleeping dogs lie" and that we can simply ignore the pervasive force of nationalism, for I am forcefully arguing for the political recognition of nations. I am not falling into the second paradox either, since I am not simply paving an easy way out for all the stateless nations. I am not indulging in an approach that would let nations secede without strong moral justifications for doing so. I am not claiming that all nations should become sovereign as long as they are able to meet some obvious general procedural rules (democratic principles, protection of minorities, primacy of the rule of law). On the contrary, I am taking for granted that there could be some appropriate arrangements for component nations within multi-nation states. It could even be argued that, in many cases, the best solution for a stateless nation is to find an arrangement within the encompassing state. Nations do not have a primary right to secede. They have a primary right only to internal self-determination and a remedial right to secede.

Finally, I am not falling into the third paradox either, for I am not suggesting that the solution is simply to transcend the actual contemporary reality of nation-states and multi-nation states, in favour of supranational organizations that would recognize only individual cosmopolitan citizens. General conditions must be met to ensure the viability of supranational organizations. These bodies must apply politics of recognition towards their component nation-states and multi-nation states, as well as towards component nations within those states. In short, the only acceptable solution is a cosmopolitan law of peoples asserting the individual rights and obligations of persons and the collective rights and obligations of nations.

NOTES

1 Ryan, "The Power of Positive Thinking," *New York Review of Books*, 16 Jan. 2003.

2 Needless to say, the same remarks apply to stateless nations vis-à-vis their own minorities. They also have the moral responsibility to recognize their own minorities.

3 Charles Taylor, "The Politics of Recognition," in A. Gutmann, ed., *Multiculturalism*. Princeton, NJ: Princeton University Press, 1994, 25–73.

4 Allen Buchanan, *Secession: The Morality of Political Divorce: From Fort Sumter to Lithuania and Quebec*. Boulder, Col.: Westview, 1991. See also "The International Institutional Dimension of Secession," in P.B. Lehning, ed., *Theories of Secession*. London: Routledge, 1998, 227–56.

5 Michael Ignatieff, *The Rights Revolution*. Toronto: Anansi Press, 2000.

6 I owe this suggestion to Anne Legaré.

7 I offer my own perspective on the Quebec–Canada relationship in "Quebec and Canada at the Crossroads: A Nation within a Nation," *Nations and Nationalism* 6, no. 2 (2000), 227–55.

8 Of course, there must be other constraints on secession. For instance, when the seceding group is itself multinational, its failure to recognize its own component minority nations would be sufficient to cast doubt on the morality of secession.

Contributors

BENEDICT ANDERSON is the Aaron L. Binenkorb Emeritus Professor of International Studies at Cornell University in Ithaca, New York. Among his publications are *Imagined Communities: Reflections on the Origin and the Spread of Nationalism* (1991) and *The Spectre of Comparisons: Nationalism, Southeast Asia and the World* (1998).

RAJEEV BHARGAVA teaches at the Centre for Political Studies, Jawaharlal Nehru University, New Delhi. Bhargava is the author of *Individualism in Social Science: Forms and Limits of a Methodology* (1992). He is editor of *Secularism and Its Critics* (1998) and co-editor of *Multiculturalism, Liberalism and Democracy* (1999) and of *Transforming India: Social and Political Dynamics of Democracy* (2000).

ROGERS BRUBAKER is professor of sociology at the University of California – Los Angeles. His books include *Citizenship and Nationhood in France and Germany* (1992), *Nationalism Reframed: Nationhood and the National Question in the New Europe* (1996), and *Ethnicity without Groups* (2004).

MARGARET CANOVAN is professor of political thought at the University of Keele. She has published *Hannah Arendt: A Reinterpretation of Her Political Thought* (1992) and *Nationhood and Political Theory* (1996).

JOCELYNE COUTURE is professor of philosophy at the Université du Québec à Montréal. She has edited or co-edited *Éthique et rationalité* (1992),

Métaphilosophie (1993), *The Relevance of Metaethics* (1996), and *Rethinking Nationalism* (1998), and she has also published many papers on nationalism and cosmopolitanism.

MATTHEW EVANGELISTA is professor of government and director of the Peace Studies Program at Cornell University in Ithaca, New York. His books include *Innovation and the Arms Race* (1988), *Unarmed Forces: The Transnational Movement to End the Cold War* (1999), and *The Chechen Wars: Will Russia Go the Way of the Soviet Union?* (2002).

LIAH GREENFELD is University Professor and professor of political science and sociology at Boston University. She is the author of numerous publications on nationalism, including the critically acclaimed *Nationalism: Five Roads to Modernity* (1992). A sequel, focusing on England/Britain, France, Germany, Japan, the Netherlands, and the United States, *The Spirit of Capitalism: Nationalism and Economic Growth*, appeared in 2001.

MONTSERRAT GUIBERNAU is reader in politics at the Open University. Her main publications include *Francoism, Nationalism: The Nation-state and Nationalism in the Twentieth Century* (1996), *Nations without States* (1999), and *Catalan Nationalism: Francoism, Transition, and Democracy* (2004). She is the editor of *Nationalism: Debates and Dilemmas for a New Millennium* (2000) and *Governing European Diversity* (2001). She has co-edited *The Ethnicity Reader: Nationalism, Multiculturalism and Migration* (1997), *Understanding Nationalism* (2001), and *History and National Destiny* (2004). She is currently researching the ESRC-funded project "Regional Identity and European Citizenship" and preparing the book *National Identity and Its Future*. She has been awarded a Leverhulme Trust Fellowship to examine the impact of migration on national identity. She has taught at the universities of Cambridge, Warwick, and Barcelona.

DAVID INGRAM is professor of philosophy at Loyola University. His publications include *Habermas and the Dialectic of Reason* (1987), *Critical Theory and Philosophy* (1990) and a companion anthology, *Critical Theory: The Essential Readings* (1991), *Reason, History, and Politics* (1995), and *Group Rights: Reconciling Equality and Difference* (2000), as well as numerous scholarly articles.

RADHA KUMAR is the author of several books, including *The History of Doing: An Illustrated Account of Movements of Women's Rights and Feminism in India 1800–1990* (1993) and *Divide and Fall? Bosnia in the Annals of Partition*

(1999). Currently a senior fellow with the Council on Foreign Relations (New York), she has held fellowships at the Institute of Development Studies (University of Sussex), the Institute of War and Peace Studies at Columbia University, the Rockefeller Foundation, and the World Institute of Economics Research (Helsinki). From 1992 to 1994, she served as executive director of the Helsinki Citizens Assembly in Prague.

AVISHAI MARGALIT is the Schulman Professor of Philosophy at the Hebrew University in Jerusalem and a regular contributor to the *New York Review of Books*. He is the author of *The Decent Society* (1996), *Views in Review: Politics and Culture in the State of the Jews* (1998), and *The Ethnics of Memory* (2002). He wrote *Idolatry* (1991) with Moshe Halbertal and was co-editor with Edna Margalit of *Isaiah Berlin: A Celebration* (1991).

DAVID McCRONE is professor of sociology at the University of Edinburgh and director of the University of Edinburgh's Institute of Governance. His recent books include *The Sociology of Nationalism: Tomorrow's Ancestors* (1998), *New Scotland: New Politics?* (2000), *New Scotland, New Society?* (2001), and *Understanding Scotland: The Sociology of a Nation* (2001). He is co-ordinator of the research programs funded by the Leverhulme Trust on Constitutional Change and National Identity (1999–2004). He is a fellow of the Royal Society of Edinburgh.

JOHN McGARRY is professor of political science at the University of Waterloo. He is the co-author of three books, *Explaining Northern Ireland: Broken Images* (1995), *The Politics of Antagonism: Understanding Northern Ireland* (1996), and *Policing Northern Ireland: Proposals for a New Start* (1999). He is the co-editor of *The Future of Northern Ireland* (1990), *The Politics of Ethnic Conflict Regulation* (1993), *State of Truce: Northern Ireland after Twenty-Five Years of War* (1995), and *Minority Nationalism in the Changing International Order* (2001). He is also the editor of *Northern Ireland and the Divided World: Post-Agreement Northern Ireland in Comparative Perspective* (2001).

KENNETH McROBERTS is principal of Glendon College, York University, Toronto, and a professor of political science. He published *Quebec: Social Change and Political Crisis* (1993). He edited *Beyond Quebec: Taking Stock of Canada* (1995) and co-edited with Patrick J. Monahan *The Charlottetown Accord, the Referendum and the Future of Canada* (1993). He is the author of *Catalonia: Nation-building without a State* (2001).

HENRY MILNER is visiting professor of political science at the University of Umea in Sweden and professor at Vanier College in Montreal, as well as adjunct professor at Laval University. He has been a visiting scholar at the University of Melbourne, at Queen's University, Turku University in Finland, and Victoria University in New Zealand. He has published *Sweden: Social Democracy in Practice* (1989) and *Social Democracy and Rational Choice: The Scandinavian Experience and Beyond* (1994). His most recent book is *Civic Literacy: How Informed Voters Make Democracy Work* (2002).

MICHAEL MURPHY is a research associate with the Institute of Intergovernmental Relations at Queen's University. His research interests include indigenous rights and governance, nationalism and self-determination, and legal norms and constitutionalism. His recent publications have appeared in the *Canadian Journal of Law and Jurisprudence*, the *Canadian Journal of Political Science*, *Citizenship Studies*, and *Ethnicities*. He is co-author of *Sub-state Nationalism: A Comparative Analysis of Institutional Design* (2002) and *In Defense of Multinational Citizenship* (2004).

KAI NIELSEN is professor emeritus at the University of Calgary and adjunct professor at Concordia University in Montreal. His recent publications include *After the Demise of the Tradition* (1991), *On Transforming Philosophy* (1995), *Naturalism without Foundations* (1997), (as co-editor) *Rethinking Nationalism* (1998), and *Globalization and Justice* (2003).

THOMAS W. POGGE is associate professor of philosophy at Columbia University. His publications include *Realizing Rawls* (1989), "An Egalitarian Law of Peoples" (1994), "Group Rights and Ethnicity" (1997), "Creating Supra-National Institutions Democratically" (1997), "On the Site of Distributive Justice" (2000), (as editor) *Global Justice* (2001), *World Poverty and Human Rights* (2002), "'Porter assistance' aux pauvres du monde" (2003), and "Can the Capability Approach be Justified?" (2003).

For many years ROSS POOLE taught at Macquarie University, Sydney, where he remains an adjunct professor in philosophy. He is currently visiting professor in politics at the New School University and a fellow at the Center for Place, Culture and Politics at the Graduate Center of the City University of New York. He is the author of *Morality and Modernity* (1991) and *Nation and Identity* (1999). His current project is entitled *Doing Justice to the Past*.

MICHEL SEYMOUR is professor of philosophy at the Université de Montréal. He has written *La nation en question* (1999) and *Le pari de la démesure* (2001), and is editor or co-editor of *Une nation peut-elle se donner la constitution de son choix?* (1995), *Rethinking Nationalism* (1998), *Nationalité, citoyenneté et solidarité* (1999), and *États-nations, multinations et organisations supranationales* (2002).

DANIEL WEINSTOCK is professor of philosophy at the Université de Montréal. He holds the Canada Research Chair in Ethics and Political Philosophy. He is also director of the Centre de recherche en éthique at the Université de Montréal. He has published many articles on nationalism, federalism, and justice in multi-nation states.

Index